Educating English Learners

Educating English Learners

Language
Diversity
in the
Classroom

Fifth Edition
(formerly *Bilingual Education:*
***History, Politics, Theory, and Practice*)**

James Crawford

BILINGUAL EDUCATIONAL SERVICES, INC.
2514 SOUTH GRAND AVENUE
LOS ANGELES, CA 90007-9979
(213) 749-6213

Fifth edition, 2004

For permission to reprint, send email to: .
  jwcrawford@compuserve.com
Or send postal mail to:
  James Crawford, c/o Bilingual Educational Services, Inc.
  2514 South Grand Avenue, Los Angeles, CA 90007-2688

Library of Congress Cataloging-in-Publication Data

Crawford, James, 1949—
Educating English learners: language diversity in the classroom /
James Crawford.
p. : ill. ; cm.
Fifth, revised edition.
Former title: Bilingual education: history, politics, theory and practice
Includes index.
Bibliography: p.
I. Education, Bilingual—United States.
LC3731.C73 1989, 1991, 1995, 1999, 2004
371.97/00973 20
ISBN 0-89075-999-5

To the memory of my father

Contents

PRACTICE

POLITICS

Preface to the Fifth Edition

Readers of my earlier editions will notice some major changes in this volume, beginning with the title page. A book that started out as *Bilingual Education: History, Politics, Theory, and Practice* – a title that no one ever seemed to remember – is now *Educating English Learners: Language Diversity in the Classroom*. I hope this will be greeted as an aesthetic improvement. But more than that, the change is meant to reflect the broadening of language-minority education in recent years. English learners and the school programs that serve them are more diverse now than in the late 1980s, when the first edition of this book appeared. Meanwhile the public policy context has evolved; the politics have changed; the research has advanced. In short, for language-educators-in-training today, there is much more to know.

Bilingual education remains an important part of the picture. Yet, for a variety of reasons that will be detailed in the chapters that follow, many teachers are now serving English learners in nonbilingual settings. It is essential for these professionals, no less than their colleagues in bilingual classrooms, to understand the basics of this field. My aim here is to provide that context as comprehensively – but concisely – as possible.

Truly revising a book is like cleaning out an attic full of treasured possessions. At first it's hard to throw anything out; later on it becomes hard to stop. In earlier editions I largely avoided this dilemma by adding new furnishings without discarding the old. This time I have made the painful decisions, eliminating dated material on policy and practice, details whose relevance has faded with time, yet striving to retain matters of historical significance. Other judgment calls involved reorganizing the text to combine some existing chapters and incorporate additional ones. Throughout, however, I have continued to stress policy as a useful prism for bringing all the diverse elements into focus.

The Fifth Edition is divided into five subject areas of three chapters each. It begins with a new section on Diversity, followed by a rescrambled lineup of History, Theory, Practice, and Politics. There are five new chapters, which cover demographic changes of the past generation, program models for English learners, U.S. language policies and their ideological roots, school "reform" in the No Child Left Behind era, and the role of advocacy in language-minority education. In addition, four existing chapters on educational research and two-way bilingual programs have been considerably expanded.

Another innovation is a CD-ROM companion disk, the Online Resource Guide, which aims to facilitate further research. It contains primary source documents – key legislation, court decisions, Congressional hearings, and government reports – along with useful articles on research and practice that are in the public domain. In addition, there are numerous Internet links to copyrighted materials relevant to educating English learners. Many of the sources cited in this book are now easily accessible on, or through, the Online Resource Guide.

Acknowledgments

After nearly two decades of writing about language-minority education, I feel indebted to an ever-expanding list of people – more, I'm afraid, that I can ever thank properly. While the judgments expressed here are my own, they reflect the contributions of countless teachers, administrators, researchers, and advocates who have patiently schooled me in the basics of the field.

At the risk of leaving out many friends, I want to mention several who have gone out of their way to help: Ellen Riojas Clark, Virginia Collier, Rosa Castro Feinberg, Michael Genzuk, Norm Gold, Kenji Hakuta, Maggie Hawkins, Wayne Holm, Martha Jiménez, Sandra Johnson, Dick Littlebear, Jim Lyons, Teresa McCarty, Reynaldo Macías, Jeff MacSwan, Dan McLaughlin, Ricardo Martínez, Geoffrey Nunberg, Carlos Ovando, Camilo Pérez-Bustillo, David Ramírez, Kellie Rolstad, Richard Ruíz, Shelly Spiegel-Coleman, Richard Tucker, Concepción Valadez, Arturo Vargas, Lucille and Philbert Watahomigie, Lily Wong Fillmore, and the late Gloria Zamora. I am especially grateful to Stephen Krashen for his scientific insights and for his inspiring example as an advocate for language-minority students.

The first edition of this book grew out of a special supplement for *Education Week* published in 1987. My editor there, Ron Wolk, generously supported that project and granted permission to reprint portions of it here. I am also thankful to my current publisher, Jeff Penichet of Bilingual Educational Services, for his fairness and professionalism.

Finally, I owe a special debt to Mary Carol Combs, who first encouraged me to investigate the English-only movement and has continued over the years to give unsparingly of her professional expertise, editorial skills, and personal support.

James Crawford

Introduction

In the beginning was the Word. And the Word was made flesh. It was so in the beginning and it is so today. The language, the Word, carries within it the history, the culture, the traditions, the very life of a people, the flesh. Language is people. We cannot even conceive of a people without a language, or a language without a people. The two are one and the same. To know one is to know the other.

Sabine Ulibarrí

The **Bilingual Education Act of 1968**[1] marked a new outlook toward Americans whose mother tongue is not English. Previously in our history, minority languages had been accommodated at certain times, repressed at others. Most often, they had been ignored. The assumption was, and is, that non-English speakers would naturally come to see the advantages of adopting the majority language as their own. Notwithstanding episodes of intolerance – most egregiously toward Native Americans – laissez-faire has usually predominated, a policy that has served to foster assimilation on a voluntary basis. Millions of immigrants have abandoned their native tongues and embraced English in what is arguably the largest, fastest, and most diverse language shift in recorded history, a phenomenon that one linguist has described as "Babel in reverse."

But the neglect of minority tongues was not entirely benign. Contrary to myth, immigrant children were more likely to sink than swim in English-language classrooms. In 1908, just 13 percent of such students who were enrolled in New York City schools at age 12 went on to high school (as compared with 32 percent of white children whose parents were native-born). Some immigrants succeeded without formal schooling, thanks to strong backs, entrepreneurial talents, or political skills; they too were in the minority.

By the 1960s, while high dropout rates persisted among language-minority children, the country's economy had changed. Upward mobility was no longer an option for those without English literacy. Prospects were doubly limited for groups who faced discrimination on the basis of race as well as language and culture: Puerto Ricans, Mexican Americans, Asian Americans, and American Indians. Public schools were largely neglecting their needs; some went so far as to punish students for speaking their native tongue.

At the same time, the civil-rights movement was beginning to energize language-minority communities. Parents who had themselves been shortchanged by English-only schools were seeking a better deal for their children. Desegregation was important, but equal opportunity demanded more than equal treatment if students could not understand the language of instruction.

New Federal Role

Recognizing this "acute educational problem," Congress moved to promote "new and imaginative programs" for educating children whose English was limited. The law, also known as **Title VII of the Elementary and Secondary Education Act**, funded experimental approaches in which students were taught partly in their native tongue and partly in English. The idea was to prepare them to succeed in English-language classrooms, to ease their transition to the mainstream.

This approach became known as **transitional bilingual education**. Though unfamiliar to most Americans at the time, it was by no means unprecedented. Minority-language schooling, bilingual and otherwise, had been widespread before World War I in localities where speakers of French, Spanish, and especially German had amassed political clout. But never before had it been endorsed as national policy.

Not that Congress had a clear idea of what bilingual education would mean in practice; only a handful of such programs even existed in 1968. The lawmakers simply resolved that *something* had to be done about the schools' negligence toward children with limited English skills. Otherwise these students would be denied an **equal educational opportunity**, a conclusion soon to be endorsed by the U.S. Supreme Court.

In 1974, the ***Lau v. Nichols*** decision made school boards, not children or parents, responsible for overcoming language barriers that impede students' access to the curriculum. Failure to do so would "make a mockery of public education," the high court said. As a matter of "simple justice," federal officials soon began to require bilingual education as a remedy where school districts had violated the civil rights of **limited-English-proficient** (LEP) children.[2] This policy was not based on a firm foundation of scientific research – which was nonexistent at the time – but rather on a determination to break decisively with past practices of English-only schooling.

In short, federal support for bilingual education was a leap of faith, an experiment based more on good intentions than good pedagogy. That is no longer a fair assessment. Bilingual approaches now reflect the latest findings in linguistics and cognitive psychology. The past three decades have brought enormous advances in curricula, methodologies, materials, and teacher training. Research-based program models have proven their effectiveness in the classroom, even in high-poverty schools where failure was once the norm. There is no question that bilingual education has benefited LEP children.

That does not mean its success has been uniform. Using students' native language for instruction is hardly a magic wand that turns mediocre schools into excellent ones. Some bilingual programs have been crudely conceived, unsupported by administrators, or "bilingual" in name only. At times teachers have lacked training in second-language acquisition or fluency in the vernacular of their students. Many English language learners have been rushed into regular classrooms prematurely, their native tongues treated as disabilities to be overcome rather than resources to be developed. Too often, academic results have been disappointing. Such weaknesses have made bilingual education vulnerable to criticism.

Cases of poor implementation, however, cannot invalidate the theoretical rationale or practical success of the best bilingual models. A four-year longitudinal study, sponsored by the U.S. Department of Education and released in 1991, reported that LEP children were thriving in programs designed to develop, rather than replace, their native language. By the 6th grade, these students were achieving at or near grade level in reading and mathematics – when tested in English – while continuing to increase their proficiency in Spanish. This finding confirmed a growing consensus among researchers in second-language acquisition: *There is no contradiction between promoting fluent bilingualism and promoting academic achievement in English; indeed, these goals are mutually supporting.*

In 1994, when Congress voted to extend the Bilingual Education Act, it made both objectives explicit for the first time. Besides teaching English to LEP children and helping them meet rigorous academic standards, the law articulated a new purpose: "developing bilingual skills and multicultural understanding." As a result, **developmental bilingual education**, including "two-way" programs serving English-proficient as well as language-minority students, began to receive substantial support for the first time. Policymakers seemed to recognize that language diversity was not just a problem to be remedied; it was also a potential asset to be valued. With this recognition, Title VII finally endorsed a cherished goal of educators: Bilingual instruction would be a way to "develop our Nation's national language resources, thus promoting our Nation's competitiveness in the global economy."

The **language-as-resource** policy proved to be short-lived. Not that it failed in the classroom or declined in popularity with parents or fared poorly in scientific studies. The problem was political. In the fall of 1994, California voters adopted Proposition 187, a crackdown on "illegal aliens" that, among other things, required educators to deny schooling to immigrant children who were undocumented and to report their families to law enforcement. Though the measure was later ruled unconstitutional in federal court, its political impact was substantial. Congress soon voted to limit the rights and benefits of all immigrants, regardless of their legal status. In 1996, the U.S. House of Representatives passed legislation recognizing English as the nation's official language and prohibiting most uses of other languages by federal government agencies and officials (the bill died without a vote in the Senate). Another English-only campaign soon erupted in California, home to 40 percent of the nation's LEP students. In 1998, voters adopted **Proposition 227**, dismantling most bilingual programs throughout the state and mandating a one-year, all-English approach. Similar measures later passed in Arizona and Massachusetts.

Perhaps the most significant blow came in 2002: repeal of the Bilingual Education Act. Under new legislation, known as **No Child Left Behind**, federal competitive grants for programs serving LEP students have been replaced by formula grants administered by the states. Not just the goal of developing native-language skills, but all references to bilingualism have been expunged from the law. While bilingual education is still eligible for funding, several new provisions – including mandatory, high-stakes testing in English – encourage schools to move toward all-English instruction. No Child Left Behind puts great stress on "scientifically based research" as a guide for program design. Thus far, however, no such basis has been offered for the federal policy reversal on educating English learners.

Sources of Opposition

Ironically, political support for bilingual education was stronger in the 1960s, when the concept was virtually untested, than it is after four decades of program experience and research that have documented its benefits. Once accepted by a majority of the American public, native-language instruction is under attack today as never before. Why is this happening?

One reason is that, with little public discussion, the Bilingual Education Act broke with a 200-year-old tradition: the federal government's reluctance to legislate on matters of language. What's more, the new policy seemed to contradict cherished assumptions about the **Melting Pot**, or more precisely, about the **Anglo-**

conformist ethic in American culture. The law's purpose was left unclear. Was it designed as a transitional program to assimilate children into the English mainstream? Or as a developmental program that encouraged students to preserve – and society to tolerate – their non-English heritage? Bilingual educators saw no contradiction between these goals, but members of the public increasingly did. While a quick transition to English was generally embraced, the idea of maintaining other languages produced skepticism and anxiety. Was the priority to give children an equal chance to succeed? Or to reinforce their ethnic identity and create jobs for Spanish-speaking teachers? In short, bilingual education has aroused passions about issues of political power and social status that are far removed from the classroom.

Second, a less restrictive immigration policy, adopted in 1965, set in motion enormous demographic changes. It increased not only the numbers of immigrants but also their racial, cultural, and linguistic diversity. Up until the 1950s, 85 percent of immigrants to the United States had come from Europe; by the 1980s, 85 percent of them were coming from the Third World, mainly from Asia and Latin America.[3] These trends continued through the 1990s, a decade in which Americans of Hispanic origin increased by 58 percent, displacing African-Americans as the nation's largest "minority." In the 2000 census, 47 million U.S. residents – nearly one in five – reported speaking a language other than English at home. For more than 28 million, that language was Spanish – a group that has grown at 10 times the rate of English-only speakers since 1980 *(see Table 1–2, page 5)*.

The new bilingualism has proved jarring to many Americans, especially to those who came of age during times of limited immigration, when monolingualism in English was considered the norm. Hearing other languages spoken freely in public or seeing government provide services in Spanish and Chinese has fostered the perception that English is losing ground, that newcomers no longer care to learn the national tongue. Bilingual education often gets the blame. Editorializing about the 2000 census, the *Washington Post* called the English proficiency of immigrant youth "shamefully low." It speculated that schools were "teaching mainly in Spanish," thereby retarding the process of assimilation.

Yet the available evidence indicates otherwise. Rather than slowing down, the shift from minority languages to English is clearly accelerating – from the classic three-generation pattern, common at the turn of the 20th century, to a two-generation pattern at the turn of the 21st. Simply put, the children of immigrants are losing their mother tongues at unprecedented rates. This is occurring despite the dramatic increase in U.S. residents who speak languages other than English. It is a paradox that many Americans have yet to grasp: while the population of minority language speakers continues to climb because of immigration, today's immigrants are learning English – and adopting it as their preferred language – more rapidly than ever before.

Nevertheless, in communities where they have concentrated, the newcomers are exerting a major and, for some of their neighbors, an unwelcome impact. A new type of nativism has emerged in response. In the early 1900s, those who felt a similar threat from "alien races" raised claims of Anglo-Saxon superiority to justify the exclusion of eastern and southern Europeans. Such explicit appeals to racial loyalty are no longer acceptable in our political discourse. Language loyalties, on the other hand, remain largely devoid of associations with social injustice. While race is immutable, immigrants can and often do exchange their mother tongue for another. To insist that they learn English seems reasonable to most Americans – including

TABLE I–1
English Language Learner Enrollment Growth by State, 1990s

	2000–01	1990–91	Growth		2000–01	1990–91	Growth
Total	3,908,095	2,202,350	77%	Missouri	11,535	3,815	202%
Alabama	6,877	1,052	554%	Montana	7,567	6,635	14%
Alaska	20,057	11,184	79%	Nebraska	10,301	1,257	719%
Arizona	135,248	65,727	106%	Nevada	40,131	9,057	343%
Arkansas	10,599	2,000	430%	New Hampshire	2,727	1,146	138%
California	1,511,646	986,462	53%	New Jersey	52,890	47,560	11%
Colorado	59,018	17,187	243%	New Mexico	63,755	73,505	-13%
Connecticut	20,629	16,988	21%	New York	239,097	168,203	42%
Delaware	2,371	1,969	20%	North Carolina	52,835	6,030	776%
Dist. of Columbia	5,554	3,379	64%	North Dakota	8,874	7,187	23%
Florida	254,517	83,937	203%	Ohio	19,868	8,992	121%
Georgia	64,949	6,487	901%	Oklahoma	43,670	15,860	175%
Hawaii	12,897	9,730	33%	Oregon	47,382	7,557	527%
Idaho	20,968	3,986	426%	Pennsylvania	31,353	15,000	109%
Illinois	140,528	79,291	77%	Rhode Island	10,161	7,632	33%
Indiana	17,193	4,670	268%	South Carolina	7,004	1,205	481%
Iowa	11,436	3,705	209%	South Dakota	5,883	6,691	-12%
Kansas	16,088	4,661	245%	Tennessee	12,475	3,660	240%
Kentucky	6,017	1,071	462%	Texas	570,022	313,234	82%
Louisiana	7,268	8,345	-13%	Utah	44,030	14,860	196%
Maine	2,737	1,983	38%	Vermont	997	500	99%
Maryland	23,891	12,701	88%	Virginia	37,385	15,130	147%
Massachusetts	44,747	42,606	5%	Washington	58,455	28,646	104%
Michigan	47,252	37,112	27%	West Virginia	1,139	231	393%
Minnesota	45,012	13,204	241%	Wisconsin	35,312	14,648	141%
Mississippi	3,225	2,753	17%	Wyoming	2,523	1,919	31%

Sources: National Clearinghouse for English Language Acquisition; U.S. Department of Education.

most immigrants themselves – as documented in public opinion surveys. Yet language politics can also provide a respectable veneer for racial politics. Hence the rise of the **English-only movement**, which has exploited anxieties about bilingualism to advance a broader nativist agenda.

Third, bilingual education is contentious, especially in school districts experiencing a rapid influx of language-minority children, for the simple reason that it disrupts established patterns. For administrators it can cause multiple headaches – the need to recruit qualified teachers, redesign curricula, reorganize class schedules – that most would prefer to avoid. Monolingual teachers fear reassignment, loss of status, or other career setbacks. English-speaking parents worry about the neglect of their own children. Taxpayers expect the bill to be outlandish, assuming (incorrectly) that all-English programs would be less expensive. While such fears usually prove to be exaggerated, school restructuring to meet changing needs is rarely painless.

Yet the demographic challenge must be faced. From 1991 to 2001, the number English learners identified by American schools nearly doubled, to an estimated 3.9 million *(see Table I–1)*. Their enrollment growth was especially dramatic in states like Nevada (343 percent), Kentucky (462 percent), Oregon (527 percent), Nebraska (719 percent), North Carolina (776 percent), and Georgia (901 percent). These students' educational needs are formidable. In study after study, a non-English-language background has been correlated with higher rates of falling behind, failing, and dropping out.

Research also shows that – contrary to the claims of some politicians – there are no quick fixes, no methodologies that offer a short-cut to second-language learning. **Structured English immersion** programs, mandated by Proposition 227 in California, were advertised as a way to teach English in one school year or less. Since voters approved the initiative, however, the annual percentage of LEP children reclassified as fluent in English has remained virtually unchanged. Banning most native-language instruction has failed to speed up the acquisition of English.

Language Attitudes

Finally, bilingual education arouses opposition because it contradicts peculiarly American ideas about language. As a people we have relatively limited experience with bilingualism on the one hand, and strongly held views about it on the other. Monolinguals in this country seldom appreciate the time and effort involved in acquiring a second language (though they may not feel up to the task themselves). Ignorance of linguistic matters is commonplace even in educated circles. Kenneth

G. Wilson, professor of English and former vice president of the University of Connecticut, sounds authoritative when he writes:

> Almost all the well-meaning claims for bilingual education turn out to be irrelevant because language doesn't work that way. ... We must do everything to introduce the second language as early as possible, the earlier the better. Nursery school is better than kindergarten, kindergarten better than first grade, and first grade better than later grades. ... Even twenty years ago we knew a fair number of things about the way children learn language. We knew many of these things only empirically then; today we have much more basic science in hand to explain these empirical data.

In fact, Professor Wilson seems to have no inkling of the recent advances in psycholinguistic research. Here he merely restates the folk wisdom that language-minority students must be taught English while they are young, before it is "too late." This notion was part of the successful sales pitch for Proposition 227. The initiative's sponsor attacked bilingual education for allegedly delaying students' exposure to English "past the age at which they can easily learn it." On that basis, many Californians bought the mandate for English-only instruction.

Yet scientific evidence has mounted steadily against the "critical period" hypothesis that, to reach full proficiency in a second language, students must acquire it before puberty. Young children do seem to have an advantage in mastering the phonological aspects of language – that is, in learning to speak without a "foreign" accent. A growing body of research, however, shows that older learners, with their greater cognitive capacity and knowledge of the world, have the edge when it comes to acquiring grammar and vocabulary.[4] Some studies have shown a very gradual, age-related decline in language-learning abilities among adults. Yet researchers have found no "cut-off" point at which they are lost. While many questions remain to be answered in this area, worries about harming LEP children by delaying all-English instruction turn out to be groundless.

Where did Professor Wilson get his information? Like most others who cherish this myth, he was able to cite only "personal anecdotal evidence ... from watching my two-to-three-year-old daughter learn Norwegian." A far cry from the "basic science" he invokes. The point here is not to single out the professor for rebuke, but to illustrate the prevalence of opinionated discourse about language. It is a subject that is dear to all of us, bound up with individual and group identity, social status, intellect, culture, nationalism, and human rights. When it comes to language, we are willing to take on the experts. Laypersons who would feel unqualified to speak on other pedagogical topics are eager to express their views about bilingual education.

Certainly this is a matter that *should* concern all Americans. It is not just a question of how we will run our schools, but of what kind of society we aspire to be: pluralist or conformist, humane or intolerant. All the more reason that the discussion should be informed. My aim in this book is to provide the factual context – the diversity, history, theory, practice, and politics of educating English learners – for those who hope to understand, and perhaps become a part of, this important field.

Notes

1. Throughout this book key terms are highlighted in boldface type.
2. For understandable reasons, the term LEP, **limited-English-proficient**, has fallen into disfavor in recent years. Rather than recognizing children for what they have – valuable skills in languages other than English – it defines them on the basis of what they lack. Unfortunately, in the author's view, none of the proposed alternatives is without drawbacks. Moreover, LEP has a precise meaning in federal and state education laws, as well as court decisions, that remains unmatched by other terminology. It also represents a conceptual advance over the term it replaced, **limited-English-speaking**, by encompassing proficiencies in reading, writing, and listening. A more neutral label, **English language learner** (ELL), is preferred by many in the field. But it, too, suggests a single-minded focus on English acquisition that tends to slight students' other pedagogical needs. Various other terms, including **speakers of other languages** (SOLs), **primary home language speakers other than English** (PHLOTEs), **potentially English proficient** (PEP) students, and **bilingual children**, tend to suffer from vagueness; none has caught on widely. All of which suggests that the quest for a perfect label is probably futile. In this volume, LEP and English learner will be used interchangeably.
3. In the 1950s the top five source countries of immigrants to the United States were (in descending order) Germany, Canada, Mexico, the United Kingdom, and Italy. By the 1980s they were Mexico, the Philippines, Vietnam, Korea, and China (including Taiwan).
4. Starting young is an advantage in the sense that proficiency in a second language takes several years to achieve. No researcher would dispute this rationale for early instruction in **English as a second language** (ESL) or **foreign languages in elementary school** (FLES). But there appears to be no pedagogical basis for hurrying LEP children into mainstream classrooms; in fact, such practices can be harmful.

Diversity

1 Bilingualism, American Style

A generation ago English learners were just a small blip on the radar screen of American educators. **Language diversity** attracted little attention because, in most parts of the United States, there was so little of it. To be sure, pockets of minority language speakers could be found in urban barrios and Chinatowns, South Florida, the rural Southwest, backwoods Alaska, northern New England, and a few Indian reservations. Children in these socially and geographically isolated communities were

targeted for assistance under the Bilingual Education Act of 1968. But they were the exceptions. By and large, to be American meant to speak English, and probably not much else – or so it was assumed.

Three decades later that premise is no longer viable. Bilingualism, both individual and societal, has become a fact of life in the United States and promises to remain so for generations to come. The reason for this trend is no mystery: immigration has reached its highest level in U.S. history, at least in numerical terms. An estimated 14 million immigrants arrived in the 1990s, legally and otherwise,[1] according to the Urban Institute. Over 90 percent of them came from non-English-speaking countries. Along with their 4 million U.S.-born children, these new Americans accounted for more than half of the nation's population growth – and more than a third of its school enrollment growth – during the decade.

As important as their numbers has been their diversity. "Never before has the United States received immigrants from so many countries, from such different social and economic backgrounds, for so many reasons," write sociologists Alejandro Portes and Rubén Rumbaut. Latin America and Asia have contributed the largest share: economic migrants from Mexico and the Caribbean,[2] political exiles from Cuba, and war refugees from Vietnam, Cambodia, El Salvador, and Guatemala. Civil strife and deprivation have brought newcomers from eastern Europe, the Middle East, and the Horn of Africa. Meanwhile globalization has created a brain drain of professional and technical workers from countries like India, Korea, the Philippines, and Taiwan.

Perhaps the most obvious result of increased immigration is the changing racial and ethnic profile of U.S. residents. Between 1970 and 2000, Asians and Pacific Islanders increased by 592 percent and Latinos by 268 percent, while blacks increased by 53 percent and non-Hispanic whites by a mere 15 percent *(see Table 1–1)*.[3] Expressed another way, one in six Americans were Asians or Latinos in 2000, up from one in 20 three decades earlier. Over the same period, non-Hispanic whites declined from 83 percent to 70 percent of the population.

TABLE 1–1
Population Growth by Self-Reported Race and Hispanic Origin, U.S. Residents, 1970–2000

	1970	1980	1990	2000	Change since 1970
White (non-Hispanic)	169,023,068	180,256,366	188,128,296	194,552,774	+15%
Black	22,539,362	26,495,025	29,986,060	34,658,190	+54%
Hispanic*	9,589,216	14,608,673	22,354,059	35,305,818	+268%
Asian, Pacific Islander	1,538,721	3,500,439	7,273,662	10,641,833	+592%
Native American	795,110	1,420,400	1,959,234	2,475,956	+211%

Source: U.S. Census Bureau.
*May be of any race.

While most of today's immigrants arrive with mother tongues other than English, increasing numbers are bilingual, well educated, and literate in English. The latter tend to prosper, often surpassing U.S. natives in earning power after a few years in this country. Many others, especially the undocumented, bring limited job skills and experience high rates of poverty. Such contradictory trends make generalizations problematic. It is safe to say, however, that immigrants are remaking America – racially, culturally, and of course, linguistically. Few communities have remained untouched.

Index of Change

The demographics are dramatic:

- One in five students in U.S. elementary and secondary schools is now an immigrant or a child of immigrants, according to the 2000 census – up from just one in 15 in 1970.
- Only 16 percent of these immigrant children are in families that came from Europe or Canada, as compared to 60 percent three decades ago.
- Today 38 percent of the newcomers are of Mexican origin, 20 percent from other Latin American countries, and 23 percent from Asia or Pacific Islands. Ten percent are undocumented, lacking most legal rights in this country.
- The Urban Institute estimates that 33 percent of immigrant students live in families with incomes below the poverty line, as compared with just 12 percent in 1970.
- Six states – California, New York, Texas, Florida, Illinois, and New Jersey – are now home to more than two-thirds of the foreign-born.
- Over the past decade, however, immigrant populations grew most rapidly in other states: North Carolina (274 percent), Georgia (233 percent), Nevada (202 percent), Arkansas (196 percent), Utah (171 percent), Tennessee (169 percent), and Nebraska (165 percent).
- A 1998 census study found that 27 percent of legal immigrants and refugees – and 58 percent of undocumented immigrants – had less than a high-school education, as compared with just 11 percent of native-born Americans.
- Paradoxically, however, legal immigrants arriving in the previous decade were more likely than the native-born to have at least a bachelor's degree (30 percent versus 27 percent). Among those who had become naturalized citizens, the rate was even higher (42 percent).
- One in four U.S. students now lives in a household where a language other

than English is reportedly spoken.

- The number of schoolchildren identified as **limited-English-proficient** (LEP) nearly doubled during the 1990s – to 3.9 million in 2000–01,[4] or more than 8 percent of K–12 enrollment *(see Table I–1, page xviii)*.
- LEP students now speak more than 460 native languages, according to the National Clearinghouse for English Language Acquisition.
- While Spanish is the mother tongue of three in four English learners, other languages spoken by at least 10,000 schoolchildren include Vietnamese, Hmong, Cantonese, Korean, Haitian Creole, Arabic, Russian, Tagalog, Navajo, Khmer, Mandarin, Portuguese, Urdu, Serbo-Croatian, Lao, Japanese, Punjabi, Armenian, Polish, French, and Hindi.

Understanding the Data

These facts and figures leave no doubt that rapid changes are under way in the U.S. student population and that schools face formidable challenges in keeping up. Considered in isolation, however, statistics can be misleading. For example, the Census Bureau created a furor when it announced that 18 percent of the U.S. population in 2000 reported speaking a language other than English at home *(see Table 1–2)*. Some doomsayers took this as evidence that diversity had gone too far, too fast: Did these 47 million minority language speakers fail to grasp their need and obligation to learn English, as earlier immigrants had done? How could our democracy continue to function without a common language? Was it time to impose tighter restrictions on immigration, or bilingual assistance programs, or both?

TABLE 1–2
Language Spoken at Home and English-Speaking Ability,
U.S. Residents, 1980–2000

	1980	%	1990	%	2000	%	Change since 1980
Speakers age 5+	210,247,455	100.0	230,445,777	100.0	262,375,152	100.0	+24.8%
English only	187,187,415	89.0	198,600,798	86.2	215,423,557	82.1	+15.1%
Other language	23,060,040	11.0	31,844,979	13.8	46,951,595	17.9	+103.6%
Spanish	11,116,194	5.3	17,339,172	7.5	28,101,052	10.7	+152.8%
Speaks English							
... very well	12,879,004	55.8	17,862,477	56.1	25,631,188	54.6	+99.0%
... not very well	10,181,036	44.2	13,982,502	43.9	21,320,407	45.4	+109.4%

Source: U.S. Census Bureau.

A closer look at the 2000 census data should allay such concerns. On the one hand, it is obvious that the number of U.S. residents who speak a language other than English at home grew disproportionately in the past 20 years – nearly seven times as rapidly as Americans who only speak English. On the other hand, about 55 percent of those from non-English backgrounds also report speaking English "very well." That is, *a majority of minority language speakers today are fluent bilinguals,* just as in 1980 and 1990. Over the past two decades, the number of fluent bilinguals has increased at roughly the same rate as the number of minority language speakers: both have doubled.

Also bear in mind that 42 percent of the immigrants counted by the 2000 census had arrived in the United States during the 1990s. Second-language acquisition does not happen overnight. It is unrealistic to expect foreign-born adults, often working long hours or isolated in the home, to attain high rates of English proficiency within a few years' time. Yet their children, who attend school and interact with English speakers in various ways, seem to be making rapid progress. Among native-born Americans who reported speaking a language other than English at home, 91 percent said they spoke English "well" or "very well."

It is important to note that the census statistics have some limitations. For one thing, they are based on **self-reports** about languages spoken and levels of English proficiency by respondents who lack expertise in such matters. Data collected in this way are clearly less reliable than those based on objective assessments. Census forms are now translated into Spanish, Chinese, Korean, Tagalog, and Vietnamese, and "assistance guides" are available in 49 other languages. But no explanations are provided for questions that many people find confusing in any language *(see page 7).*

On the other hand, nothing in these data indicates that newcomers are failing to learn English, much less threatening its hegemony as the national language. **Linguistic assimilation** seems to be proceeding quite efficiently, even though this trend is somewhat masked by the increase in recent arrivals speaking minority tongues. Large numbers of second-generation immigrants – and even some first-generation immigrants who arrived in this country at a young age[5] – are adopting English as their dominant, and sometimes their only, language.

Historical Perspective

Viewed in a broader context, today's levels of ethnic and linguistic diversity are nothing out of the ordinary. Though dramatic by the standards of the mid-20th century – an era of tight immigration quotas – they are commonplace, historically

Understanding Census Data on Language

Every 10 years the Census Bureau sets out to count the U.S. population. In the process it surveys Americans on a broad array of issues, including ethnic origins, citizenship status, and language usage. Self-reports in these areas are inherently subjective. So questions must be worded clearly to minimize inappropriate responses. That can be difficult, however, when it comes to a complicated subject like language.

Since 1980, the census "long form," which is mailed to a sample of about one in six U.S. households, has included the following:

Does this person speak a language other than English at home?
- o Yes
- o No

[If yes] What is this language? _____

[And] How well does this person speak English?
- o Very well
- o Well
- o Not well
- o Not at all

While these questions may seem straightforward, there is plenty of room for interpretation – and misinterpretation. By asking about the home language, the census is attempting to estimate the size of the linguistic minority population, that is, the number of U.S. residents who have maintained mother tongues other than English. But the question could also be taken to mean: *Does this person (ever) speak a language other than English (at any level)?* To answer in the affirmative, how fluent should one be – able to converse with native speakers or merely to give orders to household employees? How often does one need to use the language – every day or only on special occasions?

The question about English-speaking-ability is also confusing in the absence of objective criteria. When rating themselves, on what basis are respondents expected to choose *very well*, say, as opposed to merely *well* – mastery of English grammar? lack of a "foreign" accent? Guidance is obviously needed in answering these questions, all of which involve judgment calls; but none is offered. As a result, the linguistic minority numbers may be inflated to include many native English speakers whose proficiency in another language is minimal.[6] On the other hand, the 1990 census undercounted Latinos (especially recent immigrants) by nearly 5 percent. Its sampling techniques also missed many members of small or dispersed language groups.

Meanwhile self-assessments of English proficiency tend to be overstated, according to follow-up studies using objective tests. To compensate, policymakers have adopted a controversial procedure. They deem all linguistic minorities who report speaking English at any level less than "very well" to be *limited in English* for purposes of various federal programs, including the No Child Left Behind Act.

Census language data, now drawn from identical surveys in three consecutive decades, can be useful in plotting demographic trends. But their limitations should always be borne in mind.

speaking. Minority language speakers were not always welcomed by American society, but their existence was usually recognized as a fact of life. Of course, the *number of languages spoken* is larger today, thanks to global immigration patterns, but not the *proportion of Americans from non-English backgrounds*. The foreign-born population in the 2000 census, 11.1 percent of the U.S. total, appears high when compared to its all-time low of 4.7 percent reached in 1970. The current figure, however, is well below the level that prevailed from 1860 to 1930, and about average for the past century and a half *(see Figure 1–1)*.

Fluctuations in the number of foreign-born Americans correlate closely with changes in U.S. immigration policy. Before the 1920s there were few restrictions on who could come to the United States. Then Congress adopted the **national-origins quota system**, giving preference to immigrants from northern Europe, limiting those from most other nations, and almost entirely excluding Asians. This 1924 law, designed to maintain the country's racial and ethnic composition circa 1890, became an international embarrassment following World War II. It was finally repealed in 1965. Not only have national-origins preferences disappeared, but overall immigration quotas have steadily increased. As a result, the percentage of foreign-born is returning to its historic mean. Thus it is fair to say that **ethnic diversity** is not abnormal in the United States; **ethnic homogeneity** is.

The same can be said of language diversity. As Chapter 4 will elaborate, bilingualism has been a constant, if often overlooked, factor in U.S. history. Minority language groups have been prominent in all but exceptional periods. Popular notions like the **Melting Pot**, which imply a quick and simple absorption into the dominant culture, tend to conceal more than they reveal *(see Chapter 3)*. For immi-

FIGURE 1–1
U.S. Foreign-Born Population, 1850–2000

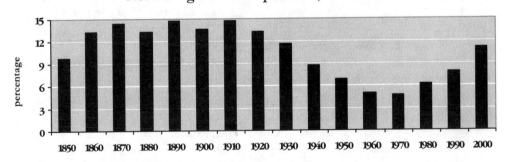

Source: U.S. Census Bureau.

grants in particular, patterns of language usage have always been complex and contradictory. Diversity increases, sometimes rapidly, as non-English-speaking groups arrive or as their homelands are annexed (e.g., in the case of Mexican Americans and American Indians). It subsides gradually as linguistic minorities and their descendants undergo a process of **Anglicization**, or adopting English as their usual language. Demographic evidence suggests that this phenomenon, more broadly described as **language shift**, has been speeding up rather than slowing down.

The recent trend is hardly surprising when one considers some of the forces driving the process. As psycholinguist François Grosjean explains, "language shift has existed for as long as languages have come into contact – the Egyptians shifted from Egyptian to Arabic, and the people of Cornwall shifted from Cornish to English – but it is especially [rapid] in immigration countries like the United States." While the causes are numerous, language shift is fundamentally about inequalities of power and status. This is not a linguistic phenomenon, because no natural language is inherently "stronger" or "weaker" than another. All are equally adaptable (e.g., capable of adding new words) to express whatever humans need to say. Language shift is therefore unaffected by Darwinian principles favoring the "fittest" species. Rather, it is a social phenomenon in which members of a less powerful and less prestigious group – who usually (though not always) comprise a demographic minority – succumb to a variety of assimilative pressures and gradually adopt a dominant group's language as their own.

There are countervailing forces, of course, social conditions and popular attitudes that encourage mother-tongue maintenance by subordinate groups. Among those cited by Nancy Conklin and Margaret Lourie, in their study *A Host of Tongues*, are relative size and geographic concentration, barriers to advancement in the wider society, continued immigration from and return migration to their homelands, loyalty to cultural and religious traditions, and various kinds of institutional support for ethnic languages. On the other hand, language shift becomes increasingly likely as a group becomes:

- more integrated into the broader society, economy, and political system;
- more urbanized and less isolated in rural enclaves;
- more exposed to mass culture in the dominant language;
- better educated, more affluent, and less dependent (socially or economically) on the ethnic community;
- intermarried with members of other language groups; and
- more identified with the nation and less with another homeland.

Factors favoring language shift are clearly stronger in the United States today than they were during the last big wave of immigration at the turn of the 20th century. It is true that newcomers still face race and class discrimination; large numbers of them speak a single language, Spanish; and those whose English is limited, Latinos in particular, tend to live in segregated neighborhoods. Yet such forces for language maintenance appear less formidable than they did in the early 1900s. It has become considerably harder to evade the reach and power of English – if not always for recent arrivals working at subsistence wages, then certainly for their children. So it is only natural that Anglicization is accelerating even as minority language speakers are increasing.

Patterns of Language Shift

Trends are difficult to plot precisely because, before 1980, the decennial census frequently changed its questions about language usage.[7] As a result, most of the historical data in this area are not directly comparable. One arguable exception is the extent of English-speaking ability in the late 19th and late 20th centuries. Responding to similar questions, five times as many Americans said they spoke "no English" at all in 1890 as in 1990 (see Table 1–3).[8] The contrast was even greater at the state level. In Montana, North Dakota, South Dakota, and Wisconsin, non-English speakers were at least 100 times more common in the earlier census. For residents of Louisiana, Michigan, Minnesota, Nebraska, New Hampshire, and New Mexico, the ratio was greater than 50 to 1. Among major cities, Milwaukee, home to many German and Polish immigrants, had the largest non-English-speaking population in 1890 (20 percent). Manchester, New Hampshire, with numerous French Canadian mill workers, was not far behind (17 percent). Other cities where at least 10 percent of residents spoke no English a century ago included Buffalo, New York; Davenport, Iowa; Detroit, Michigan; Fall River and Holyoke, Massachusetts; Lacrosse, Wisconsin; Portland, Maine; San Antonio, Texas; and San Francisco, California. In the 1990 census, no urbanized areas approached that level of non-English speakers except in South Florida and along the Mexican border.

Once again, hard numbers provide no support for the claim that English faces a threat to its dominance in the United States, or that linguistic minorities are less likely to speak English now than in the past. Indeed, these statistics suggest the opposite. Still, they are far from conclusive. Such **cross-sectional data** merely provide snapshots of different groups living at different times under different conditions. For U.S. residents being compared in 1890 and 1990, no information is available about length of time in this country, mother tongue spoken as children, or currently preferred language. Are the non-English speakers typically recent arrivals or third-generation immigrants? How many Americans who started out speaking other languages have become dominant or at least competent in English? Without answers to these questions, it is difficult to gauge changes in usage and proficiency.

The best way to measure how rapidly an ethnic minority – say, German Americans – has shifted from its mother tongue to English, would be to track rates of Anglicization over several generations, counting the number who are German monolinguals, partial or fluent bilinguals, English monolinguals, and so forth in each decade. Ideally, in other words, we should rely on **longitudinal data**, which reports a group's language behavior over time. As noted above, however, this kind of information is largely unavailable because of changing census questions and procedures.

TABLE 1–3
Percentage of Non-English-Speaking Persons,*
1890 and 1990

	1890	1990	Ratio† 1890 : 1990
U.S. population	3.6	0.8	5 : 1
New Mexico	65.1	0.9	71 : 1
Arizona	28.2	1.1	26 : 1
North Dakota	11.8	0.01	878 : 1
Wisconsin	11.4	0.1	103 : 1
Minnesota	10.3	0.1	86 : 1
South Dakota	8.8	0.02	486 : 1
Louisiana	8.4	0.1	70 : 1
California	8.3	2.9	3 : 1
Nevada	8.0	0.6	12 : 1
Texas	5.9	1.5	4 : 1
New Hampshire	5.7	0.08	72 : 1
Colorado	5.4	0.3	22 : 1
Michigan	5.2	0.1	52 : 1
Nebraska	4.9	0.06	83 : 1
Illinois	4.7	0.7	7 : 1
Rhode Island	4.7	0.8	5 : 1
New York	4.6	1.3	4 : 1
Oregon	4.5	0.3	13 : 1
Pennsylvania	4.3	0.2	28 : 1
Montana	3.7	0.02	159 : 1

Source: 1890 Census; 1990 Census.
*Age 10 and older in 1890; age 5 and older in 1990.
†Before rounding of decimals.

Without consistent statistics that can be compared in various periods, historical patterns must be traced indirectly through estimates, extrapolations, and **anecdotal data** that may or may not be representative. Such approximations are obviously less reliable than direct measurements. Nevertheless, research has yielded several generalizations about language shift in the United States that are widely accepted:

- Nonimmigrant minorities, such as Native Americans or Spanish speakers in northern New Mexico, were slower to lose their ancestral tongues than immigrants, although in recent decades these groups have also experienced rapid **language loss**.
- The process of Anglicization usually took longer for immigrants who settled in rural areas before the 20th century than for those who came later and settled in cities.
- Language shift among Europeans who arrived between 1880 and 1920 was generally completed in about three generations. According to the classic pattern, the first generation maintained the mother tongue while learning "survival English" for use outside the home; the second generation started out speaking their parents' vernacular, then acquired fluency in English; and the third generation grew up dominant, if not monolingual, in English.[9]
- The most recent waves of immigrants are becoming Anglicized even faster, with substantial attrition of **heritage languages** by the second generation in this country.

The last of these conclusions is grounded in the strongest evidence, a comprehensive database known as the 1976 Survey of Income and Education (SIE). Conducted by the Census Bureau under the supervision of the National Center for Education Statistics, the SIE featured questions about language usage that were more detailed and more precise than those of the decennial census.[10] Data from this survey are still cross-sectional, collected at a single point in time. But a great deal can be learned by observing generational differences in language usage among children, parents, and grandparents.

Based on extensive analyses of the SIE data, demographer Calvin Veltman has determined that rates of Anglicization are increasing for all linguistic minorities, including Spanish speakers. Although Latinos are more likely than other groups to retain their mother tongue – a phenomenon that Veltman attributes primarily to their high levels of immigration – they are still learning English rapidly by historical standards:

By the time they have been in the country for fifteen years, some 75 percent of all Hispanic immigrants are speaking English on a regular daily basis. … Seven out of ten children of Hispanic immigrant parents become English speakers for all practical purposes, and their children – the third generation – have English as their mother tongue.

The researcher adds that "since 1976 the principal forces driving shift to English are unlikely to have diminished in strength." Using various means to compensate for differences in survey questions, he confirmed a continuation of these trends in the 1990 census: "The data show extreme willingness on the part of new immigrants, particularly those in their prime years of schooling, not only to learn English rapidly but also to make it their principal language of communication." For such children, bilingualism is often just a brief phase between monolingualism in the native language and monolingualism in English.

TABLE 1–4
English and Heritage Language Proficiency of Second Generation* Immigrant Youth (percentages)

Ethnic Origin	Knows English		Knows HL		Bilingual Fluency†	Prefers English
	Well	Very Well	Well	Very Well		
Latin American	94.7	65.1	60.6	21.4	38.8	71.0
Colombian	98.6	70.8	59.3	19.0	43.1	70.4
Cuban	97.9	75.0	61.3	15.5	48.3	83.0
Mexican	86.1	43.7	69.1	34.9	26.1	44.8
Nicaraguan	93.0	54.9	64.0	21.7	35.5	73.6
Other Latino	96.9	71.7	55.6	20.7	41.4	75.5
Asian, Pacific Islander	90.3	57.9	20.1	8.8	7.3	73.6
Cambodian	91.6	28.4	10.9	4.3	3.3	66.3
Filipino	96.9	74.6	19.8	8.3	9.7	87.4
Laotian	76.4	28.0	12.3	3.9	1.3	55.1
Vietnamese	79.3	40.6	29.1	14.3	5.3	51.1
Other Asian	93.6	60.2	16.7	7.6	8.0	76.2
Haitian	95.4	71.4	15.2	2.0	9.3	85.6
West Indian	96.4	81.4	19.9	8.8	16.9	73.2
Other	99.0	84.2	33.7	7.8	27.6	83.5
All second-generation youth	93.6	64.1	44.3	16.1	27.0	72.3

Source: Alejandro Portes and Lingxin Hao, "*E Pluribus Unum*: Bilingualism and Language Loss in the Second Generation," *Sociology of Education* 71 (1998): 269–94.

*Second generation = Native-born with at least one foreign-born parent, or foreign-born with at least 5 years of U.S. residency.

†Bilingual fluency = Knows English very well and knows heritage language at least well.

Veltman's conclusions are consistent with findings from the Children of Immigrants Longitudinal Study, a survey of acculturation patterns in South Florida and southern California among more than 5,000 middle- and high-school students representing 77 nationality groups. Surveyed in the early 1990s, only 16 percent of these second-generation immigrants[11] said they knew their parents' language "very well," while 64 percent said they knew English "very well," and 72 percent preferred to speak English as their usual language (see Table 1–4). Only 27 percent were considered "fluent bilinguals," although there were significant variations by ethnicity, with language loss further advanced among Asians than Latinos. None of this suggests any resistance to assimilation among the children of recent immigrants.

Counting LEP Students

Critics of Veltman's approach have argued that it tends to underestimate the numbers and needs of LEP students in American schools. Children from language-minority backgrounds "do not become fluent English speakers simply because [they] speak English as their usual language," writes Dorothy Waggoner, a specialist in education statistics. She continues:

> More than half of language minority children in [a] 1978 study who usually spoke English, according to their parents, tested as limited in English proficiency. Children and adults who shift from another language to English as their usual spoken language do not thereby automatically become proficient in the English reading and writing skills necessary to succeed in English-medium schools or in the English-dominated workplace. They may never become fluent without special help.

This is one of the key insights from experience with English learner programs over the past generation: *School language and playground language are not the same.* Virtually all language-minority students will acquire the latter – also known as **oral English** skills – and most will do so with relative ease (absent any learning disability). But **academic English** skills are considerably more challenging and take considerably longer to acquire (see Chapters 8 and 9).

Timing is critical. A 4th grader arriving in the United States with no English is almost certain to learn the language eventually. But that is small comfort to the student who lacks the skills in English, literacy in particular, needed to keep up with U.S.-born 4th graders. English learners entering American schools at the secondary level are likely to encounter even greater difficulties. By the time a 9th grader, for example, has acquired the academic English needed to do cognitively demanding high-school work, high school may well be over.

Without accommodations, such as bilingual or **English-as-a-second-language** (ESL) instruction, tutoring, and counseling – appropriate to the student's age, grade, prior schooling, level of English, family situation, cultural background, and other factors – the consequences for second-language learners can be severe. For educators to meet these challenges effectively, step one is to appreciate the characteristics of this vulnerable population.

Federal and state policymakers rely on two data sources in counting LEP students: (1) responses to census questions about English-speaking ability and (2) actual enrollment figures provided each year by states and school districts. According to the census, the number of school-age children (5 to 17 years old) who spoke English less than "very well" numbered 3,493,118 in 2000, as compared with 2,388,243 in 1990 (up 46 percent). But in 2000–01, public schools identified 3,908,095 LEP students, versus 2,132,142 in 1990–91 (up 83 percent). How can these substantial differences be explained? As usual, a critical eye is essential in interpreting the data.

This is a matter of more than academic interest, because formula grants under the **No Child Left Behind Act** – the amounts allocated by the federal government to each state for English learner programs – are based on the census statistics. Millions of dollars in subsidies are at stake. Unfortunately, there are serious flaws in the census numbers, beginning with their reliance on self-reports to measure English proficiency *(see page 7)*. This procedure is dubious, since individuals who are untrained in language assessment – and frequently LEP themselves[12] – are typically asked to report this information for members of their household. A tendency by proud parents to overstate their children's English-speaking ability would hardly be surprising. Moreover, because the census asks no questions about ability to read or write in English, it surely underestimates the number of children who need help. On the other hand, its data include some school-age youth who are not enrolled in school.

Direct counts of English language learners, reported each year by state education agencies, are probably more accurate. They reflect the judgments of professional educators and consider all four components of language proficiency: **speaking, listening, reading**, and **writing**. Yet inconsistencies are pervasive in these data as well, since standards and procedures for identifying LEP students vary widely. All states now require schools to assess the English skills of children from minority language backgrounds. But while some insist that districts use strict criteria for mainstreaming students, others rely more on descriptive approaches and teacher judgments. Most states lack any detailed definition of limited English proficiency, leaving such determinations to school districts. In many cases LEP student data are incomplete because schools fail to submit their reports on time. Some districts may tend to exaggerate their enrollment of English learners to benefit from per-capita funding formulas. Others prefer to ignore these students rather than invest energy and resources in serving their needs. For all of these reasons, the state figures are also open to question. Until clear national criteria are adopted, debates over the extent of limited English proficiency are likely to continue.

Challenges for Educators

There is no question that LEP children have unique and urgent needs, beginning with – though certainly not limited to – language. Without some kind of special help, the U.S. Supreme Court has noted, "those who do not understand English are certain to find their classroom experiences wholly incomprehensible and in no way meaningful" *(see Chapter 5)*. So federal law mandates "affirmative steps" to overcome language barriers that block full access to the curriculum. Schools must not only teach English to LEP students, but do so in a way that minimizes the disruption of their academic growth. While various educational approaches have been developed, bilingual and otherwise, all of them face this legal and pedagogical challenge. Simply put, *programs for English learners must make school comprehensible*, enabling students to do academic work appropriate to their age and grade while they acquire a second language.

This is far from simple in practice. In large and medium-sized school districts today – and increasingly in urban high schools – it is not unheard of for students to speak more than 100 different languages. Researcher Stephen Krashen notes that

> many teachers today are facing a degree of diversity, of heterogeneity, that has probably never been seen before in the history of education. ... [In] a single class, [they may have] native and fluent English speakers, students who speak no English at all (and who have a poor background in the primary language), and students who speak a wide variety of first languages. Traditional solutions will not work.

It is clear that diversity on this scale poses enormous demands, even when limited English proficiency is the only **at-risk factor** schools must address. That is generally not the case. Compared to their English-speaking peers, LEP students are more likely to be poor, to live in ethnically isolated neighborhoods, and to have parents with limited education and high rates of illiteracy. Nearly two-thirds of English learners come from households where no adult speaks English very well. More than half of LEP students attend schools that are at least 30 percent LEP.[13]

Linguistically segregated schools are likely to be racially and economically segregated as well, a recipe for underperformance. In addition, LEP children who were born outside the continental United States have often had limited or sporadic education in their homelands. Sometimes their families return periodically to Mexico, El Salvador, or Puerto Rico in a "circular migration" that interrupts their children's schooling in this country.

Moreover, many immigrant and refugee children have suffered psychological traumas before or during their journey to this country. As many as 85 percent of them are separated from one or both parents in the process, according to the Harvard Immigration Project. An estimated one million are undocumented, a major stress factor for their families. Recent arrivals tend to experience profound culture shock, which may result in feelings of disorientation, isolation, and low self-worth that are compounded by language differences and the intolerance of some native English speakers. Racist receptions in their new communities, such as Ku Klux Klan organizing against Latino workers in the South, can lead to alienation and withdrawal. To teach English learners effectively, schools must cope with nonacademic as well as academic issues.

Not all LEP students face social disadvantages. Since the mid-1990s, increasing numbers have come from homes with relatively affluent and literate parents. These children, who face fewer socioeconomic hurdles, tend to experience smoother transitions into American schools and society. After learning English, many do quite well. Such students also have advantages in second-language acquisition. With more books in their homes, literacy comes easier – first in their native language, later in English. Typically they enjoy more opportunities to interact with English speakers outside the ethnic community. Their better educated parents tend to be more proficient in English and more able to help with homework.

Affluence, however, is hardly the only source of advantages in learning English. Lucy Tse, a researcher at California State University, Los Angeles, studied a group of Latino and Asian immigrants – mostly children of working-class parents with less than a high-school education – who had become fully bilingual and biliterate, done well in grades K–12, and gone on to college. In effect, they had beaten the odds, and Tse wanted to know why. After extensive interviews, she discovered what these students had in common: community and peer support for developing their native-language skills, including literacy. Over time this translated into academic success in English. Such findings offer considerable hope for children who have access to well designed and well implemented bilingual education programs.

Achievement (Data) Gaps

Unfortunately, comprehensive and reliable information on LEP students' achievement, especially over the long term, is hard to come by. This remains true despite the inclusion of English learners in **high-stakes testing** and **school accountability** mechanisms at both state and federal levels. While numerous studies have analyzed the outcomes of various instructional approaches, few if any have yielded achievement data that are representative of LEP students in general or even of broad categories, such as Spanish-background, foreign-born, or high-school English learners. So most of what passes for evidence in this area has little scientific validity. Judgments based on it should be regarded as highly speculative.

This has not stopped news media from reporting definitive-sounding data, usually drawn from standardized test scores, that tend to paint a bleak picture of English learners' performance. Such accounts are sometimes helpful in focusing public attention on the overall **achievement gap** between LEP and English-proficient students, which needs to be quantified, analyzed, and addressed. Some researchers have begun to tackle this job, with interesting if debatable results.

As interpreted by amateurs, however, raw test scores are usually misleading. Often they are exploited for political purposes. Opponents of bilingual education in Massachusetts, for example, campaigned for an English-only school initiative by highlighting LEP students' high failure rates on the Massachusetts Comprehensive Assessment System (MCAS), a test required for high-school graduation. Sponsors of a similar initiative in Arizona decried English learners' scores on the Stanford 9 achievement test, which were well below national norms in reading and mathematics.

Such results should hardly be surprising, however, when children are assessed in a language they have yet to master. These tests, which are not designed or normed for LEP students, are unreliable ways to gauge their progress in reading or math, even for those at intermediate levels; for children who are just beginning to acquire English, they are meaningless (not to mention inhumane). Although valid data about academic skills can now be gathered, at least in Spanish, through native-language achievement tests, these are administered to only about 4 percent of LEP students each year.

In any case, the question of how well children perform while they are learning English is less important than how well they perform after they join the mainstream. Research studies to measure the latter are difficult and expensive to conduct – which helps to explain the dearth of long-term outcomes data. A notable exception, which received major federal funding in the 1990s, is the Thomas-Collier study, although questions have been raised about its findings and methodology *(see Chapter 9)*.

Another crude but commonly used measure of English learners' progress is the percentage of these students "redesignated" as **fully English proficient** (FEP) each year. So-called **redesignation rates** averaged about 10 percent nationwide in 2000–01. There was substantial variation among states, ranging from a high of 31 percent in Maryland to less than 5 percent in Idaho, Mississippi, Montana, Oklahoma, Vermont, West Virginia, and Wisconsin.

Such figures tend to shock members of the public who believe children should be able to "pick up" English in a very short time. A 10 percent reclassification rate implies that it takes schools 10 years, on average, to teach English to LEP students – a startling disclosure if true. In fact, these statistics prove nothing of the kind. They do not account for the fact that LEP students come from different backgrounds, enter school at different ages, start out at different levels of English, receive different amounts of instruction, and learn at different rates, especially when it comes to academic English. Averaging out the progress of such a diverse population is not very meaningful.

In New York City, for example, more than half of all LEP students – and 62 percent of those who enter bilingual or ESL classrooms in kindergarten – exit those programs within three years, according to a 2002 report by the Puerto Rican Legal Defense and Education Fund. For older students the pattern is less encouraging. Only 45 percent of English learners who arrive in middle school and 15 percent of those who arrive in high school are *ever* reclassified as proficient in English. A substantial minority of LEP students graduate, transfer, or drop out before reaching the 40th percentile in English, a New York State requirement for redesignation as FEP (which, by definition, would not be met by 40 percent of native English speakers). Most states set the bar somewhat lower. As noted above, standards for defining English proficiency vary widely; so do school policies favoring a more or less rapid transition to English. Nevertheless, the phenomenon of "long-term English learners" – chronic underachievers – seems to be widespread. In one northern California district, teachers reported that 42 percent of LEP students in secondary schools had been classified as such for at least six years.

By contrast, English learners who are reclassified by the end of elementary school tend to prosper academically. A 1998 study in San Francisco found that redesignated FEP students, after exiting bilingual or ESL programs, performed impressively in middle and high schools. On most achievement tests in English reading and math, they outscored all other groups in the district, including those who spoke only English. Similar patterns were reported by the Children of

Immigrants Longitudinal Study: FEP high-school students[14] in San Diego enjoyed a significant edge in grade-point average over their native-English-speaking peers.

Despite the obstacles they face, many English learners are highly motivated to do well academically. "They infuse the school with a love of learning and a work ethic pitifully lacking in so many American-born students," says Patrick Welsh, a high-school English teacher in Alexandria, Virginia. "They have neither the sense of entitlement that so many lazy middle-class kids have nor the anti-achievement ethic that infects so many low-income students. No one who teaches our immigrant students is surprised that once they learn English, they often leave their American peers in the academic dust."

Notwithstanding the popular myths about second-language acquisition, the impressive performance of FEP students shows that redesignation rates are poor indicators of student progress. There is nothing about a gradual transition to English that is intrinsically harmful. To the contrary, spending several years in bilingual or ESL programs can be beneficial – provided the programs are effective. Nevertheless, this is not the experience of significant numbers of children, who continue to fall through the cracks. The problem is especially acute for late-arriving LEP students, a growing minority. According to the 2000 census, children in grades grades 6–12 are nearly twice as likely to be foreign-born as those in grades K–5.

TABLE 1–5
Generational Patterns in Dropout Rates* for Immigrants

Race/Ethnicity	Foreign-Born† (1st Generation)	Children of Immigrants (2nd Generation)	Grandchildren of Immigrants (3rd Generation)
Mexican	35.0	19.0	27.7
Other Hispanic	24.6	9.7	25.3
Asian	4.0	4.2	7.0
Non-Hispanic White	7.5	9.2	12.1
Black	16.6	5.1	16.5
All Immigrants	17.6	11.2	13.5

Source: Urban Institute; Current Population Survey, October 1995.

* Percentage of persons aged 16–24 who failed to complete high school.

†Excludes those who never enrolled in U.S. schools and Puerto Ricans, who are U.S. citizens, not immigrants.

School Completion Rates

Foreign-born students are significantly more likely to drop out of school than native-born students, for reasons that are not hard to guess: language barriers, frustrating school experiences, economic pressures, and other difficulties in adjusting to American life. A recent addition to the list is high-stakes testing. After New York State began to require passage of its academically demanding Regents exams[15] as a requirement for high school graduation, the dropout rate of LEP students nearly doubled, from 17 percent in 1998 to 32 percent in 2001.

By contrast, second-generation immigrants, many of whom start out limited in English, are more likely to complete high school than either first- or third-generation children. This pattern is remarkably consistent, despite variations in dropout rates among ethnic and racial groups *(see Table 1–5)*. Among Mexican Americans, 35 percent of first-generation immigrants aged 16–24 were not enrolled in school and had no high school diploma in 1995,[16] versus 19 percent of their second-generation and 28 percent of their third-generation counterparts. This edge for the U.S.-born children of immigrants shows that bilingualism need not be an academic disadvantage. Indeed, at 11.2 percent, their dropout rate was slightly lower than the average for *all* American youth and young adults, which was 12.0 percent that year.

Limited English proficiency nevertheless remains a risk factor for failure to complete high school. Among first-, second-, and third-generation immigrants who had previously attended U.S. schools, 23 percent of those who were LEP were recorded as dropouts in 1995, versus just 13 percent of those who were proficient in English *(see Table 1–6)*. Again, however, the picture is mixed. After students acquire English, dropout rates for some immigrant groups dip below the national average; for Latinos they remain relatively high. This suggests that factors in addition to language play a significant role. Indeed, research by Russell Rumberger of the University of California, Santa Barbara has shown that, after compensating for socioeconomic status and family variables, Latinos' "odds of dropping out are no different than those for [non-Hispanic] White students."

Social inequities, of course, have an enormous impact on children's life chances. The question for educators is how to overcome the academic effects of these inequities. What can be done to keep language-minority students in school and help them succeed? One way is to stress things that can be accomplished in the classroom: offering state-of-the-art programs to address limited English proficiency and providing trained personnel and adequate resources. Another way is to support goals that help students adjust to American life both inside and outside of school. One of these goals is **heritage language development.**

TABLE 1–6
Immigrant Dropout Rates* and English Proficiency

	LEP	Non-LEP
1st Generation†	21.5	16.0
2nd Generation	21.0	10.5
3rd Generation	38.7	13.4
Mexican	37.9	24.2
Other Hispanic	28.5	17.6
Asian	4.3	4.5
Non-Hispanic White	13.5	11.8
Black	--	16.2
All Immigrants	23.3	13.3

Source: Urban Institute; Current Population Survey, October 1995.
* Percentage of persons aged 16–24 who failed to complete high school.
†Excludes those who never enrolled in U.S. schools.

Patterns of Acculturation

The rapid assimilation of immigrants, especially when it comes to language, has been the historical norm as well as the socially preferred outcome in the United States. The result has been to maintain English in a position of overwhelming dominance. Obviously this pattern is advantageous to the eight out of 10 Americans who are fluent in no other language. They pay few costs for bilingualism as long as it remains a transitory phenomenon; the burden of adjustment falls almost entirely on linguistic minorities. But English speakers' anxiety about maintaining the status quo intensifies during periods of increasing immigration. Many begin to perceive monolingualism as natural and healthy, and diversity as abnormal and threatening *(see Chapters 3 and 6)*.

This public mood, mixed with genuine concern about the progress of immigrant students, exerts pressure on schools to teach English as quickly as possible. The No Child Left Behind Act, passed in 2002, holds states and school districts "accountable" for how well LEP students score on English-language achievement tests and how rapidly they are redesignated as FEP *(see Chapter 14)*. How well children maintain native-language skills is not an issue. The law's priority is clear: to wean them from their mother tongue and expedite their passage to monolingualism, or at least dominance, in English.

This pattern of acculturation is hardly the only alternative for LEP students – nor the most beneficial, according to the Children of Immigrants Longitudinal Study. Among second-generation adolescents in the survey, researchers Alejandro Portes and Lingxin Hao identified four basic types of linguistic adaptation:

- *English monolinguals* (48 percent) – proficient in English but no longer know the heritage language well.
- *Fluent bilinguals* (24 percent) – proficient in English and know the heritage language at least well.
- *Foreign monolinguals* (18 percent) – proficient in the heritage language but not in English.
- *Limited bilinguals* (10 percent) – not proficient in any language.[17]

About 5,000 students were interviewed to determine the impact of varying patterns of acculturation on family relations and psychosocial adjustment. While these factors are not direct measures of academic performance, they are closely correlated with it – for all students, not just immigrants.

In every category the fluent bilinguals scored higher than the other groups: family solidarity and harmony, self-esteem, and educational aspirations. English monolinguals and limited bilinguals were most likely to report conflicts within their families, often because of estrangement from the culture of immigrant communities, disrespectful attitudes toward their parents, and a general breakdown in communication. The study found that foreign monolinguals, "who have remained attached to their parents' language without learning English … display high levels of family solidarity, but have much lower self-esteem and ambition." Fluent bilinguals benefit not only from better communication with their parents. Their mastery of two languages "also helps anchor youthful identities by facilitating knowledge and understanding of parental cultures" at the same time they are learning to function in American society. This outcome, however, is achieved by only about one in four second-generation students. The researchers conclude:

> While popular with the public at large, educational policies that promote complete linguistic assimilation contain hidden costs for these children, depriving them of a key social resource at a critical juncture in their lives. Family relations and personality development suffer accordingly. … Cut these moorings and children are cast adrift in a uniform monolingual world. They, their families, and eventually the communities where they settle will have to pay the price.

As we have seen, language shift has numerous causes. Educational policies are only part of the problem, albeit a significant one considering the centrality of school in a child's life. School can also be part of the solution: English acquisition need not be a zero-sum game. LEP students are capable of developing fluent bilingualism and excelling academically – given the opportunity to do so. On the other hand, school may emphasize English and only English, treating children's native language as the central "problem" to be overcome. While this is one of the fundamental policy decisions in educating English learners, it hardly exhausts the possibilities. The next chapter will look more closely at the available program options and how pedagogical choices are made.

Suggested Reading

Grosjean, François. *Life with Two Languages: An Introduction to Bilingualism.* Cambridge, Mass.: Harvard University Press, 1982.

Portes, Alejandro, and Hao, Lingxin. "*E Pluribus Unum*: Bilingualism and Loss of Language in the Second Generation." *Sociology of Education* 71 (1998): 269–94.

Ruiz-de-Velasco, Jorge, and Fix, Michael. *Overlooked and Underserved: Immigrant Children in U.S. Secondary Schools.* Washington, D.C.: Urban Institute, 2000.

Veltman, Calvin J. "The American Linguistic Mosaic: Understanding Language Shift in the United States." In Sandra Lee McKay and Sau-ling Cynthia Wong, eds., *New Immigrants in the United States: Readings for Second Language Educators.* New York: Cambridge University Press, 2000.

Tse, Lucy. *"Why Don't They Learn English?" Separating Fact from Fallacy in the U.S. Language Debate.* New York: Teachers College Press, 2001.

See also pp. 386–87.

Online Resource Guide

Census Bureau, U.S. *Language Use and English-Speaking Ability*: 2000 (2003).

Kindler, Anneka L. *Survey of the States' Limited English Proficient Students and Available Educational Programs and Services: 2000–2001 Summary Report.* National Clearinghouse for English Language Acquisition (2002).

See also companion CD-ROM.

Internet Links

Crawford, James. "Making Sense of Census 2000." Education Policy Studies Laboratory, Language Policy Research Unit, Arizona State University (2002). http://www.asu.edu/educ/epsl/LPRU/features/article5.htm

Fix, Michael E., and Passel, Jeffrey S. "U.S. Immigration at the Beginning of the 21st Century." Testimony before the U.S. House Judiciary Committee (2001).

U.S. Census Bureau. "Language Use." http://www.census.gov/population/www/socdemo/lang_use.html

See also companion CD-ROM.

Notes

1. 9.1 million legal immigrants were admitted between 1991 and 2000, according to the Office of Immigration Statistics at the U.S. Department of Homeland Security. In addition, the Urban Institute estimates a "net inflow" of about 500,000 undocumented immigrants per year during the decade; Michael E. Fix and Jeffrey S. Passel, "U.S. Immigration at the Beginning of the 21st Century," testimony before the U.S. House Judiciary Committee, Aug. 2, 2001.

2. Along with Spanish-speaking U.S. citizens from Puerto Rico.

3. Self-reported Native Americans also increased significantly, but this seems primarily to reflect increased identification as Indians (including the fast-growing "Wanabi" tribe) rather than increased birthrates.

4. Up from 2.1 million, or 5.6 percent, in 1990–91. These figures are based on reports for public schools in the 50 states and the District of Columbia. When Puerto Rico, Guam, the Virgin Islands, and other "outlying areas" are included, the LEP population in 2000–01 totaled 4.6 million; Anneka L. Kindler, *Survey of the States' Limited English Proficient Students and Available Educational Programs and Services: 2000–2001 Summary Report* (Washington, D.C.: National Clearinghouse for English Language Acquisition, 2002).

5. Because immigrant generations are defined in different ways, these terms can be confusing. In this volume **first generation immigrants** are foreign-born persons who have relocated to the United States; their children make up the **second generation** and their grandchildren the **third generation**. But for a special definition used in the Children of Immigrants Longitudinal Study, see note 11 below.

6. Calvin Veltman, a demographer specializing in this area, has determined that 21 percent of persons who claimed to speak Japanese at home in 1990, and 20 percent of self-described Spanish speakers, failed to report Japanese or Hispanic ancestry, respectively.

7. 1890 was the first census to include a question on language, when it asked about English-speaking ability and (for non-English speakers) other languages currently spoken. In 1900, the current usage question was dropped. It was restored in 1910 and 1920, along with a new question about the mother tongue (language spoken in childhood) of the foreign-born and their children. The 1930 census retained the mother-tongue question, but on the issue of current usage it asked only whether respondents could speak English. In 1940, the mother-tongue question was extended to a sample of the general population (not just immigrants), and the question about English-speaking ability was discontinued. In the 1950 census, there was no question about language of any kind. In 1960, foreign-born persons were again asked what language was spoken in their homes *before* they came to the United States. In 1970, a rather ambiguous mother-tongue question – "What language, other than English, was spoken in this person's home when he was a child?" – was given to a sample of all U.S. residents. Since 1980, the census long form has asked about languages "other than English" now spoken at home but not about languages spoken in childhood. In addition, it has asked minority language speakers how well they speak English; *Measuring America: The Decennial Censuses from 1790 to 2000* (Washington, D.C.: U.S. Census Bureau, 2002).

8. In all likelihood, this figure is understated because the Census Bureau had fewer resources and less expertise in counting language-minority populations in 1890 than in 1990. For example, most Indian tribes were excluded from the earlier census. Another caveat worth noting is that the 1990 language data cover persons aged 5 and older, while figures from 1890 cover those aged 10 and older. Finally, self-reported data should always be approached with a critical eye.

9. Exceptions were observed among religious minorities, such as the Mennonites and Old Order Amish, whose strict isolation from the modern world enabled them to maintain their German dialects, at least until recently.

10. The SIE asked, for example: "What language was usually spoken in this person's home when he (or she) was a child?"; "What language does this person usually speak?"; and "Does this person often speak another language?"

11. "Second-generation" immigrants included both U.S.-born children with at least one foreign-born parent and foreign-born children who had lived in the United States for at least five years.

12. More than half of immigrant children reported to speak English "very well" in 2000 lived in households where all adults were limited in English.

13. By comparison, only 4 percent of non-LEP students attend such schools, according to the Urban Institute.

14. Most of these students had been reclassified from LEP.

15. In addition to an English language arts exam, graduates must pass Regents exams in math, science, and social studies. While LEP students may take the content-area exams in the native language – if they happen to speak Spanish, Korean, Chinese, Russian, or Haitian Creole – other language groups must take them only in English. Many English

learners, especially late arrivals to American schools, have not received the academic preparation needed to pass these tests in any language.

16. Counting the actual numbers of children who leave school early has always been difficult because of the extensive follow-up and record-keeping requirements for schools and districts. Thus **event dropout rates** tend to be untrustworthy. An alternative approach is to measure **status dropout rates** based on surveys of school completion among children and young adults, which are conducted annually by the Census Bureau's Current Population Survey. While these data are generally more reliable, they are inflated by recent immigrants who never attended U.S. schools – in other words, who never "dropped in." For example, a federal commission reported that the Hispanic dropout rate had reached "a staggering 30 percent" in 1994–95, a figure that has been widely circulated. But when the analysis was restricted to 16-to-24-year-olds who had attended U.S. schools, the rate fell to about 20 percent (versus 8 percent for non-Hispanic whites and 13 percent for blacks). Figures on dropout rates discussed in this chapter were adjusted by the Urban Institute to exclude foreign-born youth never schooled in the United States.

17. Such students may have limited literacy skills both in their native tongue and in English, but most linguists would disagree that a normal child could reach school age without acquiring oral competence in at least one language. The theory that some English learners are **semilingual** or speak "no language" is not only unsupported by scientific evidence; it likely to be stigmatizing and harmful in practice *(see Chapter 8)*.

2 Options for English Learners

*T*here is no **one-size-fits-all** when it comes to educating diverse groups of students. While this is a long-recognized principle of good teaching, in 1998 it became a rallying cry for educators arguing, unsuccessfully, against passage of Proposition 227 in California. As adopted by the voters, this law mandates a single all-English program, "not normally intended to exceed one school year," for English learners throughout the state – regardless of their individual needs, the desires of their parents, or the advice of professionals. Similar ballot initiatives have passed in Arizona (2000) and Massachusetts (2002; *see Chapter 13*).

Addressing Diverse Needs
Mandates vs. Realities
Key Terminology
Program Labeling
Submersion
ESL Pullout
Structured English Immersion
Transitional Bilingual Education
Developmental Bilingual Education
Two-Way Bilingual Education
Newcomer Models
Making Program Choices

The popularity of such measures stems from two widespread assumptions: (1) that there is a universally superior way to acquire a second language, "total immersion," and (2) that any young child, given intensive exposure to a second language, will acquire it in a very short time. Leaving aside for a moment the validity of these notions, the logic here is compelling. If the learning process is more or less identical for all students, then one-size-fits-all would be an efficient policy. Using the correct pedagogy and adequate quality controls, public schools should be able to turn out a uniform product that will satisfy the taxpayers. So why not require them to provide the "best" program for all students?

The problem with this reasoning is its blindness to human variation. No two children start out at the same level, have the same aptitudes, use the same learning strategies, experience the same influences outside of school, and progress at the same rates. Effective education of any kind begins with a recognition of such differences. It builds on what students already know – and on what motivates them to know more. To the extent possible, instruction is adapted to the child rather than vice versa. While none of this is easy, it is especially challenging when children come from diverse socioeconomic, cultural, and linguistic backgrounds. Schools must address, along with limited English proficiency, the widely varying needs of LEP students.

Recognizing these realities, the National Research Council offered the following advice in a 1997 report on language-minority education: "The key issue is not finding a program that works for all children and all localities, but rather finding a set of program components that works for the children in the community of interest, given that community's goals, demographics, and resources." In other words, English learners need a range of pedagogical options.

Mandates vs. Realities

Although one size never fits all, it is fair to say that some sizes often fit better than others. Program models for LEP students vary significantly in their effectiveness, as documented by research over the past generation. Some bilingual approaches have been more successful than others. In particular, those that stress **native-language development** and a **gradual transition to English** have usually proven superior in stimulating long-term achievement, at least among groups of students who are considered most **at-risk** of failing in school. Meanwhile all-English programs have generally fared poorly in head-to-head comparisons with bilingual programs *(see Chapter 9)*. The one-year immersion model adopted by California, Arizona, and Massachusetts has never been scientifically evaluated. At this writing there is no direct quantitative evidence for, or against, its effectiveness. Nevertheless, it is now the "default" program for approximately 40 percent of the nation's LEP children; similar mandates have been proposed in other states.[1]

Not long ago it was state and federal mandates for bilingual education that drew criticism. Opponents fostered the misconception that "the bilingual method" was being forced upon unwilling school districts by heavy-handed government officials. In actuality, the late Bilingual Education Act was a voluntary program, to which districts applied for federal grants on a competitive basis. While native-language approaches were favored, for much of the law's history (1968–2002) a portion of funding was also available for all-English approaches (see Chapters 5 and 6).

Only 11 states have ever required bilingual instruction, and only under certain circumstances; seven do so today.[2] These laws have generally stopped short of requiring any particular pedagogy. They merely specify some use of the mother tongue for instruction when there are enough English learners who speak it to make a bilingual approach feasible. Using two languages in the classroom hardly defines an educational program. In many cases bilingual instruction – even by this broad definition – has proved impracticable because of resource constraints, number of languages represented, shortages of qualified teachers, and political pressures both inside and outside the schools.

TABLE 2–1
Language of Instruction for English Language Learners, by State, 2000–01

	ELL Enrollment	Growth in 1990s	Instruction Incorporates L1		Instruction Does Not Incorporate L1		Language Use Not Reported	
			N	%	N	%	N	%
Total Reported	3,908,095	77%	999,879	25.6%	2,465,331	63.1%	442,885	11.3%
Alabama	6,877	554%	0	0.0%	6,877	100.0%	0	0.0%
Alaska	20,057	79%	8,565	42.7%	10,801	53.9%	691	3.4%
Arizona	135,248	106%	24,683	18.3%	100,980	74.7%	9,585	7.1%
Arkansas	10,599	430%	4,026	38.0%	6,573	62.0%	0	0.0%
California	1,511,646	53%	181,455	12.0%	1,329,844	88.0%	347	0.0%
Colorado	59,018	243%	17,510	29.7%	38,629	65.5%	2,879	4.9%
Connecticut	20,629	21%	11,322	54.9%	8,659	42.0%	648	3.1%
Delaware	2,371	20%	650	27.4%	1,721	72.6%	0	0.0%
Dist. of Columbia	5,554	64%	483	8.7%	5,071	91.3%	0	0.0%
Florida†	254,517	203%	-	-	-	-	254,517	100%
Georgia	64,949	901%	0	0.0%	64,949	100.0%	0	0.0%

Hawaii*	12,897	33%	4,441	34.4%	8,357	64.8%	99	0.8%
Idaho	20,968	426%	12,329	58.8%	8,639	41.2%	0	0.0%
Illinois	140,528	77%	106,791	76.0%	33,755	24.0%	0	0.0%
Indiana	17,193	268%	2,168	12.6%	15,025	87.4%	0	0.0%
Iowa	11,436	209%	4,968	43.4%	6,468	56.6%	0	0.0%
Kansas	16,088	245%	8,959	55.7%	6,745	41.9%	384	2.4%
Kentucky	6,017	462%	1,579	26.2%	4,128	68.6%	310	5.2%
Louisiana	7,268	-13%	2,283	31.4%	2,627	36.1%	2,358	32.4%
Maine	2,737	38%	660	24.1%	1,692	61.8%	385	14.1%
Maryland	23,891	88%	258	1.1%	23,633	98.9%	0	0.0%
Massachusetts*	44,747	5%	38,166	85.3%	5,862	13.1%	719	1.6%
Michigan	47,252	27%	41,682	88.2%	5,570	11.8%	0	0.0%
Minnesota	45,012	241%	11,204	24.9%	33,808	75.1%	0	0.0%
Mississippi	3,225	17%	415	12.9%	1,114	34.5%	1,696	52.6%
Missouri	11,535	202%	403	3.5%	11,132	96.5%	0	0.0%
Montana†	7,567	14%	-	-	-	-	7,567	100%
Nebraska	10,301	719%	186	1.8%	10,115	98.2%	0	0.0%
Nevada	40,131	343%	6,450	16.1%	33,641	83.8%	40	0.1%
New Hampshire	2,727	138%	0	0.0%	2,462	90.3%	265	9.7%
New Jersey	52,890	11%	36,675	69.3%	15,183	28.7%	1,032	2.0%
New Mexico	63,755	-13%	35,826	56.2%	27,929	43.8%	0	0.0%
New York	239,097	42%	68,250	28.5%	96,995	40.6%	73,852	30.9%
North Carolina	52,835	776%	843	1.6%	48,928	92.6%	3,064	5.8%
North Dakota	8,874	23%	3,956	44.6%	4,918	55.4%	0	0.0%
Ohio	19,868	121%	4,625	23.3%	12,440	62.6%	2,803	14.1%
Oklahoma	43,670	175%	165	0.4%	43,505	99.6%	0	0.0%
Oregon	47,382	527%	20,623	43.5%	25,419	53.6%	1,340	2.8%
Pennsylvania	31,353	109%	7,595	24.2%	23,758	75.8%	0	0.0%
Rhode Island*	10,161	33%	2,465	24.3%	7,736	76.1%	0	0.0%
South Carolina	7,004	481%	0	0.0%	7,004	100.0%	0	0.0%
South Dakota	5,883	-12%	1,146	19.5%	3,310	56.3%	1,427	24.3%
Tennessee	12,475	240%	915	7.3%	11,760	94.3%	0	0.0%
Texas	570,022	82%	284,557	49.9%	223,484	39.2%	61,981	10.9%
Utah*	44,030	196%	4,055	9.2%	37,099	84.3%	2,876	6.5%
Vermont	997	99%	0	0.0%	997	100.0%	0	0.0%
Virginia	37,385	147%	1,059	2.8%	36,326	97.2%	0	0.0%
Washington	58,455	104%	20,279	34.7%	34,476	59.0%	3,700	6.3%
West Virginia	1,139	393%	0	0.0%	1,139	100.0%	0	0.0%
Wisconsin	35,312	141%	15,209	43.1%	14,048	39.8%	6,055	17.1%
Wyoming†	2,523	31%	-	-	-	-	2,523	100%

Source: National Clearinghouse for English Language Acquisition.
* Language of instruction data are from 1999-2000.
†Did not report language of instruction data.
L1 = native language.

Mandates notwithstanding, bilingual education now serves only a minority of eligible students. In the states that submitted reports to the U.S. Department of Education for school year 2000–01, about seven in 10 English learners were being taught entirely in English, while three in 10 were receiving some type of native-language assistance (not necessarily a full bilingual program).[3] States with the least experience in serving these students – including several with rapid growth in LEP enrollments during the 1990s – were the least likely to provide bilingual education *(see Table 2–1)*.

Coming to Terms

Of course, *bilingual* can mean many things in the classroom. The term may refer to student characteristics, language of instruction, teacher qualifications, pedagogical objectives, community aspirations, or all of these things simultaneously. "'Bilingual education' is a simple label for a complex phenomenon," according to the *Encyclopedia of Bilingualism and Bilingual Education*, which lists 10 "types" and 90 "varieties" around the world. A **bilingual program** will take quite different forms for Puerto Ricans in New York, Hmong in Wisconsin, Navajos in New Mexico, and Koreans in California. While two languages are used in each case, there are important variations in students, communities, methods, and goals.

In 1994, Congress provided the following description:

> The term 'bilingual education program' means an educational program for limited English proficient students that–
> (A) makes instructional use of both English and a student's native language;
> (B) enables limited English proficient students to achieve English proficiency and academic mastery of subject matter content and higher order skills, including critical thinking, so as to meet age-appropriate grade-promotion and graduation standards in concert with the National Education Goals;
> (C) may also develop the native language skills of limited English proficient students, or ancestral languages of American Indians, Alaska Natives, Native Hawaiians and native residents of the outlying areas; and
> (D) may include the participation of English-proficient students if such program is designed to enable all enrolled students to become proficient in English and a second language.

This politically crafted definition, drawn from the final version of the Bilingual Education Act,[4] is broad enough to include a wide range of pedagogical approaches, from those that strive to develop fluent bilingualism and biliteracy to those that stress a rapid transition to English. **Native-language instruction** – that is, the use of students' mother tongue as a medium for teaching subject matter – is a required component, but not necessarily a prominent one. A 1993 study commissioned by the U.S. Department of Education reported that about a third of LEP students in nominally bilingual programs were taught more than 75 percent of the time in English; another third, from 40 to 75 percent; and a final third, less than 40 percent.

Immersion also has a variety of meanings. Water metaphors have long influenced – some would say, confused – popular conceptions of language acquisition. Richard Henry Pratt, the 19th century cavalry officer who founded a system of boarding schools for Native Americans, explained: "I believe in immersing the Indians in our civilization and, when we get them under, holding them there until they are thoroughly soaked." As a matter of government policy, linguistic assimilation became an act of coercion, achieved by placing LEP Indian children in a **sink-or-swim** situation and punishing those who violated **speak-English-only rules** *(see Chapter 4)*. Immersion in this sense has less to do with teaching than with forcing learners to adapt to harsh circumstances.

Yet there are other, less brutal approaches. Immersion can also serve as a kind of flotation device when the second language is used in ways that make school subjects comprehensible. This version seeks to adapt instruction to the students rather than vice versa – but without using their native language. Such approaches have proven successful in teaching speakers of socially prestigious and dominant languages; for language-minority students the results are less encouraging *(see Chapters 7, 8, and 9)*. In summary, immersion programs range from those that offer little or no special help to those that provide **sheltered instruction** adjusted to learners' level of understanding.

Although language of instruction is important, it is hardly the only variable in program design. California has been one of the few states to collect more detailed information in this area. Its annual Language Census asks school districts to report not merely on **program labels** but also on some of the **program components** used in educating English learners. In 1997–98, for example, the year before Proposition 227 took effect, 29 percent of the state's LEP students were provided at least some native-language instruction in subject areas, along with lessons in **English as a second language** (ESL) – the bare essentials of bilingual education *(see Table 2–2)*. Meanwhile 22 percent were taught basic ESL combined with **native-language support** in academic content areas, which generally meant tutoring by paraprofessionals working with monolingual teachers. The remainder of California's LEP students were enrolled in various kinds of all-English classrooms, including 22 percent who received ESL plus sheltered instruction in the second language; 11 percent who were taught in **mainstream** English-language classrooms, with some ESL lessons on the side; and 16 percent who got no language assistance at all.

TABLE 2–2
Instructional Services for English Language Learners
in California, 1997–98

	Total ELL Enrollment	ESL Only	ESL + SDAIE (Immersion)	ESL + SDAIE + L1 Support	ESL + L1 Instruction (Bilingual)	No ELL Services
1997–98	1,406,166	159,617	307,176	305,764	409,879	223,730
	100%	11%	22%	22%	29%	16%

Source: California Department of Education.
ELL = English language learner; SDAIE = specially designed academic instruction in English; L1 = native language.

Defining the Options

These categories, while helpful, hardly exhaust the pedagogical options for English learners. Program components can be combined in numerous ways. This helps to explain why program labels tend to be simplistic and misleading. In the mid-1980s, for example, when school officials in Elizabeth, New Jersey, replaced a "bilingual" program with an "immersion" program to participate in a research project, they told parents to expect little change: about the same (minimal) amount of Spanish would be used in the classroom. Around the same time a program was initiated in El Paso, Texas, taught primarily in English but featuring 60 to 90 minutes a day of Spanish language arts. The school district called it "bilingual immersion" to distinguish it from traditional bilingual approaches that used a bit less English. Nevertheless, it was considered to be "a true bilingual education program" because of the emphasis on developing literacy in Spanish *(see Chapter 9)*. Critics of bilingual education, however, on learning that bilingual immersion was moderately successful, portrayed the El Paso experiment as a vindication of their favored model: **structured English immersion**.[5] For them the key element was the increased **time on task** in English.

How pedagogical options are defined obviously depends on the rationales behind them – in this case, contending theories of second-language acquisition *(see Chapter 8)*. Program labels are also affected by laws that govern how they are funded. Hence the terms **transitional bilingual education** and **developmental bilingual education**. These were devised by legislators, not educators; as a result, their legal definitions are more precise than their pedagogical ones. Political controversies naturally play a role as well. **Dual language, dual immersion,** and **two-way immersion** are increasingly used as "safer" terms for what was originally known as **two-way bilingual education,** in hopes that avoiding the "B-word" will minimize opposition. Sometimes this works, though not always. Euphemisms tend to spread confusion among laypersons, for example, when "dual language" is interpreted as a synonym for any form of bilingual education.

ESL, sometimes labeled ESOL, or **English for speakers of other languages**, also describes a range of pedagogical treatments. It may be **grammar-based**, focusing heavily on "skill-building" exercises and memorization of vocabulary, or **content-based**, stressing the use of English to communicate in situations that will be meaningful to students. Again, the two approaches reflect contending viewpoints about how languages are acquired.

One content-based approach, which became popular in California in the 1990s, is divided into **English language development** (ELD) for beginners and **specially designed academic instruction in English** (SDAIE) for intermediate and advanced learners. As researchers Yvonne and David Freeman explain, "The primary goal of ELD classes is language development, and the primary goal of SDAIE classes is academic development." English is taught in self-contained classrooms rather than through special tutoring, as in the **ESL pullout** model *(see below)*. By integrating language and content instruction, ELD teachers can introduce English vocabulary when students need it and, unlike their mainstream counterparts, also provide native-language support to explain difficult concepts. This contextual approach, in contrast to the drills and memorization that characterize traditional ESL, has the added advantage of increasing students' motivation to acquire English.

In summary, **program models** that are pedagogically similar are sometimes described with different labels. Conversely, identical terminology may conceal significant variations in the classroom. Bearing such caveats in mind, let's consider the most common options for educating English learners – how they are generally understood and what they actually mean in practice.

Submersion

Submersion, another term for sink-or-swim, offers no systematic assistance for LEP students – neither ESL nor sheltered instruction nor native-language lessons – leaving them to "pick up" English on their own in English-language schools. This approach was dominant in the United States from the World War I era until 1974, when it was outlawed by the Supreme Court as a violation of minority children's civil rights. In *Lau v. Nichols,* the court ruled that school districts "must take affirmative steps to rectify the language deficiency in order to open [their] instructional program to these students" *(see Chapter 5).*

Submersion was often a product of simple neglect. Until forced to do so, most school districts preferred to ignore linguistic diversity, which they were ill equipped and poorly funded to address. It was much easier to shirk responsibility and let "problem" students bear all the costs. So English learners were typically placed in classrooms taught by and for native-English speakers. Most acquired the language eventually, but only after falling behind their peers; many never caught up.

Daniel Domenech, now superintendent of Fairfax County (Virginia) Public Schools, was one of the fortunate ones – although he hardly felt that way on arriving in the United States in 1955. He recalls:

> I was in fifth grade in Cuba, but they stuck me back in second grade in New York. There was no ESL. ... Teachers thought I was retarded because I couldn't speak English. I sat in the back of the room and looked out the window all day. It wasn't until the last years of high school that I hit my stride and could match native-born Americans in terms of grades and achievement.

A different pattern emerged in Southwestern states, especially Texas and Arizona, where submersion was part of a calculated policy of racial exclusion. Mexican American students, whatever their level of English proficiency, were routinely assigned to segregated classrooms and sometimes to segregated schools. Although the language barrier was used as a pretext, children received no special help in overcoming it. They were simply held back a year or more, "submersed" in English, and forbidden to speak Spanish on school grounds.[6] In effect, they were treated as **learning disabled** because of their ethnic and linguistic background. For most students the academic results were disastrous.

Corporal punishment for violating speak-English-only rules, a common practice, made matters worse by humiliating children and alienating them from school. Edgar Lozano, a high-school student from San Antonio, related his experience to civil-rights investigators in 1968. Throughout his school years, he said, teachers and other staff repeatedly "took a stick to me" after lecturing him that

> if you want to be American, you have got to speak English. ... I mean, how would you like somebody to come up to you and tell you that what you speak is a

dirty language? You know, what your mother speaks at home is a dirty language. [Spanish] is the only thing I ever heard at home. ... That really stuck to my mind.

More than a misguided approach to fostering English acquisition, this policy served to institutionalize white Anglo domination. As Texas state senator Joe Bernal said at the time, "schools have not given us any reason to be proud" of being Mexican Americans. Instead, "they have tried to take away our language."

Such blatant discrimination has largely disappeared, thanks to court decisions and civil-rights enforcement since the 1970s. Yet submersion persists in other forms, such as the neglect of numerous English learners who are never identified as such, or never placed in appropriate classrooms. This problem is most prevalent in states that were unaccustomed to linguistic and cultural diversity until recent years; most have been slow to respond to the arrival of immigrant children.[7] Substantial numbers of LEP students continue to go unserved or underserved as a result. In 1999, exactly a quarter century after the *Lau* decision, the Georgia Department of Education estimated that 32 of the state's school districts that enrolled English learners were providing no language assistance programs of any kind.

ESL Pullout

English-as-a-second-language instruction can take several forms. One of the most common, but least effective, of these is **ESL pullout**. Students are literally "pulled out" of mainstream – that is, submersion – classrooms for small-group tutoring in the second language, typically lasting 30 to 45 minutes per day. Hence the nickname **submersion plus ESL**. Such programs may also feature native-language support to keep students from being totally lost during unsheltered English instruction; this is often provided by aides without teaching certificates or by volunteers drawn from ethnic communities. ESL pullout teachers themselves are normally certified in their specialty.

While an improvement over sink-or-swim alone, this program is guided by a similar philosophy. Speaking a language other than English is conceived as a "language deficiency," a handicap of the students themselves. ESL pullout takes a more activist approach than submersion, by providing some remedial instruction. But it usually carries the same stigma: those enrolled are seen as slow learners who are not expected to do well in school. As a result, parents sometimes fight to keep children out of such programs. LEP students in ESL pullout soon get the negative message from teachers and peers, and many internalize it. This can lead to academic difficulties over the long term.

ESL pullout is widely regarded as inadequate to meet the needs of English learners, even as a remedial approach, because it leaves them sitting for most of the school day in classrooms that are largely incomprehensible. It is also inefficient because of the difficulty of coordinating lessons between ESL and mainstream staff. So the second language is typically taught through rote exercises rather than incorporated into meaningful instruction. Often overextended, many ESL pullout teachers have limited time for children who need a great deal of individual attention. One itinerant teacher in the suburbs of Louisville, Kentucky, interviewed in 2000, reported feelings of guilt and frustration after being assigned 47 ESL students in 11 schools spread over a large area. Because of this unrealistic workload, she said, "I don't think they get the services they truly deserve." Unable to persuade her supervisors that more ESL specialists were needed, the teacher finally transferred to another district.

At most, ESL pullout should be used as a stopgap in schools caught unprepared for a sudden influx of immigrants until a more effective program can be offered. Unfortunately, in many districts it has become a way of life, a policy of doing the bare minimum for English learners.

Structured English Immersion

Unlike the other models described here, **structured English immersion** – sometimes called **sheltered English immersion** – was conceived by government bureaucrats before it was ever tried in American classrooms. Promoted as "promising" by the Reagan administration, conservative members of Congress, and English-only activists – although the evidence for its effectiveness was speculative at best – this all-English program began to receive federal funding in the mid-1980s, over the objections of most experts in second-language acquisition. In short, structured immersion was a product of the political controversy surrounding bilingual education (*see Chapter 6*).

The term was coined by two policy analysts at the U.S. Department of Education, Keith Baker and Adriana de Kanter, authors of a 1981 report questioning the effectiveness of transitional bilingual education. "Immersion" was borrowed from **French immersion**, a Canadian program that had proven more successful than traditional foreign-language instruction in cultivating bilingualism among English-speaking students.[8] By contrast, the immersion model proposed by Baker and de Kanter was designed to assimilate minority language speakers into a monolingual English environment (an application that designers of the Canadian program opposed as potentially harmful). "Structured" was added to distinguish the Baker–de Kanter methodology from submersion, an unplanned and haphazard approach. An immersion curriculum, as they defined it, "is structured so that prior knowledge of L2 [English] is not assumed as subjects are taught. Content is introduced in a way that can be understood by the students. The students in effect learn L2 and content simultaneously."

In other words, according to the immersion theorists, teachers can effectively eliminate the language barrier by making adjustments in their use of English, thereby enabling LEP students to understand lessons in the second language, acquire English, and keep up in other subjects. This type of quick fix has obvious appeal. But how well does structured immersion deliver on its promises? So far there is little empirical evidence of its effectiveness. Theoretically speaking, there is good reason to doubt its benefits for English learners in the United States, especially those with other academic risk factors such as poverty and illiteracy in the home.

As Baker and de Kanter define it, structured immersion relies primarily on **sheltered instruction**. A component of many bilingual programs, this technique uses a controlled form of English – adjusted to students' level of proficiency – to teach them academic subject matter. To make that feasible, English learners must be taught in separate classrooms rather than mixed with native speakers of English (although they may be mixed with LEP students from other language groups). Research and experience with sheltered instruction has shown that, in appropriate contexts, children can indeed "learn L2 and content simultaneously" *(see Chapters 8 and 9)*.

One appropriate context is **foreign-language immersion**, such as the popular programs for Anglophones learning French in Canada. Students may initially be taught entirely through sheltered instruction in the second language, a model sometimes described as **early total immersion**. Yet they also receive ample support for their mother tongue outside of school, first, as speakers of the dominant societal language, and second, as members of families that are usually well educated and not impoverished. So in a Japanese immersion program in the United States,[9] for example, English-speaking children are in no danger of losing their native language, which continues to serve as a resource for cognitive growth. Moreover, such programs gradually phase in English instruction to ensure that children become both fluent and literate in two languages. They are bilingual in methods and, just as importantly, in goals. Research has shown that, on average, foreign-language immersion students meet or exceed national norms in academic achievement.

For language-minority students, however, sheltered instruction should be approached with several caveats. Thus far it has proven effective primarily for intermediate language learners, typically those in their second or third year of bilingual education, who can understand grade-level material when presented in simplified English. In other words, for students who are ready, this immersion technique can be beneficial in stimulating academic development as well as English acquisition. Sheltered instruction appears to be most effective as a component of bilingual education programs. By contrast, when it is used with beginning English learners, the curriculum must be extremely watered down to be comprehensible in the second language. In this situation structured immersion teachers tend to face a dilemma. Either they focus mainly on English, neglecting other subjects, or they present content using language that is above students' level – in effect, reverting to sink-or-swim. Both pitfalls are potentially harmful. Language-minority children who fall behind generally find it much harder to catch up, to overcome the **achievement gap** with their peers, than English-speaking children in a foreign-language immersion program *(see Chapter 9)*.

Native-language support is sometimes permitted in structured immersion programs. According to Baker and de Kanter, students may ask questions in Spanish, say, but teachers should reply in English. The voter-enacted mandates for immersion in Arizona and Massachusetts allow instructors to use "a minimal amount of the child's native language when necessary," presumably for clarification purposes. So far, however, there is no requirement in these states that immersion teachers must be fluent bilinguals, or even certified in ESL. They should at least have training in sheltered instruction methodologies, although that varies by district.

Some educators have drawn a distinction between structured immersion and **content-based ESL**. In practice, the latter programs have tended to feature hands-on projects and "discovery learning" that can be stimulating and meaningful to students. They often strive to present grade-level rather than simplified academic material. Structured immersion has been more associated with prepackaged "basic skills" approaches, such as Direct Instruction and *Open Court*, which reduce children to passive learners. In principle, however, the two program models are quite similar. To foster second-language acquisition and academic achievement, both rely entirely on sheltered English instruction, making little or no use of students' native language and no effort to cultivate fluent bilingualism. Teachers bear a heavy burden in providing lessons that are both comprehensible and grade-appropriate. Still – whether one calls it structured immersion, content-based ESL, or SDAIE – this model is generally considered superior to other all-English approaches.

Philosophically, it is based on the same **deficit model** that underlies submersion and ESL pullout: children's native language is seen as a learning "deficiency" to be "remediated." So structured immersion is likely to have similar effects on their self-esteem and identity formation. In fact, its stress on a rapid exit to the mainstream, especially in the one-year model imposed by recent ballot measures, may prove even more stigmatizing for students who fail to meet this unrealistic deadline.

Transitional Bilingual Education

Ending the neglect of LEP students, by supporting "new and imaginative elementary and secondary programs to meet [their] special educational needs," was the stated purpose of Title VII, the Bilingual Education Act of 1968. While limited guidance was available at the time from either research or practice, the failure of all-English programs was manifest. Bilingual education was an appealing alternative because it promised "a better way of teaching English, without academic retardation," according to José Cárdenas, one of the Mexican American educators who led the movement for the legislation. In other words, helping students make a successful **transition** to mainstream classrooms was seen as the principal goal. Yet not the only goal, Cárdenas hastens to add. There was also the opportunity for **maintenance** of students' mother-tongue skills, that is, for making them fully proficient in two languages. Witnesses who testified before Congressional committees in favor of the bill cited the economic, cultural, psychological, and (possibly) cognitive benefits of bilingualism. Educators recognized that children need not give up their first language to acquire a second, or to succeed academically in English. So they saw no contradiction between the goals of transition and maintenance.

But politicians did. A program that appeared to subsidize the growth of ethnic languages, in defiance of the Melting Pot tradition, was sure to provoke heated opposition (a prophecy that proved accurate over the coming years; *see Chapters 5 and 6)*. Congress initially tried to straddle the issue, leaving Title VII's specific aims open to interpretation. Policymakers gradually concluded, however, that the public would be more supportive if bilingual education was portrayed in familiar terms: as a temporary, remedial program to "compensate" for the "educational disadvantages" of poor, non-English-speaking children.

Thus **transitional bilingual education** (TBE) came into common usage as a way to articulate this limited set of goals and to draw a distinction with language maintenance approaches. The term dates from a Massachusetts law passed in 1971. Soon TBE became the cornerstone of federal policy for English learners and, in turn, the most common type of bilingual program in the United States. While there are usually no limitations on the amount of native-language instruction – when used as a *means* rather than an *end* in itself – students generally must exit TBE pro-

Program Models For Educating English Learners

PROGRAM	LANGUAGE	COMPONENTS	DURATION	GOALS
Submersion a.k.a. *Sink-or-Swim*	100% English	Mainstream instruction; no special help with English; no special teacher qualifications; illegal under *Lau v. Nichols*	---	Assimilating ELLs into English-dominant society
ESL Pullout *Submersion plus ESL*	90-100% English; may include L1 support	Mainstream instruction; ELLs 'pulled out' for 30-45 minutes of ESL daily; teachers certified in ESL	As needed	Assimilating ESLs; remedial English
Structured Immersion *Sheltered English, Content-Based ESL*	90-100% English; may include L1 for clarification	Sheltered subject-matter instruction at students' level of English; ELLs grouped for instruction; teachers trained in immersion methods	1-3 years	Assimilating ELLs; quick exit to mainstream classrooms
Transitional Bilingual Education *Early-Exit*	10-50% L1; 50-90% English	L1 and sheltered subject-matter instruction; daily ESL; initial literacy usually in L1; teacherts certified in BE, proficient in L1 and L2	2-4 years; ELLs exit on becoming English proficient	Assimilating ELLs; L2 acquisition without falling behind academically
Developmental Bilingual Education *Gradual Exit, Late Exit*	90% L1 in K–1; gradually decreased to 50% or less by grade 4	L1 and sheltered subject-matter instruction; daily ESL; initial literacy in L1; teachers certified in BE, proficient in L1 and L2; parents involved	5-6 years; former ELLs continue some classes in L1	Bilingualism and biliteracy; long-term academic achievement in English
Two-Way Bilingual Education *Dual Immersion, Dual Language Two-Way Immersion*	90/10 model: 90% L1, 10% English in early grades; 50/50 model: parity of both languages	ELLs and native-English speakers taught literacy and subjects in both languages; peer tutoring; teachers certified in BE, proficient in L1 and L2; parents involved	5-6 years	Bilingualism and biliteracy; long-term academic achievement in English

ELLs = English language learners; L1 = students' native language; L2 = second language.

grams as soon as they are proficient enough in English to function in regular classrooms. The goal is to help children keep up academically, while moving them as expeditiously as possible into the English mainstream. So this model is sometimes labeled **early-exit bilingual education**.[10]

Pedagogically speaking, there are numerous variations. Along with ESL, a near-universal component, transitional programs may also offer sheltered English instruction in subject areas. While TBE is occasionally provided for older, late-arriving students – for example, in the form of "bilingual math" or "bilingual social studies" classes – it is mostly found at the elementary level, where English learners are more likely to be concentrated. Obviously a critical mass of students from the same language group is necessary to make bilingual classrooms feasible (although this is primarily a resource issue, not a pedagogical imperative). The amount of native-language instruction differs, often depending on external pressures such as high-stakes testing in the second language. Early-exit programs featured in a major federal study of the 1980s, the **Ramírez report**, were conducted overwhelmingly in English. Others use considerably more native language, especially with beginning English learners. A majority of students exit TBE within two to four years. Typically they learn to read first in their mother tongue and later in English, although this is less common in Asian languages, whose writing systems require substantial time to master. Classroom teachers should be certified in bilingual education and proficient in both English and their students' native language. Because of personnel shortages, however, in some schools paraprofessionals end up providing much of the instruction for beginning English learners.

Transitional programs are generally equal or superior in academic outcomes to any of the all-English models but inferior to other bilingual approaches, according to evidence from evaluation research *(see Chapter 9)*. Various hypotheses have been advanced to explain this pattern. TBE's edge over all-English programs may be due to the **transfer** of subject knowledge and literacy skills from the native language to English. This not only helps students keep up academically; it also promotes second-language acquisition. But rushing children into the mainstream, with proficiency in **oral English** but not **academic English**, may squander this advantage. Meanwhile TBE's usual role as a **compensatory** program – understood to mean the "slow learner" track – may communicate self-fulfilling expectations about students' long-term prospects.

The overall goal is the assimilation of children into an English-dominant society, by steadily reducing their reliance on their mother tongue. Ironically, TBE is probably more efficient in this regard than the all-English models favored by assimilationists who object to bilingual approaches on ideological grounds. Few if any TBE programs consciously attempt to turn language-minority students into English monolinguals. Yet many have that effect in practice. They not only fail to develop full bilingualism and biliteracy, but also tend to reinforce the low status of minority tongues both inside and outside of school. Because of such negative attitudes, which pervade American society and culture, active measures are probably necessary to prevent **language attrition**, or gradual loss of proficiency, for most children from non-English backgrounds. Research suggests that failing to provide that kind of support can have academic consequences.

Developmental Bilingual Education

A language maintenance approach known as bilingual-bicultural education emerged in the 1970s as an alternative to TBE. It was part of a broader movement to stop treating minority students as "culturally deprived" and to start respecting their diverse backgrounds. This model soon came under attack, however, for allegedly placing too little emphasis on English. The criticism stemmed from the popular misconception that language acquisition is a zero-sum game: if children were encouraged to maintain their first language, what incentive would they have to master a second? To many English monolinguals at the time, bilingualism seemed like an unnatural state of affairs – and perhaps a divisive one, given the rise of Québecois nationalism in Canada. Opponents of bilingual-bicultural education argued that, on principle, schools supported by general tax revenues should seek to foster "American" values, not ethnic cultures. Such ideas were hardly restricted to the extremist fringe. They were also espoused by liberal elites such as the *Washington Post*, whose education editor led the charge against language maintenance *(see Chapter 5)*.

As a result, such programs were declared ineligible for federal funding in 1978. Congress voted to support native-language instruction *only* until LEP students could make the transition to English. The maintenance model made a comeback in the 1984 reauthorization of the Bilingual Education Act under a new label: **developmental bilingual education** (DBE). Nevertheless, these programs remained out of favor in Washington, and relatively rare at any level, until the early 1990s. While precise figures are lacking, it is safe to say that they are still outnumbered by transitional programs.

To the untrained eye DBE looks a lot like TBE, at least in the early years. The two models usually share the same essential components: ESL instruction, initial literacy in the native language, and subjects taught in sheltered as well as native-language classrooms. Yet these programs are quite distinct in strategies and outcomes. TBE is a **remedial treatment** for limited English proficiency, understood as a malady that must be "cured" to make children fit for regular classrooms. DBE recognizes and values the potential of LEP students to become fluent in two languages; thus it offers them an **enrichment experience** above and beyond a school's regular offerings. The former tries to compensate for what English learners lack, while the latter seeks to build on what they already know.

TBE's approach to bilingualism is **subtractive**, based on the belief that a quick transition to English is students' best hope of catching up with their English-speaking peers. DBE's approach is **additive**. Its designers start with the premise that – given a rigorous curriculum, qualified teachers, and sufficient time – English learners can meet high expectations of both academic achievement and bilingual fluency. The contrasting philosophies make for significant differences in how such programs are perceived and, frequently, in how students perform.

A popular form of DBE has been called **late-exit** or, more precisely, **gradual-exit bilingual education**. English learners are moved in stages from native-language instruction to content-based ESL to mainstream classes. In DBE, English instruction is limited in the beginning – typically about 10 percent of class time in kindergarten and 1st grade – and is phased in gradually until, by the 4th or 5th grade, it is predominant. From the outset LEP children are mixed with fluent English speakers in subjects that are not linguistically challenging, such as art, music, and physical education. This social contact, along with basic ESL, promotes oral English development, while beginners study core subjects in their native language. As their English improves, intermediate and advanced students are taught increasingly through sheltered and mainstream instruction, starting with math and science, which are easier to make comprehensible in English, and later in language arts and social studies. After they become fully fluent in English, students continue to take one or two classes in the native language. Generally such opportunities end when children leave elementary school because (at present) DBE and other **heritage language** models are scarce at the middle- and high-school levels.

As Stephen Krashen, who helped design the gradual-exit model for the Case Studies project in California *(see Chapter 10)*, explains:

> This kind of plan avoids problems associated with exiting children too early from first-language instruction (before the English they encounter is comprehensible) and provides instruction in the first language where it is most needed. [It] also allows children to have the advantages of advanced first-language development.

Another benefit is that the more the native language is used in the classroom, the more limited-English-speaking parents are likely to help with homework and to take an active interest in their children's schooling overall. Research shows that, when consistently implemented by qualified staff, gradual-exit programs avoid any trade-off between academic achievement and English acquisition. By the 6th grade, students are significantly more likely to have overcome the achievement gap than their counterparts in TBE or structured immersion.

Nevertheless, DBE remains the most controversial approach for educating English learners, and probably the least understood. Because it serves disempowered constituencies – immigrants, Native Americans, or Puerto Ricans – it is especially vulnerable to political attack, regardless of its pedagogical results. Yet there is an important exception to this rule. When developmental bilingual programs are opened to English-speaking children, there is a significant increase in public acceptance. In this "two-way" context, the goal of bilingualism often seems less threatening.

Two-Way Bilingual Education

Along with its political advantages, there are some persuasive pedagogical arguments for **two-way bilingual education**, beginning with its unique use of **peer models**. Students of different backgrounds learn from each other – potentially a powerful factor in second-language acquisition. In some respects, this hybrid approach combines DBE for language-minority children acquiring English with foreign-language immersion for language-majority children acquiring Spanish, Korean, Navajo, or various other languages. It differs, however, in one important respect. With native speakers of different languages mixed together in the same classroom, it becomes more difficult to make instruction comprehensible for both groups at the same time. Ultimately two-way bilingual education may prove more effective than either DBE or immersion alone, although (at this writing) data from **controlled scientific studies** remain limited.

Increasingly these programs are described as **dual immersion**, a label that both appeals to popular beliefs about language learning and emphasizes the benefits for native English speakers. When the word *bilingual* goes unmentioned, members of the public may fail to notice that minority children are involved. Even when they do, the activism of English-speaking parents often helps to counteract negative perceptions. Following passage of Proposition 227 and similar English-only initiatives, many bilingual education programs have been dismantled, but so far almost none of these have been two-way programs.[11] Nationwide the popularity of this approach has soared in recent years. According to the Center for Applied Linguistics, which compiles an annual directory, between 1987 and 2003 the number of two-way programs increased nearly tenfold.

The appeal is easy to understand. Two-way instruction promises the "best of both worlds," as **bilingual movement** enthusiasts liked to say in the 1970s. It gives students a chance that is quite rare in the United States to become fluent in two languages and to excel academically at the same time. The idea is exciting to a growing number of parents who want the cultural and career advantages of bilingualism for their children. It has special resonance in immigrant and Native American communities, where younger generations might otherwise lose the heritage language.

Two-way bilingual education is also hard to fault at the level of public policy. It has the potential to develop language skills that not only benefit individuals but also meet vital needs of government and business. Richard Riley, U.S. secretary of education during the Clinton administration, challenged American schools to increase the number of these programs to 1,000 by 2005. "It is high time we begin to treat language skills as the asset they are, particularly in this global economy," he said. "Proficiency in English and one other language is something that we need to encourage among all young people."

While there are several variations of two-way bilingual education *(see Chapter 12)*, two are especially common. The **50/50 model**, as the term implies, teaches all subjects in both languages, using more or less equal amounts of English and the minority tongue throughout the program. The **90/10 model** is similar to the "one way" form of DBE, beginning with 90 percent minority-language instruction in the early years and phasing English in gradually. According to Kathryn Lindholm-Leary, a leading researcher on two-way programs, this typically means 10 percent English instruction in grades K–1, 20 percent in grades 2–3, and 50 percent in grades 4–6. Both models stress **language separation**, as opposed to **concurrent translation**, so that students will focus on lessons taught in their weaker language rather than wait for the mother-tongue version *(see Chapter 8)*. The goal is to make second-language "input" comprehensible, as in sheltered instruction. As noted above, however, this can be challenging for the teacher when beginning learners are mixed with native speakers of the **target language** in the same classroom. Some programs separate the two groups for language arts instruction (in one or both languages) for part of the day; others do not. Ideally, there should be a 50/50 split between English learners and minority-language learners to maximize the impact of peer modeling and peer tutoring. Social interaction motivates students to learn to communicate in each others' vernacular and provides a meaningful context for doing so.

Research evidence on two-way models, while tentative, is encouraging for both language-majority and language-minority students when it comes to fostering bilingualism and biliteracy. The native-English speakers, a self-selected and often socially "advantaged" group, generally do well academically. So do the English learners in many (though not all) programs; according to a few studies, they outperform comparable students in one-way DBE. If there is an edge here for two-way approaches, it may result in part from the high status accorded to the minority language. English learners are recognized for the valuable skills they bring from home and are encouraged to share with other students. Playing this role can enhance their self-confidence and enthusiasm for school, with positive effects on achievement.

Because of its promise and popularity, two-way bilingual education is sometimes promoted as a model for all U.S. students. One day that may be realistic. But meanwhile there are high hurdles to clear before such programs can serve even a sizable fraction of English learners in the United States; at most, about 2 percent were enrolled in 2001–02. For two-way approaches to work as intended, relatively stable enrollments are necessary. This requires a steady stream of kindergartners whose parents are willing to commit them to a five- to six-year program that is experimental and may be traumatic at first. Finding enough native-English speakers is often difficult. Transience among minority language speakers can also be a problem. Teachers must be fully bilingual, well trained, and thoroughly collegial to present a rigorous curriculum in two languages. Parent involvement – on the part of both language groups – is essential. So is strong leadership to pull it all together.

Newcomer Programs

Some recent immigrants and refugees – those who are older, non-English-proficient, unschooled in their homelands, suffering from social and psychological difficulties, or not uncommonly, all of the above – may need more assistance than the normal bilingual or ESL program can provide. Districts with substantial numbers of such students have come to recognize the advantages of **newcomer programs** that provide a sheltered and supportive environment, along with intensive tutoring and counseling, to ease the transition to life in the United States. These schools, or sometimes schools-within-schools, have been described as "cultural and educational shock-absorbers." They are more often found at the secondary level, where new arrivals' adjustment problems tend to be more severe.

Newcomer programs focus not only on academic and linguistic needs; they also provide an orientation to the American education system and teach some of the survival skills that children will need, especially in urban high schools. Teachers are specially trained to help newcomers cope with culture clash. In addition to counseling for children, the schools make special efforts to assist immigrant families obtain social, medical, and mental health services. Enrollments are normally limited to one year or less, while students are preparing to enter other language-assistance or mainstream programs.

Pedagogical components and methods vary. Some newcomer programs are heavy on ESL remediation and sheltered instruction, while others offer native-language classes to get students up to speed in academic subjects and sometimes in vocational training. A few, such as Liberty High School in New York City, seek to develop bilingualism and biliteracy. This 9th grade newcomer school accepts recent immigrants aged 14 and above, who may enter at any time during the year. Most depart after one or two semesters to enter regular high schools. But speakers of Chinese, Polish, and Spanish who have underdeveloped literacy skills may remain for up to two years, or until they reach the 9th grade level in the native language.

Not surprisingly, newcomer programs – which are generally smaller and more generously staffed with psychologists, supplemental teachers, and paraprofessionals – cost significantly more per student than mainstream programs. The Los Angeles Unified School District, whose immigrant enrollment increases by about 10,000 each year, once operated an elementary newcomer school in affluent Bel Air, busing in students from tough inner-city neighborhoods. The school was a one-year stopover for children who had limited education or traumatic experiences in their home countries. It was largely supported by federal funding under the Emergency Immigrant Education Act. After that law expired in 2002, the district closed its elementary newcomer center and started assigning all recent arrivals to regular schools.

Evaluating the effectiveness of newcomer programs is obviously difficult, given the variety of their offerings and the diverse characteristics of their students. Some civil-rights groups have objected to any approach that segregates immigrants, even temporarily, from native-born students. Meanwhile English-only proponents have objected to any reliance on bilingual instruction. Yet where newcomer programs exist, they remain popular with parents and teachers. Children at these schools usually have high attendance rates and often do well after transferring out. For example, those who pass through the Academy for New Americans, another newcomer high school in New York, have graduation rates above the citywide average for all students; many go on to college. The nurturing environment can make a big difference in their lives. Around the time that Los Angeles closed its elementary newcomer program, a student who had learned English there a decade earlier said:

"I'm graduating from Oregon State University this summer, and I know that the Bellagio Road Newcomer School is one of the reasons why."

Making Program Choices

How do school districts select one or more program models for educating English learners? According to the Center for Research on Education, Diversity, and Excellence (CREDE), such choices should ideally be based on "careful consideration of a [school] district's goals, resources, and the needs and characteristics of its students."

When it comes to goals, educators no longer have the option of setting low standards, officially or otherwise, for "problem" groups. The No Child Left Behind Act of 2002 is designed to "hold schools accountable" for ever-increasing – many would say unrealistic – test scores by students in general and by English learners in particular.

A key question for districts is whether to focus entirely on English acquisition and academic performance assessed in English, to which high stakes are attached by the new law, or whether – in addition – to pursue the goals of full bilingualism and biliteracy. Opting for the first alternative would mean choosing ESL pullout, structured immersion, or transitional bilingual programs. Opting for the second would require developmental bilingual programs, either one-way or two-way, which are appropriate for meeting all three goals. This is not an easy decision, however, because the academic payoff of DBE is long-term, while the pressure to pump up test scores is immediate. Failing to meet yearly performance targets under No Child Left Behind can bring severe sanctions against districts, schools, and educators *(see Chapter 14).*

The question of resources should not be a decisive factor in choosing program models. Federal courts have ruled that inadequate funding is no excuse for short-changing English learners. Program decisions should be based on serving children's needs, not appeasing taxpayers. In a less than ideal world, of course, resources matter a great deal to those who set school policies. Sometimes it may be legitimate to rely on stopgap measures – for example, when there are no bilingual- or ESL-certified professionals available to serve an unexpected influx of immigrants – until adequate programs can be developed. Yet a growing number of districts make long-term pedagogical choices based on expediency, financial and otherwise. Hiring one or two itinerant ESL teachers, for example, is much easier and less expensive than getting expert advice and designing an effective English learner program. Over time, however, this approach fails to serve anyone's best interests. Not only does the district invite civil-rights investigations and lawsuits, but an ESL pullout program, when faithfully implemented, is considerably more expensive than a full-fledged bilingual or immersion program.

Because of the complexities of school finance, studies of the **incremental costs** of educating LEP students (i.e., those above and beyond average per-pupil expenditures) are notoriously difficult to design. So reliable research in this area has been limited. One exception is a study commissioned by the California legislature in the late 1980s. Using sophisticated techniques to disaggregate school expenses, researchers found that ESL pullout was by far the most costly program alternative, because it meant hiring a corps of supplemental teachers. The expense of two-way bilingual education was also above average because of complex administrative requirements. TBE, DBE, and structured immersion – all provided in self-contained classrooms by qualified teachers – cost roughly the same *(see Table 2–3)*. The researchers caution that only well designed and well implemented programs were selected for the study; so it may not be representative of all California schools. Obviously, because of inflation, the totals would be higher today. But there is no reason to believe that the relative expense of each model would be substantially different.

TABLE 2–3
Supplemental Costs Per LEP Student, by Program Model, Selected California Schools, 1989–91

	ESL Pullout	Structured Immersion	TBE	DBE	Two-Way Bilingual
Direct Instruction	$1,042	$3	$20	$59	$186
Administration and Support	$99	$106	$129	$90	$472
Language Assessment	$46	$60	$43	$22	$24
Inservice Training	$11	$6	$22	$9	$194
Total Costs	$1,194	$175	$214	$180	$876

Source: Jay Chambers and Tom Parrish, *Meeting the Challenge of Diversity: An Evaluation of Programs for Pupils with Limited Proficiency in English*, vol. IV, *Cost of Programs and Services for LEP Students* (Berkeley, Calif.: BW Associates, 1992).

Other important factors in pedagogical decision-making involve student characteristics and needs. Bilingual instruction is difficult when LEP children come from such diverse backgrounds that several language groups may be represented in a single classroom. Recruiting enough qualified bilingual teachers may be impossible, especially in languages that are seldom taught in the United States such as

Hmong, Gujarati, or Serbo-Croatian. In such cases structured immersion may be the best option that schools can realistically provide. Students who already speak some English and have support at home from well educated family members – for example, the children of foreign diplomats or business executives – may be adequately served by such programs. Sometimes parents may favor a quick transition to English or distrust the school to develop native-language skills (sometimes with good reason); in this situation TBE may be the best option. Two-way programs may be feasible where sufficient numbers of English-speaking parents are eager to support them, but often that is not the case. Certainly this is no reason to deny DBE to language-minority students who could benefit from it. Indeed, research suggests that developmental approaches are the best choice for many English learners, although they also tend to arouse the most controversy.

As these examples suggest, real-world policymaking is a complex process that goes well beyond balancing goals, resources, and student needs. More is involved than weighing the research evidence and making a rational decision about which program would work best. There are significant external factors – public attitudes, power struggles, and national traditions – that influence and, especially in this field, tend to determine the outcome. It is to this **language policy** context that we now turn.

Suggested
Reading

August, Diane, and Hakuta, Kenji, eds. *Improving Schooling for Language-Minority Children: A Research Agenda.* Washington, D.C.: National Academy Press, 1997.

Baker, Colin, and Jones, Sylvia P. *Encyclopedia of Bilingualism and Bilingual Education.* Clevedon, U.K.: Multilingual Matters, 1998.

Freeman, Yvonne S., and Freeman, David E. *ESL/EFL Teaching: Principles for Success.* Portsmouth, N.H.: Heineman, 1998.

McDonnell, Lorraine M., and Hill, Paul T. *Newcomers in American Schools: Meeting the Educational Needs of Immigrant Youth.* Santa Monica, Calif.: Rand Corporation, 1993.

See also pp. 387–88.

Online
Resource
Guide

Crandall, Joann. *Content-Centered Language Learning*. ERIC Clearinghouse on Languages and Linguistics (1994).

Friedlander, Monica. *The Newcomer Program: Helping Immigrant Students Succeed in U.S. Schools*. Washington, D.C.: National Clearinghouse for Bilingual Education (1991).

Rennie, Jeanne. *ESL and Bilingual Program Models*. Washington, D.C.: ERIC Clearinghouse on Languages and Linguistics (1993).

Riley, Richard W. "Excelencia para Todos – Excellence for All: The Progress of Hispanic Education and the Challenges of a New Century" (2000).

See also companion CD-ROM.

Internet
Links

Genesee, Fred, ed. *Program Alternatives for Linguistically Diverse Students*. Santa Cruz, Calif.: Center for Research on Education, Diversity and Excellence, 1999. http://www.cal.org/crede/pubs/edpractice/EPR1.htm

See also companion CD-ROM.

Notes

1. These measures allow parents, under certain circumstances, to seek "waivers" of the English-only rule – e.g., for students aged 10 and older and for those with "special needs." In California, a flexible interpretation of the latter provision has enabled many bilingual education programs to continue. In Arizona and Massachusetts, however, the wording of the initiatives was tightened to limit parents' ability to qualify for such exemptions. Even if waivers are granted, none of these states requires school districts to provide bilingual instruction *(see Chapter 13)*.
2. Alaska (1975), Connecticut (1977), Illinois (1973), New Jersey (1975), Rhode Island (1974), Texas (1973), and Wisconsin (1975). Mandates for bilingual education in California (1976), Colorado (1975), Massachusetts (1971), and Michigan (1974) were later repealed.
3. States such as Arkansas, Idaho, Kansas, and Oregon reported that "instruction incorporates the native language" for substantial numbers of English learners, but this often meant "native-language support" by teacher aides rather than instruction by bilingual teachers. Data were provided for 3,510,292 out of 3,908,095 LEP students nationwide; Florida, Montana, and Wyoming failed to submit reports on language of instruction. Figures for Puerto Rico, Guam, and other "outlying areas" have been excluded for purposes of this analysis.

4. The No Child Left Behind Act, which replaced it in 2002, makes no mention of bilingual education.

5. Much of the evidence favoring the effectiveness of structured immersion for LEP students in the United States comes from studies of this El Paso program, which no longer exists.

6. Native American students received similar treatment in federal Indian schools, parochial schools, and public schools on and off the reservation.

7. E.g., Kentucky reported a 462 percent increase in LEP students during the 1990s, while the census reported only a 252 percent increase in LEP residents of the state, aged 5–17. This suggests that substantial numbers of English learners went unidentified in 1990 as compared with 2000. Yet the problem may persist. In 2000, the state continued to report significantly fewer LEP children (6,017) than the census did (10,896).

8. Soon this model inspired similar approaches for English speakers in the United States, beginning with a highly regarded Spanish immersion program in Culver City, California. Baker and de Kanter also cited programs for language-minority students in the Philippines, South Africa, and McAllen, Texas, that they categorized as structured immersion, but the label in each of these cases has been disputed *(see Chapters 7 and 9)*.

9. According to a national directory compiled by the Center for Applied Linguistics in 2002, foreign-language immersion programs are also available in Cantonese, French, German, Native Hawaiian, Mandarin, and Spanish.

10. A **late-exit model** of bilingual education, which provides considerably more native-language instruction, is sometimes described as another form of TBE because children generally exit at the end of elementary school, in the 5th or 6th grade. Yet late-exit programs differ qualitatively from the early-exit approach by continuing to develop LEP students' native-language skills after they are reclassified as fully English-proficient (FEP). Thus, in the author's view, this approach is more appropriately classed as a form of **developmental bilingual education.**

11. See Chapter 12, note 8.

3 Language Policies in the U.S.A.

*S*trictly speaking, the United States has never had a language policy, consciously planned and national in scope. It has had **language policies** – ad hoc responses to immediate needs or political pressures – often contradictory and inadequate to cope with changing times. The absence of a national consensus in this area means, among other things, that local decisions on how to educate English learners are a continuing source of controversy.

Mixed Feelings about Diversity
Language Policies Elsewhere
American Exceptionalism
Linguistic Laissez-Faire
Language Ideologies, National Myths
Bilingual Double Standard
Questions of Power
Assimilationism vs. Pluralism
Multicultural Anxieties
School Policies and Politics
'Orientations' in Language Planning
Individual Rights, Group Rights

Nevertheless, as the country grows more diverse, government cannot avoid language policymaking in various forms. Deciding when to provide essential services in languages other than English, how to define and combat language-based discrimination, and where to find the language skills deemed critical to national security are some obvious examples. Yet each of these questions is approached in isolation. At the federal level, for example, no agency or official is responsible for coordinating decisions, resources, or research on the wide array of language issues that challenge and sometimes divide Americans.

So confusion persists about some very basic questions: Should linguistic diversity be treated primarily as a threat to be contained, if not eliminated, through restrictive legislation? Or as an asset to be conserved and exploited in pursuit of national goals? Should it be seen as a reality that the country must actively accommodate to ensure civil and political rights for newcomers? Or as a source of recurrent but minor complications that can be addressed on a piecemeal basis? Over the past generation, federal and state policies have vacillated erratically among these alternatives.

So it is hardly surprising that these policies tend to work at cross purposes. By the early 1990s, the U.S. government was spending an estimated $1 billion annually on foreign-language education, mainly to train its own personnel and to subsidize college-level programs; this is not an official figure because there is no central source of information on such costs. At the same time, the federal treasury was providing at least $1 billion – again, the exact amount is difficult to quantify[1] – to support elementary- and secondary-school programs that were mostly designed to assimilate native speakers of foreign languages into an all-English environment.

A decade later, aside from a stronger emphasis on "holding schools accountable" for student performance in English, not much has changed. Skills in so-called **critical languages,** those deemed essential to national security functions, remain in short supply. To meet their personnel needs, federal intelligence agencies, along with the State and Defense departments, rely heavily on training English monolinguals to speak these languages, an expensive and inefficient approach.[2] Meanwhile

> **Language Policy** *n.* 1. What government does officially – through legislation, court decisions, executive action, or other means – to (a) determine how languages are used in public contexts, (b) cultivate language skills needed to meet national priorities, or (c) establish the rights of individuals or groups to learn, use, and maintain languages.
>
> 2. Government regulation of its own language use, including steps to facilitate clear communication, train and recruit personnel, guarantee due process, foster political participation, and provide access to public services, education, proceedings, and documents.

the government largely continues to ignore language resources that already exist in immigrant communities and could be developed with a relatively modest investment. Such contradictory practices are difficult to justify, even from the narrow perspective of cost-effectiveness. Yet they tend to go unnoticed when there is no comprehensive approach to language policy.

Why Not U.S.?

Efforts to deal with language issues in a holistic fashion are common in many countries with diverse populations. Among other things, such policies regulate government operations, define legal rights, authorize funding, set educational priorities, and assign responsibility for implementation. For example:

- Canada's policy of **official bilingualism** within a multicultural context gives equal status to English and French in federal government services, proceedings, and employment, while subsidizing the maintenance of other languages and cultures. Provinces retain considerable autonomy to adopt their own policies, more (e.g., New Brunswick) or less (e.g., Québec) sensitive to minority rights.
- India has designated English and Hindi as official languages at the national level, while constitutionally recognizing 17 other **regional languages** used by state governments, an approach aimed at promoting both efficiency and social harmony in a country where there are more than 400 languages with at least 10,000 speakers.
- Switzerland seeks to manage a multiethnic polity while minimizing ethnic divisions with its territorial approach to recognizing **language rights**; German, French, and Italian are designated as official languages of government in parts of the country where each language group is concentrated; Romansch, spoken in isolated areas, has honorary status as a "national language."
- South Africa, since the overthrow of apartheid, has "officialized" nine indigenous languages in addition to English and Afrikaans for government operations, documents, broadcasting, and education; any of the official languages may be used as a medium of instruction in public schools, which actively promote multilingualism.
- Australia maintains a national policy on languages that aims to: (1) foster English literacy for all, (2) conserve and develop skills in immigrant languages, (3) prevent the extinction of Aboriginal tongues, and (4) encourage English speakers to learn one of 10 target languages that have been singled out as essential to trade and diplomacy.

While these language policies vary considerably in approach and effectiveness – many have formidable obstacles to overcome – by definition they specify a key role for government in mitigating conflicts and pursuing national goals.

Transnational bodies such as the European Union have also devoted substantial time and resources to **language planning**, or organized efforts to engineer social behavior with regard to language.[3] Seeking to promote multilingualism through lifelong learning, for example, the Council of Europe calls on member states "to offer pupils, as far as possible, the opportunity to learn two, or where appropriate, more languages *in addition to* their mother tongues" (emphasis added). At the country level, more elaborate policies have been developed and government ministries have been established to oversee language affairs.

Why is there nothing comparable in the United States? Our most sweeping language initiative to date is Executive Order 13166, issued by President Clinton in 2000, requiring federal agencies, grantees, and contractors to develop plans "to improve access" to their activities by persons whose English is limited. It puts the Civil Rights Division of the U.S. Justice Department in charge of coordinating these efforts and providing regulatory guidance. On paper, the presidential directive appears to signal a significant change in policy. Yet the requirements remain vague and thus far compliance has been limited. As of early 2004, for example, the U.S. Department of Education had yet to submit its plan.

To be sure, this country has its own unique traditions and preferences; language policies that work elsewhere may not be appropriate here. Yet the United States faces many of the same challenges – including questions of equity, productivity, ethnic relations, and resource development – found in the nations mentioned above. In fact, its linguistic-demographic makeup is strikingly similar to Australia's, except for the dominant position of Spanish among U.S. minority languages.[4] Americans' overall response to diversity, however, remains largely unplanned. What accounts for our failure to develop a comprehensive national language policy?

Some have argued that the United States never needed such a policy in the past because, until quite recently, it was a "unilingual" nation and newcomers were quick to adapt to that reality. English was indisputably the language of government and the "common bond" of civil society, according to this view. Thus language barriers were generally a transitory phenomenon, requiring little or no involvement by the state – unlike the situation today, when large numbers of immigrants are failing to assimilate and instead are demanding special programs in their native tongues. What America needs now, these advocates say, is a language policy that would clarify and protect the dominant status of English. To that end they have advanced legislative proposals to designate English as the nation's official language and to restrict, in various ways, public usage of other languages *(see Chapter 6)*.

While appealing to many Americans who are troubled by the quantity (and in some cases the "quality") of today's immigrants, this line of reasoning enjoys little support from objective evidence. Indeed, it asserts precisely the opposite of what demographic research has documented. As discussed in Chapter 1, **Anglicization rates** are probably higher today than at any point in U.S. history, even as linguistic minority populations expand, because of a rapid shift to English among second-generation immigrants. Language diversity in North America has ebbed and flowed, reaching its lowest level in the mid-20th century. But it has existed in every era, since long before the United States constituted itself as a nation.

American Exceptions

Among the factors that have distinguished this country from many others are its immigrant roots, promise of social mobility (at least for those of European origins), and libertarian, individualist traditions. From the outset **American identity** was defined in terms of political principles, not involuntary ties of ancestry. The new nation self-consciously strived to be, in Thomas Paine's words, "an asylum for the persecuted lovers of civil and religious liberty from *every part* of Europe." In theory, anyone could become an American, not just those of a certain ethnicity, simply by swearing loyalty to democratic ideals.

Thus ethnic differences were neither to be encouraged nor discouraged by the state,[5] in hopes that a policy of tolerance would serve to make conflicts more manageable, less antagonistic. Rather than repress competing interests and factions, James Madison believed that a well designed government could balance them all against each other, for the good of the whole. Indeed, he warned that too much popular unity could be dangerous. To guard against this threat, which has come to be known as the **tyranny of the majority**,[6] Madison advocated a structure of **political pluralism** in which minority rights of all kinds would be protected. Our early leaders had some significant blindspots – race in particular – which distorted these ideals by limiting their application.[7] Nevertheless, what was in the late 18th century a unique form of nationalism served to discourage rigid ethnic divisions, common in Europe, in which language differences loomed large and produced intractable conflicts.

While America's streets were never paved with gold, to the surprise and disappointment of many newcomers, opportunities for individual advancement have often been greater here than elsewhere. This is not to say that immigrants have routinely been welcomed. To the contrary, nativist reactions have flared up repeatedly, especially in hard economic times. Yet language has been a relatively minor theme in these attacks. Indigenous and conquered peoples, primarily racial minorities, have been more likely than immigrants to bear the brunt of English-only policies, used for purposes of social control and expropriation of resources *(see Chapter 4)*. To the extent that ideological justifications were offered for language restrictions, they more often involved a call to impose "civilization" on "primitive" peoples than asserted any claim for English as a symbolic unifier of Americans. Only in the early and late decades of the 20th century did outbreaks of xenophobia mutate into virulent strains of linguistic nationalism.

Historically speaking, language has been a less salient factor in social conflicts among Americans than race, religion, or class. Because the dominance of English was usually taken for granted, immigrants' foreign speech tended to draw fewer reactions from the native-born than, say, their Catholicism or poverty or swarthy complexions. Notwithstanding exceptional times and places, such as the World War I era and California during the Gold Rush, officially sponsored discrimination on the basis of language was far less common in America than in many of the homelands from which immigrants came.

> ## Safeguarding Minority Rights
>
> It is of great importance in a republic not only to guard the society against the oppression of its rulers, but to guard one part of the society against the injustice of the other part. Different interests necessarily exist in different classes of citizens. If a majority be united by a common interest, the rights of the minority will be insecure. There are but two methods of providing against this evil: the one by creating a will in the community independent of the majority – that is, of the society itself; the other, by comprehending in the society so many separate descriptions of citizens as will render an unjust combination of a majority of the whole very improbable, if not impracticable. ... Whilst all authority in it will be derived from and dependent on the society, the society itself will be broken into so many parts, interests, and classes of citizens, that the rights of individuals, or of the minority, will be in little danger from interested combinations of the majority.
>
> **James Madison, *The Federalist* (1788)**

When European regimes found an ethnic minority troublesome, typically the first response was to repress its native tongue. This often had serious consequences, as sociologist Herbert Kelman explains:

> Since language is so closely tied to group identity, language-based discrimination against the group is perceived as a threat to its very existence as a recognizable entity and as an attack on its sacred objects and symbols. The issue is no longer merely a redistribution of power and resources, but it is

self-preservation of the group and defense against genocide. The conflict becomes highly charged with emotion and increasingly unmanageable. Genocide, after all, is not a matter for negotiation but for last-ditch defense.

Immigrants have encountered little of this in the United States, where they could generally establish schools, attend religious services, hold public meetings, and publish newspapers in any language without state interference. Paradoxically, the laissez-faire climate tended to weaken rather than strengthen their linguistic loyalties over time. As Nathan Glazer has observed, "languages shriveled in the air of freedom, while they had apparently flourished under adversity in Europe." Issues of bilingualism thus tended to decline in significance for second- and third-generation Americans.

Still, this is not quite the whole story. Glazer might have also mentioned the role of tight immigration quotas enacted in the 1920s, targeting eastern and southern Europeans in particular, which severely limited the flow of non-English speakers into the United States. Immigration from Greece, for example, was restricted to less than one percent of its pre–World War I level. The effect on minority languages was devastating. As the children and grandchildren of immigrants shifted to English, few newcomers were arriving to replenish the ranks of Greek, Italian, Polish, or Yiddish speakers, to name a few. German Americans, smarting from the wartime repression of their language *(see Chapter 4)*, began to assimilate in large numbers. By the 1960s, when a mass exodus occurred from white ethnic neighborhoods to deracinated suburbs, speakers of non-English mother tongues were advancing in age and dwindling in numbers. For immigrants' children and grandchildren, Anglicization was virtually complete. The major exceptions to this pattern were speakers of Spanish, Chinese, and Native American languages. Located primarily in the Southwest and a few urban centers, these groups tended to lack the political influence to make their demands heard.

So, at a time when the federal government was rapidly expanding, launching a variety of Great Society initiatives, language diversity ranked relatively low on the national agenda. It was conceived – when noticed at all – primarily as a regional issue and a "racial" problem of secondary importance to the African-American civil-rights struggle.

The federal government's belated, piecemeal response, as exemplified by the Bilingual Education Act of 1968, was probably inevitable.[8] Rather than work toward a national language policy, it simply opened a new front in the War on Poverty. This approach proved to be effective politics at the time, facilitating an expeditious and uncontroversial response to the needs of English learners. Yet, by consciously avoiding issues of linguistic assimilation and pluralism, policymakers failed to engage the American public in any substantive discussion about the rationale and implications of bilingual education. As a result, they merely postponed and possibly exacerbated the English-only reaction to come.

Language Ideologies

The political backlash was – or should have been – predictable. Despite lacking a national language policy, Americans have some characteristic ways of thinking and behaving where language is concerned, certain **language ideologies**. These are belief systems that shape, and are shaped by, everyday practices. Not necessarily true or false, consistent or inconsistent, ideologies are nevertheless rooted in social reality, growing directly out of the lived experience of various identity groups (defined, e.g., by nationality, class, ethnicity, or gender).[9] More or less coherent opinions about language, sometimes described as **folk linguistics**, are acquired from friends, relatives, media, community leaders, advocacy organizations, and other nonspecialist sources. They are popularized not merely through repetition but, more importantly, through reinforcement by society's dominant institutions. Language ideologies may involve, for example:

- *Family legends*: "My great-grandfather came to this country without a word of English and he succeeded without bilingual education."
- *Conventional wisdom:* "The best way to teach English is 'total immersion,' the earlier the better, because young children can easily 'pick up' a second language."
- *Political principles*: "Immigrants who came here to enjoy the blessings of America have a patriotic obligation to speak America's language."
- *Ethnic paranoia*: "English may be spreading throughout the world, but Spanish is taking over in the U.S.A."

Though casually acquired, such convictions often come to be deeply felt as they are incorporated into **national myths**, larger narratives about who we are as Americans. Among the best known of these is the **Melting Pot**, a term popularized by a play of that name by Israel Zangwill, a Jewish immigrant from England, in 1908. The metaphor suggests a fusion of many cultures and genetic stocks into something entirely new, "a nation of immigrants" in which ethnic divisions would disappear and mutual respect would thrive. The play's central character, a Russian Jew named David Quixano, sums it up as follows:

America is God's crucible, the great Melting Pot where all the races of Europe are melting and re-forming! Here you stand, good folk, think I, when I see them at Ellis Island, here you stand in your fifty groups, with your fifty languages and histories, and your fifty blood hatreds and rivalries. But you won't be long like that, brothers, for these are the fires of God you've come to – these are the fires of God. A fig for your feuds and vendettas! Germans and Frenchmen, Irishmen and Englishmen, Jews and Russians – into the Crucible with you all! God is making the American.

Zangwill's idealist dream, however, was no match for the political realities of that period. Popular revulsion against Jews, Slavs, Italians, and other so-called "new immigrants" led to a coercive campaign for **Anglo-conformity**. Rather than incorporating what newcomers had to offer, according to sociologist Milton Gordon, this movement "demanded the complete renunciation of the immigrant's ancestral culture in favor of the behavior and values of the Anglo-Saxon core group." One result was that by 1919, in the name of **Americanization**, a majority of states adopted English-only instruction laws. Bilingual education, which had thrived in many areas, was largely eradicated *(see Chapter 4)*.

Owing to this historical experience, the Melting Pot has come to mean **assimilation**, a path to becoming American that involves the sacrifice of "un-American" (i.e., ethnic) traits, rather than **acculturation**, a process of adding the new without discarding the old. In the 1980s advocates of the latter approch began to promote the image of the **Salad Bowl**, suggesting that cultures should blend without losing their distinct flavors. This alternative national myth was designed to celebrate bilingualism and biculturalism. Dueling metaphors continue to play a prominent role in debates over English-only legislation.

Other nations have also elaborated language ideologies, specific to their own histories and politics, expressing their own identities, hopes, prejudices, and fears. **Ethnocentrism**, or the tendency to regard one's own group as the standard for judging others, frequently plays a role. By and large, however, the anxiety that many Americans express about linguistic diversity today remains rare. No doubt one reason is that, outside the United States, mastering two or three languages is more commonly a lived, as opposed to an imagined, experience. Even in countries with highly charged language politics – Canada, for example – bilingualism is generally regarded as a response to necessity rather than a deviant phenomenon. While this hardly ensures peace among language groups, familiarity tends to bring increased understanding; parochialism does not.

Bilingual Double Standard

In recent years the following joke has achieved international popularity, no doubt more for its message than its wit:

> *What do you call someone who speaks three languages?*
> Trilingual.
> *What do you call someone who speaks two languages?*
> Bilingual.
> *What do you call someone who speaks one language?*
> American.

The stereotype is rather out of date, following three decades of rising immigration. Yet it is fair to say that fluent bilingualism in the United States remains a largely ethnic phenomenon. For the majority of Americans, a complacent monolingualism is still the norm. Although foreign-language enrollments have increased substantially since the 1950s, largely in response to stiffer requirements for college entrance and graduation, there is no evidence that this trend has led to substantial increases in foreign-language proficiency. American students' limitations in this area, though periodically bemoaned in government reports, are seldom acted upon. What accounts for our resistance to serious language-learning, which distinguishes us from so many fellow inhabitants of the planet?

Geographic isolation is sometimes cited as a cause; yet that has hardly discouraged Japan from stressing the study of foreign languages, with considerable success. Another possibility is the growing role of English as a **lingua franca**, or common language, in international relations, business, media, and science. Why, then, is Australia actively conserving and developing multilingual skills, recognizing their importance in an era of globalization, while the United States is not? A stronger explanatory factor may be the limited demand for bilinguals in our domestic employment market; without the promise of a financial payoff, there is less incentive to spend the time (and often the expense) needed to acquire a second language. As immigrant communities grow, however, this argument becomes less tenable. Not only teachers but social service providers, health care workers, police officers, and even convenience store clerks in cities like Miami are increasingly called upon to use Spanish, Vietnamese, Haitian Creole, or other languages on the job (although they are not always well compensated for doing so).

While practical incentives, or lack thereof, surely affect Americans' language-learning practices, **language attitudes** are usually decisive. We tend to value bilingualism in certain contexts – and certain people – and to devalue it in others. In short, explains sociolinguist Rolf Kjolseth, we have a "schizophrenic" mentality:

> There are bilinguals whom we admire and praise as individuals. They are scholars, diplomats, celebrities, businesspersons, and members of the jet set. There are other bilinguals whom we disparage, pity, or despise. They are members of ethnic groups: Mexicans, Cubans, Puerto Ricans, French Canadians, Vietnamese, Laotians, ad infinitum. ... Although we hold the one in awe and the other in disdain, the persons referred to may be equally skillful bilinguals. Still, we feel no sense of contradiction. ... **Individual bilingualism** is "good" and **group bilingualism** is "bad." [Emphasis added]

Ironically, because group bilingualism is acquired in a natural context, such as growing up in a community where two languages are spoken, it is likely to be more proficient than individual bilingualism, which is normally acquired by English speakers in an artificial (i.e., classroom) environment. Yet the latter type of bilingualism is typically praised, while the former is ignored or discouraged or taken for granted. In opinion polls Americans overwhelmingly agree that immigrant children should learn English without delay – and if not, their schools must be doing something terribly wrong *(see Chapter 15)*. Meanwhile we tolerate high levels of failure in foreign-language programs, from which students routinely emerge without basic conversational skills, or even the ability to order a meal in a foreign restaurant, after several years of instruction. Where does this "bilingual double standard" originate?

Power Plays

As the linguist Noam Chomsky postulates, "questions of language are basically questions of power." Speakers of a dominant tongue, for example, are seldom as willing to acquire a second language as members of linguistic minorities. In the mid-1960s, when Canada adopted its policy of official bilingualism, members of the Anglophone majority were six times less likely to be bilingual than their Francophone counterparts. Assuming that the two groups were equally capable of learning each other's languages, speaking the more powerful tongue had apparently bred apathy or arrogance or perhaps a combination of the two.

Consciously or not, language attitudes express social and political attitudes. The fact that group bilingualism in the United States today is associated with low-status, nonwhite, impoverished minorities, and individual bilingualism with well educated, affluent members of the dominant culture helps to explain our contradictory views. Of course, these generalizations are simplistic, misleading, and out of date. No matter. The point is that they are widely believed, reflecting and reinforcing prejudices that already exist concerning immigrants and their impact.

"Although American society is highly stratified and marked by great inequalities," Kjolseth argues, "we are ideologically committed to egalitarianism, equality of opportunity and distributive justice." How can this disturbing contradiction between the ideal and the reality be resolved? One solution is to think of linguistic minorities as culturally "deprived" and "disadvantaged": *It's too bad those poor people don't speak enough English to get ahead.* Society finds it easy to blame the victims for their victimization. By contrast, Kjolseth says, "if a group was seen as *advantaged* culturally ... by virtue of being bilingual, then the reasons for its subordination would have to be sought elsewhere, namely in the economic and political spheres" (emphasis added). This is hardly the kind of criticism that power elites like to encourage. They prefer to emphasize the **cultural deprivation** analysis *(see Chapter 4)*, which lays an ideological foundation for paternalistic responses, ranging from the subtractive (transitional bilingualism) to the coercive (English-only mandates).

Loyal Americanism

We must have but one flag. We must also have but one language. That must be the language of the Declaration of Independence, of Washington's Farewell address, of Lincoln's Gettysburg speech and second inaugural. We cannot tolerate any attempt to oppose or supplant the language and culture that has come down to us from the builders of this Republic with the language and culture of any European country. The greatness of this nation depends on the swift assimilation of the aliens she welcomes to her shores. Any force which attempts to retard that assimilative process is a force hostile to the highest interests of our country. It is a force, which, if allowed to develop, will, for the benefit of this group or that, undermine our national institutions and pervert our national ideals.

Theodore Roosevelt, "The Children of the Crucible" (1917)

These types of language policies address the "problem" without disrupting established power relationships. Assimilation is a one-way street.

The purported beneficiaries of such policies are increasingly conceived as *immigrants* to America rather than as *linguistic-minority* Americans. News media nowadays tend to portray bilingual education and ESL as programs designed exclusively for recent arrivals to the United States. In 2002, the *Washington Post* excitedly reported its discovery that substantial numbers of LEP students are U.S.-born – a pattern that was just as evident in 1968 or 1984. This is now considered news, however (as well as an implicit criticism of schools), because limited English proficiency is assumed to be a condition that primarily affects the foreign-born. The shifting focus is significant. Because immigrants have made a voluntary decision, at least in theory, to come to the United States, it is much easier to dismiss their aspirations to maintain native languages and cultures than it is for, say, Spanish speakers in the Southwest who have resided there for generations. So the latter tend to be squeezed into the immigrant "frame." Recognizing indigenous bilingualism creates ideological complications.

For many Americans **linguistic assimilation**, or the effective displacement of minority languages by English, is the obvious "solution" to linguistic diversity. It appears beneficial both to society at large, by eliminating language barriers, and to immigrants themselves, by cultivating skills that are critical to their upward mobility. Assimilation also has a strong symbolic appeal for the native-born. Insisting that newcomers shed their foreign traits, language in particular, is a way to reassert the Americanization myth about who must adapt to whom. Immigrants are expected to demonstrate their loyalty to the United States by embracing "American" ways. When government endorses such policies, for example, by declaring English the official language, it makes a statement about power, clarifying who is on top – and who is not.

Assimilationist ideology was on prominent display at a 1998 conference sponsored by the Georgia Department of Education, which chose as its theme: "English: The Language That Unifies U.S." State superintendent of schools Linda Schrenko set the tone when she told ESL and migrant education teachers:

> English has been the language that has enabled all Americans, regardless of heritage, to communicate with one another. For the past several years the population of limited English proficient students in Georgia has experienced a tremendous increase. This trend is likely to continue for many years. As educators, we must utilize the most effective proven methods for teaching English to these students so that they too can realize the American dream. We must also teach them about our great culture and our great country so they will feel that they are Americans and learn about our civic duties, rights and privileges.

The conference program was filled with patriotic illustrations and epigraphs, including Theodore Roosevelt's famous assertion that "there is no room in this country for hyphenated Americanism." In a similar vein, it quoted the leader of a veterans' group: "Americanism is humanity's most glorious experiment in the science of living. If this experiment should fail, civilization itself may well be doomed."

Development of English learners' native-language skills was not among the goals that Georgia officials were prepared to endorse. Until leaving office in 2002, Schrenko used the authority of the state to discourage and, when necessary, to block school districts from offering any form of bilingual instruction.[10] Despite paying lip service to "effective proven methods for teaching English," the state education department made little if any effort to justify its English learner policies on the basis of scientific research. Rhetoric about the imperatives of assimilation proved sufficient with a majority of the public. Not only in Georgia but throughout the United States, this ideology remains dominant where language questions are concerned. The burden of justification, and a heavy one at that, falls on those who would challenge it.

Contested Terrain

Dominant, of course, is not the same as exclusive. Ethnic minorities and their allies have often tended toward different perspectives, notably those grounded in **cultural pluralism**. Neither integrationist nor separatist, the pluralist ideal is one of unity-in-diversity. It seeks to extend the principles of liberty and equality to all comers, without pressuring any group to give up its native language, culture, or identity.

To be sure, some immigrants have acquiesced in the Americanization ethic and refused to pass on heritage languages to the next generation, hoping (usually in vain) that English monolingualism would spare their children from discrimination in school and society. Internal debates over whether to use English or minority languages for instruction, media, or religious services have divided virtually every ethnic group at one time or another. While some immigrant leaders have preached the benefits of total assimilation, they have generally been the exception.

Certainly this viewpoint was unusual among the largest linguistic minority for most of U.S. history, German Americans.[11] Until World War I, according to the historian John Hawgood, "the Germans used their language as a weapon to ward off Americanization and assimilation, and used every social milieu, the home, the church, the school, the press, in the fight to preserve the German language, even among their children and grandchildren." These efforts to avoid Anglicization succeeded for generations in rural areas of the Midwest, and continue to succeed in isolated religious communities such as the Amish and Old Order Mennonites.

As a result, says Milton Gordon, "cultural pluralism was a fact in American society before it became a theory." The term came into common usage in the 1950s, although its leading proponent, the philosopher Horace Kallen, began elaborating the theory much earlier. In his 1915 critique of the Americanization campaign, the English-only movement of its time, this German-Jewish immigrant advocated an alternative vision of American democracy, which he described as "a federation or commonwealth of nationalities":

> The common language of the commonwealth, the language of its great political tradition, is English, but each nationality expresses its emotional and voluntary life in its own language, in its own inevitable aesthetic and intellectual forms. The common life of the commonwealth is politico-economic, and serves as the foundation and background for the realization of the distinctive individuality of each *natio* [sic] that composes it. ... [E]ach ethnic group is the natural instrument, its spirit and culture are its theme and melody, and the harmony and dissonances and discords of them all make the symphony of civilization.

Writing a bit more succinctly in 1924, Kallen explained: "Democracy involves not the elimination of differences but the perfection and conservation of differences." This was a bold – many would say, utopian – viewpoint in an era that was debating whether, given their ethnic distinctiveness, eastern and southern Europeans were "assimilable" at all. (American elites soon concluded they were not, and largely slammed the door on further immigration by non–Anglo-Saxons.) Cultural pluralism initially attracted few adherents other than Zionists and foreign-born radicals.[12] By the time it gained broader acceptance, largely in reaction to Nazi atrocities in World War II, English was not just the common but frequently the only language spoken by descendants of European immigrants. Other than religion, most of the ethnic differences that remained among white Americans were superficial at best. This made cultural pluralism more palatable to members of the majority, less a challenging social agenda than a vague expression of good will, a celebration of diversity that was largely in the past. Not unlike the national motto, *E pluribus unum*, "Out of many, one."

Conversely, **multiculturalism** – the ideological offspring of cultural pluralism – attracts heated opposition today not so much for its radicalism as for its social and political implications in a period of demographic transformation. When power is being redistributed, insecurities abound and symbolic struggles take on great significance. Multiculturalism has become a natural target because it celebrates what many Americans find threatening: ethnic differences that are considerably more profound than those of a generation ago. In other words, it champions the *pluribus* rather than the *unum* at a time of uncertainty about what it is that defines the nation and holds it together.

While the new diversity is hardly limited to language, bilingualism arouses special ire among today's "culture warriors" because it serves as a convenient symbol for the impact of immigration. Legislating English-only restrictions in itself cannot restore the homogeneous America of the 1950s. But by "sending a message to immigrants," it appeases English speakers who feel disgruntled, even dispossessed, by social change and who are nostalgic for a time when minority language speakers "knew their place." Anxieties about social status are at the heart of this movement (see Chapter 6).

Yet a countertrend is also emerging. The more common it is to encounter minority languages in public places or popular culture, the less threatening they become. Mass marketers have clearly noticed the change in attitudes. The 2003 Grammy awards, a mainstream television broadcast to 25 million viewers, featured a toothpaste commercial delivered entirely in Spanish. Bilingualism is losing its shock value and, for most Americans, its sinister overtones. In fact, the English-only backlash has begun to generate a backlash of its own. Efforts to restrict the use of other languages are increasingly perceived as bigoted – and not just by their targets. Politicians of all stripes, including President George W. Bush, now recognize the importance of Latinos as potential swing voters, and many of them make a symbolic point of speaking Spanish in public (although, with Bush, it seldom goes beyond "Mi casa es su Casa Blanca").[13]

Attitudes about the practical dimensions of multilingualism are also in flux, thanks to globalization, not only of trade and capital markets but also of ethnic strife, nuclear weapons, threats to public health, climate change, and environmental degradation. The status of English as a world lingua franca makes it easier for monolingual Americans to travel and live overseas. But it hardly eliminates the need to know other languages, whether to learn about other cultures, sell products, or combat terrorism.

The events of September 11, 2001, highlighted Americans' vulnerabilities in this area. In the aftermath of al Qaeda's attacks, U.S. security agencies were so desperate for translators of Arabic and other languages of south Asia that they were forced to place want-ads in newspapers.[14] The National Foreign Language Center at the University of Maryland reports that, when U.S. forces invaded Afghanistan to hunt down the terrorists, five of the country's seven major languages – including Pashto, spoken by 8 million Afghans – were not even taught in U.S. colleges and universities.[15] Americans' lack of proficiency in these tongues certainly complicated the military effort and may have contributed to the escape of most Taliban and al Qaeda leaders.

There should be no question that, in a complex and dangerous world, the value of proficient bilingualism is on the rise. As growing numbers of English-speaking parents seek meaningful language-learning opportunities for their children, **two-way bilingual education** is more popular than ever before *(see Chapter 12)*. So are **heritage language programs** designed to help minority students reclaim their ancestral tongues. Over time these incremental developments could revolutionize the way Americans perceive linguistic diversity, or at least open more eyes to alternative viewpoints.

Policy and Politics

As long as a nation remains conflicted over whether to celebrate, accommodate, or stamp out bilingualism, its responses will be confused and contradictory. Language issues like bilingual education continue to flare up periodically, generating an emotional debate and sometime hasty decisions. **Policy formation** – ideally a rational process of analyzing problems, gathering data, considering options, and setting goals – becomes in practice a highly politicized activity, sensitive to opinion polls and pressure groups. Decisions tend to be made on an ideological basis, appeasing passions of the moment with simplistic, one-size-fits-all solutions, rather than considering factual evidence about, say, which pedagogical approaches would work best for diverse groups of students. Politicization of complex issues is quite likely to occur when instruments of **direct democracy**, such as ballot initiatives, replace the deliberative processes of legislatures and administrative agencies. In these situations minority voices are easily drowned out, thus eliminating the need for compromise and inviting extreme outcomes.

In a representative democracy, of course, **advocacy** by individuals as well as interest groups is an inevitable factor in policymaking – as it should be. Public education is inherently *political*, an activity that affects all members of the community, one way or another, whether they have school-age children or merely pay school taxes, and stakeholders naturally want to exert an influence. This complicates decision-making but also serves useful purposes. School officials need input from the public, both to design effective policies and to give communities a sense of ownership. When policymaking becomes an elite and unaccountable process, schools can be perceived as alien institutions, inspiring parental resistance rather than support (indeed, this has often occurred in minority communities). While educators need autonomy to apply their expertise and experience, the surest way to achieve that is by winning the trust and respect of those they serve. Politics, in this broad sense, is inescapably part of the job.

By contrast, when education becomes *politicized,* external considerations – questions of power, social status, material interests – take precedence over the merits of an issue. Ideology determines pedagogy, even if that means overriding professional judgment and research evidence about what approaches would best serve students. This is a recipe for unworkable policies and, more often than not, for social polarization.

California's Proposition 227 is a classic example. The sponsor of this ballot measure, a wealthy entrepreneur and aspiring politician named Ron Unz, recognized bilingual education as a target of opportunity, a poorly understood program that was widely opposed by English-speaking taxpayers. Rather than consult research or seek expert advice on how to improve the education of English learners, Unz took folk linguistics as his starting point: the "common sense" notion that young children can acquire a second language virtually overnight if "totally immersed." Accordingly, he drafted legislation to impose a one-year, all-English program as the default model for English learners *(see Chapter 13).* California's disproportionately white, affluent, childless electorate then approved the measure, over the opposition of most Latino voters, limiting the educational options of Latino and other language-minority children. Political battles over English-only initiatives continue. Although the full story of their impact remains to be written, an apt title might be: *Policymaking as Tyranny of the Majority.*

'Orientations' in Language Policy

Richard Ruíz, an expert in language planning, offers another approach for analyzing and critiquing policy decisions in this area. He proposes the concept of **orientations,** ideological frames that "delimit the ways we talk about language and language issues," including the questions that are asked, the conclusions that are drawn, even the data that are gathered. "In short," Ruíz says, "orientations determine what is *thinkable* about language in society" (emphasis added). He identifies three basic types:

- *Language-as-problem* focuses on complications created by linguistic diversity, usually in the context of treating larger social ills (poverty, illiteracy, ethnic hostilities).
- *Language-as-right* emphasizes principles of social justice, such as ensuring minorities' equal access to schools, courts, voting booths, and other public institutions.
- *Language-as-resource* values linguistic skills of all kinds as cultural capital, recognizing the social benefits of conserving and developing these assets.

Orientations can be useful in analyzing the assumptions, whether explicit or unconscious, that go into formulating alternative language policies, as well as the implications of these policies when put into practice. Thinking of limited English proficiency as a *problem*, for example, a *disability* of children who are *disadvantaged* by their linguistic-minority backgrounds, implies the need for *remediation* to bring English learners up to standard, to *compensate* for their cultural *deprivation*. It thus becomes "natural" to respond with a single-minded emphasis on English; in other words, a policy of **subtractive bilingualism**. Whether bilingual or all-English, school programs are likely to stress linguistic assimilation at the expense of developing native-language skills.

The policy response would be decidedly different if students' proficiency in, say, Chinese, were conceived as a *resource*: a useful *tool* not only for academic achievement but also for English acquisition; a way to *enhance* cultural identity, familial ties, and social adjustment; a future *advantage* in the job market because of its growing *value* to employers; and a potential *contribution* to monolingual American students (the deprived group in this context) where schools are able to exploit the *opportunity*. This orientation tends to encourage **additive bilingualism** through approaches such as developmental and two-way bilingual education.

Thus a clear message is conveyed, intentionally or not, by policies and practices that treat language as a problem as opposed to a resource, or vice versa. Children are quick to receive it. They can sense from the behavior of adults whether their mother tongue is regarded as a threat, a nuisance, or a handicap, or whether it is seen as an asset worth preserving. When educators favor assimilationist approaches, they place a stamp of authority on negative messages about students' backgrounds and, by implication, about students themselves. These stigmas tend to be internalized, weakening English learners' self-confidence about their abilities, already under pressure because of the language barrier, and denigrating their ethnic and family origins. Children are forced to choose, in effect, between the values of home and those of school. None of this is conducive to academic performance.

By contrast, policies that validate the native language and culture, treating them as worthy of respect and relevant to classroom instruction, are associated in the research literature with positive outcomes. School becomes more meaningful as it builds on children's experience. By making biculturalism an option, it can also strengthen their sense of who they are, helping to mitigate the identity conflicts that are virtually inevitable for linguistic minorities approaching adolescence in America. Language-as-resource is a key component of what Jim Cummins calls **empowerment**, or "transformative pedagogy," in which teacher-student interactions reflect "collaborative relations of power" instead of the coercive, hierarchical relations that characterize the wider society *(see Chapter 8)*.

Collaboration is an even stronger feature of the language-as-right orientation, which gives linguistic minorities a participatory role in policies that affect them. In other words, it extends the principles of democracy to questions of culture and ethnicity. One approach is to ensure "first class" citizenship to individuals – an equal right to education, due process, and public services – regardless of their proficiency in English. Alternatively, language-as-right may involve the prerogative of ethnic communities to maintain their linguistic autonomy, to govern themselves in the minority language, or to revitalize ancestral tongues, with state support when necessary. For example, Canada's policy of official bilingualism, according to a former Commissioner of Official Languages, effectively guarantees Francophones the "right *not* to assimilate, the right to maintain a certain difference."

The concern for **group rights**, unlike the protection of individual rights, has few precedents in the United States.[16] Litigation to improve the education of English learners in American schools has rarely claimed an **ethnic entitlement** to schooling in the native language, a principle often asserted in other nations. Instead, it has demanded native-language (or other) accommodations to ensure an **equal opportunity** for any language-minority child to succeed. This narrow tradition has made it more difficult to challenge the hegemony of assimilationist assumptions in policymaking. Indeed, a version of language-as-right has been embraced by opponents of bilingual education who champion minority children's "right" to be taught in English.

Orientations, while useful in analyzing language policy outcomes and the thought processes behind them, nevertheless tell only part of the story. They are better at describing the *what* than the *how* or *why*. It would also be a mistake to assign orientations any direct causal role – as if government officials made decisions by explicitly choosing the language-as-problem alternative, say, over language-as-resource. This is not how real-world policies are formulated. One reason is that debates about language are seldom simply debates about language. In fact, they are generally *less about language* than about underlying social and political conflicts. Developments in language policy must therefore be understood holistically, in the context of broader historical forces.

Suggested Reading

Crawford, James. *At War with Diversity: U.S. Language Policy in an Age of Anxiety*. Clevedon, U.K.: Multilingual Matters, 2000.

Gordon, Milton M. *Assimilation in American Life: The Role of Race, Religion, and National Origins*. New York: Oxford University Press, 1964.

Higham, John. *Send These to Me: Jews and Other Immigrants in Urban America*. New York: Atheneum, 1975.

Kjolseth, Rolf. "Cultural Politics of Bilingualism." *Society* (May-June 1983): 40–48.

Ruíz, Richard. "Orientations in Language Planning." *NABE Journal* 8 (1984): 15–34. Rpt. in Sandra Lee McKay and Sau-ling Cynthia Wong, eds., *Language Diversity: Problem or Resource?* Cambridge, Mass.: Newbury House, 1988.

See also pp. 389–90.

Online Resource Guide

Executive Order 13166. *Improving Access to Services for Persons with Limited English Proficiency* (2000).

Kallen, Horace. "Democracy versus the Melting Pot" (1915).

Roosevelt, Theodore. "Children of the Crucible" (1917).

Tocqueville, Alexis de. "Unlimited Power of the Majority in the United States, and Its Consequences." In *Democracy in America* (1835).

See also companion CD-ROM.

Internet Links

James Crawford's Language Policy Web Site.
http://ourworld.compuserve.com/homepages/jwcrawford/

Mercator: Linguistic Rights and Legislation.
http://www.ciemen.org/mercator/index-gb.htm

National Foreign Language Center: "Language and National Security."
http://www.nflc.org/security/background.htm

Nunberg, Geoffrey. "The Official English Movement: Reimagining America."
In James Crawford, ed., *Language Loyalties: A Source Book on the Official English
Controversy*. Chicago: University of Chicago Press, 1992:
http://ourworld.compuserve.com/homepages/jwcrawford/nunberg.htm

See also companion CD-ROM.

Notes

1. The estimate of foreign-language expenditures comes from J. David Edwards, "Foreign Languages and the State of the Union," Joint National Committee for Languages, March 1993. While the combined budget for bilingual and immigrant education programs was around $200 million at that time, the lion's share of federal funding for English learner programs came from Title I; unfortunately, the latter amounts were not disaggregated.

2. E.g., the Defense Language Institute in Monterey, California, provides a beginning 63-week course in Arabic for military personnel, at an estimated cost of $33,500 per student, not counting room, board, and military salaries. Students who successfully complete the course reach basic proficiency levels that remain well below what is required for intelligence work.

3. The language historian Heinz Kloss has made a distinction between **corpus planning**, which seeks to regulate features of the language itself, such as grammar and vocabulary, and **status planning**, which governs the usage of various languages in particular social contexts.

4. Like the United States, Australia has a dominant English-speaking majority – largely monolingual – but is also home to hundreds of indigenous languages, most of which are threatened with extinction. Immigrant languages are even more prevalent there, with a foreign-born population of 23 percent (versus 11 percent in the U.S.A.) Chinese and Italian speakers are Australia's largest linguistic minorities, accounting for 2.1 and 1.9 percent of the population, respectively, in 2001. By comparison, nearly 11 percent of U.S. residents (aged 5 and above) reported speaking Spanish at home in 2000.

5. An important precedent was set in 1818, when Congress rejected a petition by Irish immigrants for a land grant in the West. Although the U.S. government had millions of acres to distribute, it wanted to avoid "a patchwork of foreign settlements," explains historian Marcus Lee Hansen. "Probably no decision in the history of American immigration policy possesses more profound significance. By its terms the immigrant was to enjoy no special privileges to encourage his coming; also he was to suffer no special restrictions. His opportunities were those of the native, nothing more, nothing less"; *The Immigrant in American History* (New York: Harper Torchbooks, 1964), p. 132.

6. The term was coined by Alexis de Tocqueville, in *Democracy in America* (1835).

7. In 1790, for example, the nation's first elected Congress voted to restrict naturalization to "free white persons." Well into the 20th century, this law was still being used to bar citizenship to Asian and Middle Eastern immigrants; it was finally repealed in 1952. The last racial criteria in U.S. immigration policy were removed in 1965.

8. Other examples are the Voting Rights Act amendments of 1975, which guaranteed bilingual ballots for certain minority language groups in certain jurisdictions (mostly in the Southwest) where English literacy rates were low, and the Federal Court Interpreters Act of 1978, which required the translation of some, but not all, legal proceedings for limited English speakers.

9. The term **ideology** is notorious for its multiplicity of meanings. For an in-depth discussion, see Terry Eagleton, *Ideology: An Introduction* (London: Verso, 1991).

10. E.g., in 1998, state officials refused to approve the Hall County school system's application for a federal Title VII grant. The Georgia Department of Education ruled that the proposed two-way bilingual education program was inconsistent with "the expeditious acquisition of the English language. ... While the concept of teaching Spanish to English-speaking elementary school children is worthy of consideration, it is the goal of the Department to promote English proficiency programs to LEP students."

11. Spanish speakers outnumbered German speakers for the first time in the 1950s.

12. One obvious source of supporters, African-Americans, were excluded from Kallen's vision – not for any principled reason but because his focus was exclusively on European ethnics. "The pluralist thesis from the outset was encapsulated in white ethnocentrism," concludes historian John Higham.

13. In a spontaneous moment, the president's contradictory feelings about language came through. The occasion was a joint press conference in Paris with Jacques Chirac, the president of France, in May 2002. An American reporter asked Bush a question, in English naturally, then turned to Chirac and asked him, in French, to comment as well. Obviously surprised by the journalist's bilingual ability, Bush responded: "Very good. The guy memorizes four words, and he plays like he's intercontinental. ... I'm impressed. Que bueno. Now I'm literate in two languages." Was this American anti-intellectualism talking? Resentment of Old Europe? A C student's jealousy? Whatever the source, it is hard to imagine a similar reaction from any other world leader.

14. In 1993, the shortage of such skills left Americans vulnerable to the first attack on the World Trade Center. Three years earlier U.S. authorities had acquired documents, in Arabic, that outlined plans for blowing up the twin towers but they lacked the resources to translate them until after the terrorists acted; "FBI Agents Ill-Equipped to Predict Terror Acts," *Washington Post*, Sept. 24, 2001.

15. About 600 U.S. students were learning Farsi, the dominant language of Iran, which is a relative of Dari, spoken by about 5.6 million Afghans. Meanwhile there were four U.S. students studying Uzbek, which has 1.4 million speakers in Afghanistan; NFLC, "Language and National Security Briefing," Jan. 16, 2002.

16. A notable exception to this pattern is the Native American Languages Act of 1990 *(see Chapter 11).*

History

4 A Forgotten Legacy

Bilingual education figures nowhere in the immigrant myth: the bootstraps rise to success, the fight for social acceptance, the sink-or-swim imperative of learning English. For many Americans today, the idea of teaching children in other languages is an affront to sacred traditions. Yesterday's immigrants allegedly prospered without special programs; glad to blend into the Melting Pot, they struggled to master the language of their adopted homeland. By operating in English only, public schools weaned students from other tongues and opened a new world of opportunities.

Ancestral legends die hard. While some early newcomers were quick to assimilate and advance themselves, "melting" was more often a process of hardships that lasted for several generations. The immigrants' children were typically the first to achieve fluency in English, their grandchildren the first to finish high school, and their great-grandchildren the first to grow up in the middle class. Moreover, language minorities who were also racial minorities never had the option of joining the mainstream, whether they learned English or not, before the civil-rights reforms of the 1960s. Melting Pot mythology obscures the diversity of cultures that have flourished in North America since the colonial period, and the aggressive efforts to preserve them, among both immigrants and indigenous minorities. In this history bilingual education has played a central, if overlooked, role.

In 1664, when the settlement of New Netherland was ceded to the British crown and renamed New York, at least 18 tongues were spoken on the island of Manhattan, not counting Indian languages. Although the hegemony of English over the American colonies (except for Québec) had been decided by the late 17th century, the sounds of German, Dutch, French, Swedish, Irish, and Welsh were frequently heard at the time of the American Revolution, and Spanish was dominant in several soon-to-be-acquired territories. Bilingualism was common among the working classes as well as the educated, especially in the middle colonies of New York, Pennsylvania, New Jersey, and Delaware. In the mid-18th century, newspaper advertisements for runaway servants, both black and white, made frequent reference to their bilingual or trilingual proficiencies. For example:

> Run away ... from *John Orr,* near *Skuylkill, Philadelphia,* a Servant Man named *James Mitchel.* ... He has been a Traveller, and can talk Dutch [probably German], Spanish and Irish. ...
> Run away also ... an *Irish* Servant Man named Peter Kelley. ... He speaks good *French.* ...
> Run away from *Joseph Forman*, of New-York ... a Negro Man named JOE. ... [This] country born, speaks good English and Dutch.[1]

Wherever Europeans established schools in the New World, vernacular education was the rule, whether in English or another tongue. New arrivals naturally strived to preserve their heritage; **language loyalties** were strong. Indeed, these were among the values that had brought the Pilgrims to America. During a brief exile in Holland, religious freedom had come at a high cost: their children had begun to lose English. In Plymouth these refugees sought a climate where not only their Puritanism but their culture could thrive.

German-speaking Americans were operating schools in their mother tongue as early as 1694 in Philadelphia.[2] Sometimes bilingual and sometimes not, German-language schooling prevailed until the early 20th century, notwithstanding periodic attempts to replace it with English as the medium of instruction. In the 1750s Benjamin Franklin promoted one such project under the auspices of a missionary group called the Society for the Propagation of Christian Knowledge. All went smoothly until German parents learned that linguistic assimilation, not religious instruction, was the real purpose of these schools; whereupon they refused to enroll their children. Soon afterward the Pennsylvania Germans helped to vote Franklin out of the colonial assembly.[3] As a political pamphleteer, Franklin expressed alarmist concerns about bilingualism that have a familiar ring today. Citing the increased use of German in public situations, he predicted that interpreters would soon be

> necessary in the Assembly, to tell one half of our Legislators what the other half say; In short unless the stream of their importation could be turned from this to other Colonies ... [Germans] will soon so out number us, that all the advantages we have will not in My Opinion be able to preserve our language, and even our Government will become precarious.

Yet such views were rare among the nation's founders. Not only was bilingualism generally accepted as a fact of life, but the Continental Congress actively accommodated politically significant groups of non-English speakers. During the Revolutionary War it published many official documents in German and French, including the *Artikel des Bundes und der immerwährenden Eintracht zwischen den Staaten*, or Articles of Confederation.

No Official Language

Anti-British sentiment aroused by the American Revolution inspired a variety of schemes to discard English in favor of German, French, Greek, or Hebrew as the national language. Notwithstanding the legend that Congress came within one vote of adopting German as our official tongue, no alternative language was seriously considered. As one clever patriot observed at the time: "It would be more convenient for us to keep the language as it was and *make the English speak Greek.*"

Like England, the United States has adopted neither an official language nor a government-sanctioned body to regulate speech. In 1780, John Adams's proposal to establish an American language academy "for refining, correcting, improving, and ascertaining" the English tongue was ignored by the Continental Congress.

Evidence suggests that the framers of the Constitution believed that a democracy should leave language choices up to the people rather than imposing them from above.[4] They had no interest in promoting diversity, to be sure; the concept of **cultural pluralism** had yet to be invented *(see Chapter 3)*. But according to anthropologist Shirley Brice Heath, our early leaders placed a higher premium on political liberty than on linguistic homogeneity. Hence they adopted, in effect, "a policy not to have a policy" on language.

Benjamin Rush, a leading physician and a signer of the Declaration of Independence, hoped to encourage the assimilation of the Pennsylvania Germans without compromising the principles of the new nation. His solution: bilingual higher education. A federally funded German College, he argued, would "open the eyes of the Germans to a sense of the importance and utility of the English language and become perhaps the *only possible means*, consistent with their liberty, of spreading a knowledge of the English language among them." Like most of the founders, Rush was eager to promote a common tongue but felt the goal could be

Did German Almost Become the Official U.S. Language?

A persistent myth, popularized after the Civil War and revived by the German-American Bund in the 1930s, is that German failed by a single vote to become the official language of the United States. Apparently the tale draws on two unrelated events involving Frederick A. C. Muhlenberg, a Pennsylvania German who served as the first Speaker of the U.S. House of Representatives.

One of these involved a petition by Virginia Germans seeking the publication of important federal laws in their language. In 1795, the House defeated this proposal on a 42-41 vote, in which Muhlenberg may have stepped down from the Speaker's chair to break a tie. The limitations of early records, however, make it impossible to ascertain what role, if any, the Speaker played. It is known that he was never fluent in German and was widely suspected of Anglophilia.

In a second, better documented episode, Muhlenberg broke a tie vote in favor of executing the Jay Treaty, which authorized payment of a ransom for American sailors held by the British. This act brought the Speaker both political and personal grief. Pennsylvania voters, who regarded the treaty as a humiliating sellout, defeated Muhlenberg in the 1796 election; whereupon his own outraged brother-in-law attacked him with a knife.

A combination of poor record-keeping, suspicions about Muhlenberg's divided loyalties, and German cultural pride breathed life into this captivating but absurd story. English has never been forced to weather a challenge, serious or otherwise, in the U.S. Congress. Neither has it been granted official status, despite the recent efforts of English-only advocates *(see Chapter 6)*.

better achieved by voluntary rather than dictatorial means. Benjamin Franklin lent his considerable influence to the project, having modified his opinion about German Americans now that they were supporting Federalism (and opposing his political enemies). Founded in 1787 at Lancaster, Pennsylvania, this was the nation's first institution of higher education conducted primarily in German. It continues today as Franklin and Marshall College.

The work of defining and standardizing the "American language" was left to unofficial – that is, nongovernmental – arbiters. With his dictionary and speller, Noah Webster sought to differentiate what he called **Federal English** from the "corrupted" language of the mother country. "As an independent nation," he argued in 1789, "our honor requires us to have a system of our own, in language as well as government." There was also the danger that regional and class differences in speech might divide the new nation, he warned. "Our political harmony is therefore concerned in a uniformity of language." Nevertheless, the young Webster confidently predicted that the competitors of Federal English "will gradually waste away – and within a century and a half, North America will be peopled with a hundred millions of men, *all speaking the same language.*"

Annexing Diversity

Although his prophecy proved remarkably accurate, Webster could hardly have anticipated the language diversity produced by a century of expansion and immigration. In 1803, the Louisiana Purchase doubled the territory of the United States, while annexing large enclaves of French and Spanish speakers, not to mention scores of Indian tribes. President Thomas Jefferson initially tried to impose an English-only administration on the new territory. He soon relented, however, as residents of New Orleans, overwhelmingly Francophone at the time, came close to rebellion over the language issue. When Louisiana entered the Union in 1812, it was the first (and last) state to do so with a non-English-speaking majority. As a requirement for admission, Congress insisted that Louisiana's laws and official records be published in the language "in which the Constitution of the United States is written." But nothing prevented the state from operating in other languages as well, and it did so on a regular basis. Governor Jacques Villeré, elected in 1816, always addressed the legislature in French because he spoke no English.

Meanwhile, back East, the dominance of English was increasing, albeit temporarily, at the expense of rival tongues. From 1790 to 1830, European military conflicts and efforts to check emigration to the Americas, combined with the War of 1812, made the trans-Atlantic passage difficult to impossible. Without reinforcement by new arrivals, colonial languages like French, Dutch, and German declined, especially among the young. Ethnic schools increasingly offered bilingual and sometimes all-English instruction.

By the 1830s, however, the tide was turning once again, as progressively larger waves of immigrants began to arrive on U.S. shores; Germany alone provided more than five million newcomers during the 19th century. This brought another expansion of non-English-speaking enclaves, where it was considered only natural for children to be schooled in their native tongues. Still, no uniform **language policy** prevailed. Bilingual education was likely to be accepted in areas where language-minority groups had influence and to be rejected where they had none.

By mid-century, public and parochial German-English schools were operating in such cities as Baltimore, Cincinnati, Cleveland, Indianapolis, Milwaukee, and St. Louis. An Ohio law of 1839 authorized instruction in English, German, or both in areas where parents requested it. In 1847, Louisiana adopted the identical statute, except that it substituted French for German. The Territory of New Mexico, two years after its annexation in 1848, authorized Spanish-English bilingual education. Altogether more than a dozen states passed laws that provided for schooling in languages other than English, either as a subject or as a medium of instruction. Elsewhere bilingual education was common without explicit authorization, as local school boards provided classes in languages as diverse as Swedish, Danish, Norwegian, Italian, Polish, Dutch, and Czech.

"Ethnic politics" rather than discussions of "the psychological advantages or disadvantages of bilingual training" determined the structure of these programs, according to Joel Perlmann, an education historian. "The debates did not focus on whether kids would learn math better in German or in English, or whether they were emotionally better off learning German skills first. The central issues, the ones that were always raised, had to do with being a good American and creating a good America."

For most 19th century educators, linguistic assimilation was the ultimate goal for immigrant students. Yet coercive means were usually seen as counterproductive, especially for groups like the Germans, who felt strongly about maintaining their heritage. William Torrey Harris, St. Louis school superintendent in the 1870s and later U.S. commissioner of education, believed that the schools must "Americanize" language-minority children. At the same time, he preached cultural tolerance, arguing that "national memories and aspirations, family traditions, customs and habits, moral and religious observances cannot be suddenly removed or changed without disastrously weakening the personality." Harris was also a realist. He knew that dissatisfied parents had the option of Catholic or Lutheran schools, which were actively competing for students. So it was important to address their aspirations: "If the German children can learn to read and write the language of the fatherland in the public schools, they will not need separate ones."

'Americanization' Efforts

A resurgence of nativism in the late 19th century, led by the American Protective Association (APA), a secret society dedicated to anti-Catholic agitation, marked the beginning of a gradual decline for bilingual education. Earlier opponents of immigration, such as the Native American ("Know Nothing") Party of the 1840s and 1850s, had attacked the Germans mainly for their religion, politics, or lifestyle – rarely for their foreign speech. By the 1880s, however, language legislation was discovered to be a convenient weapon against Catholic schools. The *Chicago Tribune* editorialized against "the arrogance and presumption ... of an Italian priest living in Rome" for encouraging immigrants to send their children to non-English schools. Ironically, at that time in the Midwest, a parochial-school education – whether Catholic or Lutheran – was practically synonymous with a German-language education. So, in 1889, Protestant schools became unintended victims when Wisconsin and Illinois enacted the APA's proposal to mandate English as the sole language of instruction in all schools, public and private.

Despite the religious bigotry behind the new language laws, the American Catholic hierarchy was ambivalent in its response: disturbed by state meddling with parochial education, yet not averse to the new English requirements. Language was becoming a focus of contention within the church, as splits developed along nationality lines and Irish Americans fought to maintain their hegemony. In Wisconsin, however, there was no hesitation among German Americans. Catholics and Lutherans united across sectarian lines to resist this encroachment on their religious and linguistic rights. When was it decided that "Americanization" was synonymous with Anglicization? they asked. "There is no reason we should hate English, nor is there any reason why a true American should not look upon German with tender regard," argued Colonel Conrad Krez, a decorated Civil War veteran in Milwaukee. Wisconsin's defenders of English-only schools, such as Governor William D. Hoard, tried to cast the issue as "the *duty* of the State to require, and the *right* of the children of the State to receive, instruction in the language of the country." But immigrant voters soon expelled the governor, along with most of his fellow-Republican officeholders. After Democrats took over, the law was speedily repealed. A virtually identical scenario played out simultaneously in Illinois, bringing to power the progressive governor John Peter Altgeld. Parochial schools were again free to teach as they chose, although in practice most increased their use of English.

Indeed, German-language schooling may have already begun to decline before these conflicts erupted. Around this time several cities abandoned bilingual education in their public schools. St. Louis did so after German voting strength was sapped by gerrymandering and Irish immigrants gained control of the school board. Louisville and St. Paul banished German to the status of a foreign language offered only in the upper grades. Assimilationist pressures from German parents themselves may have also played a role in promoting English instruction. Nevertheless, surveys conducted in 1900 reported that more than 600,000 children – or about 4 percent of the U.S. elementary school population at the time, public and parochial – continued to receive instruction partly or exclusively in the German language. This figure is probably conservative, according to historian Heinz Kloss, who estimates that the total was closer to one million, or 7 percent. It also does not include the significant, if undetermined, numbers of students who were receiving bilingual instruction in other languages.

'New' Immigrants

By this time novel strains of xenophobia had begun to multiply as Italians, Jews, and Slavs began to outnumber Irish, Germans, and Scandinavians in the immigrant stream. The so-called **"new immigrants"** were more culturally diverse than their predecessors from northern Europe and more likely to settle in cities, now that the best lands in the West had been claimed and the frontier was largely "closed" to additional homesteaders. So the appearance, manners, living habits, and speech of these groups attracted more public notice and comment – usually negative. A poem published by the *Atlantic Monthly* in 1892 illustrates the horror that they inspired in many of the native-born:

> Wide open and unguarded stand our gates,
> And through them presses a wild motley throng –
> Men from the Volga and the Tartar steppes,
> Featureless figures from the Hoang-Ho,
> Malayan, Scythian, Teuton, Kelt, and Slav,
> Flying the Old World's poverty and scorn;
> These bringing with them unknown gods and rites,
> Those, tiger passions, here to stretch their claws.
> In street and alley what strange tongues are these,

Accents of menace alien to our air,
Voices that once the Tower of Babel knew!

Responding to such sentiments, Senator Henry Cabot Lodge of Massachusetts organized the Immigration Restriction League, seeking to bar entry to any foreigner unable to pass a literacy test.[5] In 1906, Congress passed the first federal language law of any kind, an English-speaking requirement for naturalization.

Not all Americans were so unsympathetic. Muckrakers exposed squalor and exploitation in urban slums, while social reformers sought to improve immigrants' lot through protective legislation and self-help. Settlement houses worked to ease their adjustment to a new culture. Operating through organizations like the YMCA, philanthropists financed large-scale adult English instruction for the first time, while also indoctrinating immigrants in "free enterprise" values. After the Lawrence textile strike of 1912,[6] a campaign to "Americanize the immigrant" was organized by industrialists hoping to counter the influence of foreign labor agitators. In 1915, the National Americanization Committee launched an "English First" project in Detroit, with the cooperation of the local Board of Commerce. Employers such as Henry Ford made attendance at after-hours English classes mandatory for their foreign-born workers.

As Americanization took a coercive turn, proficiency in English was increasingly equated with political loyalty; for the first time, an ideological link was forged between speaking good English and being a "good American." The U.S. Bureau of Education became active in this propaganda effort, sponsoring conferences on "Americanization work" and publishing an *Americanization Bulletin* and other literature, all financed by private benefactors. The goal was explicitly stated: to replace immigrant languages and cultures with those of the United States. As explained by the superintendent of New York City schools in 1918, Americanization would cultivate "an appreciation of the institutions of this country [and] absolute forgetfulness of all obligations or connections with other countries because of descent or birth." Ellwood P. Cubberly, dean of the Stanford University School of Education, viewed the issue through the "racial" lens then popular among the power elite:

> Our task is to break up [immigrant] groups or settlements, to assimilate and amalgamate these people as part of our American race, and to implant in their children, as far as can be done, the Anglo-Saxon conception of righteousness, law and order, and our popular government, and to awaken in them a reverence for our democratic institutions and for those things in our national life which we as a people hold to be of abiding worth.

The Rise of Language Restrictionism

Americanization represented a break with the principle of treating other nationalities in ways "consistent with their liberty." So did the nation's new policy of imperialism, as articulated by one of its leading exponents, Senator Albert J. Beveridge of Indiana: "The rule of liberty, that all just governments derive their authority from the consent of the governed, applies only to those who are capable of self-government. ... God has ... been preparing the English-speaking and Teutonic peoples for a thousand years [as] master organizers of the world to establish system where chaos reigns." Cultural jingoism flowed directly out of military jingoism. Following the Spanish-American War, the U.S. government imposed English as the medium of instruction in its new colonies of Puerto Rico, Hawaii, and the Philippines.

In Puerto Rico, where the population was virtually monolingual in Spanish, the policy was an educational disaster but it was justified as a political necessity. One candid official noted in 1902: "Colonization carried forward by the armies of war is vastly more costly than that carried forward by the armies of peace, whose outposts and garrisons are the public schools of the advancing nation." Another maintained that "English is the chief source, practically the only source, of democratic ideas in Porto Rico [sic]." Puerto Ricans had no say in the matter. Indeed, the island's legislature passed repeated condemnations of the English-only mandate, to no avail. As a result, students spent much of their time parroting lessons in a language they had no occasion to use outside of school. Few found much value in such education. A 1925 study by Teachers College at Columbia University reported that 84 percent of Puerto Rican children were dropping out by the 3rd grade. Although the language policy was modified periodically, first to allow Spanish instruction in the early grades and later to restore initial reading in English, it remained largely intact until 1949.

Back on the mainland, former President Theodore Roosevelt applied a similar philosophy to immigrants: "We have room for but one language in this country and that is the English language, for we intend to see that the crucible turns our people out as Americans, of American nationality, and not as dwellers in a polyglot boarding house." He advocated, on the one hand, expanded opportunities for immigrants to learn English and, on the other, the deportation of those who failed to do so within five years. Roosevelt framed language differences as a loyalty issue – a problem of "hyphenated Americanism" – to counter German Americans' pleas for U.S. neutrality as World War I approached.

After the United States entered the war in April 1917, anti-German feeling crested in an unprecedented wave of **language restrictionism**. Several states passed laws and emergency decrees banning German speech in the classroom, in church, in public meetings, even on the telephone. Authorities in St. Louis and Milwaukee closed down German theaters and opera houses. The town of Findlay, Ohio, imposed a $25 fine for anyone who spoke the enemy's language on the street. In the Midwest by 1921, at least 18,000 persons were charged under such laws. The hysteria did not end with Armistice Day; to the contrary, it intensified in 1919. Governor James M. Cox of Ohio sought legislation to remove all uses of German from his state's elementary schools, public and private, arguing that the language posed "a distinctive menace to Americanism, and a part of a plot formed by the German government to make the school children loyal to it." The state legislature quickly approved Cox's bill.

Under legal pressure or not, around this time most public school systems in the United States curtailed study of the German language. They did so with the blessings of such establishment voices as the *New York Times*, which editorialized: "Some German-American parents want German to be taught. It pleases their pride, but it does not do their children any good." German-language teachers, suddenly thrown out of work, were often reassigned to instruct children in "Americanism" and "citizenship." Mobs raided schools and burned German textbooks; in Lima, Ohio, they were led by the local school superintendent. In nearby Columbus the school board sold its German books to a waste paper company for 50 cents per hundredweight.

Soon the fervor of **Anglo-conformity** spilled over into hostility toward all minority tongues. "Patriotic" associations, such as the National Security League and the American Defense Society (a favorite of Roosevelt's), campaigned against foreign-language advertising in the New York subways, which they associated with "aliens ... neither speaking nor thinking American." Naturally schools were targeted as well. In the year following the war, according to legal historian Arnold Leibowitz, 15 states legislated English as the basic language of instruction.[7] Several followed Ohio's example of forbidding any foreign-language study in the elementary grades. The most restrictive of these laws were later struck down by the U.S. Supreme Court in ***Meyer v. Nebraska,*** a case involving a parochial school teacher whose "crime" had been to read a Bible story in German to a 10-year-old child. In reversing Meyer's conviction, the court said:

> The desire of the legislature to foster a homogeneous people with American ideals prepared readily to understand current discussions of civic matters is easy to appreciate. Unfortunate experiences during the late war and aversion

toward every characteristic of truculent adversaries were certainly enough to quicken that aspiration. But the means adopted, we think, exceed the limitations upon the power of the State and conflict with rights assured ... in time of peace and domestic tranquility. ...

The protection of the Constitution extends to all, to those who speak other languages as well as to those born with English on the tongue. Perhaps it would be highly advantageous if all had a ready understanding of our ordinary speech, but this cannot be coerced by methods which conflict with the Constitution – a desirable end cannot be promoted by prohibited means.

By the time the court handed down this ruling in 1923, the frenzy of Americanization was already starting to subside. Attempts to legislate loyalty to English were on the decline. Big city school systems were beginning to lift bans on German studies. Yet public attitudes had changed fundamentally: learning in languages other than English now seemed less than "American." European immigrant groups felt stronger pressures to assimilate and diminished enthusiasm for preserving old-country ways. Minority tongues were devalued in the eyes of the younger generation. Meanwhile the stream of non-English-speaking newcomers slowed to a trickle after 1924, when Congress enacted the strictest immigration quotas in the nation's history.

Bilingual instruction continued in some parochial schools and a few public ones, mainly in rural areas of the Midwest, but by the late 1930s it was virtually eradicated throughout the United States. Interest in the study of foreign languages also fell off dramatically. Next to Latin, German had been the most popular foreign language in 1915, with 24 percent of American secondary school students enrolled; by 1922, less than one percent were studying German. Overall enrollments in modern language classes declined from 36 percent of secondary students in 1915 to 14 percent in 1948.[8]

Within a generation the Americanizers' goal of transforming a polyglot society into a monolingual one was largely achieved. "This linguistic equivalent of 'book burning' worked admirably well" in promoting assimilation, writes Josué González, former federal director of bilingual education. "But it worked best with the Northern European immigrants," who had a "cultural affinity" with American values and shared a "Caucasian racial history." For other language minorities, especially those with darker complexions, English-only schooling brought difficulties. While their cultures were suppressed, discrimination barred their full acceptance into American life. In addition, it was these groups – conquered peoples and racial minorities – who had suffered linguistic repression in the 19th century, a departure from the habitual laissez-faire treatment of European immigrant languages.

English as a 'Civilizing' Influence

The U.S. government recognized the language rights of the Cherokee tribe under an 1828 treaty and agreed to subsidize the first newspaper published in an Indian tongue, the *Cherokee Phoenix*. Like most of the solemn promises made to American Indians, however, these were soon broken. In the early 1830s President Andrew Jackson initiated a policy of forcible **Indian removal** from the eastern United States. When the Cherokees used their printing press to advocate resistance, it was confiscated and destroyed by the state of Georgia. Their ordeal became known as the Trail of Tears, as more than a third of tribal members died en route to Oklahoma. After resettlement they established an educational system of 21 schools and two academies. Using Sequoyah's **syllabary**, or phonetic writing system, tribal members achieved a 90 percent literacy rate in the Cherokee language. According to a U.S. Senate report on Indian education, in the 1850s these schools "used bilingual materials to such an extent that Oklahoma Cherokees had a higher English literacy level than the white populations of either Texas or Arkansas." Other tribal and missionary schools also made effective use of native-language instruction.

Successful or not, such experiments in bilingual education were doomed by the federal government's hostility to **Indian self-determination**. In 1868, the Indian Peace Commission reported: "In the difference of language to-day lies two-thirds of our trouble. ... Schools should be established, which children should be required to attend; their barbarous dialects should be blotted out and the English language substituted." Beginning in 1879, federal officials began separating Indian children from their families and forcing them to attend off-reservation boarding schools. Students were punished when caught speaking their tribal tongues, even if they could speak no English. Senator Ben Nighthorse Campbell of Colorado, a member of the Northern Cheyenne tribe, describes the experience: "Both my grandparents were forcibly removed from their homes and placed into boarding schools. One of the first English words Indian students learned was *soap*, because their mouths were constantly being washed out for using their native language."

This policy coincided with a broader campaign to contain Indians on reservations by repressing their cultures, for example, by banning native religious ceremonies and hair braids for Indian men. The rationale was that such "civilizing" measures, including compulsory use of English, would acclimate nomadic peoples to reservation life. "To teach Indian school children in their native language is practically to exclude English, and to prevent them from acquiring it," declared J. D. C. Atkins, commissioner of Indian affairs, in 1887. "This language, which is good enough for a white man and a black man, ought to be good enough for the red man." In defense of the **speak-English-only rule**, Atkins asked: "Is it cruelty to the Indian to force him to give up his scalping knife and tomahawk? Is it cruelty to force him to abandon the vicious and barbarous sun dance, where he lacerates his flesh, and dances and tortures himself even unto death?"

Senator Henry Dawes of Massachusetts used a similar line of argument to justify "allotment" of reservation lands to individual Indians. It would assimilate them into American culture, he predicted, by teaching "selfishness, which is at the [basis] of civilization." In practice, the Dawes Severalty Act of 1887 made them vulnerable to exploitation, foreclosure, and theft. Federal policy succeeded mainly in "severing" Indians from millions of acres to which they were entitled by treaty. In the early 1900s, when whites demanded access to lands in Oklahoma, Congress dissolved the autonomous tribal governments of the so-called Five Civilized Tribes – Cherokees, Choctaws, Creeks, Chickasaws, and Seminoles – along with their independent school systems. The Cherokees' printing press, which had been used to produce native-language teaching materials, again was confiscated. This time it was shipped to Washington, D.C., and put on display at the Smithsonian Institution. Tribal schools were taken over by the Bureau of Indian Affairs (BIA) and English-only policies were instituted. From that point on, educational attainment among Oklahoma Indians began a long, slow decline. By 1969, 40 percent of Cherokee adults in the eastern part of the state were functionally illiterate, up to 75 percent of their children were dropouts in some schools, and in one county 90 percent were receiving welfare. But virtually all of them spoke English.

In 1934, Indian Commissioner John Collier rescinded the BIA's official policy of repressing Indian vernaculars. He even tried to introduce native-language instruction in some community schools, hoping to encourage bilingualism and biliteracy. On the Navajo reservation, the BIA hired linguists to compile a Navajo dictionary and develop Navajo teaching materials. But this experiment with bilingual education was limited by a severe shortage of trained Indian teachers and by budget cuts during World War II. Despite their best efforts, Collier and his fellow reformers also failed to change the culture of BIA educators, many of whom continued to forbid children to "talk Indian" in school. Punishments for violating English-only rules continued unofficially into the 1940s and 1950s, as many Native American adults can testify from personal experience. Parents were understandably skeptical when federal policy reversed itself again in 1968 and Indian bilingual programs were suddenly encouraged (see Chapter 11).

Strangers in Their Own Land

Spanish speakers endured similar treatment in the Southwest. As a conquered people following the Mexican-American War, they too faced repression of their language and culture to a far greater extent than European immigrants did. The 1848 Treaty of Guadalupe Hidalgo promised that these new Spanish-speaking citizens of the United States "shall be maintained and protected in the free enjoyment of their liberty and property, and secured in the free exercise of their religion without restriction." While not mentioned explicitly, a guarantee of certain language rights was strongly implied.[9] Yet such rights have rarely been respected.

Although California's 1849 constitution required the publication of all laws in both Spanish and English, the practice was soon abandoned. Political power shifted abruptly as the Gold Rush attracted hordes of Anglo-American miners and land speculators, along with immigrants from all over the world. Amid the competition for wealth, language became a tool of advantage. In 1855, the legislature mandated English-only instruction in all schools, along with other measures designed to discriminate against the Spanish-speaking residents, known as Californios. Forced to prove title to their lands in a language and legal system that was foreign to them, over time the Californios were expropriated from most of the 14 million acres they had held on the eve of statehood (40 percent of their holdings went to pay the fees of English-speaking lawyers).

Californians met to rewrite their state constitution in 1878–79 during a period of unabashed nativism. One delegate proclaimed: "This State should be a State for white men. ... We want no other race here. The future of this republic demands that it shall be a white man's government, and that all other races shall be excluded." After stripping Chinese immigrants of virtually all civil rights, the convention took aim at the Californios (not one of whom was present as a delegate). As adopted, the new constitution featured the following provision: "All laws of the State of California, and all official writings, and the executive, legislative, and judicial proceedings shall be conducted, preserved, and published in no other than the English language."[10]

Spanish speakers enjoyed a different experience in New Mexico, where they remained a majority of the population until the early 20th century. In the 1870s the territorial legislature still operated mainly in Spanish, with laws later translated into English. Jury trials were held in English in only two of 14 counties. A mere 5 percent of New Mexico's schools used English as the language of instruction, while 69 percent taught in Spanish and 26 percent were bilingual. With the arrival of railroads in the 1880s, the territory's demography began to change, but not its tradition of tolerance. When New Mexico finally became a state in 1912, its first constitution provided guarantees against language discrimination and for the training of Spanish-language teachers.

Texas represented the opposite extreme. There Mexican American children were commonly segregated in inferior schools, if not discouraged from attending school altogether. English-only instruction was strictly enforced. Beginning in 1919, the Texas legislature made it a criminal offense to teach in any other language (although foreign-language instruction was permissible in the upper grades). Children were likewise punished for using any language but English on school grounds. As a young man, Lyndon B. Johnson taught for one year at a segregated "Mexican" school in Cotulla, Texas, where the future president became known for severely spanking children he overheard speaking Spanish during recess. In the Rio Grande Valley, **Spanish detention**, or being kept after school for violating English-only rules, persisted well into the late 1960s, according to an investigation by the U.S. Commission on Civil Rights. One south Texas principal, quoted in the commission's 1972 report, explained the disciplinary policy in this way:

> Our school is predominantly Latin American – 97 percent. We try to discourage the use of Spanish on the playground, in the halls, and in the classroom. We feel that the reason so many of our pupils are reading two to three years below grade level is because their English vocabulary is so limited. We are in complete accord that it is excellent to be bilingual or multilingual, but we must ... stress the fact that practice makes perfect – that English is a very difficult language to master. Our pupils speak Spanish at home, at dances, on the playground, at athletic events. ... We feel the least they can do is try to speak English at school.

As late as 1970, a teacher was indicted in Crystal City, Texas, for using Spanish in a high school history class. The case was subsequently dismissed, however. Unbeknownst to the prosecutor, state legislators had repealed the English-only instruction law the previous year.

'Cultural Deprivation' Era

George I. Sánchez, a psychologist at the University of Texas, protested the schools' single-minded emphasis on English and became an early advocate of bilingual approaches. "Imagine the Spanish-speaking child's introduction to American education!" Sánchez wrote in 1940.

> He comes to school, not only without a word of English but without the environmental experience upon which school life is based. He cannot speak

Timeline: Language Diversity in America

1664 New Netherland is acquired by the British and becomes New York; at least 18 languages are spoken on Manhattan Island

1694 German-language school is founded in Germantown (Philadelphia)

1754 Benjamin Franklin organizes a project to assimilate German children under the guise of religious instruction; parents refuse to cooperate

1764 Pennsylvania Germans rally against Franklin, helping to vote him out of the colonial assembly

1780 John Adams proposes an American Language Academy; no interest expressed in the Continental Congress

1787 U.S. Constitution is ratified, with no official language provisions

1803 Louisiana Purchase brings U.S. citizenship to speakers of French, Spanish, and numerous Native American languages

1812 Louisiana becomes first (and last) state to enter the Union in which English speakers are a minority

1828 Treaty recognizes Cherokee language rights; U.S. government subsidizes tribal newspaper, the *Cherokee Phoenix*, printed in Sequoyah's syllabary

1839 Ohio enacts first state law authorizing bilingual education, in English and German

1845 Louisiana's second constitution adopts a form of official bilingualism, recognizing French and English as coequal languages in state legislature

1847 Louisiana adopts Ohio's bilingual education law, substituting French for German

1848 Treaty of Guadalupe Hidalgo ends the Mexican-American War, with implicit guarantee of Spanish language rights in territories ceded to U.S.

1849 First constitution of California provides for publication of laws in both English and Spanish

1855 California imposes English-only instruction statewide, although the mandate is poorly enforced

1868 Indian Peace Commission proposes to use schools to "blot out ... barbarous dialects" spoken by Native Americans

1879 Second California constitution bans official publications and proceedings in languages other than English

1879 System of off-reservation boarding schools is established for American Indians; speak-English-only rules are brutally enforced

1889	Wisconsin and Illinois adopt English-only instruction laws aimed at parochial schools; measures are repealed after outcry by German Americans
1893	U.S. Marines overthrow the government of Queen Liliuokalani of Hawai'i; soon after, English is imposed as the island's sole language of instruction
1898	Puerto Rico becomes a U.S. colony following the Spanish-American War; English is imposed as the island's sole language of instruction
1900	From 4 to 7 percent of U.S. elementary school children are receiving part or all of their instruction in the German language
1906	Congress passes first language legislation at the federal level, an English-speaking requirement for naturalization
1912	New Mexico becomes a state; its constitution bans discrimination against Spanish speakers and requires training of Spanish-proficient teachers
1915	English First project in Detroit requires foreign-born workers to attend English and citizenship classes as condition of employment
1917	U.S. enters World War I; campaign to "Americanize" immigrants receives federal support; states adopt emergency measures to restrict German usage
1919	Fifteen states enact English-only instruction laws, bringing the national total to 34; bilingual education is dismantled in much of U.S.
1919	Ohio bans any use of German in its public schools
1919	Texas legislature makes it a criminal offense to use any language but English as the medium of instruction
1922	Less than one percent of U.S. secondary-school students are learning German as a foreign language, down from 24 percent in 1915
1923	In *Meyer v. Nebraska*, U.S. Supreme court strikes down laws that restrict the teaching of foreign languages
1924	Congress adopts national-origins quota system, the most restrictive immigration policy in U.S. history
1934	Bureau of Indian Affairs ends English-only policy for students, but it persists unofficially for another three decades
1948	Puerto Rico achieves Commonwealth status; English-instruction policy is soon terminated, despite objections by President Truman
1958	Congress passes National Defense Education Act, authorizing the first federal subsidies for foreign-language instruction
1963	Two-way bilingual education program established for Spanish- and English-speaking children at Coral Way Elementary School in Miami

to the teacher and is unable to understand what goes on about him in the classroom. He finally submits to rote learning, parroting words and processes in self-defense. To him, school life is artificial. He submits to it during class hours, only partially digesting the information which the teacher has tried to impart. Of course he learns English and the school subjects imperfectly!

Gradually other educators began to recognize the futility of coercive assimilation. But few were ready to accept the alternative advanced by Professor Sánchez: that the school should *build upon*, rather than dismantle, the minority child's language and culture. Instead, reformers sought more effective ways to adapt the child to the school – in particular, to treat his or her "language disability."

Cultural deprivation theory, which came to dominate educational psychology in the 1950s, rejected the genetic (i.e., racist) explanations for underachievement by minority students that had prevailed in the early 20th century. It pointed instead to environmental factors, although these too involved blaming the victims: the failure of parents to stress educational attainment, "lower-class" values that favored "living in the present" rather than planning for the future, limited literacy, and inadequate English-language skills. "To make it in America," declared the sociologist W. I. Thomas, what these "culturally inferior" children needed most was to master the language and values of the dominant society. The job of the schools, he argued, was to "change their culture," that is, to overcome students' handicaps of ethnic background.

Explaining school failure on the basis of culture naturally involved contrasting the experiences of different immigrant nationalities. Jews were cited as a positive example, whose success in the first half of the 20th century was attributed to the high value they placed on intellectual accomplishment, ingenuity, and perseverance. Catholic immigrants, on the other hand, were often stereotyped as fatalistic, uncompetitive, and unsupportive of their children's education, traits that had allegedly kept Italians, Irish, Poles, and others from rising as rapidly. The same thought process is evident today in invidious comparisons that are drawn between Asian Americans, the "model minority," and various Latino groups.

Needless to say, this line of argument is advanced primarily by educated persons who see themselves as representing a "superior" culture (whether acquired through hard work or judicious choice of parents); as such, it can easily be dismissed as a form of self-flattery, not to mention class bias. The important question, however, is whether the cultural explanation of school failure can be supported empirically.

As it happens, there is plenty of historical evidence to contradict it. Stephen Steinberg, a sociologist at Queens College, analyzed the background of Jewish immigrants in the early 1900s and traced their relative prosperity to urban roots in Eastern Europe. Though largely poor and non-English-speaking, most brought literacy as well as academic and employment skills to their new homeland. By contrast, Jews who came from peasant backgrounds and lacked these skills tended to fare no better than their non-Jewish peasant counterparts from Italy, Ireland, or Poland. At the time, few children of rural immigrant parents advanced beyond the early grades, irrespective of their cultural traits. Thus for these groups, economic integration – that is, entry into the "middle class" – became a multigenerational process.

Assimilationist Schooling

As the cultural deprivation hypothesis gained hegemony, it naturally fostered assimilationist models of education. **English as a second language**, a methodology developed in the 1930s to meet the needs of foreign diplomats and university students, was now prescribed for language-minority children. Pullout classes, the most common form of ESL, removed students from regular classrooms, typically two to five times a week for a 45-minute period of compensatory instruction (*see Chapter 2*). Unlike remedial reading, ESL took account of a child's lack of oral English proficiency. Still, its availability was not widespread. In a Civil Rights Commission survey, only 5.5 percent of Mexican American children in California, Arizona, New Mexico, Colorado, and Texas were enrolled in ESL classes in 1968–69; about half that number were receiving bilingual instruction.

While ESL was an improvement over sink-or-swim English instruction, its effectiveness usually remained limited. "By dealing with the student simply as a non-English speaker," the commission observed in 1972, "most ESL classes fail to expose children to approaches, attitudes, and materials which take advantage of the rich Mexican American heritage." Excluding minority cultures, or providing only fantasy stereotypes like "caballeros and senoritas with gardenias behind their ears," was undercutting children's self-image. Instruction that strives to change students "into something else" inevitably discourages academic achievement, notes Josué González. "When children are painfully ashamed of who they are, they are not going to do very well in school, whether they be taught monolingually, bilingually, or trilingually."

From a strictly academic standpoint, ESL students were learning English too slowly to keep up in other content areas. So there was little improvement in their long-term achievement. In the 1960s the dropout rate for Puerto Rican students in

New York City was estimated at 60 percent; those who stayed in were almost automatically assigned to vocational tracks. In 1963, the city's public schools awarded 331 academic diplomas to Puerto Ricans, representing no more than one percent of the total Puerto Rican enrollment; of these graduates only 28 went on to college.

Meanwhile language difficulties were often ignored; students were simply labeled slow learners, or worse. Based on their performance on IQ tests administered in English, disproportionate numbers of language-minority children ended up in **special education** classes. As late as 1980, Hispanic children in Texas were overrepresented by 315 percent in the learning-disabled category.

Bilingual Education Reborn

The renaissance of bilingual education occurred not among Mexican Americans or Puerto Ricans, but among a relatively privileged minority: Cuban exiles who had fled to Miami after the 1959 revolution in their homeland. The early arrivals were of European stock, light-skinned, and largely from the business and professional classes. Proud of their Spanish heritage, they brought with them education and job skills, if little ready cash. Many had taught school in Cuba, and the state of Florida helped them become recertified. Generous subsidies were available through the federal Cuban Refugee Program.

To serve this politically favored group, the Dade County Public Schools provided ESL instruction and, in 1961, initiated **Spanish-for-Spanish-speakers** classes. Two years later the district established a full-fledged bilingual program, in all likelihood the nation's first since the 1920s. Launched at the Coral Way Elementary School, the experiment was open to both English and Spanish speakers. It was anything but a compensatory approach: the objective was fluent bilingualism for both groups. Pauline Rojas and Ralph Robinett, ESL specialists who had worked in Puerto Rico, directed the effort with the help of well trained Cuban educators.

Beginning in September 1963, Coral Way's 350 1st, 2nd, and 3rd graders were grouped by language. Cuban children received their morning lessons in Spanish and their afternoon lessons in English; for English-speaking children, the schedule was reversed. During lunch, music, and art, as well as on the playground, the two groups were mixed. Results were immediately promising, as students appeared to progress academically and in both languages. A 1966 report by the district concluded: "The pupils in Coral Way are rapidly becoming 'culturally advantaged.' They are learning to operate effectively in two languages and two cultures."

Indeed, Coral Way was in many respects a success. In English reading both language groups did as well as or better than their counterparts in monolingual

English schools, and the Cuban children achieved equivalent levels in Spanish. The one disappointment was among the Anglo students; as a group, they never reached national norms in Spanish reading achievement. "In retrospect," observes psychologist Kenji Hakuta, "the difference between the two groups was not unexpected, since the predominant language of the environment [was] English." The Cuban children had an advantage because, unlike their English-speaking peers, they received high-quality exposure to the target language outside as well as inside the classroom. In any case, Hakuta writes, "the feasibility of bilingual education was established."

News of Coral Way's success soon spread beyond Dade County. Educators of English learners began to visit the district to learn about bilingual pedagogy. Impressed by what they saw, many returned home to adapt the Coral Way model to their own communities. By 1967, according to historian Diego Castellanos, bilingual programs had been introduced in Rough Rock, Arizona; Calexico and Marysville, California; Hoboken and Long Branch, New Jersey; Las Cruces and Pecos, New Mexico; and Del Río, Edinburgh, Laredo, San Antonio, and Zapata, Texas. These experiments were welcomed by language-minority parents and progressive educators alike, who were eager for alternatives to sink-or-swim.

Bilingual programs would likely have remained just that, however – promising, small-scale experiments – absent a unique confluence of events. These included:

- *the civil-rights movement* of the 1960s, which activated not only African-Americans but also Latinos and Asian Americans in struggles against discrimination, especially in the schools;
- *antipoverty initiatives* by the Kennedy and Johnson administrations, which put issues of social equality on the national agenda; and
- *the Cold War*, which pitted the United States against a scientifically advanced enemy, thus dictating an expanded role for the federal government in education funding and policymaking.

As the next chapter will illustrate, this history helped to shape English learner programs and policies as we know them today.

Suggested
Reading

Baron, Dennis. *Grammar and Good Taste: Reforming the American Language.* New Haven: Yale University Press, 1982.

Crawford, James. *Hold Your Tongue: Bilingualism and the Politics of "English Only."* Reading, Mass.: Addison-Wesley, 1992.

Higham, John. *Strangers in the Land: Patterns of American Nativism, 1860–1925.* 2d ed. New Brunswick, N.J.: Rutgers University Press, 1988.

Kloss, Heinz. *The American Bilingual Tradition.* 2d ed. Washington, D.C.: Center for Applied Linguistics, 1998.

Schlossman, Stephen L. "Is There an American Tradition of Bilingual Education? German in the Public Elementary Schools, 1840–1919." *American Journal of Education* 91 (1983): 139–86.

See also pp. 390–92.

Online
Resource
Guide

Leibowitz, Arnold H. *Educational Policy and Political Acceptance: The Imposition of English as the Language of Instruction in American Schools.* Washington, D.C.: ERIC Clearinghouse for Linguistics, 1971.

Meyer v. Nebraska (U.S. Supreme Court, 1923)

U.S. Commission on Civil Rights. *The Excluded Student: Educational Practices Affecting Mexican Americans in the Southwest.* Mexican American Education Study, Report III. Washington, D.C.: 1972.

See also companion CD-ROM.

Internet
Links

Ovando, Carlos J. "Bilingual Education in the United States: Historical Development and Current Issues." *Bilingual Research Journal* 27, no. 1 (2003): 1–24. http://brj.asu.edu/content/vol27_no1/documents/art1.pdf

See also companion CD-ROM.

Notes

1. Apparently monolingualism was unusual enough to be noteworthy: "Run away from his Master, *Theodorus Van Wyck*, of *Dutchess* County, in the Province of *New York*, a Negro Man named JAMES, aged about 22 Years ... can talk nothing but English, and has a low Voice." These and other Colonial advertisements are quoted in Allen Walker Read, "Bilingualism in the Middle Colonies, 1725-1775," *American Speech* 12 (1937): 93-99.

2. German Americans were the nation's largest ethnolinguistic minority in every decennial census from 1790 to 1950. In an analysis of the 1790 census, the American Council of Learned Societies estimated that persons of German background represented 8.6 percent of the population of the original 13 states. See "Report of the Committee on Linguistic and National Stocks in the Population of the United States," in the *Annual Report of the American Historical Association for the Year 1931*, pp. 103–441.

3. They were especially incensed by a passage in Franklin's *Observations on the Increase of Mankind* (1755) in which he wrote:

   > Why should the *Palatine Boors* be suffered to swarm into our Settlements, and by herding together, establish their Language and Manners, to the Exclusion of ours? Why should *Pennsylvania*, founded by the *English*, become a Colony of *Aliens*, who will shortly be so numerous as to Germanize us instead of our Anglifying them, and will never adopt our Language or Customs, any more than they can acquire our Complexion.

   Apparently regretting his intemperate language, Franklin excised this passage from later editions of his writings. Ironically, in 1732 he had founded the first German-language newspaper in America, *Die Philadelphische Zeitung*, although he did not speak the language himself. Its editor, a French Huguenot, used an odd variety of German that drew ridicule from the locals, and the venture soon failed as more qualified German printers arrived in Pennsylvania.

4. Seventy years earlier the British monarchy had rejected a similar scheme by Jonathan Swift, a notorious language scold who condemned the "corruptions" of English during the Restoration era. Daniel Defoe, another enthusiast of an English language academy, wanted to make it "as criminal ... to coin words as money." Samuel Johnson, however, in the preface to his *Dictionary*, described the idea of arresting language change by fiat as not only futile, but contrary to "the spirit of English liberty"; Albert C. Baugh and Thomas Cable, *A History of the English Language*, 3rd ed. (Englewood Cliffs, N.J.: Prentice-Hall, 1978), pp. 254–69.

5. The standard was an ability to read 40 words in any language. Congress passed such legislation four times beginning in 1897, but each time it was met with presidential vetoes. The literacy test finally became law in 1917, when Congress mustered the two-thirds majority needed to override President Wilson's veto. By that time its effectiveness as a barrier had declined, as a larger percentage of "new immigrants" could now read and write.

6. Led by the Industrial Workers of the World, this strike in Lawrence, Massachusetts, was a watershed event in U.S. labor-management relations. Victorious despite brutal repression, the strikers demonstrated the solidarity potential of an unskilled immigrant workforce composed of many nationalities. Organizers overcame ethnic divisions by conducting strike meetings in more than 20 languages. See Richard O. Boyer and Herbert M. Morais, *Labor's Untold Story* (New York: United Electrical, Radio and Machine Workers of America, 1955).

7. This brought the total to 34 states. At the national level, a bill to designate English "the language of instruction in all schools, public and private," failed to pass the 66th Congress. For many Americans, federal language legislation – not to mention federal intrusion into the jurisdiction of local school boards – remained anathema.

8. According to the American Council on the Teaching of Foreign Languages, these enrollments (in public schools, grades 9–12) climbed to 27.7 percent in 1968, then fell to 21.9 percent in 1982 before rebounding to 38.4 percent in 1990 and 42.5 percent in 2000. Generally speaking, the number of students taking modern language courses has paralleled trends in college entrance and graduation requirements.

9. This interpretation is consistent with statements by Nicholas Trist, the treaty's chief U.S. negotiator. In a letter to Secretary of State James Buchanan, Trist italicized what he perceived to be an "overpowering" concern of the Mexican delegates: *a perfect devotion to their distinct nationality, and a most vehement aversion to its becoming merged in or blended with ours."* Hence they insisted on "the right of Mexicans residing there to continue there, retaining the character of Mexican citizens." Thirty years later, several delegates to a California constitutional convention cited the Treaty of Guadalupe Hidalgo in opposing an English-only mandate for state government, but they were voted down.

10. California thus became the second English-only state, after Illinois (1845).

5 The Evolution of Federal Policy

When Proposition 227 took effect in 1998, dismantling most of California's bilingual education programs, two school districts were not directly affected. San Francisco and San Jose remained under court orders dating from 1974 and 1985, respectively, that required them to provide native-language instruction to English learners. Years earlier, parents had sued the districts, alleging that they were violating civil-rights law by neglecting the needs of these students. Federal courts agreed.

To remedy the problem, judges in both cases mandated bilingual education as a way to open up the curriculum to children who had been effectively excluded. Under the U.S. Constitution, federal authority generally takes precedence over state and local authority where national concerns such as civil rights are at stake. Therefore, these court decisions "trumped" Proposition 227 in San Francisco and San Jose. The two districts were obligated to continue providing bilingual programs for LEP students, just as they had done before passage of the ballot initiative, while other districts in the state were being forced to eliminate bilingual programs.

As applied in this situation, the legal logic is clear enough. Considered more broadly, however, it raises a number of questions. One might reasonably ask, for example, why LEP students in the rest of California should be treated any differently from those in San Francisco and San Jose. If bilingual education is required to safeguard the civil rights of English learners in those districts, why not in all? For that matter, why was Proposition 227 itself permissible? By banning a program deemed to be effective in helping LEP children overcome language barriers – and imposing an unproven alternative pedagogy – how could California's law *not* conflict with the students' federally guaranteed right to an equal education?

These were among the arguments raised in federal court by advocates for bilingual education in seeking to overturn Proposition 227 statewide. But the judge in this case found them to be unpersuasive. He declined to block the measure from taking effect, ruling that the plaintiffs had shown no threat of "irreparable harm" to children *(see Chapter 15)*. The decision did little to dispel the general confusion and contention over these issues.

Unlike many countries, the United States has historically left responsibility for funding and operating public schools largely to state and local governments. Federal involvement was minimal before the 1960s, except in specialized fields such as vocational and Indian education. The **National Defense Education Act of 1958**, passed in response to *Sputnik* (the satellite that demonstrated the Soviet Union's early lead in space exploration), was the first effort at the national level to strengthen mathematics, science, and foreign-language instruction. While initial subsidies and requirements were modest, the federal role increased steadily under the Great Society reforms of the 1960s. Key legislation included the **Civil Rights Act of 1964**, which banned race, sex, and national-origin discrimination in public facilities, and the **Elementary and Secondary Education Act of 1965** (ESEA), which addressed the academic needs of poor children. Both laws have been instrumental in improving the schooling of English learners. At the same time, they have greatly complicated the lines of authority among federal, state, and local officials over public education. Laws and regulations have proliferated, often changing without much notice to stakeholders. So it is no wonder that uncertainty persists about schools' legal options and obligations in serving LEP students.

Much of the confusion has arisen from the "two track" approach that has characterized the federal government's role. On the one hand, it has provided financial aid to support programs for English learners; on the other, it has taken steps to ensure that these children have an equal chance to succeed. Although policies on both tracks have aimed at enhancing educational opportunities, they have not always run side by side. Funding for bilingual education programs came first, before federal authorities had begun to grapple with the problem of discrimination against English learners in the schools.

Genesis of Title VII

On January 2, 1968, when President Lyndon B. Johnson signed the **Bilingual Education Act** into law, the U.S. government signaled its first commitment to assisting students with limited English skills. Also known as **Title VII** of the ESEA, it authorized resources to support educational programs, train teachers and aides, develop and disseminate instructional materials, and encourage parental involvement. In spite of its name, the original Bilingual Education Act did not require schools to use a language other than English in order to receive funding.[1]

The law's focus was explicitly compensatory, aimed at children who were both poor and "educationally disadvantaged because of their inability to speak English." Yet a key question of goals – whether the act was meant to speed the transition to English or to promote bilingualism – was left unresolved. Senator Ralph Yarborough, the measure's prime sponsor, did nothing to clarify this issue when he told fellow lawmakers: "It is not the purpose of the bill to create pockets of different languages throughout the country ... not to stamp out the mother tongue, and not to make their mother tongue the dominant language, but just to try to make those children fully literate in English."

Although Senator Yarborough and President Johnson were both liberal Democrats from Texas, for some years there had been bad blood between the two, and it was the White House that put up the strongest resistance to the legislation. By 1967, spending for Great Society programs and the Vietnam War had put a squeeze on the federal budget. In its precarious political position, the Johnson administration hoped to avoid further tax increases and thus sought to head off new demands on the federal treasury. Testifying before Yarborough's special subcommittee on bilingual education, Commissioner of Education Harold Howe II argued against creating a new "title" of the ESEA. Some additional assistance, he said, could be provided under the existing Titles I and III, which were already financing 18 bilingual and ESL programs in the Southwest.

Howe also endorsed the major criticism of Yarborough's proposal: it would have aided only Spanish-speaking children, ignoring the needs of others who might benefit from bilingual instruction. Explaining his rationale for targeting a limited population, the senator responded:

> If you take the Italians, Polish, French, Germans, Norwegians, or other non-English-speaking groups, they made a definite decision to leave their old life and culture. ... That decision to come here carried with it a willingness to give up their language, everything. That wasn't true in the Southwest. We went in and took the people over. They had our culture superimposed upon them.

Hispanic leaders quickly recognized the political risks of this position. Representative Henry B. González of Texas argued for the coverage of Louisiana Cajuns, American Indians, and other native-born language minorities. "In view of our continuing efforts to promote mutual respect and tolerance," he said, "we would be inviting grave and justly deserved criticism from many ethnic groups if we recognize the problems of only one."

The critics were pacified when Representative James Scheuer of New York drafted a compromise extending the program to all "children who come from environments where the dominant language is other than English," but giving preference to those from low-income families.[2] Senator Yarborough was soon won over and the Johnson administration, finding itself outflanked, reluctantly agreed to support a new Title VII.

By the late 1960s political winds favored increased attention for Spanish-speaking Americans, who had been largely passed over by antipoverty legislation. The National Education Association (NEA) had drawn attention to the plight of Mexican American children with its Tucson Survey of 1965–66. Its pamphlet *The Invisible Minority, Pero No Vencibles* painted a picture of educational neglect in that Arizona city: inadequate facilities, a lack of trained teachers, and the scandal of sink-or-swim schooling. Throughout the Southwest veteran educators like José Cárdenas of San Antonio were beginning to conclude that "just about anything was better than the existing situation." Simultaneously a number of academic researchers and Romance language teachers were coming to the conclusion that a bilingual approach was theoretically viable. The NEA brought these forces together, along with Senator Yarborough and Texas state senator Joe Bernal, at a conference in Tucson on October 30–31, 1966. Politically speaking, this marked the birth of what came to be known as the **bilingual movement**.

Notwithstanding differences over minor details, at the time there was remarkably little controversy about the idea of federal support for bilingual education. In endorsing Yarborough's bill, Senator George Murphy, a conservative Republican from California, noted that Governor Ronald Reagan had recently signed legislation repealing California's English-only school statute. (Five years later Reagan would approve the state's first bilingual education law.) As with any idea whose time has come politically, members of Congress scrambled to affix their names. Thirty-seven bilingual education bills were introduced in the 90th Congress (1967–68), including one sponsored by George H. W. Bush, then a freshman Representative from Houston.

Expenditures were another matter. Under pressure from the White House, Congress approved no funding for Title VII in the first year. For 1969 it appropriated $7.5 million, just enough to finance 76 projects serving 27,000 children. Even this meager subsidy doubled the number of students enrolled in bilingual classrooms in the United States. By 1972, the total rose to 112,000 of the estimated five million language-minority children of school age.

Beginning with New Mexico in 1969, states began to pass laws authorizing instruction in languages other than English. In 1971, Massachusetts became the first to mandate bilingual education in school districts with enough LEP students to make it practical. Thirty-two states now have statutes expressly permitting native-language instruction and, of these, seven require it under certain circumstances.[3] Laws in seven other states, most dating from the World War I era, still prohibit any instruction in languages other than English.[4] While those outright bans are no longer enforced, Proposition 227 in California and similar measures in Arizona and Massachusetts restrict the availability of bilingual education to varying degrees.

'Simple Justice'

The second track of federal policy began to take shape in 1970, largely as a response to civil-rights activism. A few months earlier La Raza Unida Party, a militant Chicano group, had taken matters into its own hands. In Crystal City, Texas, it organized school boycotts to protest the unequal treatment of Spanish-speaking students. Bilingual education was among its demands and, after the party had won a majority of seats on the local school board, among its innovations. Meanwhile Mexican American, Puerto Rican, and Chinese American parents began to file lawsuits challenging the schools' failure to address their children's language needs.

Until that time thinking about civil rights had been heavily influenced by the U.S. Supreme Court's 1954 decision in ***Brown v. Board of Education,*** which outlawed segregated schools as inconsistent with equal education. Now the parents of

English learners advanced a novel claim of discrimination: that *equal treatment* for their children – in other words, "submersing" them in mainstream classrooms designed for English-background children – meant *unequal opportunities* to succeed. There was no question that large numbers of language-minority students were falling behind and dropping out. At issue was whether local school officials should be held accountable. The Civil Rights Act had forbidden discrimination on the basis of national origin, but thus far federal authorities had focused most of their attention on race discrimination against African-Americans. Nevertheless, **de facto** and **de jure segregation** of Mexican American children remained prevalent in schools throughout the Southwest.

Finally, on May 25, 1970, the U.S. government entered the fray. J. Stanley Pottinger, director of the federal Office for Civil Rights (OCR), sent a memorandum to "school districts with more than five percent national-origin-minority group children" informing them of their obligations under the Civil Rights Act. While the law prohibits discrimination in a variety of contexts, the relevant section was **Title VI**, which involves government programs. As President John F. Kennedy said in proposing the legislation, "Simple justice requires that public funds, to which all taxpayers of all races contribute, not be spent in any fashion which encourages, entrenches, subsidizes, or results in racial discrimination." OCR interpreted this to mean that public schools had a responsibility to guarantee all students, regardless of their background, an equal opportunity to succeed. So when children's English skills were limited, Pottinger wrote, "the district must take affirmative steps to rectify the language deficiency in order to open its instructional program to these students."

Although the memorandum did not direct school officials to establish bilingual education programs, it demanded that they offer some kind of special language instruction for children who needed help with English. It prohibited the assignment of students to classes for the handicapped "on the basis of criteria which essentially measure or evaluate English language skills." No longer could schools shuttle children along vocational tracks toward an "educational dead-end" instead of teaching them English. Finally, administrators had to communicate with parents in a language they could understand.

While Pottinger's memorandum carved out new territory for OCR's enforcement of Title VI, including the threat to terminate federal education subsidies as a last resort, the immediate reaction in school districts was muted. There was no stampede to comply with the federal directive. Most schools continued to offer little more than sink-or-swim. Education historian Colman B. Stein reports that in

Beeville, Texas, the superintendent's only response was to redesignate vocational programs, where Latino students were concentrated, as "career education."

If the executive branch was slow to get results, the federal courts were not. A lawsuit by Mexican American parents in New Mexico, *Serna v. Portales Municipal Schools*, led to the first court mandate for bilingual education. Based on expert testimony in this 1972 case, a federal judge ordered instruction in the children's native language and culture as part of a desegregation plan. Upholding the decision two years later, the 10th U.S. Circuit Court of Appeals ruled that Title VI gave Hispanic students "a right to bilingual education."

Other landmark cases followed. ASPIRA, a Puerto Rican advocacy group, sued New York City on behalf of 150,000 Hispanic students. In 1974, it won a **consent decree,** or court-approved settlement, guaranteeing bilingual instruction for the city's Spanish-dominant children. In *Ríos v. Read* (1977), a federal judge ruled that the Patchogue-Medford, New York, school district had violated the rights of LEP students by providing a half-hearted bilingual program that relied mainly on ESL and included no bicultural component. "While the District's goal of teaching Hispanic children the English language is certainly proper," the court said, "it cannot be allowed to compromise a student's right to a meaningful education before proficiency in English is obtained."

The most sweeping order came in 1981. U.S. District Judge William Wayne Justice found that the state of Texas had not only segregated students in inferior "Mexican schools," but had "vilified the language, culture, and heritage of these children with grievous results." Accordingly, Judge Justice mandated bilingual education in grades K–12 throughout Texas. The following year, however, a federal appellate court reversed this ruling in the case, *U.S. v. Texas*, on factual grounds. Evidence of discriminatory practices had been insufficient to justify such a broad remedy, it said; moreover, the Texas legislature had recently enacted a strong mandate for bilingual education.

Lau Decision

The major court decision on the rights of language-minority students, and the only such ruling by the U.S. Supreme Court, is ***Lau v. Nichols.*** The case originated in 1970, when a San Francisco poverty lawyer, Edward Steinman, learned that a client's child was failing in school because he could not understand the language of instruction. Steinman filed a class-action lawsuit on behalf of Kinney Lau and 1,789 other Chinese-background students in the same predicament.[5] These children, he alleged, were being denied "education on equal terms" (the court's standard in *Brown v. Board of Education)* because of their limited English skills. San Francisco school officials responded that, unlike the *Brown* case, *Lau* involved no discrimination because there was no segregation or disparate treatment. The same instruction was offered to all students, without regard to national origin. If the Chinese children had a "language deficiency," that was unfortunate but the district was not to blame.

Federal district and appeals courts sided with the school officials, although in a strong dissent Judge Shirley Hufstedler of the 9th Circuit (later U.S. secretary of education) dismissed the school district's premises as irrelevant:

> The state does not cause children to start school speaking only Chinese. Neither does a state cause children to have black skin rather than white nor cause a person charged with a crime to be indigent rather than rich. State action depends upon state responses to differences otherwise created.
>
> These Chinese children are not separated from their English-speaking classmates by state-erected walls of brick and mortar, but the language barrier, which the state helps to maintain, insulates the children from their classmates as effectively as any physical bulwarks. Indeed, these children are more isolated from equal educational opportunity than were those physically segregated Blacks in *Brown*; these children cannot communicate at all with their classmates or teachers. ... Invidious discrimination is not washed away because the able bodied and the paraplegic are given the same state command to walk.

In 1974, the Supreme Court unanimously overruled the lower courts and embraced Hufstedler's logic. "There is no equality of treatment," wrote Justice William O. Douglas, "merely by providing students with the same facilities, textbooks, teachers, and curriculum; for students who do not understand English are effectively foreclosed from any meaningful education." Under Title VI of the Civil Rights Act, the Chinese-speaking children were entitled to special assistance to enable them to participate equally in the school program, the court said. Sink-or-swim was no longer acceptable. The ruling invoked no Constitutional guarantees – or, in legal parlance, it "did not reach" the equal protection clause of the Fourteenth Amendment. Title VI, whose implications were spelled out by OCR's 1970 memorandum, was sufficient basis for requiring extra help for children with limited English skills, according to the court.[6]

The decision stopped short of mandating bilingual education, an omission that the program's critics have interpreted as upholding "flexibility" for school districts to use alternative methods. The plaintiffs, however, had earlier dropped their demand for bilingual instruction. So the lack of an explicit order for this approach was in keeping with the court's customary reluctance to address issues not raised in a case. *Lau* said nothing for or against the principle of local option. Justice Douglas wrote in the preface to his opinion:

> No specific remedy is urged upon us. Teaching English to the students of Chinese ancestry who do not speak the language is one choice. Giving instructions to this group in Chinese is another. There may be others. Petitioners ask only that the Board of Education be directed to apply its expertise to the problem and rectify the situation.

In the end San Francisco officials signed a consent agreement to provide bilingual education for the city's Chinese, Filipino, and Hispanic children. (As approved and supervised by the federal district court, this order remains intact, shielding the district from most provisions of Proposition 227.)

The *Lau* ruling attracted little public notice at the time; it received a one-sentence mention in the January 22, 1974, edition of the *New York Times*. But the Office for Civil Rights immediately grasped the magnitude of the enforcement job ahead. In 1975, OCR investigators made preliminary visits to 334 school districts with large numbers of language-minority children. "Most [districts had] utterly failed to meet their responsibilities," according to David Tatel, director of OCR during the Carter administration. A task force led by Martin Gerry began drawing up guidelines for "educational approaches which would constitute appropriate 'affirmative steps' to be taken by a noncomplying school district 'to open up its instructional program.'"

U.S. Commissioner of Education Terrel Bell announced these so-called **Lau Remedies** on August 11, 1975. The guidelines told districts how to identify and evaluate children with limited English skills, what instructional treatments would be appropriate, when children were ready for mainstream classrooms, and what professional standards teachers should meet. They also set timetables for meeting these goals. Most significant, the remedies went beyond the *Lau* decision, requiring that where children's rights had been violated, districts must provide bilingual education for elementary-school students who spoke little or no English. "English as a second language is a necessary component" of bilingual instruction, the guidelines said, but "since an ESL program does not consider the affective nor cognitive development of the students ... an ESL program [by itself] is *not* appropriate." For older students, compensatory ESL instruction would generally be permissible.

Interviewed a decade later, Gerry explained this decision: "If we had given school systems a choice between bilingual instruction and ESL, they would have all gone to ESL because it was cheaper and politically popular with a lot of people – reasons that had nothing to do with the educational needs of the kids." Despite the limited research on bilingual-bicultural approaches at that time, Gerry had become "sold on" their effectiveness while serving as a court-appointed monitor of civil-rights orders in Texas, he said. "These were the only programs that were working." Nevertheless, he recalled, OCR's intent was to move children into English-language classrooms as quickly as possible – not to make them proficient in two languages, as some Hispanic educators had urged.

Hastily drafted, with no opportunities for public comment, the Lau Remedies lacked the legal status of federal regulations. In practice, however, they had the full force of the federal government behind them as OCR embarked on a campaign of aggressive enforcement. Where investigators found civil-rights infractions, they used the Lau Remedies as a basis to negotiate consent agreements, or **Lau Plans**, with offenders. Threatened with a loss of federal funding if they resisted, such districts had little choice but to adopt bilingual education.

Contradictions of Title VII

By 1973–74, when the Bilingual Education Act came up for reauthorization, it had won influential allies on Capitol Hill. Title VII's budget of $45 million now sponsored 211 school projects in 26 languages, including Russian, French, Portuguese, Cantonese, Pomo, Cree, Yup'ik, and Chamorro. Still, the program was serving only about 6 percent of eligible children. Besides the problem of insufficient funding, the Senate Labor and Public Welfare Committee expressed concern about "continuing inertia on the part of the Office of Education in developing a comprehensive set of goals, directions, and policies for the Title VII effort. ... Equally disappointing [is the fact that] virtually no Title VII funds have been spent for ... teacher training and professional development."

In response to these complaints, Senators Edward Kennedy and Walter Mondale moved to expand the program. As amended, the 1974 law required school programs funded under Title VII to spend at least 15 percent of their grants on inservice training of bilingual teachers. It also required them – for the first time – to include instruction in students' native language and culture "to the extent necessary to allow a child to progress effectively through the educational system." Finally, the new law expanded eligibility for participation in Title VII programs to all children of "limited English-speaking ability," regardless of their family's income or the dominant language of their homes.

While bilingual education was sanctioned as a route to English acquisition, the amendments again failed to resolve the tension between the goals of **transition** to English and **maintenance** of the native language. Both approaches remained eligible for funding. With their growing political clout, Hispanics provided a strong constituency for an enrichment rather than a compensatory model, for programs that promoted fluency in two languages rather than just one. Puerto Rico's Congressional delegate, Santiago Polanco-Abreu, had articulated this ideal during 1967 deliberations on the Bilingual Education Act:

> I wish to stress that I realize the importance of learning English by Puerto Ricans and other minority groups living in the States. But I do not feel that our educational abilities are so limited and our educational vision so short-sighted that we must teach one language at the expense of another, that we must sacrifice the academic potential of thousands of youngsters in order to promote the learning of English, that we must jettison and reject ways of life that are not our own.

He proposed

> the establishment of programs which (a) will utilize two languages, English and the non-English mother tongue, in the teaching of the various school subjects, (b) will concentrate on teaching *both* English and the non-English mother tongue, and (c) will endeavor to preserve and enrich the culture and heritage of the non-English-speaking student.

Though these goals were not adopted explicitly, neither were they rejected in the original enactment of Title VII. The Department of Health, Education, and Welfare appeared to endorse them in its 1971 instructions for grant applicants: "It must be remembered that the ultimate goal of bilingual education is *a student who functions well in two languages* on any occasion" (emphasis added). In 1974, the department's undersecretary, Frank Carlucci, expressed a different interpretation of Congressional intent. "The cultural pluralism of American society is one of its greatest assets," he said, "but such pluralism is a private matter of local choice, and not a proper responsibility of the federal government. ... [The goal of Title VII is] to assist children of limited- or non-English speaking ability to gain competency in English so that they may enjoy equal educational opportunity – and *not* to require cultural pluralism."

Politically speaking, the language maintenance issue would become bilingual education's Achilles heel. Prompted by a resurgence of ethnic pride among both whites and racial minorities, in 1972 Congress had passed the Ethnic Heritage Studies Act, which authorized federal aid to establish research centers and develop curriculum materials. But the trend proved to be short-lived. By the mid-1970s a backlash began to develop against subsidies to preserve minority languages and cultures. Critics argued against diverting federal dollars from the twin imperatives of teaching English and assimilating children into the mainstream. Albert Shanker, president of the American Federation of Teachers, wrote in a 1974 editorial:

> The American taxpayer, while recognizing the existence of cultural diversity, still wants the schools to be the basis of an American melting pot. While the need for the child to feel comfortable and be able to communicate is clear, it is also clear that what these children need is intensive instruction in English so that they may as soon as possible function with other children in regular school programs.

Fuel was added to the controversy by the American Institutes for Research (AIR), which in 1977–78 released the first large-scale evaluation of bilingual education in the United States. AIR's conclusions shocked practitioners: researchers could find no evidence for the overall effectiveness of bilingual approaches, as compared with sink-or-swim instruction. The study's methodology, however, drew sharp criticism from other researchers in the field, who argued that bilingual education was a new approach that varied enormously in program quality, teaching methods, student characteristics, and other factors that AIR had failed to consider *(see Chapter 7).*

In its most explosive finding, the study reported that federally funded bilingual programs were defying the will of Congress. When AIR had asked Title VII directors about the duration of bilingual instruction, 86 percent responded that Spanish-speaking children were retained even after they had learned enough English to join mainstream classrooms. Most programs aimed to maintain minority languages rather than to speed the transition to English, AIR concluded. Whether that goal was achieved in practice, however, was doubtful in light of another of the report's findings: 50 percent of "bilingual" teachers interviewed admitted they lacked proficiency in their students' mother tongue. Nevertheless, critics seized on the first statistic to argue that schools were violating the law by providing bilingual instruction beyond "the extent necessary" for English proficiency.

An especially influential critic was Noel Epstein, education editor of the *Washington Post.* In 1977, he published a monograph indicting federal policy on bilingual education, entitled *Language, Ethnicity, and the Schools.* Epstein characterized language maintenance programs as "affirmative ethnicity," linking this pedagogical approach to the legal concept of affirmative action, which was also coming under attack at the time. The implication was that both ideas were misguided attempts to compensate for past discrimination. "Cultural pluralism in the schools" was fine, Epstein said. His quarrel was not with "efforts to teach 'each about every,' to promote greater tolerance and respect across ethnic and racial groups." But he objected to government-financed programs to foster children's allegiance to minority identities. Inculcating ethnic pride was a function best "left to families, religious groups, ethnic organizations, private schools, ethnic publications, and others."

Even President Jimmy Carter, who liked to show off his own knowledge of Spanish and who had appointed officials favorable to bilingual maintenance programs, told his Cabinet: "I want English taught, not ethnic culture." By 1978, as Congress prepared to fine-tune Title VII, the pendulum was swinging back toward the transitional approach.

Segregation Question

Perhaps the most compelling concern was that of school desegregation, a goal that some educators saw as contradictory to any program that smacked of language maintenance. "Without any serious national debate," argued civil-rights expert Gary Orfield in 1977,

> it seems that we have moved from a harsh assimilationist policy to a policy of linguistic and cultural separation. ... I believe that there is a better middle position, one which would encourage integration of Hispanic children into schools which respect their cultural tradition and encourage children of diverse backgrounds to voluntarily study Spanish language and literature in classes that actually have bilingual student bodies.

Moreover, according to historian Diego Castellanos, some Hispanic leaders began to express fears that "bilingual tracks" might become an institutionalized form of de facto segregation. Another civil-rights advocate, Alfredo Mathew, warned that

> bilingualism [could] become so insular and ingrown that it fosters a type of apartheid that will generate animosities with other groups, such as Blacks, in the competition for scarce resources, and further alienate the Hispanic from the larger society. ... Only to the extent that bilingual programs remain open to the possibilities of involving Blacks and Whites of all nationalities will bilingualism become an important and challenging alternative.

There was no question that bilingual programs in the late 1970s tended to separate language-minority students from their English-speaking peers. Yet segregation was nothing new in Hispanic schooling, bilingual or otherwise. In the year the Bilingual Education Act was passed, 65 percent of Spanish-background children in elementary school and 53 percent of those in high school were attending predominantly minority institutions, according to a study by ASPIRA. By 1976, the figures had increased to 74 percent and 65 percent, respectively. Most Title VII grants were going to highly segregated school districts.

Bilingual education was a complicating factor in several civil-rights cases, as federal courts sought to reconcile the goals of racial balance and quality programs for English learners. According to José Cárdenas, speaking from long experience as a school superintendent in Texas, "desegregation efforts consistently have jeopardized special programs for minority populations," dispersed Latino students, and undermined parental control. In a response to Epstein, Cárdenas blamed administrators' insensitivity for this contradiction, rather than any separatist agenda among bilingual education advocates. He added that multicultural instruction was neither a subsidy for "affirmative ethnicity," nor an attempt to emphasize cultural differences, but an overdue recognition of the role of minorities in American culture.

Once again, Congress grappled with these contending views in its 1978 amendments to the Bilingual Education Act. This time it succeeded in clarifying the law's goals. The native language would be used *only* "to the extent necessary to allow a child to achieve competence in the English language." Although this formulation made little sense in pedagogical terms, its political meaning was clear. Henceforth Title VII programs would be strictly transitional; no funds would be available for language maintenance. At the same time, student eligibility for assistance was expanded to all children of **limited English proficiency** – that is, those who needed help with reading and writing skills in English, even if their speaking skills seemed adequate. The new law addressed the problem of national-origin desegregation by allowing up to 40 percent enrollment of English-speaking children in bilingual programs as a way to assist LEP students in learning English.

OCR: One Step Forward, Two Steps Back

Throughout the late 1970s, the federal Office for Civil Rights continued to monitor school districts' performance in serving language-minority children. Where it found violations OCR required districts to initiate bilingual education programs and other changes under the Lau Remedies. By 1980, it had negotiated 359 Lau Plans to remedy past discrimination, enabling many LEP children to receive special help for the first time.

A majority of districts cooperated, albeit with some grumbling about federal heavy-handedness. The schools of Alhambra, California, for example, had no bilingual education and only minimal ESL instruction in 1977, when OCR cited the district for multiple civil-rights violations. Ten years later the district had 120 bilingual classrooms, featuring instruction in Spanish, Vietnamese, Cantonese, and Mandarin. Elsewhere there was sporadic resistance to OCR's enforcement. A group of Texas school districts sought Congressional intervention after federal authorities found their services to LEP students inadequate and suspended federal aid under the (now defunct) Emergency School Assistance Act. OCR officials were hauled before a Congressional subcommittee and accused of making unreasonable demands that exceeded the agency's legal mandate, especially its insistence on bilingual instruction.[7]

With its controversial policy on *Lau*, OCR's lack of formal rules was becoming a handicap. To settle a 1978 lawsuit by a consortium of Alaska school districts, the federal government pledged to go through the legal process of proposing regulations, soliciting public comment, and issuing final rules on school districts' obligations under Title VI of the Civil Rights Act. Unlike the unofficial Lau Remedies, the new regulations would have the force of law. OCR took its time, however, in studying the legal issues, and the process of creating the new U.S. Department of Education added to the delays.

On August 5, 1980, just three months before Election Day, President Carter finally acted. In what was widely interpreted as a political move to win Hispanic votes, his administration released a proposal that was even more prescriptive than the original Lau Remedies. Under the formal **Lau Regulations**, bilingual education would be mandated in all schools where at least 25 LEP children of the same minority language group were enrolled in two consecutive grades in elementary or middle schools.

Reaction was immediate and overwhelmingly negative from educators' groups; strong support came only from the National Education Association and the National Association for Bilingual Education. The Department of Education received an unprecedented 4,600 public comments, most of which opposed the proposal. Feeling the election-year heat, Congress voted to block the rules from taking effect before mid-1981. Education Secretary Hufstedler exacerbated the backlash when she dispatched representatives of the bilingual education office to defend the Lau Regulations proposal at hearings around the country. The effect was to strengthen the popular misconception of Title VII as a heavy-handed federal mandate rather than a voluntary grant program.

Fairfax County, Virginia, an affluent suburban district near Washington, D.C., had been fighting since 1976 against OCR's pressure to establish a bilingual program. Local administrators argued that, with LEP students representing more than 50 language groups, intensive ESL was the only practical treatment. Based on glowing reports of students' progress and the district's financial commitment to serving them, in late 1980 federal officials relented. Still catching heavy flak for the Lau Regulations, OCR wanted to show that it could be flexible. So in the Fairfax case it approved the first Lau Plan featuring an ESL-only approach. The *Washington Post* hailed the "Fairfax model" as a triumph for local control over "a hard-line government policy." **Content-based ESL**, a common component of bilingual programs, was now portrayed as a promising "alternative method." (Subsequent research, however, has failed to confirm these expectations; *see Chapter 9.*)

If there had been any hope of salvaging the Lau Regulations, it was buried under Ronald Reagan's landslide victory and his promise to "get government off our backs." Terrel Bell, the incoming Secretary of Education, withdrew the proposed rules on February 2, 1981, calling them "harsh, inflexible, burdensome, unworkable, and incredibly costly." Ironically, Bell was the same official who had issued the Lau Remedies six years earlier. Now he condemned the mandate for native-language instruction as "an intrusion on state and local responsibility. ... We will protect the rights of children who do not speak English well, but we will do so by permitting school districts to use any way that has proven to be successful."

Notwithstanding this even-handed statement of policy, the new administration's rhetoric began to tilt sharply against the bilingual alternative. In off-the-cuff remarks shortly after taking office, President Reagan made his personal views clear:

> Now, bilingual education, there is a need, but there is also a purpose that has been distorted again at the federal level. Where there are predominantly students speaking a foreign language at home, coming to school and being taught English, and they fall behind or are unable to keep up in some subjects because of the lack of knowledge of the language, I think it is proper that we have teachers equipped who can get at them in their own language and understand why it is they don't get the answer to the problem and help them in that way. *But it is absolutely wrong and against American concepts to have a bilingual education program that is now openly, admittedly dedicated to preserving their native language and never getting them adequate in English so they can go out into the job market and participate.* [Emphasis added]

A new era had begun.

Legislative Fallout

During the first few months of the Reagan administration, attention focused anew on the effectiveness issue. Large-scale evaluation studies had thus far failed to prove the superiority of bilingual education; in the AIR study, some children fared better in sink-or-swim classrooms. As a result, alternatives like the Fairfax ESL model and **structured immersion** in English began to gain credibility. The heaviest blow was dealt by an Education Department review of the research literature by Keith Baker and Adriana de Kanter. Widely publicized in the fall of 1981, the study created a sensation by concluding that evidence for the effectiveness of bilingual education was tenuous at best *(see Chapter 7)*. Policymakers began to ask: Why mandate a pedagogical approach whose benefits had yet to be demonstrated? Why not adopt a policy of "local flexibility," not only in meeting civil-rights obligations but also in qualifying for Title VII funds? Why not explore English-only alternatives, especially in districts that had trouble recruiting adequate numbers of bilingual teachers?

In 1982, Bell proposed to eliminate the native-language requirement for districts receiving Title VII grants. Echoing the Reagan rhetoric on social spending, he argued that "reduced federal resources available for education [should be] focused on students who are most in need of special programs." Senator S. I. Hayakawa, the California Republican who sponsored the Reagan administration's bill, was more candid in explaining its intent:

> I believe that given the flexibility to choose their own program, local schools will emphasize English instruction. Without the expensive requirement of a full academic curriculum in foreign languages, schools will be able to teach more non-English-speaking students for the same cost [and will enable them] to join the mainstream of our society more quickly. . . . Well-intentioned transitional bilingual education programs have often inhibited [immigrants'] command of English and retarded their full citizenship.

The 1978 amendments to Title VII, Hayakawa warned, were encouraging demands for **official bilingualism** and thereby threatening to splinter American society into disparate cultural groups. Besides passage of a bill to limit bilingual education, he urged ratification of a constitutional amendment designating English as the sole official language of the United States.

Congress failed to act on either measure that year. But with Title VII up for reauthorization in 1983, its opponents were optimistic about winning major changes, perhaps even blocking an extension. They introduced several bills to restrict bilingual programs or to redirect federal aid to all-English classrooms.

Sensing this adverse climate, supporters of existing law postponed the battle until the election year of 1984 – an astute decision, as it turned out. Republicans were actively courting the Hispanic vote for the first time. Suddenly the president had words of praise for "effective bilingual programs"; a White House aide described Ronald Reagan's "growing sensitivity on the issue."

Two House Democrats, Dale Kildee of Michigan and Baltazar Corrada of Puerto Rico, introduced legislation reauthorizing Title VII that had largely been drafted by James J. Lyons, lobbyist for the National Association for Bilingual Education (NABE). To the surprise of most observers, the bill moved quickly thanks to a deal worked out with two Republicans, John McCain of Arizona and Steve Bartlett of Texas. The compromise permitted, for the first time, a portion of Title VII funds to support **special alternative instructional programs** (SAIPs) that did not use English learners' native language. Under a complicated formula, 4 percent of total appropriations up to $140 million would be reserved for SAIPs, along with half of any excess above that amount, up to a ceiling of 10 percent. The idea was to give the administration an incentive to boost Title VII funding overall by allowing an increasing share for its favored alternative methodologies.[8]

In exchange for this concession, NABE won several new grant programs:

- *family English literacy*, aimed at assisting the parents of children in Title VII classrooms;
- *special populations*, which would respond to the needs of preschool, gifted and talented, and special education students of limited English proficiency;
- *academic excellence*, designed to replicate exemplary instructional models; and
- *developmental bilingual education*, which reintroduced a modest authorization to support native-language maintenance – a purpose prohibited since 1978.

The amendments also put a stronger emphasis on teacher training. The academic goals of Title VII, which had been vaguely defined, were restated as "allow[ing] a child to meet grade-promotion and graduation standards." Taken together, Lyons said, these changes helped Title VII "break out of the compensatory mold." No longer would it be regarded as a single-purpose remedial program – or so he hoped.

To bilingual education advocates, the 4 percent concession to proponents of alternative methods seemed a small price to pay for the gains they had achieved. Yet, while the practical effects of the change were small, the long-term implications proved substantial. The tiny breach in the dike would grow, releasing a torrent of legislative conflicts in the coming years.

OCR's Retreat

Secretary Bell's withdrawal of the Lau Regulations had thrown civil-rights enforcement into disarray. OCR went back to the drawing board to develop rules that would give districts more leeway, while defining standards to ensure that LEP children's needs were addressed. Almost immediately it encountered opposition. Daniel Oliver, the Department of Education's new general counsel, argued that the *Lau* decision might no longer be valid, in light of subsequent decisions by the U.S. Supreme Court *(see below)*. In line with the Reagan administration's philosophy on civil rights, Oliver argued that OCR should have to prove "discriminatory intent," rather than merely documenting "discriminatory effects," to find that a district had violated Title VI of the Civil Rights Act. Certainly, he said, a failure to provide *any* special services to LEP children would violate the law. On the other hand, "a school district which implements reasonably a program based upon a theory deemed sound by experts [would] demonstrate a lack of discriminatory purpose" unless federal officials could prove otherwise. Oliver's approach generated considerable controversy within the Education Department. A consensus was never reached on what regulations to propose, and in late 1982 the idea of issuing revised Lau Regulations was abandoned. "Districts have been left free to pursue any approach based on informed educational judgment," wrote Harry Singleton, the assistant secretary for civil rights. By default, Oliver's hands-off position had prevailed.

OCR operated without any publicly stated policy until December 1985, when it announced it would enforce *Lau* on a "case by case basis." It did not specify what a *Lau* violation might look like, but OCR compliance officers would presumably know one when they saw one. "There is considerable debate among educators about the most effective way to meet the educational needs of language minority students," the memorandum explained. "OCR does not presume to know which educational strategy is most appropriate in a given situation."

The Lau Remedies – a detailed set of requirements for LEP student identification, assessment, exit criteria, teacher certification, staff-student ratios, and bilingual instruction – gave way to a broad statement about the obligation to provide "services ... to meet the educational needs of LEP children." Virtually all decisions about what services would be appropriate were left up to the school district, which merely had to find an "expert" to endorse them. An expert was rather loosely defined as "someone whose experience and training expressly qualifies him or her to render such judgments." The measure of success was similarly vague: to give students access to the regular educational program "within a reasonable period of time." Advertising its new flexibility, the memorandum advised "districts faced with a shortage of trained teachers, or with a multiplicity of languages" that they might not be able to staff "an intensive ESL program or a bilingual program. OCR does not require a program that places unrealistic expectations on a district" or that would require it "to divert resources from other necessary educational resources and services." Not much reading between the lines was required. Districts would have little to fear from OCR as long as they could claim to be "serving" LEP children in some fashion.

Timeline: Language Policy Developments, Part I

1954	In *Brown v. Board of Education*, Supreme Court outlaws "separate but equal" public schools
1964	Civil Rights Act passes Congress; Title VI prohibits race, sex, and national origin discrimination in government-funded programs
1965	As part of the War on Poverty, Congress passes Elementary and Secondary Education Act
1965–66	Tucson Survey documents educational neglect of Mexican American students in the Southwest
1966	Tucson conference brings together language-minority educators and politicians, launching the "bilingual movement"
1967	37 bilingual education bills are introduced in Congress
1968	Bilingual Education Act (Title VII of Elementary and Secondary Education Act) becomes law
1969	Texas decriminalizes teaching in languages other than English
1970	Office for Civil Rights issues memorandum on school districts' obligation to take "affirmative steps" to overcome language barriers for LEP students
1970	*Lau v. Nichols* lawsuit is filed, alleging that San Francisco schools are neglecting the needs of Chinese-background students
1971	Massachusetts passes first state law mandating bilingual education where enough English learners speak the same native language
1973	Illinois and Texas pass laws requiring districts to offer bilingual education under certain circumstances
1974	Federal appeals court in *Serna v. Portales Municipal Schools* upholds a "right to bilingual education" for Mexican American children

1974   Unanimous Supreme Court decision in *Lau v. Nichols* outlaws sink-or-swim instruction as a "mockery of equal education"

1974   Congress passes Equal Educational Opportunities Act, making *Lau* decision part of the U.S. Code

1974   ASPIRA Consent Decree mandates bilingual instruction for Latino children in New York City

1974   Bilingual Education Act is reauthorized; professional development stressed; use of students' native language and culture required in funded programs

1975   OCR task force issues Lau Remedies, requiring bilingual education as a remedy where districts have violated English learners' civil rights

1976   California mandates bilingual education

1977–78   AIR report returns mediocre report card for Title VII, highlights programs' efforts to maintain Spanish

1978   Bilingual Education Act reauthorized; language maintenance banned – funding restricted to transitional programs

1978   In *Regents of University of California v. Bakke*, Supreme Court limits civil-rights claims to cases in which intentional discrimination can be proved, weakening legal basis of *Lau v. Nichols*

1980   Fairfax County, Virginia, becomes first district allowed to use all-ESL program to meet its obligations under Lau Remedies

1980   Lau Regulations are issued, mandating bilingual instruction where at least 25 LEP students speak same language in two consecutive grades

1981   Lau Regulations are withdrawn by incoming Reagan administration; called "harsh, inflexible, burdensome, unworkable, and incredibly costly"

1981   Virginia legislature designates English as state's official language; local districts shielded from mandates for bilingual education

1981   U.S. Department of Education leaks Baker–de Kanter report questioning the effectiveness of transitional bilingual education

1981   Federal appeals court in *Castañeda v. Pickard* sets "three-prong" test for school districts in meeting obligations to English learners

1982   Federal court order in *U.S. v. Texas*, requiring bilingual education statewide in grades K–12, is overturned on appeal

1983   Denver schools fail to meet obligations under *Castañeda* standard; court orders stronger bilingual programs

1984   Bilingual Education Act is reauthorized; modest funding allowed for developmental bilingual and "special alternative" (all-English) programs

In 1985, as part of a broad initiative to revamp federal policy on educating English learners *(see Chapter 6)*, the Reagan administration invited districts that had previously adopted Lau Plans to renegotiate these agreements. The implication was clear. Those who wanted to eliminate native-language instruction could now do so with the blessings of OCR. As it happened, however, few districts were eager to dismantle their bilingual programs. Six months later the Education Department acknowledged that only 14 districts had responded, including several that sought to expand their use of native languages.

Not surprisingly, OCR's *Lau* enforcement fell off sharply during this period. Data compiled by the agency in 1986 at the request of Congress, showed that school districts were nine times less likely to be monitored for *Lau* compliance under the Reagan administration than from 1975 to 1980, under the Ford and Carter administrations. When OCR personnel did visit school districts, they found violations 58 percent of the time; yet follow-ups were rare. Nationwide, in 1985, OCR's *Lau* enforcement consisted of 10 investigations of complaints against school districts, 11 reviews to ensure compliance with the law, and two monitoring visits to determine whether local officials were abiding by their Lau Plans. In 1980, the comparable figures were 136 complaint investigations, 69 compliance reviews, and 195 monitoring visits.

Critics accused the Reagan administration of abdicating its obligation to safeguard the civil rights of language-minority students. "OCR has disappeared from the field as far as any meaningful enforcement goes," charged civil-rights attorney Camilo Pérez-Bustillo. Peter Roos, his colleague in the Multicultural Education Training and Advocacy (META) project, added: "If you had a real case – anything you had a legal handle on – you wouldn't bring it to OCR [because] it would get so tied up in the bureaucracy. The regional offices don't have authority to act on their own. By the time a case gets to Washington, it's lost."

There was little change during the administration of President George H. W. Bush, other than efforts to tone down the strident rhetoric against bilingual education. The trend of declining enforcement efforts continued. OCR reported 12 compliance reviews in 1991, which it described as "the largest number ... in recent years." Between 1976 and 1980, the average number had been 115.

President Clinton's appointee to head OCR, Norma Cantú, had been a litigator for the Mexican American Legal Defense and Educational Fund. On her arrival in 1993, one of her first acts was to double the frequency of *Lau* reviews. Yet the Clinton administration never showed any interest in reopening the question of appropriate instruction for LEP students or in specifying minimum standards that districts must meet, for example, in providing adequate resources and qualified personnel for language-minority programs. In effect, OCR continued to enforce *Lau* case by case. This policy continues under President George W. Bush.

Castañeda Standard

Parents frustrated by OCR's inaction retain the option of taking their complaints directly to federal court. A useful tool in such cases has been the **Equal Educational Opportunities Act of 1974** (EEOA), as interpreted by the 5th Circuit Court of Appeals in *Castañeda v. Pickard.* Section 1703(f) of the EEOA requires school districts to take "appropriate action to overcome language barriers that impede equal participation by its students in its instructional programs."

Obviously, a great deal hinges on the meaning of "appropriate action." *Castañeda* represents one attempt to define it. In its 1981 ruling, the 5th Circuit acknowledged "serious doubts about the continuing vitality of Lau" raised by the Supreme Court's decision in *Regents of University of California v. Bakke* (1978). In that case the court ruled that government actions with "a racially disproportionate impact" are not necessarily illegal under Title VI of the Civil Rights Act, or unconstitutional under the Fourteenth Amendment, unless there is a **discriminatory intent**. In other words, teaching all children in English, regardless of their language abilities, might now be permissible. If a history of discrimination could not be documented, affirmative steps to overcome limited English proficiency might no longer be required.

In *Castañeda*, however, the appellate court relied on the EEOA – not the *Lau* decision – to mandate special help for English learners. It ruled that, in passing this law, Congress had thrown its weight behind *Lau*, thus affirming that educational neglect violated the civil rights of language-minority children, whether or not they had been victims of deliberate discrimination.

The decision added that "good faith efforts" did not discharge school officials of their responsibilities. Since Congress had failed to define appropriate action, the court did so, by outlining three criteria for a program serving LEP students:

- It must be based on "a sound educational theory."
- It must be "implemented effectively," with adequate resources and personnel.
- After a trial period, it must be evaluated as effective in overcoming language handicaps.

Using this analysis, in 1983 the META lawyers argued that the Denver Public Schools were providing only a half-hearted program in transitional bilingual education. A federal court agreed. Rejecting officials' claims of "good faith," it ordered Denver to adopt sweeping changes, including criteria for evaluating staff qualifications, better training of teachers and aides, and improvements in language assessment. Other courts have applied the EEOA – and *Castañeda's* "three-prong" test – to state education agencies that had failed to ensure that local districts were meeting their obligations to LEP students. Illinois and Florida were among the states required to adopt minimum standards for compliance, for example, in correctly identifying and placing LEP children.

The *Castañeda* standard remains in effect, at least in the 5th Circuit and arguably throughout the country. In 1991, OCR formally adopted the test as the cornerstone of its *Lau* enforcement. In the federal courts, however, its usefulness has waned, as judges appointed by conservative presidents have become less sympathetic to civil-rights claims. Moreover, the first criterion under *Castañeda* is quite easy to meet, since "experts" have been willing to endorse a wide range of pedagogical treatments, including the one-year immersion model mandated by Proposition 227 *(see Chapters 13 and 15)*.

META lost its first major lawsuit in 1989, *Teresa P. v. Berkeley*, which focused on the second test: allegedly inadequate resources, staff, assessment, and placement procedures for LEP students in the Berkeley, California, schools. A central complaint was the district's failure to recruit a sufficient number of credentialed teachers to staff its bilingual classrooms. But Judge D. Lowell Jensen, a former Reagan administration official, was unconvinced. "Good teachers are good teachers, no matter what the educational challenge may be," he ruled. While applying the *Castañeda* test, he found no factual support for any civil-rights violation.

Teresa P. was not decided in a social vacuum. At a time of increasing hostility toward bilingualism, the Berkeley school board dipped into emergency reserves for $1.5 million to defend the lawsuit – more than three times the amount that the district spent each year on LEP students. Resisting the demands of Hispanic parents proved popular, even in a community renowned for its liberalism, and it attracted substantial support from outsiders as well. Expert witnesses were recruited, friend-of-the-court briefs were filed, and press coverage was orchestrated by U.S. English, a group that advocated a "unilingual" America through what it called "the legal protection of English." The debate over bilingual education policy now raged in a broader, more politicized context.

Suggested Reading

Castellanos, Diego. *The Best of Both Worlds: Bilingual-Bicultural Education in the U.S.* Trenton, N.J.: New Jersey State Department of Education, 1983.

Epstein, Noel. *Language, Ethnicity, and the Schools: Policy Alternatives for Bilingual-Bicultural Education.* Washington, D.C.: Institute for Educational Leadership, 1977.

Lyons, James J. *Legal Responsibilities of Education Agencies Serving National Origin Language Minority Students.* Washington, D.C.: Mid-Atlantic Equity Center, 1988.

Stein, Colman B., Jr. *Sink or Swim: The Politics of Bilingual Education.* New York: Praeger, 1986.

See also pp. 393–94.

Online Resource Guide

Castañeda v. Pickard (5th Circuit Court of Appeals, 1981).

Department of Health, Education, and Welfare, U.S. "Memorandum to School Districts with More Than Five Percent National Origin-Minority Group Children" (1970).

Lau v. Nichols (U.S. Supreme Court, 1974).

Office for Civil Rights, U.S. "Task-Force Findings Specifying Remedies Available for Eliminating Past Educational Practices Ruled Unlawful under *Lau v. Nichols*" (Lau Remedies, 1975).

Serna v. Portales Municipal Schools (10th Circuit Court of Appeals, 1974).

See also companion CD-ROM.

Internet Links

Crawford, James. "Language Politics in the U.S.A.: The Paradox of Bilingual Education." In Carlos Ovando and Peter MacLaren, eds., *The Politics of Bilingual Education and Multiculturalism: Students and Teachers Caught in the Crossfire.* New York: McGraw-Hill, 2000.
http://ourworld.compuserve.com/homepages/jwcrawford/paradox.htm

See also companion CD-ROM.

Notes

1. In practice, however, all of the early Title VII programs made use of students' native language in one way or another, according to Albar Peña, the first federal director of bilingual education.

2. In the final House-Senate agreement, the bill targeted funding to schools with high concentrations of students from households whose incomes were below $3,000 a year.

3. See Chapter 2, note 2.

4. Alabama, Arkansas, Delaware, Nebraska, North Carolina, Oklahoma, and West Virginia. In 1981, Virginia adopted an **Official English** law relieving school boards of any "obligation to teach the standard curriculum, except courses in foreign languages, in a language other than English" but permitting them to provide bilingual instruction on a voluntary basis.

5. Of the district's 100,000 students, 16,574 were of Chinese background, of whom 2,856 were deemed to need special help in English; 633 received one hour of remedial language instruction daily and 433 received six hours. Only one-third of the 59 remedial teachers were fluent in both Chinese and English.

6. While Justice Douglas wrote on behalf of a unanimous court, Justices Stewart and Blackmun, joined by Chief Justice Burger, wrote concurring opinions that expressed some reservations. "I merely wish to make plain," Blackmun said, "that when, in another case, we are concerned with a very few youngsters, or with just a single child who speaks only German or Polish or Spanish or any language other than English, I would not regard today's decision … as conclusive upon the issue whether the statute and the [OCR] guidelines require the [federally] funded school district to provide special instruction. For me, numbers are at the heart of this case and my concurrence is to be understood accordingly."

7. Following a stern admonition from George Mahon, the Texas Democrat who chaired the House Appropriations Committee, the hearing recessed so that a compromise could be reached between OCR's Cynthia Brown and the school district officials.

8. Like many domestic programs in the Reagan years, bilingual education was a vulnerable target for budget cutters. Its funding declined from $167 million in 1980 to $133 million in 1986. While it increased to $147 million in 1988, after adjustment for inflation this still represented a reduction of more than 40 percent from the pre-Reagan level *(for historical Title VII budgets adjusted for inflation, see Figure 6–1, page 145).*

6 English Only or English Plus?

When Americans first learned about the campaign to declare English the nation's **official language**, the prevailing reaction was: *Isn't it already?* That's what two-thirds of respondents said in a 1987 survey to test citizens' knowledge of the U.S. Constitution. In fact, the country had gotten by for 200 years without giving English any special status in law, or even debating the wisdom of doing so, no doubt because its dominant status in society was never in question. Congress

Official Language Question
Roots of U.S. English
Charges of Racism
Hidden Agendas
English Plus Alternative
English Only vs. Bilingual Education
Secretary Bennett's Broadside
Research Debate
1988 Battle over Title VII
Stanford Working Group
Improving America's Schools Act

considered such legislation for the first time in 1981, when it was proposed by Senator S. I. Hayakawa of California.[1]

A longtime critic of schooling in languages other than English, Hayakawa hoped to recast the issue from a question of equal opportunity, the dominant paradigm of the 1960s and 1970s, to a question of internal security. In short, he warned that fostering diversity could lead to civil strife. Arguing that bilingual education had departed from its original mission of assimilating immigrants, he pointed to "a growing split among ethnic groups based on their native languages. With each trying to become more powerful than the other, the function of language could change from a means of communication to a tool of cultural assertion. Such a struggle for supremacy could have catastrophic consequences."

His proposed remedy was a constitutional amendment to designate English as the official language of the United States. The measure further specified:

> Neither the United States nor any State shall make or enforce any law which requires the use of any language other than English. This article shall apply to laws, ordinances, regulations, orders, programs, and policies. No order or decree shall be issued by any court of the United States or of any State requiring that any proceedings, or matters to which this article applies, be in any language other than English.

In other words, government at all levels would be required to function in English only. Oddly enough, considering the senator's rhetorical assaults on bilingual education, the one exception to this mandate would allow "educational instruction in a language other than English as required as a transitional method of making students who use a language other than English proficient in English."

Hayakawa's English Language Amendment, like similar constitutional proposals over the next two decades, never advanced beyond the hearing stage or came to a vote in Congress, even in committee.[2] In 23 states, however, voters or legislators have adopted some form of **Official English** legislation.[3] While the legal effects have been minimal thus far, the political effects have been significant. By crystallizing concerns about immigrants and their social impact, the **English-only movement** has led many Americans to view "bilingualism" as a social problem, thereby putting bilingual assistance programs of all kinds on the defensive. In 1986, for example, 73 percent of California voters approved Proposition 63, an amendment to their state constitution instructing elected officials to "take all steps necessary to insure that the role of English as the common language of the State of California is preserved and enhanced." Shortly thereafter, Governor George Deukmejian vetoed an extension of California's bilingual education law, arguably the nation's strongest at the time. The English-only movement had begun to realize

Hayakawa's strategic objective, by reframing the policy debate on how to serve English learners.

In the civil-rights era, policymakers had asked: Given the obvious failure of sink-or-swim schooling, wasn't it time to try something new? What pedagogical approaches, what mix of languages in the classroom, would provide English learners an equal chance to succeed? By the mid-1980s they wanted to know: How could children be taught English as quickly as possible, so as to mitigate the impact of linguistic diversity? Might the goal of assimilation be better achieved without resorting to native-language instruction? Bilingual education, once conceived as a way to expand opportunities for LEP children and a superior approach to teaching English, was now denounced as a barrier to students' full participation in American life and a potential source of ethnic strife. To understand how this reversal in perceptions took place, and how English-only advocates came to be so influential, it is helpful to analyze the movement's origins and premises.

Roots of 'English Only'

After retiring from Congress in 1983, Hayakawa joined forces with Dr. John Tanton, a Michigan ophthalmologist and immigration-restriction activist, to found an organization to champion the English-only cause. They named it U.S. English. The fledgling group was an instant media sensation – "The Mother Tongue Has a Movement," announced the *New York Times* – and soon it won celebrity endorsements from the likes of Saul Bellow, Alistair Cooke, Walter Cronkite, Eugene McCarthy, and Arnold Schwarzenegger. Using sophisticated direct-mail techniques, U.S. English grew rapidly; by 1988, it reported a dues-paying membership of 350,000 and an annual budget of $7 million.[4]

The U.S. English message was simple: our common language is threatened by the "mindless drift toward a bilingual society." In this nation of immigrants, the English language has been our "social glue" – not just "*a* bond, but *the* bond" that has held Americans together and allowed us to resolve our differences – according to Gerda Bikales, the group's first executive director. But now the status of English was "threatened" by the encroachment of other tongues. In a fundraising letter sent to millions of recipients, Hayakawa alleged that "prolonged bilingual education in public schools and multilingual ballots threaten to divide us along language lines." U.S. English was needed, he said, to create a "countervailing force to the special interest groups pressing for language separatism." In another article Hayakawa was more explicit, blasting "the ethnic chauvinism of the present Hispanic leadership [that] threatens a division perhaps more ominous in the long run than the division between blacks and whites."

The English Language Amendment, he explained, was necessary to head off a movement for **official bilingualism** – that is, coequal status for Spanish in the United States – and to "send a message" to immigrants that English-speaking ability is an obligation of American citizenship. This message would take a very practical form: the elimination of a wide a range of government services now provided in minority languages. While U.S. English was sometimes hard to pin down on specifics, at various times its leaders called for a ban on bilingual 911 operators, health services, drivers' tests, and voting rights; endorsed English-only rules in private workplaces; petitioned the Federal Communications Commission to limit foreign-language broadcasting; protested Spanish-language menus at McDonald's; opposed Pacific Bell's *Páginas Amarillas en Español* and customer assistance in Chinese; and complained about the availability of federal tax forms in Spanish.

In recent years U.S. English has sought to distance itself from the English-only label,[5] denying any interest in interfering with private uses of other languages or in curtailing emergency services for non-English speakers. Yet it has refused to repudiate the concept of language restrictionism, the idea that all Americans should be required to speak English in certain contexts. "There is a price to entering the social and economic and political mainstream," Bikales insisted in a 1986 interview, speaking from her personal experience as a German-Jewish immigrant:

> In return for freedom and opportunity, one learns English. … Cultural displacement, cultural loss, is extremely painful. It doesn't come free. No one can be excused from paying it. Government should not stand idly by and let the core culture, the shared culture formed by generations of earlier immigrants, slip away. [It] should not allow its own citizens to feel like strangers in their own land. If anyone has to feel strange, it's got to be the immigrant – until he learns the language.

This line of argument found a receptive ear among Americans of diverse backgrounds and political persuasions, liberal and conservative, Democrat and Republican, foreign- and native-born. But it proved especially appealing to those who made no secret of their animus toward linguistic minorities. In 1985, when the Reagan administration initiated an effort to shift federal funding from bilingual education to all-English alternative approaches, U.S. English generated the bulk of comments, many of which were openly hostile to immigrant groups:

> We here in Southern California are overrun with <u>all</u> sorts of aliens – Asian, Spanish, Cuban, Middle East – and it is an insurmountable task if these mil-

lions are not required to learn English. Many are <u>illerate</u> [sic] <u>in their native language</u>. [Rolling Hills, California] …

At the rate the Latinos (and non-whites) reproduce, [we] face a demographic imbalance if we do not change several of our dangerously outdated laws. Make English the official language everywhere in the U.S.A. [Jersey City, New Jersey] …

No other ethnic group has made the demands for bilingual education as have the Cubans. The more you give them, the more they demand. WHOSE AMERICA IS THIS? ONE FLAG. ONE LANGUAGE. [North Miami, Florida]

These sentiments were by no means isolated. In an internal survey conducted in 1988, U.S. English asked its members what had prompted them to support the organization. Forty-two percent cited the statement: "I wanted America to stand strong and not cave in to Hispanics who shouldn't be here."[6]

Charges of Racism

Such candid racism among its followers became an embarrassment for U.S. English, and a rallying point for its critics. Leaders of Hispanic and Asian communities, along with elected officials ranging from Tom Bradley, the Democratic mayor of Los Angeles, to William Clements, the Republican governor of Texas, denounced the English-only movement as racially divisive. Attorney General James Shannon of Massachusetts, a Democrat, warned that enacting an Official English measure in his state would intensify "bigotry, divisiveness, and resentment of minority groups." Senator Pete Domenici, Republican of New Mexico, called the proposed English Language Amendment "an insult to all Americans for whom English is not the first language. … It won't help anyone learn the English language. It won't improve our society. It won't lead to a more cohesive nation. In fact, it will create a more divided nation."

Stung by charges of anti-Hispanic bias, in mid-1987 U.S. English hired Linda Chávez as its president. Formerly staff director of the U.S. Commission on Civil Rights and an advisor in the Reagan White House, Chávez was sophisticated in the ways of Washington. Immediately she began working to dispel the organization's exclusionist image and to replace it with a beneficent one. She championed Official English as a way to bring newcomers into the mainstream. In frequent public appearances, she advertised the presence of immigrants on the U.S. English board of directors, including S. I. Hayakawa, who had once been barred from this country under the Asian exclusion provisions of U.S. immigration law. Chávez frequently cited her own Hispanic roots dating back three centuries in New Mexico. "Contrary to any anti-immigrant sentiment pervading the official English movement, quite the opposite concern motivates" U.S. English, she maintained.

> Unless we become serious about protecting our heritage as a unilingual society – bound by a common language – we may lose a precious resource that has helped us forge a national character and identity from so many diverse elements. I truly believe that the official English movement will help protect the future integration of new Americans, as it has helped make Americans of so many generations of immigrants in the past.

It was an effective argument, delivered by an effective spokesperson. Chávez boosted the credibility of U.S. English, especially on Capitol Hill. Representative Don Edwards, a liberal Democrat from California, convened the first House sub-committee hearings on the English Language Amendment. Leaders of language-minority communities continued to attack U.S. English as xenophobic. But such claims had limited force when a prominent Latina was leading the Official English campaign and portraying it as a civil-rights measure.

Tanton Memo Scandal

For Linda Chávez and U.S. English, the honeymoon ended abruptly in the fall of 1988. First came the publication of a confidential memorandum by John Tanton, chairman of the board of U.S. English, who predicted a Hispanic political takeover in the United States unless something was done about Hispanic immigration and high birthrates:

> *Gobernar es poblar* translates "to govern is to populate." In this society, where the majority rules, does this hold? Will the present majority peaceably hand over its political power to a group that is simply more fertile? ... Can *homo contraceptivus* compete with *homo progenitiva* if borders aren't controlled? ... Perhaps this is the first instance in which those with their pants up are going to get caught by those with their pants down. ... As Whites see their power and control over their lives declining, will they simply go quietly into the night? Or will there be an explosion? ... We are building in a deadly disunity. All great empires disintegrate; we want stability.

Tanton's memo, written for a private discussion group, also enumerated a range of cultural threats posed by Spanish-speaking immigrants: "the tradition of the *mordida* (bribe), the lack of involvement in public affairs"; Roman Catholicism, with its potential to "pitch out the separation of church and state"; low "educability" among children and high school-dropout rates; failure to use birth control; limited concern for the environment; and, of course, language divisions.

A second damaging disclosure involved two large contributors to U.S. English and the Federation for American Immigration Reform (FAIR) – an allied group also headed by John Tanton – which had financed racist propaganda about immigrants and advocated policies of eugenic sterilization.[7] Chávez expressed dismay to learn of these connections, as well as what she termed the "anti-Hispanic and anti-Catholic" views of Dr. Tanton, and she quit her job in protest. Meanwhile Walter Cronkite announced his resignation from the U.S. English advisory board and told the group to stop using his name in its fundraising. Tanton also stepped down, issuing a bitter statement in which he denied any racist intent and denounced the opponents of Official English for their "McCarthyite tactics of guilt by association." He was later replaced by Mauro Mujica, a Chilean immigrant, whose Hispanic origin was featured in an advertising campaign to rehabilitate the image of U.S. English.[8]

Inclusion or Exclusion?

Disclosure of Tanton's memo made many federal officials nervous about endorsing the English-only agenda, which now seemed a lot less benign than before. Yet it did little to slow the campaign's momentum at the state level. Two weeks after the scandal broke, voters approved Official English laws by overwhelming margins in Colorado and Florida. By an extremely close vote, Arizonans adopted an initiative mandating that "this state and all political subdivisions of this state shall act in English and no other language." But the highly restrictive measure never took effect because it was blocked by federal and state courts on constitutional grounds. Among other things, it would have forbidden Arizona's teachers and school administrators from communicating with parents in languages other than English – a clear violation of the First Amendment right to freedom of speech. An English-only law in Alaska was later struck down for similar reasons.

Ironically, by outlawing bilingual services, such legislation probably makes it "harder for immigrants who have not yet mastered English to enter the social and economic mainstream," argues Geoffrey Nunberg, a linguist at Stanford University. Meanwhile none of the Official English laws thus far have offered non-English speakers any practical help in learning the language. "The fact is that immigrants are desperate to learn English," Nunberg says, noting that when Proposition 63 passed in California, there were 40,000 adults on waiting lists for ESL instruction in Los Angeles alone.

To remedy the acute shortage of such classes nationwide, in 1988 the Congressional Hispanic Caucus sponsored the English Proficiency Act, which authorized up to $25 million a year for adult ESL (although Congress "zero-funded" the program for most of its existence; it expired in 1994). Remarkably, U.S. English declined to support this legislation. Instead, it called for the private sector – Spanish-language media in particular, which it blamed for fostering "language ghettos" – to subsidize ESL classes. Later the organization launched its own charitable effort, Project Golden Door, to support such instruction, devoting about one percent of its budget to this purpose. The lion's share of its spending continued to sponsor efforts to restrict bilingualism, leading critics to charge that the real objective of English-only advocates is the exclusion, not the integration, of immigrants.

Why the sudden concern for the "functional protection of English"? asks sociolinguist Joshua Fishman. How is English endangered in a country where it is spoken by more than nine out of ten residents; where "linguistic minorities overwhelmingly lose their mother tongues by the second or at most the third generation"; and where "no ethnic political parties or separatist movements exist"? Fishman maintains that U.S. English and allied groups are promoting "a hidden agenda," seeking scapegoats for social ills that have little or nothing to do with language. He characterizes "the English-only movement [as] a displacement of middle-class fears and anxieties from difficult, perhaps even intractable, real problems in American society, to mythical, simplistic, and stereotypic problems. ... [It is] another 'liberation of Grenada' relative to the real causes of unrest in the world."

Concerned by the growing influence of this movement, in 1985 the League of United Latin American Citizens and the Spanish American League Against Discrimination (SALAD) launched a campaign known as **English Plus**. There should be no dispute over the importance of English proficiency in America, stressed Osvaldo Soto, a leader in this effort. "But English is not enough. We don't want a monolingual society. This country was founded on a diversity of language and culture, and we want to preserve that diversity." Offering a positive alternative to language restrictionism, these advocates argued that the national interest would be better served by encouraging mastery of English Plus other tongues.

The idea soon caught on among broader ranks of education, civil-rights, and ethnic advocacy groups – many shocked into action by the passage of Proposition 63 in California – who came together to create the English Plus Information Clearinghouse (EPIC), a national effort to oppose the English-only movement. EPIC called for a reaffirmation of "cultural and democratic pluralism" and the "need to foster multiple language skills." A policy of English Plus, it argued, would promote equal opportunities, increase cross-cultural understanding, safeguard minority language rights, and enhance the nation's position in world trade and diplomacy. Effective means to achieving those goals were already available: developmental and two-way bilingual education. It would be several years, however, until policymakers took notice.

English Only vs. Bilingual Education

Although the Reagan administration took no formal position on the English Language Amendment, nothing prevented its officials from working closely with English-only proponents. Carol Pendás Whitten, the federal director of bilingual education from 1985 to 1987, met frequently with leaders of U.S. English to discuss their views on the education of LEP children. She even commissioned one of the group's consultants, Gary Imhoff, to review the "objectivity and accuracy" of materials used in bilingual teacher-training programs. A prolific writer on behalf of U.S. English and FAIR, Imhoff had warned that native-language instruction may serve as a "crutch," making students "excruciatingly slow" to learn English.[9] After Imhoff's hiring drew protests, Whitten was forced to cancel his contract, but her ties with English-only activists continued.

U.S. English also focused its efforts at the state level. In California it lobbied for reduced state subsidies to programs serving English learners and, following the court decision in *Teresa P. v. Berkeley (see Chapter 5)*, it pressured school districts to adopt all-English approaches. In New York the organization rallied public opposition to a plan to use more stringent criteria for mainstreaming English learners to regular classrooms. It took out full-page newspaper advertisements and flew in "expert" witnesses, but ultimately failed to influence the State Board of Regents. By the late 1980s U.S. English was spending hundreds of thousands annually on such efforts and on those of independent groups. The latter included Learning English Advocates Drive (LEAD), a group of teachers opposed to bilingual education in California and New York, and the Institute for Research in English Acquisition and Development (READ), which supported studies by academic enthusiasts of structured immersion. READ's first director was Keith Baker, of **Baker–de Kanter report** fame *(see Chapters 5 and 7)*. His successor was Rosalie Porter, a former ESL director and author of *Forked Tongue: The Politics of Bilingual Education*.

In her book Porter criticized the English Language Amendment as divisive, portraying herself as a moderate who belonged to neither of "the extremist camps – the doctrinaire official-English supporters [or] the strident proponents of full bilingualism." When confronted with READ's financial dependence on the English-only movement, she insisted that "these grants are without strings."[10] In fact, Porter's views on bilingual education were indistinguishable from those of U.S. English, which purchased 300 copies of *Forked Tongue* and mailed them to policymakers.

The book was accessible and well received by editorial writers – and not just conservatives. But it had no credibility with researchers, even the tiny handful that agreed with her conclusions. Keith Baker, for example, called *Forked Tongue* "heavily biased" against bilingual education. In particular, he faulted Porter for claiming the "superiority" of an ESL-only program she had administered in Newton, Massachusetts, while citing "not a shred of evidence." Baker noted that the book provides "no test scores, data on dropout rates, or other empirical indicators. Instead, all that is offered is the author's personal opinion that she is right and everybody else is wrong."

Porter represented an academic viewpoint that flowered in the 1980s: scorn for bilingual education as a creature of ethnic politics, a program that was ideologically motivated and thus pedagogically suspect. One need not favor English-only legislation to take this position; those who articulate it best generally do not. Their ranks include both neoconservatives like E. D. Hirsch[11] and traditional liberals such as Arthur Schlesinger, Jr.

This critique was powerful, first, because of the widespread ignorance about bilingual pedagogies (which extended to many of the critics), and second, because it formed part of a broader complaint about demographic diversity and social fragmentation. Hirsch's best-selling book, *Cultural Literacy*, faulted public schools for emphasizing skills over content, thereby failing to transmit the factual elements of a unitary, Anglo-American national culture – things that all students "need to know." Bilingual education was not only a distraction from this central task but a concession to a dangerous form of diversity, Hirsh argued: "Linguistic pluralism ... is much different from Jeffersonian pluralism, which has encouraged a diversity of traditions, values, and opinions." To encourage the former "increases cultural fragmentation, civil antagonism, illiteracy, and economic-technological ineffectualness" – in other words, social breakdown. Schlesinger issued a similar jeremiad in *The Disuniting of America*, another bestseller of that period:

> Bilingualism shuts doors. It nourishes self-ghettoization, and ghettoization nourishes racial antagonism. ... The bilingual campaign has created both an educational establishment with a vested interest in extending the bilingual empire and a political lobby with a vested interest in retaining a Hispanic constituency. ... Most ominous about the separatist impulses is the meanness generated when one group is set against another.

As bilingual education was subsumed into the debate over multiculturalism, the issue was framed increasingly as a matter of politics and ideology: ethnic pride to the point of separatism, vested interests in protecting Hispanic jobs, political bosses with hidden agendas, perhaps even threats to civil order – who knew where "bilingualism" might lead?[12] The pedagogical specifics, when mentioned at all, were reduced to insignificance. Evidence about what worked in the classroom for English learners played little or no role in a discussion dominated by political charges and countercharges. Bilingual education thus became ensnared in the same net with Afro-centrism, cultural relativism, "political correctness," and other demons (real or imagined) that troubled many Anglo-Americans during the 1980s. In this climate advocates of all-English instruction saw their opportunity.

Bennett's Broadside

William J. Bennett had never set foot in a bilingual classroom on September 26, 1985, the day he launched a broadside against two decades of federal policy on the schooling of language-minority children. Like most Americans, the new U.S. secretary of education had only a vague notion of what bilingual education meant in practice. Speaking in New York City, he asserted that the program "had lost sight of the goal of [teaching] English," and instead had become "a way of enhancing students' knowledge of their native language and culture."

These were not the criteria that Bennett's department used in awarding grants under **Title VII of the Elementary and Secondary Education Act**. Nor did they reflect the *transitional* character of the vast majority of bilingual programs in the United States, most of which featured English as the predominant language of instruction. A California survey had recently found that the native language was used, on average, only 8 percent of the time – and sometimes it was never used – in so-called "bilingual" classrooms. Nevertheless, Bennett's characterization echoed public misconceptions about bilingual education, as fostered by critics such as U.S. English and increasingly by news media.

Calling the Bilingual Education Act "a failed path ... a bankrupt course," he said that "too many children have failed to become fluent in English," while the Hispanic school dropout rate remained "tragically as high now as it was twenty years ago. ... After seventeen years of federal involvement, and after $1.7 billion of federal funding, we have no evidence that the children whom we sought to help – that the children who deserve our help – have benefited." The secretary was especially critical of Title VII's requirement that programs make some use of students' native language and culture, arguing that "a sense of cultural pride cannot come at the price of proficiency in English, our common language." While bilingual education could be beneficial "in some circumstances," he conceded, research indicated that it

> was no more effective than alternative methods of special instruction using English, and in some cases … was demonstrably less so. Indeed, the English language skills of students in bilingual education programs seemed to be no better than the skills of those who simply remained in regular classrooms where English was spoken, without *any* special help. … We believe that local flexibility will serve the needs of these students far more effectively than intrusive federal regulation.

The widely reported speech reopened a national debate over bilingual education, shattering the compromise achieved just a year earlier on Capitol Hill *(see Chapter 5)*. Title VII's 4 to 10 percent share for alternative programs, created by the 1984 amendments, had represented a concession on the part of bilingual education advocates, but to many critics it now seemed parsimonious. News accounts styled Secretary Bennett as a champion of innovative approaches who dared to challenge "the powerful bilingual education lobby." Journalists reported the controversy largely as he portrayed it – between defenders of English instruction and proponents of cultural maintenance, between local option and federal control. "Secretary Bennett makes sense," the *Washington Post* editorialized. "The rigidity of federal policy is hampering this program." The *New York Times* agreed, adding that "often instruction in the foreign language goes on too long, impeding the student's mastery of English."

Bennett's tactics were a model of purposeful ambiguity. He decried the "failure" of bilingual education *policy*, not of bilingual education itself – a claim for which he had no evidence. At the same time, the secretary surely knew that the distinction would be lost on much of his audience, including headline writers throughout the country. The speech thus conveyed two messages: an insistence that native-language instruction be used for transitional purposes only, appeasing the program's harshest critics, and a call for responsible experimentation with various methodologies, appealing to Americans with open minds but without much information, for example, about what local flexibility had meant before *Lau v. Nichols*.

Although Bennett gave no credit where it was due, these had been Senator Hayakawa's primary themes on bilingual education since the late 1970s and they were now prominent in the platform of U.S. English. Elaborating on the connections between language and citizenship, the secretary declared that Americans "should be conversant" with the Constitution and the Declaration of Independence *in English.* "They should be able to read them and understand what those words mean as they were written." Though he stopped short making the link explicit – *speak good English to be a good American* – to many Latino and Asian American leaders the implication was troubling. At a time of rising ethnic tensions, thanks in no small measure to English-only activism, the nation's top education official appeared to be siding with those who questioned the loyalty and patriotism of minority language speakers. English Plus advocates were incensed. "To say that we make our country stronger because we make it 'U.S. English,'" charged SALAD, "is like saying that we make it stronger by making it 'U.S. White.' It is as insidious to base the strength or unity of the United States in one language as it is to base that strength or unity in one race."

Research Debate

Bilingual educators now found themselves defending their program on several flanks: clarifying its goals, including but not limited to English proficiency; communicating the complexities of research on second-language acquisition; refuting charges about linguistic "divisiveness"; and countering attacks on their own motives. These were formidable tasks, considering the level of public confusion about Title VII and about the pedagogical philosophy it embodied.

Researchers and practitioners criticized Bennett's insinuation that bilingual education barred the way to English. "The time spent teaching children in their native language is not merely a contribution to their ethnic pride, but also an investment in their eventual success as school learners and as speakers of English in addition to the native language," wrote Catherine Snow, an educational psychologist at Harvard. While true flexibility could prove beneficial, she said, if Bennett's policy "simply means that many non-English-speaking children receive no native-language instruction, the likely result is that such children may learn English a little faster, but not so well, and that they will be more likely to fail in school as a result." José Cárdenas, director of the Intercultural Development Research Association, took issue with Bennett's assertion that all-English alternatives to bilingual instruction looked promising. To the contrary, Cárdenas maintained, there were

> no data to suggest the success of the structured immersion approach. Though the replacement of bilingual programs by immersion programs has long been an [aim] of the Reagan administration, scholars have never taken this recommendation seriously due to the absence of a single study showing this method as a feasible approach to the education of limited-English-proficient students in the United States.

Criticism of Bennett's position intensified in the spring of 1986, when interim results leaked out from a major longitudinal study comparing structured immersion with various forms of bilingual education. For enthusiasts of English-only approaches, the news could not have been worse. Children in both early-exit and late-exit bilingual programs were significantly outperforming the immersion students in all subjects, including English reading. Generally speaking, the more exposure children had to their native language, the better they were doing. Spokespersons for the Department of Education insisted that no conclusions about immersion should be drawn from these preliminary data *(see Chapter 9)*.

Officials pointed instead to the 1981 Baker de–Kanter study, which had reviewed the research literature and concluded that the case for bilingual instruction was inconclusive. Because there was no demonstrably superior "method" for teaching English learners, the study concluded, there should be no limitations on federal funding for English-only instruction. Accordingly, the Reagan administration now proposed to undo the 1984 compromise on Title VII, striking the complex formula for allocating appropriations among bilingual and alternative programs. It would then be free to support, in Secretary Bennett's words, "any type of instructional approach which a local educational agency considers appropriate for educating its limited-English-proficient children." Flexibility indeed.

Congress, however, would need to approve any such deal, and it was far from ready to do so. Augustus Hawkins, the California Democrat who chaired the House Education and Labor Committee, was especially skeptical. To shed some light on the research debate, he asked the General Accounting Office (GAO), the investigative arm of Congress, to try to gauge the consensus, if any, among experts in the field. Was there any scientific basis to continue favoring bilingual education in federal funding allocations? Or did the evidence support Bennett's claims about the inconclusiveness of research on English learner programs?

What the GAO produced was one of the strongest endorsements of bilingual instruction yet to emerge from the federal government. Its independent panel of experts, a majority of whom had been recommended or cited as authorities by the Department of Education, were asked to review relevant studies and try to bring some clarity to the policy process. The panel was unambiguous in its rejection of Bennett's arguments:

- "The research showed positive effects for transitional bilingual education on students' achievement of English-language competence."
- "Evidence about students' learning in subjects other than English," although

less abundant than data on second-language acquisition, also "supported the requirement for using native languages."

- Research provided no reason to believe that all-English methodologies like structured immersion or stand-alone ESL offered promise for language-minority children in the United States.
- There was no scientific basis for claiming that high Hispanic dropout rates reflected the failure of bilingual education, because of limited data on this issue.
- Overall, the research was hardly inconclusive; there was enough evidence to indicate both the validity of native-language instruction and the groups of children most likely to benefit from it.

Armed with the GAO's conclusions, in early 1987 advocates for bilingual education believed they were in a strong position to keep Title VII intact, perhaps even to achieve some modest gains. Democrats had recently recaptured the Senate, restoring Senator Edward Kennedy, a longtime ally of the program, as chairman of the Labor and Human Resources Committee. On the House side of the Capitol, Chairman Hawkins lent his considerable clout to the cause by sponsoring legislation to extend the Bilingual Education Act, with only minor changes, until 1993. To the National Association for Bilingual Education (NABE) and its allies, the GAO report seemed to come at the perfect time, providing a scientific vindication of

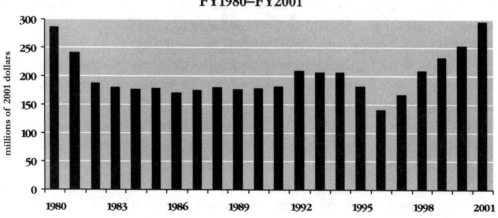

FIGURE 6–1
Title VII Appropriations, Adjusted for Inflation
FY1980–FY2001

Source: U.S. Department of Education.

native-language instruction. At last, here was a chance for research to shape policy, for scientific consensus to triumph over political expediency. But the vagaries of the legislative process dictated otherwise. In the final outcome, the researchers' views would play no discernible role at all.

Wavering Allies

The first hint of trouble came in the Senate. Without holding hearings to consider expert views on bilingual education, Kennedy and Senator Claiborne Pell of Rhode Island began to look for common ground with Republicans. They entered into negotiations with Senator Dan Quayle, sponsor of the administration's bill seeking to eliminate the "4 percent cap" on funding for all-English programs. A bipartisan compromise was soon achieved. It proposed to divert 25 percent of the Title VII budget to support **special alternative instructional programs** (SAIPs) that made no use of students' native language. In addition, at the suggestion of Senator Pell, a child's enrollment in a Title VII classroom would be limited to three years.

Before the Senate committee voted on the bill, the General Accounting Office was called upon once more for advice. Was there a factual basis to Senator Quayle's argument that bilingual education was infeasible where LEP children were geographically dispersed or divided into several language groups? After a quick survey of nine state education departments that collected data at the school level, the GAO issued its tentative finding: 22 percent of LEP children "were in low concentration areas" – that is, in schools where classrooms had fewer than 10 to 20 speakers of the same minority language. The study made no determination of whether bilingual education was feasible in various settings. For Senator Kennedy and members of his committee, however, the GAO's conclusion seemed tailor-made to justify the new funding formula, and they adopted the compromise bill on a 15-1 vote, avoiding a protracted debate over bilingual education.[13]

Emboldened by the Democrats' retreat in the Senate, Republicans dug in their heels to resist the Hawkins bill in the House, now part of a larger measure to reauthorize 18 federal programs aiding elementary and secondary education. With Title VII the last thorny matter to resolve and English-only sentiment rising in opinion polls, most House Democrats were as eager to compromise as their Senate counterparts. Despite some resistance from members of the Congressional Hispanic Caucus, a similar deal was reached, providing a larger slice of federal funding for nonbilingual programs. As Representative Dale Kildee, one of the Democratic negotiators, explained afterward, the decision was based on political

Timeline: Language Policy Developments, Part II

1981	English Language Amendment is introduced in Congress for first time
1983	U.S. English is founded to lobby for Official English
1985	Secretary of Education William J. Bennett launches broadside attack on bilingual education
1986	Voters approve Proposition 63 in California, the eighth state to declare English its official language
1987	California Governor George Deukmejian vetoes an extension of state's bilingual education law
1987	Official English measures are considered by legislatures in 37 additional states, passing in five
1987	English Plus Information Clearinghouse (EPIC) is founded
1987–88	Congress reauthorizes Title VII, diverting up to 25 percent of funding for all-English programs
1988	Scandal over Tanton memo brings resignations at U.S. English; voters pass English-only measures in Arizona, Colorado, and Florida
1991	Education Department releases Ramírez study documenting superior academic outcomes in developmental bilingual education
1993	Stanford Working Group recommends policy of promoting bilingualism for all American students
1994	Congress reauthorizes Title VII for last time, gives funding priority to programs that cultivate English learners' native languages
1996	House of Representatives passes "English Language Empowerment Act" to restrict federal government's use of other languages; bill dies in Senate
1998	California voters adopt Proposition 227, replacing most bilingual programs with all-English immersion for LEP students
2000	Arizona voters pass Proposition 203, a stricter English-only mandate for public schools
2002	Massachusetts voters pass Question 2 and Colorado voters reject Amendment 31 – similar anti-bilingual legislation
2002	Iowa declares English its official language, bringing the number of states with active Official English laws to 23
2002	Bilingual Education Act is repealed and replaced by No Child Left Behind Act

rather than pedagogical realities: "In substance, I certainly believe that transitional bilingual education is a very effective method," he said defensively. "But it's not understood [by most members of Congress]. The anti-bilingual smear job is growing. The attacks are real in both [party] caucuses. It's not a Democrat-Republican issue. ... I can count votes."

Title VII represented less than 2 percent of the total funding authorized in the omnibus education measure, and the amounts in dispute were relatively small. Yet deliberations on the bill, especially in the House, were dominated by debates over how to divide these sums between native-language and all-English instruction. Funding to support school programs was an important issue, following several years of deep cuts in Title VII spending *(see Figure 6–1)*. Yet more than money was at stake. As New York State Commissioner of Education Gordon Ambach noted during hearings on the bill, there was also the "message the federal government is sending" about bilingual education, which had a considerable impact on state and local policies.

By the spring of 1988, when the final shape of the legislation was hammered out, it was the Senate formula that largely prevailed. NABE won a few concessions on secondary issues, but failed to budge lawmakers on Senator Pell's three-year rule. To educators the idea of limiting services to English learners on this arbitrary basis was disturbing. While allowing exceptions based on individual student evaluations, the new requirement implied that three years of bilingual (or all-English) instruction was enough; that additional language support might prove harmful to the child; and that programs featuring a longer transition to English were inferior or misguided. No research had been cited to justify the change, no determination that the "average" English learner could become fully proficient in English within three years – only a public mood of impatience with the perceived duration of bilingual programs. The question of arbitrary time limits would become increasingly significant, both as a research issue and as a political issue, over the coming decade *(see Chapters 9 and 13)*.

Defusing the Controversy

Advocates for bilingual education learned some painful lessons from the 1987–88 reauthorization battle. Regardless of what research showed or what experts said about the benefits of native-language programs, defending their preferential treatment under Title VII made the law increasingly vulnerable to political attacks. Continuing to debate funding formulas linked to **language of instruction** would also tend to "overshadow ... virtually all other issues associated with the education of limited-English-proficient Americans," wrote James J. Lyons of NABE. The organization hoped "to resolve this distracting controversy so that the nation might focus on the critical problems confronting language-minority students and the schools they attend." Teacher recruitment and certification, academic standards, appropriate assessment, and numerous other concerns would continue to get short shrift unless the policy discussion could be broadened.

Fortuitously, or so it seemed, a broader movement for **school reform** was now gathering steam, as governors in several states strived to overcome years of neglect, underfunding, and low standards in the public schools. A 1989 "summit meeting," convened by the National Governors Association and the first Bush administration, adopted an ambitious set of education goals *(see Chapter 14)*. In these developments advocates for English learners saw exciting opportunities, but also some dangers – in particular, the danger of being left out. While scores of Washington-based interest groups, representing virtually every aspect of education, were poised to take advantage of the favorable climate for change, few of them had much acquaintance with the needs of language-minority students, thus far a low priority for **standards and goals** enthusiasts.

'Reinventing' LEP Programs

Hoping to remedy this situation, an ad hoc collection of bilingual educators, researchers, and activists came together under the leadership of Kenji Hakuta of Stanford University. The school reform train was coming down the track, as Hakuta put it, and there were only two choices: either get on board and work hard to represent the interests of English learners, or get run over. With support from the Carnegie Corporation of New York, the group's first step was to sponsor a series of meetings to evaluate federal policy for LEP students and to consider the potential rewards and risks of comprehensive reform. While diverse views were represented, a consensus gradually emerged from the panel, which became known as the Stanford Working Group. Its report, entitled *A Blueprint for the Second Generation*, was released in June 1993 as the Clinton administration began to develop its legislative agenda for education.

The Working Group broke with the past in two significant ways. First, it actively sought to overcome the isolation of bilingual and ESL educators from the school reform movement. Having grown under the aegis of **categorical funding** and civil-rights enforcement to serve a "special" group of students, these fields were often ignored or viewed with skepticism by other sectors of the education community. Insularity had served a purpose when new pedagogies were being developed to remedy the failures of mainstream schooling. But it also limited the ability of language educators to influence broad changes of the kind that now seemed inevitable. Like it or not, the new standards and goals would directly affect the teaching of English learners. So, rather than defending the status quo, the Working Group adopted a pragmatic strategy of working within the framework of the reform movement to get the best possible deal for LEP students under less-than-ideal circumstances.

Second, the Working Group widened the policy focus to include programs other than Title VII. **Chapter 1**, for example, enjoyed stronger Congressional support and promised more generous funding,[14] despite its compensatory approach and poor record in addressing language barriers. In several states limited English proficiency had been considered a legal impediment to participation in Chapter 1 programs, even though LEP children were three times more likely to attend high-poverty schools than their English-speaking peers. So the Working Group saw it as essential to make Chapter 1 more responsive to the needs of English learners.

The *Blueprint* detailed its recommendations in the context of "two overarching principles":

1. Language-minority students must be provided with an equal opportunity to learn the same challenging content and high-level skills that school reform movements advocate for all students.
2. Proficiency in two or more languages should be promoted for all American students. Bilingualism enhances cognitive and social growth, competitiveness in a global marketplace, national security, and understanding of diverse peoples and cultures.

The second recommendation was especially timely in light of the **Ramírez study**, released in 1991, which reported significant academic advantages for students in developmental bilingual education *(see Chapter 9)*.

The Clinton administration readily endorsed these ideas. It also appointed Eugene García, a respected researcher and member of the Working Group, to direct the federal Office of Bilingual Education and Minority Languages Affairs (OBEMLA). The administration's legislative proposals on Title VII and, to a lesser extent, on Chapter 1 were closely modeled on the Stanford recommendations. Highlights that became law include:

- *Restructuring Title VII grants.* Rather than continue to categorize school programs by the amount of native language used (transitional, developmental, or special alternative), grants were redefined by functional category (program development and implementation, program enhancement, comprehensive school program, or systemwide improvement). The intent was both to depoliticize the appropriations process and to encourage holistic approaches. While the 25 percent allowance for all-English programs was retained, like a vestigial organ it served little if any function.

- *Encouraging bilingual skills.* Developmental bilingual programs received preference in federal funding for the first time. In awarding grants OBEMLA was instructed to give priority to applicants seeking to develop "bilingual proficiency both in English and another language for all participating students." It was also authorized to fund programs designed to conserve endangered Native American languages *(see Chapter 11).*
- *Enhancing the state role.* To strengthen "systemic" planning on how to serve English learners, state education agencies were given the responsibility to review Title VII proposals before they were submitted to OBEMLA (except for Native American projects, which were exempted from this process).
- *Opening up Chapter 1.* A legal provision that had previously excluded LEP children was dropped from the program, which was renamed **Title I**. School districts were also required to take various steps to identify these students, address their language needs, assess them equitably, and involve their parents in decision-making.

Extension of the Elementary and Secondary Education Act, now known as the **Improving America's Schools Act of 1994**, proved far less contentious than it had six years earlier. While skirmishes broke out over a few social issues, most of these had nothing to do with bilingual education. Republicans put up some resistance when the bill reached the House floor, as Representative Toby Roth of Wisconsin, leader of the most extreme English-only faction, proposed to repeal Title VII. ("I want all Americans to be the same," Roth explained. "That is my mission.") The amendment attracted just 58 votes, although some of these came from Republican leaders who would come to power a few months later.[15]

Opponents did exact a potentially important concession. The 25 percent funding limit for SAIPs could be waived under certain conditions, namely, when school districts could show that bilingual instruction was impractical because of a shortage of qualified teachers or a diverse student population. But the Clinton administration, which generally favored a **language-as-resource** approach, never exploited this loophole. It has since become moot because this reauthorization of the Bilingual Education Act proved to be the last *(see Chapter 14).*

On balance, the 1994 legislation was greeted as a major victory by advocates for English Plus. With the fever of English-only activism apparently in remission, the future of bilingual education seemed secure. The euphoria proved to be short-lived, as nativist sentiment began to spread again in the mid-1990s. Nevertheless, the new law opened many possibilities at the classroom level. While the "Republican Revolution" on Capitol Hill would soon bring cuts in funding for Title VII overall, federal spending increased for developmental and two-way bilingual education. The more these programs succeeded, the more popular they became with states and localities, which in turn took more initiative in developing their own policies for English learners. Ironically, among the far-reaching innovations of the 1994 law was a lessening of federal influence.

Suggested Reading

Adams, Karen L., and Brink, Daniel T., eds., *Perspectives on Official English: The Campaign for English as the Official Language of the U.S.A.* Berlin: Mouton de Gruyter, 1990.

Crawford, James, ed. *Language Loyalties: A Source Book on the Official English Controversy.* Chicago: University of Chicago Press, 1992.

Padilla, Amado M. et al. "The English Only Movement: Myths, Reality, and Implications for Psychology." *Journal of the American Psychological Association* 46, no. 2 (Feb. 1991): 20–30.

Schmid, Carol L. *The Politics of Language: Conflict, Identity, and Cultural Pluralism in Comparative Perspective.* New York: Oxford University Press, 2001.

See also pp. 394–96.

Online Resource Guide

General Accounting Office, U.S. *Bilingual Education: A New Look at the Research Evidence* (1987).

House Education and Labor Committee, U.S. *Compendium of Papers on the Topic of Bilingual Education* (1986).

House Judiciary Subcommittee on Civil and Constitutional Rights, U.S. *English Language Constitutional Amendments* (1988).

Senate, U.S. S. J. Res. 72. *Proposing an Amendment to the Constitution Establishing English as the Official Language of the United States* (1981).

See also companion CD-ROM.

Crawford, James. "Hispanophobia." In *Hold Your Tongue: Bilingualism and the Politics of "English Only."* Reading, Mass.: Addison-Wesley, 1992.
http://ourworld.compuserve.com/homepages/jwcrawford/hytch6.htm

"Language Legislation in the U.S.A."
http://ourworld.compuserve.com/homepages/jwcrawford/langleg.htm

Teachers of English to Speakers of Other Languages (TESOL) Sociopolitical Concerns Committee. *Official English? No!* (1996).
http://www.ncela.gwu.edu/miscpubs/tesol/official/

Internet Links

Notes

1. The only previous official-language bill – a 1923 attempt to recognize the "American language" – was hardly a serious proposal. Its sponsor, Representative Washington J. McCormick of Montana, wanted to strike a blow against literary Anglophiles, not against bilingualism. He argued that making American the official language "would supplement the political emancipation of '76 by the mental emancipation of '23. America has lost much in literature by not thinking its own thoughts and speaking them boldly in a language unadorned with gold braid. ... Let our writers drop their top-coats, spats, and swagger-sticks, and assume occasionally their buckskin, moccasins, and tomahawks." The proposal died in committee but was adopted that same year by the state of Illinois, where Irish American legislators saw an opportunity to disrespect the British Empire.
2. A statutory version applying to the federal government alone passed the House of Representatives in 1996 *(see Chapter 13)*.
3. In chronological order they are: Nebraska (constitutional amendment, 1920); Illinois (statute replacing "American" with English, 1969); Virginia (statutes, 1981 and 1996); Indiana, Kentucky, and Tennessee (statutes, 1984); California (constitutional amendment, 1986); Arkansas, Mississippi, North Carolina, North Dakota, and South Carolina (statutes, 1987); Arizona, Colorado, and Florida (constitutional amendments, 1988); Alabama (constitutional amendment, 1990); Montana, New Hampshire, and South Dakota (statutes, 1995); Georgia and Wyoming (statutes, 1996); Alaska and Missouri (statutes, 1998); Utah (statute, 2000); and Iowa (statute, 2002). Hawaii is officially bilingual, recognizing both English and Native Hawaiian (constitutional amendment, 1978). Arizona's Official English measure, Proposition 106, was struck down in 1998 as a violation of the U.S. constitution. In 2002, Alaska's statute was overruled for violating that state's constitution (although the decision is on appeal), leaving a net total of 23 Official English measures in effect at the state level.
4. In 2003, the organization claimed to have 1.7 million members, while estimating its annual budget at $4 million – about half the level of the early 1990s; *Hispanic Link Weekly Report*, Nov. 10, 2003.

5. In fact, U.S. English originated the term in 1984 when it sponsored a California ballot initiative entitled "Voting Materials in English Only." The label was then popularized by journalists who believed that it accurately summarized the group's agenda.

6. For 25 percent this was a "major reason," for 17 percent a "minor reason," for 53 percent "not a reason," and 5 percent had no opinion. No inquiry was made about attitudes toward Asians or other linguistic minorities. The survey also reported a "membership profile" of U.S. English that was disproportionately male (67 percent), elderly (75 percent were at least 60 years of age), affluent (33 percent had incomes above $50,000), college educated (60 percent), conservative (67 percent), Republican (71 percent), and northern European in origin (68 percent). Among the 385 respondents who identified their ethnic heritage, there were no Mexican Americans, no Cubans, two "other Hispanics," two Asians, and three blacks. The telephone survey, conducted by the Gary C. Lawrence Co. of Santa Ana, California, was based on a random sample of 400 U.S. English members, with a margin of error of plus or minus 5 percent.

7. The funding sources were Cordelia Scaife May, an heiress to the Mellon fortune, and the Pioneer Fund, a little-known foundation dedicated to "racial betterment" through eugenics. During the 1980s May contributed at least $5.8 million to U.S. English, FAIR, and several affiliated organizations through the Laurel Foundation and family trust funds. In 1983, Laurel financed distribution of *The Camp of the Saints*, a futuristic novel by the French writer Jean Raspail, in which Third World immigrants destroy European civilization. Linda Chávez said she had once reviewed this "sickening book," describing it as "racist, xenophobic, and paranoid," and had been disturbed to see a U.S. English staff member reading it.

    The Pioneer Fund was created in 1937 by Harry Laughlin, former director of the Eugenics Record Office at Cold Spring Harbor, New York. Laughlin described the foundation's objectives as "practical population control ... by influencing those forces which govern immigration, the sterilization of degenerates, and mate selection in favor of American racial strains and sound family stocks." The Pioneer Fund's first project was to popularize "applied genetics in present-day Germany" – that is, Adolf Hitler's program of forced sterilization for persons judged to be genetically inferior. John B. Trevor, Jr., a current officer of the Pioneer Fund, testified against the 1965 immigration law, warning that repeal of the national-origins quota system would produce "a conglomeration of racial and ethnic elements" and lead to "a serious culture decline." In the 1970s the Pioneer Fund financed genetic research by William Shockley and Arthur Jensen purporting to prove that blacks have lower IQs than whites. In the 1980s it supported experiments to explore hereditary differences in learning between Chinese and American children. Tanton disclaimed any knowledge of these activities by the Pioneer Fund, although he had served as chairman of FAIR from 1982 to 1986, a period during which it received $370,000 from the eugenics foundation; by 1993, the total exceeded $1 million.

8. In a 1992 interview, however, when asked how he – as a Hispanic – felt about Tanton's memo, Mujica replied: "I don't consider myself a Hispanic. I'm a Basque."

9. In his contract with Whitten's office, Imhoff agreed to determine whether the texts "value ... the maintenance of non-English languages and the preservation of traditional cultures more highly than the attainment of English language proficiency and the ability to acculturate to this society." Although the consultant professed an open mind on this question, his writings suggest otherwise. "Bilingual programs have held sway for political, not educational, reasons," Imhoff alleges in *The Immigration Time Bomb*, which he coauthored with former governor Richard Lamm of Colorado. Hispanic leaders support bilingual education as a jobs program and as a way to maintain their ethnic "power base," the book continues. Assimilation must take precedence, even if that means lowered expectations for student achievement: "The measure of success cannot be that students enrolled in any special program for those with limited English-language ability have the same degree and amount of success as those with no language handicap. That is an unrealistic and unreachable goal. ... If we can't afford school dropouts, who are a natural by-product of displacement and cultural shock, then we can't afford immigration."

10. Founded in 1989 with a $62,500 grant from U.S. English, READ continued to enjoy its support through the early 1990s. Other grants have come from the Laurel Foundation, the major benefactor behind U.S. English and FAIR; English Language Advocates, a California group that campaigned for Proposition 63; the Smith Richardson Foundation, a funder of numerous New Right causes; and the Fordham Foundation, headed by Chester E. Finn, Jr., former assistant to Secretary of Education William J. Bennett. After running READ for several years out of her home in Amherst, Massachusetts, in 1998 Porter affiliated the "institute" with the Center for Equal Opportunity, a Washington, D.C.-based "think-tank" founded by Linda Chávez to oppose affirmative action and multiculturalism.

11. Hirsch, a professor of English at the University of Virginia, has never been directly linked to advocates of language and immigration restrictions. Yet his Cultural Literacy Foundation has received substantial support from Cordelia Scaife May *(see note 6 above)*, the largest funder of U.S. English and other projects linked to its founder, John Tanton, in the 1980s.

12. While Hirsch and Schlesinger only hinted at this last possibility, it was made explicit by R. E. "Rusty" Butler, an aide to Senator Steve Symms, an Idaho Republican who took over as lead sponsor of the English Language Amendment after Hayakawa retired. In a monograph entitled *On Creating a Hispanic America: A Nation Within a Nation?* Butler wrote:

> Bilingual education was to be a form of atonement for the nation's sins against Hispanics, and a means of easing America's 'guilt.' ... The ethnic politician has a high stake in bilingual education: By it, students are molded into an ethnically conscious constituency. Pride in their heritage and language, and an allegiance to their roots rather than their country, helps to diminish a sense of Americanism. ...
>
> A dependence on the home language and culture plays into the hands of unscrupulous politicians by isolating Hispanics. Assimilation into the main-

stream culture would make political control difficult, if not impossible [by Latino leaders]. ...

Many scholars argue that bilingual education breeds and fosters a separatist mentality which has both economic and political implications. ... Dutch criminal psychologist Dick Mulder has said that "there is a danger that the language situation could feed and guide terrorism in the U.S." Therefore, bilingual education and the ideal of Aztlán as a potential Hispanic homeland has [sic] national security implications.

13. Senator Kennedy had become solicitous toward Republicans on bilingual education when Senator Quayle threatened to derail the Star Schools program, a pet project of the Massachusetts Democrat. After Quayle withdrew his objections to the latter bill, a deal on Title VII was quickly hatched.

14. In 1993, the Chapter 1 budget of $6.8 billion was 35 times as large as the Title VII budget of $195 million.

15. Members of the House leadership in the 104th Congress who voted in 1994 to abolish Title VII included Majority Leader Richard Armey, Majority Whip Tom DeLay, Ways and Means Committee Chairman Bill Archer, and Rules Committee Chairman Gerald Solomon. House Speaker Newt Gingrich did not vote on the Roth amendment, but had previously cosponsored English-only legislation.

Theory

7 The Effectiveness Question

Does bilingual education really work? Politicians and pundits remain obsessed with this simplistic issue, a perennial focus of journalistic investigation and partisan debate. Never mind that most researchers and practitioners in language-minority education feel they answered the question long ago. Four decades of experience in the classroom, refinements in curriculum and methodology, and gains in student achievement have made believers out of countless

Narrow Focus on Language
Federal Research Agenda
Flawed Evaluation Studies
AIR Report
Methodology Matters
Role of Theory
Basic Research vs. Evaluation Research
Standards of Scientific 'Proof'
Baker–de Kanter Report
Willig's Meta-Analysis
Rossell and Baker vs. Greene

parents, teachers, administrators, and school board members. While generalizations are problematic – the label *bilingual education* describes a variety of pedagogies, some better designed and implemented than others – there is no question that bilingual approaches have helped to dismantle language barriers for millions of English learners since 1968. Data from numerous scientific studies support this conclusion, while data supporting the effectiveness of all-English approaches remain shaky at best.

Does this mean that using students' mother tongue in the classroom always "works," that it guarantees rapid progress in English and academic content areas? Of course not. **Language of instruction** is no more the sole determinant of success for Tagalog- , or Russian- , or Crow-speaking students than it is for English-speaking students. Often it plays a less significant role in achievement than factors such as program design and resources, teacher qualifications, administrative leadership, school culture, parental and community influences, and socioeconomic status, to name a few. Moreover, as a **program component**, language may be used in various ways, to foster various goals: additive, subtractive, assimilationist, pluralist *(see Chapter 2)*. Why, then, has so much heated discussion surrounded the question: *Which "method" is more effective – bilingual or English-only instruction?*

Politics is one obvious reason. As long as members of the public remain anxious about whether immigrants are assimilating and skeptical about the concept of learning in two languages, such concerns will be voiced by their elected representatives. It has become a familiar scenario over the past two decades. Debates over English learner policies flare up, highlighting stark, symbolic differences rather than gray areas of uncertainty or potential common ground. Stakeholders, whether practical or ideological, choose "sides" between pro- and anti-bilingual positions, largely ignoring other pedagogical variables. Hyperbolic news coverage serves to intensify the conflict and increase polarization. Expert opinion and research evidence are overshadowed by notions of **folk linguistics**: that young children "pick up" new languages quickly and effortlessly; that prolonged reliance on the native tongue reduces incentives to learn English; that bilingualism confuses the mind and retards school achievement. Until such fallacies are convincingly addressed, bilingual education is likely to remain a volatile issue, easy to exploit for political purposes.

Research Agenda

A second, less obvious reason for the preoccupation with language of instruction is the federal research agenda itself, which has been tailored to the needs of policymakers, not educators. Large-scale studies have been designed primarily to justify or repudiate existing policies on language-minority education. Thus they have tended to neglect **basic research** on second-language acquisition and its effects on academic achievement, and instead have focused primarily on **program**

evaluation. Was the government getting good value for its money? Were students learning English as rapidly as Congress intended? Did the outcomes of native-language programs warrant a continued funding preference under Title VII? Or was all-English instruction a more promising approach? Certainly these were significant issues. Yet the heavy stress on policy-related research came at the expense of more complex investigations into the learning of diverse student populations under diverse conditions. Generally speaking, pragmatism reigned while theory was slighted. Simplistic questions were asked and, as a result, the answers were often of limited pedagogical value.

In 1997, National Research Council issued a vigorous critique of this one-sided emphasis in federally sponsored research. While costly national evaluation studies over the past 25 years had produced some "general lessons," the NRC's expert panel found, overall these projects "yielded disappointing results" because of faulty and inappropriate research methods, poorly articulated goals, and lack of theoretical grounding. Most were dominated by a narrow fixation on "which type of program is best." Yet despite pressures to vindicate one political viewpoint or another, the panel said, these studies often produced murky answers to the effectiveness question.

For partisans, this conclusion may be the only common ground in the entire debate – a recognition that evaluation research, often poorly conceived and executed, has failed to make an ironclad case for the superiority of bilingual instruction. This is not to say, however, that evaluations have yielded nothing. Numerous local programs have been judged successful by various criteria: language-minority students stay in school, graduate, and go on to college at higher rates than before; parents are more approving of, and more involved in, their children's education; staff qualifications and morale are high, thanks to strong and creative leadership. To anyone connected with such schools, English learners are clearly progressing, whether or not that progress is fully reflected on standardized tests. As early as 1978, researcher Rudolph Troike summarized a dozen bilingual experiments whose results were encouraging with diverse groups of students, including Navajos in Arizona, Chinese in California, Latinos in New York, and Francophones in Maine. Yet relatively few such exemplary programs have ever been subjected to rigorous scientific evaluations, while many of those that have been studied turned out to be less than impressive.

In an influential 1986 article, Kenji Hakuta and Catherine Snow argued that "evaluation studies are doing a poor job of measuring" the benefits of bilingual education. Despite the release of more sophisticated studies since that time, notably the **Ramírez report** in 1991 and a Dade County, Florida, study published in 2002 *(see Chapter 9)*, evaluation research remains subject to varying interpretations and methodological criticisms. Disputes over its relevance often turn on arcane statistical points that are inaccessible to the public and uninteresting to the news media. Thus the language-of-instruction debate rages on.

More often than not, bilingual educators get the blame for the underdeveloped state of research in their field. Yet, as holder of the purse-strings, the federal government has always been the dominant influence – when and if funding has been forthcoming. In the first decade of Title VII, Congress appropriated about $500 million for bilingual programs, but only one-half of one percent went for research. The Bilingual Education Act was originally intended to finance demonstration projects from which others would learn. Since native-language approaches were largely untested in 1968, following a half-century hiatus in the United States, summarizing experience was seen as vital. So all Title VII grants for instructional programs had to include an evaluation component. Many of the required evaluations, however, were of such poor quality that in 1975 the U.S. Office of Education destroyed all those that had been submitted thus far. Although members of Congress lodged frequent complaints over the years, they never appropriated sufficient resources under Title VII to ensure high-quality reports from grantees. A 1993 study for the Department of Education found that the average allocation for this purpose – $3,000 to $4,000, which bought four to five days of an evaluator's time – tended to yield pro forma evaluations that focused mainly on achievement outcomes rather than on analyses aimed at improving instruction. Scientific studies featuring comparison groups or statistical controls were, of course, out of the question for that price.

Inadequate funding has hardly been the only problem. Since the mid-1970s the U.S. Department of Education has devoted substantial resources to a handful of major studies. Yet research designs were often unable to overcome the numerous difficulties that are inherent in assessing educational treatments for English learners. Such studies have tended to be crude in conception, failing to consider what was already known – or to extend theoretical understanding – about language and learning. These weaknesses are best illustrated by analyzing some of the studies that have had a significant impact on policymaking.

The AIR Study

The initial progress report on Title VII appeared in 1977–78, a national evaluation by the American Institutes for Research (AIR). The study encompassed Spanish-English bilingual programs in 38 school districts, involving 8,200 children in 10 states, at a cost of nearly $1 million. It remains the largest single evaluation of Title VII–supported programs ever conducted.[1] After nearly a decade of federal funding, AIR concluded, there had been "no consistent significant impact" on the education of LEP children. The study compared the progress of English learners in bilingual education with that of Spanish-background students enrolled in all-English mainstream classrooms. It concluded there was little difference in outcomes between the two models. This was the first of several evaluation studies (and studies summarizing other studies) that could find nothing conclusive to say about bilingual education. Press accounts of the AIR report stressed the absence of positive results – in English reading, children actually scored higher in sink-or-swim classrooms – and critics of Title VII were quick to use the ammunition. Why should government mandate native-language instruction, they asked, or give it preference in funding, when its effectiveness remained in doubt?

Bilingual education advocates responded that such poorly designed research would never yield useful findings. Rather than testing an ideal instructional model, AIR had examined widely varying approaches labeled "bilingual" that had received Title VII grants for at least three years, then compared their overall outcomes with those of nonbilingual approaches. "In such an analysis," wrote Tracy Gray and Beatriz Arias of the Center for Applied Linguistics,

> the positive effects found with the good programs are often canceled out by the negative effects found with the bad programs. ... It avoids the reality that bilingual programs develop and exist in districts that differ markedly in terms of variability of linguistic needs, demographics, availability of well-trained teachers, adequate curricula, district commitment, and level of politicization of constituencies.

Not surprisingly, when all the academic effects were averaged out, the end results were mediocre.

Closer analysis turned up additional problems with AIR's methodology, raising serious questions about validity of its conclusions. In a **controlled scientific experiment** designed to gauge the effects of an educational treatment, **background variables** – factors other than those being studied – need to be "held constant" to avoid biasing the results. For example, if students in bilingual classrooms are slower learners or start out with less English proficiency than students in mainstream classrooms, such pre-existing differences will "contaminate" attempts to compare the two groups' progress over time. The bilingual students might score lower because bilingual education is ineffective, or merely because the mainstream students, on average, had a higher academic aptitude and a head-start in English. Unless such variables are controlled – by making sure that students in the **experimental** and **comparison groups** share characteristics that are indeed comparable – it would be impossible to say for sure.

This was precisely the challenge faced by the AIR study. The research subjects were children at many different stages of linguistic and academic development. For example, 28 percent of students in the Title VII (experimental) group were reported to be dominant or monolingual in Spanish, versus only 5 percent of those in the non–Title VII (comparison) group. Meanwhile 26 percent of the Title VII students were classified as English monolinguals and 47 percent as English-dominant bilinguals, as compared with 83 percent and 12 percent of the non–Title VII students, respectively. Compensating for such differences in language proficiency was complicated by the fact that the assessments themselves were suspect. Children were classified as Spanish- or English-dominant not on the basis of objective tests but according to teachers' subjective evaluations, which numerous studies have shown to be unreliable. Assessed by this procedure, only a small minority of students in both groups were deemed to be "limited-English-speaking." Other researchers in the field found this hard to accept, since English reading scores hovered in the 20th to 30th percentile range for both groups. Many of the children, given objective assessments, would likely have met the more expansive definition of limited English *proficiency* adopted by Congress in 1978 *(see Chapter 5)*. In hindsight, of course, it is impossible to say with certainty.

Still more remarkable was the fact that at least two-thirds of the mainstream students had previously been enrolled in native-language classrooms for at least one year. Many had apparently been transferred from bilingual programs after being judged proficient in English. Yet the study neglected to take into account this or other aspects of students' prior educational experiences. It does not take a Ph.D. to understand why "graduates" of bilingual education would tend to outperform English learners who had yet to be mainstreamed. In effect, the individual success stories of Title VII were being cited as evidence of its failure.

How did such anomalies affect the study's overall findings? In calculating the achievement outcomes of bilingual versus mainstream programs, the researchers made statistical adjustments in an effort to control for variables including "student social-economic status level, student pretest score, student preference for and use of English and Spanish, and the number of school days between pretesting and posttesting." Yet, for many critics of the AIR study, it remained unclear exactly who was being compared with whom.

'Gold Standard'

Many of these "comparability" problems could have been avoided through a research technique known as **random assignment**. If AIR's pool of 8,200 research subjects had been divided between the Title VII and non–Title VII programs on the basis of chance alone – rather than, say, level of English proficiency or parental preferences – the probability that comparisons might be contaminated by pre-existing differences in student characteristics would be extremely small. Random assignment is often described as "the gold standard" in scientific research, the surest way to control for variables that could bias a study's conclusions. It is specifically mentioned in the **No Child Left Behind Act** as the methodology preferred by the federal government in determining whether educational programs are "scientifically based" *(see Chapter 14)*.

In the real world of schools, however, this ideal is extremely difficult to achieve, especially in a large-scale or long-term study involving English language learners. Immigrant students in particular are a mobile population, arriving at various times throughout the school year and frequently exiting bilingual programs as they acquire English or follow their families to other communities. This leads to "attrition" of subjects from experimental or comparison groups, which undermines their randomness and distorts the analysis of program outcomes. Meanwhile parental preferences, school priorities, legal and ethical constraints, and other factors prevent researchers from treating English learners as lab animals without rights that must be respected. For example, research using "no treatment" as a comparison group – that is, sink-or-swim instruction – has been outlawed since the 1974 *Lau v. Nichols* decision.[2]

Random assignment can sometimes be achieved in small-scale experiments with the informed consent of parents, although volunteerism itself can lead to problems of **selection bias**. Children are often enrolled in two-way bilingual education, for example, by families that are more activist than average in fostering bilingualism and cultural awareness – factors likely to affect their school performance *(see Chapter 12)*. When random assignment is impossible, as is usually the case, re-searchers must conduct a **quasi-experiment**, using statistical means to control for pre-existing differences. Such techniques are imperfect, however, and their reliability is often questioned. While it is feasible to adjust statistically for factors like socioeconomic status and parental education levels, variations in initial English proficiency and academic aptitude are often more problematic. The National Research Council has sharply criticized "the use of elaborate statistical methods intended to overcome the shortcomings" in study designs.

Also bear in mind that, while controlled experiments are important, they are certainly not the only means by which science advances. Indeed, in many disciplines they are impossible. Researcher Jim Cummins cites the example of climatologists, who are obviously unable to stage weather events – hurricanes, say – in order to study them under controlled conditions. "What scientists do to generate knowledge in this discipline (and many others)," he says,

> is to observe phenomena (e.g., the conditions under which hurricanes appear) and build up theoretical models that attempt to predict these phenomena. With further observations they test and refine their predictive models. There is no control group, for obvious reasons, yet theory-based predictions are constantly being tested and refined.

Like education research, climate research is sometimes controversial for external political reasons that have nothing to do with the validity of its findings. But few would claim that it is any less scientific.

When thinking about research methodology, it is also helpful to remember the computer programmer's dictum: *garbage in, garbage out.* Even a "true experiment" featuring random assignment of subjects does not guarantee valid or meaningful results. If the **independent variable** (the educational treatment) is not carefully controlled, it is likely to bias the **dependent variable** (the educational outcome). The AIR study lumped together diverse treatments, defining them entirely by their use, or nonuse, of students' native language. It also tended to blur distinctions between bilingual and nonbilingual instructional models, for example, on the matter of staff characteristics. One-quarter of the teachers and aides in the all-English programs had at least two years of professional experience in bilingual programs, and a majority had attended inservice training in bilingual methodologies. Seventy-nine percent said they spoke both English and Spanish. No doubt English learners in "mainstream" classrooms with these teachers received something quite different from the typical sink-or-swim treatment. The students may well have benefited, but the study did not. It was as though, in weighing the outcomes of purportedly bilingual and nonbilingual programs, someone put a thumb on the scale to favor the latter. Once again, what AIR actually measured is difficult to determine.

Another crucial issue in research design is its **theoretical framework**, which is influential regardless of whether it is clearly articulated. If a study's assumptions about second-language acquisition are erroneous, for example, its findings are unlikely to be relevant to English learner programs and policies. A major complaint about the AIR study was its short time span – roughly five and one-half months between pretest and posttest[3] – which, critics like Gray and Arias argued, was too limited to gauge the impact of the bilingual treatment. It was widely understood, even at that early stage of research in second-language acquisition, that LEP students need considerably more than five and one-half months to make significant progress in English.

Bilingual programs based on this understanding were designed accordingly. Rather than rushing English learners into the mainstream, they featured native-language instruction in subject areas for an extended period, facilitating a gradual transition designed to avoid disrupting students' academic development. Empirical evidence was beginning to confirm the benefits of this strategy. A **longitudinal study** tracking the multiyear progress of Navajo English learners in Rock Point, Arizona (also released in 1978), found a slight advantage for an all-ESL approach by grade 3, but a significant edge for bilingual education by grade 6.

Judging such programs on the basis of short-term outcomes made little sense, then, unless the aim was to discredit bilingual education. More likely, the research design agreed upon by AIR and the Department of Education was a case of ignoring educational theory for the sake of administrative expediency. A longer-term study would obviously have been more complex and costly and, as always, policymakers were impatient for answers about English learner programs. This helps to explain why the answers they got were frequently unsatisfying.

Standards of Success

"While the AIR study can and should be faulted for its inaccuracies," wrote Rudolph Troike at the time, "not all of the negative findings can be easily dismissed, and bilingual educators should take this report seriously as a challenge to improve the quality of programs." Rather than an indictment of the concept of bilingual instruction, AIR's findings indicated there were problems with its implementation, he concluded. "Unfortunately, there are still too many bad programs in this country."

Critics of bilingual education had no trouble endorsing this last statement. But they rejected it as an explanation for the relatively poor showing of native-language programs in evaluation research. "Without some independent measure of the success of implementation of each project, the implementation hypothesis is a meaningless tautology," argued Keith Baker and Adriana de Kanter of the U.S. Department of Education. It was just as likely, they added, that "those few projects with positive outcomes were successful *despite* their use of bilingual instruction. ... No consistent evidence supports the effectiveness of TBE [transitional bilingual education]. ... Findings of *no significant difference* predominate" (emphasis added).

Whatever the case, they wrote, it might "be more cost-effective to switch to alternative instructional methods [than] to undertake large-scale efforts to redesign and properly implement TBE programs."

Indeed, from a policymaker's perspective, AIR's inconclusive report did suggest that Title VII was failing to meet expectations. Notwithstanding a handful of exemplary programs, if bilingual education was not making much of a difference overall, why should the federal government spend millions of dollars and put legal pressure on local school districts to adopt it?

Yet, drawing on theories of second-language acquisition, some researchers came to an entirely different conclusion. In an early review of evaluation studies, Laraine Zappert and Roberto Cruz explained:

> A non-significant finding is not a negative finding with respect to bilingual education. A non-significant effect, that students in bilingual education classes are learning at the same rate as students in monolingual classes, demonstrates the fact that learning in two languages does not interfere with a student's academic and cognitive performance.

In other words, when there is "no difference," students in bilingual education are learning just as much English, even though they receive *less English instruction* than their counterparts in nonbilingual programs. Meanwhile they are keeping up in content areas and developing fluency in two languages. Such results may well prove "nonsignificant" in short-term comparisons with all-English programs, but they also contradict the theory that diverting students from **time on task** in English will retard English acquisition. More important, these findings strengthen the hypotheses underlying bilingual education, such as the **transferability** of skills and knowledge between languages *(see Chapter 8)*.

Role of Theory

Here, as in many disputes over studies in this field, differing interpretations reflect fundamentally different assumptions about the role of theory in guiding educational research and educational practice. Policymakers tend to seek "bottom line" results on which they can base decisions. *Whether* a pedagogical approach proves successful in actual classrooms is more important for their purposes than *why;* hence their focus on evaluation research. While this information is also useful to practitioners – assuming that evaluations produce valid conclusions – educators tend to place higher value on studies that help them understand and improve what goes on in their classrooms. Such insights are more likely to come from a mode of scientific inquiry loosely described as **basic research**. Rather than simply asking "what works," it uses empirical data to confirm or reject hypotheses about why LEP students succeed or fail in school; how factors like age, social status, and native-language proficiency affect the process of acquiring English; and how linguistic development interacts with cognitive development.

In short, basic research produces **theoretical knowledge** that can be applied to diverse conditions. Not only is such knowledge useful in designing educational programs; it is also essential in analyzing their successes and failures in various contexts. Theory helps to explain, for example, why second-language immersion tends to be more effective for some students (language-majority students from well educated households) than for others (language-minority students who live in poverty; *see Chapter 9*). By contrast, research that is uninformed by theory – like many evaluation studies – has no basis for analyzing program successes or failures. It cannot explain why a model that works for, say, Puerto Ricans in Connecticut yields disappointing results with Vietnamese in Louisiana. Unable to predict which pedagogical elements are appropriate in which contexts, such research offers little more than a trial-and-error method for making program choices.

Hakuta and Snow argue that basic research can and should play a much larger role in policymaking for English learners. They cite several findings about bilingualism – or more accurately, theories supported by an accumulating body of evidence – that are directly relevant to decisions in this area:

- Early childhood is not the optimum age to acquire a second language; older children and adults are "more efficient language learners." Thus the "sense of urgency in introducing English to non-English-speaking children and concern about postponing children's exit from bilingual programs" are misplaced.
- "Language is not a unified skill, but a complex configuration of abilities. ... Language used for conversational purposes is quite different from language used for school learning, and the former develops earlier than the latter."
- Because many skills are transferable to a second language, "time spent learning in the native language ... is not time lost in developing English." To the contrary, a child with a strong foundation in the first language will perform better in English over the long term.
- For the same reason, "reading should be taught in the native language, particularly for children who, on other grounds, run the risk of reading failure. Reading skills acquired in the native language will transfer readily and quickly

to English, and will result in higher ultimate reading achievement in English."

- "There is no cognitive cost in the development of bilingualism in children. Very possibly, bilingualism enhances children's thinking skills."

Such developments in basic research have exerted an increasing influence on the design of bilingual education programs. In the early 1980s the California Department of Education launched an innovative model known as Case Studies in Bilingual Education – using a theoretical framework developed by Jim Cummins, Stephen Krashen, and others – which emphasizes the benefits of native-language development and a gradual transition to English *(see Chapters 8 and 10)*.

Nevertheless, getting policymakers to pay attention to basic research has been a challenge. Some of the obstacles have been political, others philosophical. Since evaluation research provides weaker support for bilingual approaches, it has naturally been favored by enthusiasts of all-English approaches, who rarely address or even acknowledge the insights of basic research. This emphasis also appeals to the **pragmatist ideology** that tends to dominate policy deliberations, attaching paramount importance to "real-world results" while treating theory as a kind of airy speculation.

In 1988, Edward Fuentes, the federal director of bilingual education research, was asked for an assessment of Cummins's work. The Department of Education had none, he said. Pressed for his own opinion, Fuentes ventured: "I think he has a theory, and his theory has yet to be proved. It's one of many explanations. That's the nature of social science. People have to continue investigating." By implication, findings from basic research on bilingualism, second-language acquisition, and bilingual pedagogies were "just theory." They had no relevance to bilingual education policy as far as the Reagan administration was concerned. Officials professed to care only about "hard facts" that would show which "method" would "work best."

'Burden of Proof'

Opponents of bilingual education in the 1980s enjoyed a tactical advantage in the debate over its effectiveness. Where evidence is contradictory, the easiest position to defend – and the hardest to disprove – is that results are inconclusive. Reagan administration officials contended that, as long as the findings of evaluation studies remained mixed, effectively *nothing was known* to guide policymakers. Therefore, the Bilingual Education Act should favor no particular approach in funding programs for English learners. "Let us permit diversity, innovation, experimentation, and local options to flourish," proposed Chester E. Finn, Jr., assistant secretary for educational research. In other words: *Let us seize this opportunity to divert federal funding from bilingual to nonbilingual programs.* Finn elaborated the administration's official agnosticism as follows:

> The logical test underlying scientific research is the question of rejection of the null hypothesis. That is to say, the burden of proof rests on those who assert that some effect or event occurs. The presumption in all scientific research is that there is no difference until proven otherwise. Thus … it is not incumbent on the Department of Education to prove that "transitional bilingual education" is ineffective. Rather, the burden of proof is on those who assert that such education *is* effective. When results are inconclusive, the correct scientific conclusion is to accept the null hypothesis, i.e., to conclude that those who assert effectiveness have failed to prove their claims. … It is the inconclusive nature of the research that supports the Department's view that this unproven method ought not be mandated by law.

Science does indeed insist on high standards of proof. It does not restrict itself, however, to politically generated hypotheses, such as whether or not programs labeled TBE are "effective," or to a single type of evidence, such as program evaluation data. In opposition to Finn's **empiricist** outlook, which regards science as a simple process of marshalling facts to "prove claims," researchers engaged in basic research, such as Jim Cummins and Stephen Krashen, have expounded a more expansive view. They conceive science to be a process of building on existing knowledge, as summarized by theory, to generate new hypotheses, which are then subjected to rigorous empirical tests, helping to refine theory and thereby produce more sophisticated hypotheses, leading to additional experiments that advance knowledge … in a continuing cycle.

For example, it is well documented that literacy "transfers" between languages, even between those with radically different alphabets such as English and Chinese. This bit of evidence supports the theory that developing native-language skills helps to support second-language learning. One hypothesis that logically follows is that English language learners would benefit by acquiring initial literacy in the mother tongue. Of course, it is necessary to put this proposition to an empirical test (and, indeed, research continues in this area). The effects of such an approach, positive or negative, might or might not be detectable in a large-scale evaluation study with many variables in play. Smaller, better targeted and controlled studies – the kind that the Reagan administration considered irrelevant – are more likely to measure its impact.

If researchers truly seek to advance knowledge about how children learn, rather than merely to vindicate positions that they already hold, they will be ruthless in testing hypotheses. Cummins explains that,

> while no individual research finding can "prove" a theory or confirm a hypothesis, any research finding can disconfirm or refute a theory or hypothesis. Thus, the criterion of validity for any hypothesis is extremely stringent: it must be consistent with *all* of the research data or at least be able to account for inconsistencies (e.g., poor implementation of a program).

To be scientific, theoretical frameworks must be **falsifiable**, in the terminology of philosopher Karl Popper. That is, they must be testable on empirical grounds. This means that the hypotheses they generate must be "endangered" experimentally, placed in situations where they could be *dis*proven.

The perennial problem for policymakers is how to proceed when science has yet to provide conclusive answers to the questions they need to answer – which is often the case. Do they remain agnostic and indecisive? Or do they act on the best evidence available, as crystallized in the form of theory? In this respect, Finn's claims about the scientific "burden of proof" put the Department of Education at odds with most scientists working on second-language pedagogies at the time. While acknowledging that many questions remained to be answered, a strong consensus of experts endorsed Title VII's preference for native-language instruction *(see Chapter 6)*. "It's hard to do the perfect experiment," Krashen observed in a 1987 interview.

> Some of the [evaluation] study designs have been awful. But the results are very consistent over hundreds of studies. Evidence, which varies in quality, supports [the hypothesis that] bilingual education works. ... All scientific hypotheses are fragile. One bit of contradictory evidence can destroy them. But we owe it to the kids to use [bilingual instruction] because it's our best guess as to what works best. I can't imagine any other way.

Baker–de Kanter Report

Nevertheless, the Reagan administration insisted that the vast majority of these "hundreds of studies" were rendered meaningless by their unscientific methodologies. Officials argued that only studies meeting rigorous criteria should be considered as a basis for policy decisions and that this research, taken together, offered little or no support for bilingual education. To bolster their position, they pointed to a controversial report by the U.S. Department of Education on the state of research in the field.

In August 1980, as the Carter administration prepared to issue its ill-fated Lau Regulations *(see Chapter 5),* officials at the White House asked the department to review the research literature on the effectiveness of bilingual education. The job went to the Office of Planning and Budget,[4] which had earlier directed the AIR study. It was assigned to Keith Baker and Adriana de Kanter, respectively a sociologist and a management intern. Although the Reagan administration withdrew the Lau proposal in February 1981, the research project continued under the new Secretary of Education, Terrel Bell.

Baker and de Kanter defined the study in legal-political terms, asking:

1. Is there a sufficiently strong case for the effectiveness of TBE for learning English and nonlanguage subjects to justify a legal mandate for TBE?
2. Are there any effective alternatives to TBE? That is, should one particular method be exclusively required if other methods are also effective?

Equally important, perhaps, was what the researchers failed to ask. They made no attempt to describe the features of successful and unsuccessful bilingual programs, but only to determine whether "the instructional method is uniformly effective."

After reviewing more than 300 studies (about half of which were primary evaluations of actual programs), Baker and de Kanter judged most to be methodologically unsound. In the end they threw out all but 28 because of design weaknesses. They rejected studies without control groups that compared the progress of LEP students against national norms on achievement tests. As such children learn English, the researchers argued, they may record "spectacular gains" by better understanding the language of the test and not because they have progressed academically. Also excluded were studies that did not feature random assignment of students, unless statistical measures were taken to control for extraneous variables. Other studies were disqualified for using grade-equivalent scores, which the researchers said were "almost impossible to interpret." Among the evaluations left out were all 12 cited by Troike, along with many of bilingual education's best-publicized success stories. Among those included was the AIR report, which the reviewers described as "the only American [research] designed to be nationally representative," despite the widespread criticisms of its methodology.

Baker and de Kanter analyzed the "acceptable" studies to determine whether they supported one program type or another, or whether the results were inconclusive. Then they "counted the votes" for or against each model and added up the totals. Conclusion: there was "no consistent evidence" that programs using the native language were effective. In a majority of the 28 evaluations, Baker and de

Kanter found that differences in student performance were too small to be statistically significant when transitional bilingual education was compared with submersion, or sink-or-swim. Among the studies that showed one approach to be superior, the score was split about evenly between the two.[5] The researchers also concluded that, in some cases, TBE and submersion were less effective than either ESL or structured immersion.

Summarizing the study's policy implications, Baker and de Kanter maintained that

> too little is known about the problems of educating language minorities to prescribe a specific remedy at the federal level. ... Each school district should decide what type of special program is most appropriate for its own unique setting. ... Although TBE has been found to work in some settings, it also has been found ineffective and even harmful in other places. Furthermore, both major alternatives to TBE – structured immersion and ESL – have been found to work in some settings. ... An occasional, inexplicable success is not reason enough to make TBE the law of the land.

The researchers made no effort to conceal their own preference, calling for "a widespread, structured immersion demonstration program" to test this all-English approach. Perhaps that was because they could cite only one, unpublished study touting the benefits of immersion for language-minority children in the United States. It involved a kindergarten curriculum in McAllen, Texas, which was labeled "a modified immersion program" despite the fact that it included an hour of daily Spanish instruction.

The authors' enthusiasm for all-English instruction was based largely on evaluations of Canadian immersion programs, which have proven highly effective in teaching French to English-speaking children. The researchers who designed this model, however, have cautioned against extrapolating from its success to justify immersion for language-minority children in the United States. They have also noted that the Canadian model is a bilingual approach. Its participants are children of the dominant language group, whose mother-tongue development is reinforced rather than threatened outside of school. For speakers of low-status minority languages, an all-English immersion program would likely be harmful, the Canadian researchers have warned.

Rejecting these objections as "untested theoretical arguments," Baker and de Kanter said that "immersion may not transfer successfully from Canada to the United States, but this is an empirical question that must be answered by direct test." Little additional evidence was available in January 1987, when the Department of Education resubmitted to Congress a proposal to allow increased funding for alternatives to bilingual education. Edward Fuentes could cite only one primary study asserting the promise of structured immersion in this country, a program evaluation in Uvalde, Texas. Moreover, initial results from the Ramírez longitudinal study, then supervised by Keith Baker, showed unpromising results for structured immersion when it was compared with various types of bilingual education *(see Chapter 9)*.

Critiquing the Critics

Though never officially endorsed by the department, a draft of the Baker–de Kanter report surfaced in the press in September 1981. Its conclusions were widely regarded as an indictment of Title VII. "Bilingual Education May Be Scrapped," blared a typical headline, suggesting that funding might soon be redirected to more "promising techniques" like all-English immersion. While the authors disavowed such interpretations, the Baker–de Kanter study has frequently been cited by the enemies of bilingual education. During the 1980s it became easily the most-quoted federal pronouncement on the education of LEP children, and probably the most criticized as well.

As with the AIR study three years earlier, bilingual education supporters protested the report's methodology, attacking its program labels as oversimplified and misleading. How to characterize educational treatments was disputed in several cases, either because studies contained inadequate program descriptions or because of theoretical differences over the use of native-language instruction in so-called "immersion" approaches. Baker and de Kanter were also accused of using a double standard of methodological acceptability to exclude evaluations favorable to bilingual education and to include those that found it harmful. Once again, the vote-counting approach of tallying studies on each side of the effectiveness question was assailed as a primitive research technique at best.

The most ambitious rebuttal appeared in 1985. Psychologist Ann Willig used a sophisticated statistical procedure known as **meta-analysis** to create a new synthesis of the Baker–de Kanter data. This technique enabled her to combine mean **effect sizes**, or differences in program impact, some of which were too small to be statistically significant in individual studies. It also avoided a major weakness of vote-counting, which treated all studies equally regardless of size. For example, if bilingual education was slightly worse than immersion in research involving 20 children and substantially superior in research involving 2,000, the two studies would cancel each other out using the Baker–de Kanter procedure. Meta-analysis enabled Willig to convert these outcomes into weighted averages, thus allowing for a precise measurement of overall differences in student achievement between bilingual and nonbilingual classrooms. She also adjusted for 183 variables that Baker and de Kanter had not taken into account, ranging from student and teacher characteristics to instructional methods to the language of achievement tests. Perhaps most important, Willig was able to control for design weaknesses in the evaluations under review.

The Willig study reanalyzed 23 of the 28 evaluations included in the Baker–de Kanter report (excluding foreign and nonprimary studies). She thereby accepted the federal researchers' decision to disqualify, on methodological grounds, a large number of studies supporting the superiority of bilingual approaches. Nevertheless, her meta-analysis of the Baker–de Kanter data "consistently produced small-to-moderate differences favoring bilingual education," Willig reported. The pattern prevailed in reading, language skills, mathematics, and total achievement, as tested in English, and listening comprehension, reading, writing, total language, mathematics, social studies, and attitudes toward school and self, as tested in Spanish.

According to Willig, these "significant positive effects" became visible only when statistical controls were applied for methodological flaws. In other words, the better a study's design, the better bilingual education fared. Where evaluations used random assignment of subjects to experimental and comparison groups, the effect size was largest in favor of bilingual programs. Conversely, the weaker research designs tended to be stacked heavily against native-language instruction, such as the AIR study's use of comparison groups including many so-called "submersion" students who had previously been enrolled in bilingual classrooms. In other studies results were sometimes distorted because comparison students were already judged to be English-dominant rather than LEP, or were taught by bilingual teachers who made frequent use of students' native language. Often English learners were exited from bilingual programs during the experiment and replaced by incoming LEP students, who naturally depressed aggregate scores. Or teacher turnover and disorganization were problems in the bilingual classroom, but not in the comparison classroom.

Critics had previously shown that such factors were biasing evaluation studies against bilingual education. Willig's contribution, using meta-analysis, was to isolate each design flaw, calculate the amount of distortion (including interactions among variables), and adjust the program comparisons. On a level playing field, she proved, bilingual education could outscore the competition: "In every instance where there did not appear to be crucial inequalities between experimental and comparison groups, children in the bilingual programs averaged higher than the comparison children." At the same time, she warned that "until quality research in bilingual education becomes a norm rather than a scarcity," educators will be handicapped in addressing the needs of language-minority children.

Willig's research was cited by several experts polled in 1986 by the U.S. General Accounting Office as evidence against Reagan administration claims that the case for bilingual education remained unproven *(see Chapter 6)*. In response, the Department of Education issued its first comment on her work: "The Willig meta-analysis reviewed a non-representative and very small sample of the existing research and used an inappropriate methodology. It is by no means a comprehensive review of the literature." Asked to explain why Willig's study was any less comprehensive than the Baker–de Kanter report – after all, it relied on virtually the same body of evaluation research – Keith Baker responded that Willig had reviewed fewer studies than a 1983 version of his report. (The later edition, which encompassed 39 rather than 28 studies, reached conclusions identical to those of the 1981 draft.)

Alan Ginsburg, Baker's superior in the Office of Planning, Budget, and Evaluation, argued further that meta-analysis was an inappropriate research tool. The issue, he said, was not whether bilingual education is effective "on average, but [whether there are] programs that might be appropriate in one community, but not in another. The averaging effect of meta-analysis is quite limiting." Averaging, of course, was what reviews of the literature like the Baker–de Kanter report and evaluations like the AIR study were all about. Willig had simply refined the process. Baker expanded on Ginsburg's reasoning in a 1987 article for the *Review of Educational Research*:

> Willig's [finding of] a net average positive effect does not necessarily justify a federal mandate for TBE, especially if many programs produce negative results and successful alternatives exist. ...The advantage of a narrative review over meta-analysis is clear in this situation. Where the methodology of the literature being synthesized is very complex and problematical, only the narrative reviewer can fully assess the strengths and weaknesses of a study and evaluate it as a whole to determine what is and is not valid in a study. The mechanistic checklists used in meta-analysis cannot assess the gestalt of a study.

Responding to Baker in the same issue of the journal, Willig noted that the computer "coding system" at the heart of meta-analysis, "forces one to scrutinize every aspect of a study" in a way that minimizes subjective judgments. "In contrast, the narrative reviewer may omit important factors when assessing the value of a study, either because of the overload of information or ... reviewer bias." Willig observed that Baker and de Kanter had consistently ignored flaws in evaluation studies or used partial data in ways that confirmed negative assessments of bilingual education.

Rossell and Baker vs. Greene

More than a decade later, a similar review of the literature, followed by a similar meta-analysis, generated claims and counterclaims about program effectiveness along nearly identical lines. In 1996, Baker joined forces with Christine Rossell, a political scientist at Boston University, in publishing an analysis of 72 evaluation studies deemed "methodologically acceptable" (out of 300 reviewed). This time the vote totals were even less favorable to transitional bilingual education. The researchers reported that TBE was "better than regular classroom instruction" only 22 percent of the time when students were compared in English reading, while 33 percent of the studies showed that submersion was superior and 45 percent were inconclusive. TBE was "never better than structured immersion" in reading, and 83 percent of the time it was "worse." It also fared poorly when compared to other forms of ESL, and was rated superior to just one program model: developmental bilingual education. Presented in this way, the case against native-language instruction seemed formidable indeed.

Again, however, there were serious questions about the methodology of the review itself, many of which echoed criticisms of the Baker–de Kanter report in the 1980s:

- *Phantom studies.* Other researchers had difficulty assessing the review's conclusions because it included numerous evaluations that were difficult to locate. Stephen Krashen reported that only two of the 20 studies purporting to show that "submersion beats TBE" had been published in peer-reviewed journals (which also cast doubt on their methodological rigor.) Another researcher, Jay Greene, found that several of the obscure studies were impossible to track down, even with the help of Professor Rossell.
- *"Translating" from the Canadian.* Most of the studies cited in favor of structured immersion, a monolingual approach, involved programs designed to cultivate French-English bilingualism among Anglophone students in Canada. (Jim Cummins pointed out that some of these "were actually *trilingual* programs

involving instruction in French, English, and Hebrew.") The idea of equating two models with such different methods, goals, student characteristics, and sociolinguistic contexts has no support whatsoever from experts in second-language pedagogies *(see Chapter 9)*. In addition, the "partial immersion" approaches in Canada that were used as surrogates for transitional bilingual education in the United States had nothing to do with assimilating immigrants. In fact, they seemed to resemble TBE in just one respect: amount of native language used in the first two or three years. Rossell later acknowledged that, "in many cases, we had to 'translate' the programs into U.S. terminology." Important pedagogical details seem to have been lost in the process.

- *Program (mis)labeling.* Reported success stories for structured immersion in the United States are quite rare; even in these cases their characterization is often challenged. A so-called "bilingual immersion" program in El Paso, Texas, for example, was championed by Rosalie Porter, Russell Gersten, and others as an example of the superiority of structured immersion (although its edge over a traditional bilingual approach was quite modest). Meanwhile the program's designers conceived it as a form of bilingual education because it offered up to 90 minutes a day of "native language cognitive development ... [designed] to develop concepts, literacy, cognition, and critical thinking skills in Spanish." At one point Keith Baker agreed that this model resembled two-way bilingual education. Later he changed his mind and described it as "structured English immersion." In the study he coauthored with Rossell, the program was labeled "submersion." This is not an isolated example. Many evaluations in the review provided little or no description of program components other than language of instruction. With numerous uncertainties about what pedagogical approaches are being compared, it is difficult to place much confidence in the overall conclusions.

- *Disputed outcomes.* Rossell and Baker's reporting of study results sometimes departed from those of the studies' authors. Kathy Escamilla of the University of Colorado took sharp issue with the characterization of a publication she had coauthored: "Rossell and Baker report the results in a unidimensional way. That is, they report only one overall finding. We had multiple findings, none of which matched those reported by Rossell and Baker." Contrary to what the reviewers claimed, Escamilla's research featured no comparisons of reading achievement. Instead, it focused on oral language acquisition in Vietnamese, Spanish, and English.

- *Inconsistently applied criteria.* In about 20 percent of the studies that Rossell and Baker judged to be methodologically sound, students received native-language instruction in both control and experimental groups, making valid comparisons impossible. Some of the included studies either failed to evaluate any form of bilingual education or measured its effects over a very short time – as little as seven weeks. A few studies duplicated results from the same research, thereby inflating the number of "votes" against native-language programs. Others had sample sizes that were quite small; one compared 28 structured immersion students to 16 bilingual education students. Krashen notes that "if only a few students had slightly different scores, the [overall] results could have looked very different."

- *Exclusion of relevant research.* As in the Baker–de Kanter study, Rossell and Baker excluded as unscientific a large number of studies that found bilingual approaches to be effective. Krashen agrees that the failure of an evaluation study to use random assignment or statistical controls for pre-existing differences is a "flaw" that should be weighed in evaluating research results. "But there are reasons to hypothesize that it is not fatal," he argues:

> If we look at many studies with nonrandom assignment, and have no reason to believe that subjects in different treatments differ in relevant ways, it can be argued that randomization of subject assignment has, in fact, occurred, because of the large number of studies. In other words, many slightly flawed studies can be combined to arrive at a valid analysis.

Dividing the research on bilingual education into "acceptable" and "unacceptable" studies – that is, meaningful versus meaningless – may advance partisan ends, but it squanders potentially valuable insights.

If there was a common theme in these complaints about the Rossell-Baker study, it was the suspicion of researcher bias, a perennial weakness of the vote-counting approach. So a meta-analysis released in 1998 by the Tomás Rivera Policy Institute, provided a welcome antidote. Perhaps to avoid charges of liberal bias itself, the Latino-oriented research center commissioned Jay Greene, a fellow at the conservative Manhattan Institute and a leading advocate for school vouchers, to conduct the review. As Willig had done with Baker–de Kanter, Greene adopted the selection criteria of Rossell and Baker but excluded from their body of studies those that failed to meet their criteria or that came from outside the United States. In the end, he found 11 acceptable studies to include in the meta-analysis. Finally, rather than accept questionable program labels, he based his comparisons simply on programs' use – or nonuse – of English learners' native language for instruction.

Greene's conclusions were striking not so much for contradicting Rossell and Baker (hardly a surprise, with the Canadian studies omitted) as for duplicating Willig's findings of 13 years earlier. First, there was a modest edge for bilingual education. In reading, Greene found an effect size of .21 of a standard deviation, identical to Willig's calculation; in total language, .74, as compared to Willig's .73; and in math, .12 versus .18.[6] Second, the advantage for bilingual education grew as studies became more rigorous, just as in Willig's research. "Despite the relatively small number of studies," Greene concluded, "the strength and consistency of these results, especially from the highest quality randomized experiments, increases confidence in the conclusion that bilingual programs are effective at increasing standardized test scores measured in English."

Other researchers have agreed that these findings are impressive. The fact they so closely paralleled Willig's "adds to the plausibility and reliability of his results," Krashen says, adding that "the similarity is not because both researchers looked at the same studies. Only four studies were included in both analyses."

The recalculations by Greene and Willig added up to a powerful refutation of claims that there was no scientific support for native-language instruction. Nevertheless, the question *bilingual or not?* remains a limited focus for investigation, which excludes a wide array of program variables. Tabulating the results of crude studies, even with the aid of statistical magic, yields limited insights into how children make academic progress while acquiring a second language. Such questions are the province of basic research.

Suggested Reading

Baker, Keith A., and de Kanter, Adriana A. "Federal Policy and the Effectiveness of Bilingual Education." In *Bilingual Education: A Reappraisal of Federal Policy. Lexington*, Mass.: Lexington Books, 1983.

Krashen, Stephen D. *Inquiries and Insights: Second Language Teaching, Immersion and Bilingual Education, Literacy.* Hayward, Calif.: Alemany Press, 1985.

Rossell, Christine H., and Baker, Keith. "The Educational Effectiveness of Bilingual Education." *Research in the Teaching of English* 30, no. 1 (1996): 7–74.

Willig, Ann C. "A Meta-Analysis of Selected Studies on the Effectiveness of Bilingual Education." *Review of Educational Research* 55, no. 3 (1985): 269–317.

See also pp. 397–98.

Online
Resource
Guide

Crawford, James. *Best Evidence: Research Foundations of the Bilingual Education Act.* National Clearinghouse for Bilingual Education (1997).

Dulay, Heidi, and Burt, Marina. *Bilingual Education: A Close Look at Its Effects.* National Clearinghouse for Bilingual Education (1980).

Tucker, G. Richard. *Implications for U.S. Bilingual Education: Evidence from Canadian Research.* National Clearinghouse for Bilingual Education (1980)

See also companion CD-ROM.

Internet
Links

August, Diane, and Hakuta, Kenji, eds. *Improving Schooling for Language-Minority Children: A Research Agenda.* Washington, D.C.: National Academy Press, 1997. http://www.nap.edu/books/0309054974/html/index.html

Cummins, Jim. "Educational Research in Bilingual Education." (1999). http://www.iteachilearn.com/cummins/educationalresearch.html

Greene, Jay. *A Meta-Analysis of the Rossell and Baker Review of Bilingual Education Research* (1998). http://brj.asu.edu/archives/23v21/articles/art1.html

See also companion CD-ROM.

Notes

1. Using a methodology that departed radically from that of traditional evaluation studies, the Thomas-Collier report of 1997 included data from "more than 700,000 student records" to compare the academic outcomes of various program models for English language learners *(see Chapter 9)*.
2. At the time the AIR study collected its data in 1975–76, the federal Office for Civil Rights was only beginning to enforce the ruling.
3. Students were tested in reading, oral comprehension, and mathematics in English, and in reading and oral comprehension in Spanish.
4. Later renamed the Office of Planning, Budget, and Evaluation; since 2001 it has been known as Policy and Program Studies Services.
5. According to a later article by Baker, one in three studies showed "significant positive effects" for TBE; one in four for submersion.
6. For a simple frame of reference, consider that the achievement gap between LEP and English-proficient students is typically about one standard deviation.

8 Basic Research on Language Acquisition

*M*ost educated Americans can testify to the difficulty of becoming bilingual. Despite years of schooling in French, Spanish, or German, how many can carry on a real-life conversation in a language other than English? The American Council on the Teaching of Foreign Languages estimated in 1987 that "only 3 percent of American high school graduates, and only 5 percent of our college graduates, reach a meaningful proficiency in a second language – and many of these students come from bilingual homes." No doubt those

Language-Learning Methodologies
Chomskyan Revolution
Critical Period Hypothesis
Input Hypothesis
Interdependence Hypothesis
BICS and CALP
Threshold Hypothesis
Empowering Minority Students
'Semilingualism' and Deficit Models
Challenge to BICS/CALP Distinction
Krashen's Critics
Cognitive Effects of Bilingualism

rates have increased somewhat, thanks to stiffer language requirements in higher education and the rapid growth of linguistic minority populations. Still, there is no reason to believe that foreign-language instruction has markedly improved. While it may produce passable reading skills, rarely does it equip students to communicate. They may earn high marks for recalling grammatical rules or parroting classroom exercises or producing flawless compositions. Yet oral exchanges with native speakers can be an ego-jarring experience.

Frustrated at having invested so much effort for so little return, monolinguals tend to rationalize:

- *I started learning a language too late; the longer you wait, the harder it is.*
- *I never had a chance to use the language outside of class, and now I'm embarrassed to try.*
- *I just don't have any aptitude for memorizing grammar and vocabulary.*

Each of these reactions expresses a popular "theory" of second-language acquisition. As generalizations, they are inadequate to explain student failure, but they do reflect persistent problems with foreign-language teaching. Conversational facility is indeed difficult to acquire when there are limited opportunities to engage in actual conversations. An emphasis on grammar drills not only bores students; it seldom trains them to *speak* the target language. Older learners tend to be especially self-conscious when forced to participate in exercises detached from any purposeful context. For years students have lodged such complaints, with little effect on the way foreign languages are taught in this country.

Historically speaking, the focus on form over function seems to be a recent development in second-language education. During the Roman Empire scholars achieved a high level of grammatical knowledge of Latin and Greek, often in connection with the rhetorical arts. Yet apparently such studies were never regarded as a route to language acquisition. In the bilingual schooling of Roman children, conversational dialogues were used to develop fluency in Greek. Latin, the **lingua franca** of culture and scholarship in medieval Europe, was taught for centuries with a stress on oral skills as well as reading and writing.

"Toward the end of the Renaissance," writes psychologist Barry McLaughlin, when Latin began to die out as a spoken tongue,

> emphasis began to shift from the learning of language as a practical tool to the learning of language as a means to an end – that of developing the mind. Latin and Greek were taught because it was thought that the study of grammar was good mental discipline. Since these languages were not living languages, little attention was given to oral communication. Texts were read and translated, and this – together with the study of grammar – became the essence of language training.

By the 19th century the **grammar-translation approach** was being used to teach modern languages as well. Students spent their time conjugating verbs, memorizing vocabulary, learning syntactic rules and their exceptions, taking dictation, and translating written passages. Since communicative proficiency was not an important goal, oral use of the second language was minimal. In the United States such methods predominated well into the 1950s.

Acceptance of the grammatical approach has never been universal. The English philosopher John Locke wrote in 1693:

> Latin is no more unknown to a Child, when he comes into the World, than English. And yet he learns English without Master, Rule, or Grammar; and so might he Latin too, as Tully [Cicero] did, if he had some Body always to talk to him in this Language. . . . [In this way] a Child might without Pains or Chiding, get a Language, which others are wont to be whip'd for at School six or seven Years together.[1]

Perceptive educators have long recognized the potential of more natural approaches to language acquisition. Over the years a number of **direct methods** – the most famous being that of Maximilian Berlitz – have used varieties of partial or total immersion. Oral language is heavily emphasized and translation is avoided; students are encouraged to think in the second tongue. Meanwhile grammar is taught inductively, rather than through the application of rules. Such techniques have proved successful among diplomats, business people, and others with strong incentives to learn. Yet they make for highly structured, teacher-centered lessons that have been less appealing to younger learners. More recently, efforts to involve students actively, by engaging them in meaningful communication, led to innovations in ESL teaching such as the Natural Approach, Suggestopedia, and Total Physical Response. In high school and college foreign-language programs, however, communication-based methods remain the exception.

By 1957, when the shock of *Sputnik* revived Americans' interest in foreign languages, there was widespread dissatisfaction with the grammar-translation method, which was producing few if any functional bilinguals. The prevailing diagnosis was that, while students might become sophisticated grammarians, they were getting too little "practice" in conversation. Still, there was no rush to adopt direct methods, whose approach to grammar seemed haphazard to many educators. What filled the vacuum became known as the **audiolingual method**. With backing from the Modern Language Association, it emerged as a popular alternative to the grammar-translation approach and remains in use today.[2]

Influenced by the fields of behavioral psychology and structural linguistics, audiolingualism begins with the premise that each language is a distinct set of "speech habits." Since students already have well developed habits in their mother tongue, the logic goes, they need systematic practice to learn new habits in the second language. Special attention must therefore be paid to differences between the two grammars; otherwise learners tend to graft new vocabulary onto first-language syntax (a pitfall of direct methods, in the audiolingualists' view). Accordingly, the audiolingual method relies on oral "pattern drills" and "memorization and mimicry" to teach grammar in a planned sequence. The idea is that, through repetition, students' use of the second language becomes automatic, allowing them to produce sentences of their own. When it comes to communication skills, however, practice apparently does not make perfect. Evaluations have shown that audiolingual students, like their predecessors in grammar-translation classrooms, seldom reach more than a novice level of oral proficiency in the second language.

Revolutionary Theory

Audiolingualism suffered a major setback when the reigning **paradigm**, or theoretical system, that sponsored it was overthrown by the **Chomskyan revolution** in linguistics. In the **behaviorist** view espoused by B. F. Skinner, language learning is just another branch of learning – that is, the mind grasps grammatical forms in the same way it draws generalizations from all experience. Therefore, like other behavioral patterns, correct speech habits must be developed through imitation and reinforcement, assisted by frequent repetition. (This assumption also underlies the **time-on-task theory** of language acquisition; *see Chapter 9*.) Implicit in Skinner's premises is the notion that as children acquire language, they internalize a finite set of linguistic responses for all the stimuli they will encounter in life. This is an absurd claim, according to Noam Chomsky.

In any language the number of sentences is infinite, Chomsky points out; there is no limit to the grammatical combination of words. Moreover, while exposed to relatively small amounts of data, children master complex syntactic structures in their native tongue. Rather than merely repeating a limited linguistic repertoire, they learn to produce utterances that have never been heard before, by themselves or by others, which are nevertheless "correct" and comprehensible to fellow speakers of the language. Thus, in Chomsky's theory, language use is a creative, open-ended process rather than a closed system of behavioral habits. That this ability could be acquired empirically – entirely through generalizations from experience – is highly implausible.

Instead, Chomsky hypothesizes, human beings have an innate cognitive capacity for language. The mind is endowed with **linguistic universals** that enable us to formulate rules from the verbal sounds we hear. Such rules depend on the structure of language – for example, the subject-predicate relationship – rather than on easily mimicked features such as word order. Natural human languages differ in particulars while sharing a **universal grammar**, or set of principles that determines the grammars the mind may "construct." Conversely, according to Chomsky, these same universals "exclude other possible languages as 'unlearnable.'" Or, to use another metaphor, heredity has "hard-wired" the human mind with an ability to acquire certain kinds of linguistic structures. Environmental stimuli – messages received in a natural language – "throw switches" to activate the "circuits" of a possible grammar in the brain.

The rapidity and efficiency of the process is remarkable. "During the most active acquisition period (ages 2 to 6)," explain linguists Jeff MacSwan and Kellie Rolstad of Arizona State University, "children learn approximately 10 to 12 new words a day, often on one exposure and under highly ambiguous circumstances. Children know things about elementary aspects of sentence structure for which they have no evidence at all." By school age their mastery of the morphological and syntactic rules of their native language is "essentially indistinguishable from [that of] adults."

Under certain conditions – mental retardation or extreme social deprivation, for example – children may never fully acquire a natural language. But for the vast majority of the human species, the **language faculty** is part of our biological endowment. There are substantial variations in language usage, of course, depending on race, class, ethnicity, gender, education, work, interests, and a host of other characteristics. For example, **linguistic registers**, or communication styles, differ substantially between social groups and situations. Unfamiliarity with "school language" can be a source of academic difficulties, just as unfamiliarity with "street language" or Valley Girl speech or the jargon of computer geeks can cause problems in other **language domains**. But all normal children have the capacity to acquire new registers, given sufficient exposure to them. Chomsky makes an important distinction between **linguistic competence**, or underlying knowledge of language that enables the speaker to "generate" an infinite number of sentences, and **linguistic performance**, or how language is used in real-world contexts.

Beginning in the early 1960s, Chomsky's theory of generative grammar had an enormous impact. Language acquisition, no longer a subset of general learning theory, became the focus of experimental research by psychologists who were also linguists. In studying the actual speech of children, these researchers departed from Chomsky's theoretical approach, which was unconcerned with linguistic behavior in its raw state. Nevertheless, the psycholinguists were able to confirm empirically many of Chomsky's hypotheses about the language faculty and its relation to other cognitive functions. Studies determined, for example, that there is a **natural order** for children's mastery of grammatical structures in both first and second languages, with certain forms acquired later than others.

The Chomskyan revolution raised unsettling questions for language educators. If normal children learn their first language naturally – without behavioral guidance and reinforcement – do teachers have a significant role to play? Indeed, are languages "teachable" in any meaningful sense? Some theorists have answered no to both questions. Yet empirical evidence has shown that individuals differ widely in their ability to learn second languages after early childhood. How could this be true if the process were genetically "programmed"?

One explanation is the **critical period hypothesis**, which posits that lateralization of the language function in the left hemisphere of the brain – a process completed before puberty – impairs the capacity for natural language acquisition. The strongest evidence for this hypothesis comes from case studies of **language deprivation**, unusual circumstances in which children fail to acquire a mother tongue in their early years. But its application to second-language acquisition is dubious, according to many researchers. After all, adults can and do learn one or more additional languages, sometimes approaching native-like fluency.[3] Some research indicates that older learners may be at a phonological disadvantage, unable to shed their "foreign accents" as easily as children. Other studies suggest that adults may experience a long, gradual decline in their aptitude for acquiring other aspects of language. As researchers Ellen Bialystok and Kenji Hakuta argue, however, the literature shows no point at which language-learning potential declines drastically. Indeed, there is considerable evidence that older language students outpace younger language students, at least in the short term.

Another finding relevant to the teachability question is that schoolchildren also vary substantially in second-language acquisition. In a study of LEP students aged 8 through 10, Lily Wong Fillmore and Barry McLaughlin found that 60 percent became "fairly proficient" in English after three years of schooling, 30 percent "were just beginning to make sense of the new language," and 10 percent "had learned virtually no English at all." While "differences in learners" played a role, these alone could not account for the dramatic disparities. At least as important, the researchers concluded, were "differences in those who provide learners with linguistic input, that is, the speakers of the target language, and ... differences in the social settings in which the language is learned." In other words, the quality of teaching appears to be a significant variable in second-language acquisition.

The implications of Chomsky's work were not immediately self-evident in the classroom. Since generative grammar posits that language development is a process of rule formation, not habit formation, some of Chomsky's followers devised the so-called **cognitive approach**: a return to the deductive teaching of grammatical rules, combined with exercises to practice them. Yet this approach has proved no more successful than the audiolingual method in developing communicative competence. Both models have been unpopular with students, who tend to describe them as boring and repetitive. These varying methodologies seem to have produced roughly equivalent, mediocre results. Why should this be so?

What both approaches lack is an adequate **theory of second-language acquisition** that can account for the strengths and weaknesses of instructional programs. Why have grammar-based and audiolingual approaches failed to develop communicative skills in foreign-language classrooms, while direct methods have been more successful? Why do second-language immersion approaches benefit some students, but not others? Why do some bilingual education programs produce dramatic gains, while others do not? Why does *more* English exposure sometimes lead to *less* English acquisition by language-minority students?

Theory is essential to developing, testing, and improving an educational treatment, argues Stephen Krashen. It is not enough simply to apply the results of studies showing an advantage for one method over another. "Moving directly from research ... to teaching is incorrect," he says. "We run the danger of choosing the wrong characteristics to utilize in class. Without theory we cannot distinguish the crucial or distinctive features from the noncrucial or nondistinctive features."

Such a theory has emerged in the past two decades. Its best-known exponents are Krashen, a linguist at the University of Southern California, and Jim Cummins, an educational psychologist at the University of Toronto. But it incorporates the work of many researchers in Canadian immersion, bilingual education, and ESL. More than foreign-language teaching, these three fields are furnishing the data – and reaping the benefits – of a revolutionary new conception of language development.

Learning, Acquisition, and the Input Hypothesis

At its basic level the theory draws a distinction between language **acquisition** and language **learning**. Krashen hypothesizes that fluency in a second tongue cannot be learned; that is, conscious knowledge of grammar and vocabulary does not prepare us to use the language for communicative purposes. Instead, this proficiency must be acquired, or appropriated by the mind, in essentially the same way in which we master our first language. As Locke recognized three centuries ago, babies do just fine without grammar books and dictionaries. Traditionally, human beings of all ages have developed language skills "through communicative practice in real situations," Krashen says. "Even today, with the vast amount of linguistic knowledge available about the languages of the world, it is likely that most ability to communicate in another language is acquired" outside the classroom.

How does acquisition occur? "In one fundamental way," according to Krashen. "We acquire language when we understand it. What is spectacular about this idea is that it happens incidentally, involuntarily, subconsciously, and effortlessly." The key factor is **comprehensible input**: messages in the second language that make sense – ideally, just beyond the competence of the listener, who must strain a bit to understand (Krashen calls this $i + 1$). Both vocabulary and grammar are internalized in this way, as we receive communications in which they are "encoded."

What counts most is the *quality* of second-language exposure, not the *quantity*. As tourists thrown among strangers speaking a strange tongue, we get plenty of input but absorb little of what we hear. On the other hand, when our foreign hosts take the trouble to make themselves intelligible through gestures, context, or simplified speech, we can pick up survival levels of their language. Taking a beginning language course before our trip might facilitate interaction with native speakers, enabling us to acquire much more. So would learning something about the country we plan to visit.[4]

The **input hypothesis** draws on Chomsky's theory of the language faculty, our genetically evolved **language acquisition device** that functions more or less identically in all members of the human species. When this "mental organ" receives intelligible messages in a second language, Krashen explains, the brain has "no choice but to acquire that language, just as the visual system has no choice but to see, and the pancreas has no choice but to operate as pancreases do." We acquire grammatical structures in their natural order, provided that we get sufficient amounts of high-quality input. As our language organ processes this "essential environmental ingredient," Krashen says, it generalizes rules from verbal stimuli – not empirically, but "according to innate principles" of universal grammar.

"The obvious implication," he concludes, "is that language teaching should be based on giving people messages they understand." A non-English-speaking child gets little or no comprehensible input in a sink-or-swim classroom. By contrast, if the child is first provided background knowledge, such as a lesson taught in the native language, English instruction becomes more intelligible. "The first ratio-nale for bilingual education," he postulates, "is that information, knowledge that you get through your first language, makes English input much more comprehensi-ble. It can take something that is utterly opaque and make it transparent."

Krashen likes to illustrate this point with an exercise in decoding a nonsense word, *rouche*. It goes as follows:

> Favorable conditions are necessary to do this activity. That is, you have to have enough *rouche*. If there is too much *rouche*, the object might break. But if conditions are too calm, you will have problems because the *rouche* makes the object go up. If there are obstacles, a serious problem can result because you cannot control the *rouche*. Usually, the *rouche* is most favorable during the spring.

Confronted with this problem by researcher Shirley J. Adams, only 13 percent of experimental subjects could define *rouche*. After background information was pro-vided, 78 percent guessed correctly. The context that made the difference was: "This passage is about flying a kite." (For the benefit of the remaining 22 percent, if they are still wondering, *rouche* means "wind.")

English instruction in subjects other than language can provide a rich source of comprehensible input for LEP children. In such high-context situations, stu-dents readily acquire new words and syntax in the second language, Krashen says, especially if they already know something about the subject being discussed: "For ESL students, a well-taught geography lesson, if it's comprehensible, is a language lesson. In fact, it's better than an ESL class, [where] we're always wondering what to talk about." This methodology, known as **sheltered instruction** – sometimes called **sheltered English** or **sheltered subject-matter instruction** – tailors lessons to LEP students' proficiency in English. Since the early 1980s it has increas-ingly been incorporated into bilingual education programs, with excellent results.

On the other hand, the input hypothesis explains the pitfalls of an early (and sometimes still practiced) methodology in bilingual education known as **concur-rent translation**. Using this approach, a teacher gives a lesson in two languages at once, translating each idea on the spot. Naturally children tend to "tune out" the second language and wait for the translation. Having no reason to pay attention, they receive no comprehensible input in English. (For the same reason, Krashen notes, few Americans have learned the Celsius scale: our thermometers alternately display temperatures in the familiar Fahrenheit scale.) Meanwhile the teacher using concurrent translation has little incentive to make the lesson understandable in the second language, that is, to help the students "negotiate meaning." The ineffective-ness of this method has been confirmed empirically by researchers including Dorothy Legaretta-Marcaida and Lily Wong Fillmore. Various ways of alternating language use – morning-afternoon, different days, "preview-review" lessons – have proven more beneficial. Without instantaneous translations, children become more attentive and motivated to figure out what the teacher is saying in English.

Krashen's theory also underscores the futility of traditional approaches to ESL and foreign-language teaching that stress form over function, whether through memorizing rules (grammar-translation and cognitive methods) or through mind-less exercises to illustrate "the structure of the week" (audiolingual method). Because such techniques have nothing to do with real communication, students have trouble focusing on content; comprehensible input is limited.

"Learning about" a language, gaining conscious knowledge of its syntax and usage, can serve a **monitor,** or editing, function. By applying grammatical rules, we can produce more "correct" speech or writing. But conscious knowledge alone is inadequate in communicative situations, for three reasons. First, grammar books are woefully incomplete when compared with the complex set of rules internalized by native speakers of a language. Linguists "have described only a fraction" of the structure of any natural language (including English), Krashen says, and the per-centage taught in class is even smaller. Second, most people are unable or unwilling to learn all these rules. Third, for the tiny minority who can successfully "focus on form" while communicating, the process of recall is still too slow to sustain a nor-mal conversation.

Another misplaced emphasis is teachers' impatience for oral production in the second language before students are ready. "Speaking per se does not cause lan-guage acquisition," Krashen argues, but follows from it as "a result of obtaining comprehensible input." This corollary of the input hypothesis explains why LEP children typically exhibit a **silent period** of as much as six months after entering school and then suddenly start speaking in English. "When they begin to speak, they are not beginning their acquisition," he says. "They are showing off their com-petence."

That this process occurs naturally does not mean it is smooth or easy. Psychological and attitudinal factors can, and usually do, interrupt the functioning of the language acquisition device. Krashen groups such negative influences under the term **affective filter.** These include anxiety, lack of self-confidence, and inade-quate motivation to speak the second language, any of which can retard acquisition by keeping comprehensible input from "getting through." Adults seem to be especially hindered by such barriers.

In this respect young children appear to have an advantage over their elders. Before puberty they tend to be less self-conscious about performance in a new tongue and more comfortable in their interactions with native speakers, an important source of comprehensible input. On the other hand, **low self-esteem** – which is common among poor, minority children who speak a low-status language – often coincides with anxiety or hostility toward learning in general and toward English in particular. Such attitudes "raise the affective filter," or reduce the amount of input that is comprehensible, thus slowing the acquisition of English.

Instructional techniques have a strong impact in the affective realm, either reinforcing or reducing the obstacles to language acquisition. Teachers who encourage students' attempts to communicate real messages tend to "lower" the affective filter. By contrast, calling attention to students' errors is likely to heighten their self-consciousness. Failing to respect a child's silent period and attempting to force speech production, rather than allowing English to "emerge" on its own, can be counterproductive. According to Tracy Terrell, creator of the Natural Approach to ESL, this mistake "will at best delay language acquisition ... and at worst may create blocks to [it], blocks which later could prove to be quite difficult to remove."

It is here, in the affective realm, that native-language instruction can supply an antidote to common problems in second-language teaching. A bilingual-bicultural curriculum, merely by recognizing the value of a minority language and culture, can enhance a LEP child's self-esteem and provide a more comfortable environment for English acquisition. And this is only the beginning of bilingual education's benefits, Krashen says – benefits that he, as a longtime ESL professional, only came to recognize in mid-career.

While research is steadily demonstrating that native-language instruction facilitates English acquisition, the conclusion remains controversial. For many educators as well as lay persons, the notion of "go East to get West" – or study Spanish to learn English – appears to defy common sense. Krashen's own conversion, he recalls, came around 1980, during a discussion of Jim Cummins's work on native-language literacy.

Interaction of First and Second Languages

In exploring how first-language skills influence both second-language acquisition and academic achievement, Cummins challenged the conventional wisdom about bilingualism. He began in the mid-1970s with a critique of oversimplified notions on both sides of the bilingual education debate. First, Cummins says, there was the "intuitively appealing argument ... that deficiencies in English should be remediated by intensive instruction in English." In other words, teaching LEP students in their mother tongue seemed to be a costly diversion from English acquisition. Second, there was the popular rationale for bilingual instruction – indeed, the argument had shaped the first decade of federal policy – that children cannot learn in a language they have yet to master. Cummins believed that neither hypothesis could stand up to theoretical examination and that both were contradicted in practice by successful programs.

The "insufficient exposure" idea, still a mainstay of opposition to bilingual education, was summed up by the late Representative John Ashbrook of Ohio. He charged that Title VII was

> actually preventing children from learning English. Some day somebody is going to have to teach those young people to speak English or else they are going to become public charges. ... When children come out of the Spanish-language schools or Choctaw-language schools which call themselves bilingual, how is our educational system going to make them literate in what will still be a completely alien tongue?

Despite the persistence of such assumptions, Cummins says, they are strongly contradicted by research: "The results of virtually every bilingual program evaluated during the past 50 years show either no relationship or a negative relationship between amount of school exposure to the majority language and academic achievement in that language."

Moreover, there is no reason to believe that first and second languages function independently in the brain, or that knowledge and skills acquired in one are not transferable to the other. An implicit "theory" of **separate underlying proficiency** – which logically follows from the view that native-language development comes at the expense of second-language development – has "not one shred of evidence" to support it, Cummins says. Taken to its logical extreme, this cognitive model would "leave the bilingual in the curious predicament" of being unable to "communicate with himself." When switching languages, such persons would be hard-pressed to translate what they had heard or said.

In opposition to this notion, Cummins has advanced a theory of **common underlying proficiency**. That is, skills in different languages inhabit the same part of the brain, reinforcing each other at the base while differing at the surface. In this "dual iceberg" model of the bilingual mind, features that are most cognitively demanding and most detached from contextual aids, such as literacy, "are interdependent across languages." On the other hand, the "surface aspects" of language differ substantially between, say, English and Swahili. Cummins's **interdependence hypothesis** predicts that a child who has mastered the basics of reading and thinking in the first language will perform well on entering a second-language environment. Because of common underlying proficiency, students do not need to relearn these skills.

Successful bilingual programs provide empirical support for Cummins's theory. The full range of proficiencies known as literacy appears to transfer readily, an effect that has been documented even for languages whose writing systems differ radically, such as Vietnamese and English, Japanese and English, or Turkish and Dutch. Krashen puts it quite simply: "Once you can read, you can read." Empirical studies have also shown that knowledge and skills in subjects like mathematics or social studies, once acquired in the first language, are retained when instruction shifts to the second language. Given achievement tests in English, students often perform well even though they learned the material in Spanish.

For the input hypothesis, the implications are significant. An English learner who has kept up in math through Spanish instruction will benefit doubly when studying the subject in a sheltered English classroom. "He will not only get more math; he'll get more English," Krashen explains, as compared to a student who has less contextual knowledge to make math lessons comprehensible in English. He adds that "the goal of bilingual programs is English literacy. The route is through the first language. ... You learn to read by reading, by making sense out of print. Vocabulary grows, grammar grows, spelling ability grows, good writing style grows. It's easier to make sense out of print in a language you understand."

Two Types of Language Proficiency

Cummins also took issue with the dominant paradigm supporting bilingual education in the 1970s, the common-sense idea that children are inevitably handicapped when there is a "mismatch" between the languages of home and school. The U.S. Commission on Civil Rights articulated this view in 1975: "Lack of English proficiency is the major reason for language-minority students' academic failure. Bilingual education is intended to ensure that students do not fall behind in subject matter content while they are learning English." In other words, children cannot succeed academically in a language they have yet to fully acquire. Cummins responds that, however well intentioned, this explanation has been invalidated by the success of immersion programs for English-speaking children in Canada and the United States. From the outset such students learn through the medium of the second language, with English instruction phased in later.

At a theoretical level, he argues, the **language mismatch hypothesis** reflects "an inadequate understanding of what is meant by 'English proficiency.'" Instruction in a child's first language is "much more than an interim carrier of subject matter content. Rather, it is the means through which the communicative proficiency … is developed" that underlies literacy, in both English and the native language. Cummins is not referring to linguistic ability in general but to the kind of linguistic skills that are essential for success in school. Fostering, rather than disrupting, children's native-language development thus becomes critical to their long-term academic performance. Yet the heavy emphasis on transitional forms of bilingual education, long favored by policymakers in the United States, has worked against this goal. Cummins warns that hurrying children into the English mainstream "is likely to result in the creation of **academic deficits** in language-minority students" (emphasis added). This may well explain the disappointing results of many TBE programs.

In considering the nature of language proficiency, Cummins looked for ways to explain two well documented phenomena that the linguistic mismatch hypothesis could not account for:

- Disproportionate numbers of children from linguistic minority backgrounds, judged by their teachers to be fluent in oral English, were nevertheless falling behind academically after being reassigned to regular classrooms.
- Such students tended to perform poorly not only in English but also in their mother tongue, a syndrome sometimes described as "illiteracy in two languages."

One explanation, Cummins hypothesized, was that educators were failing to differentiate between two very different types of second-language proficiency. He termed these **basic interpersonal communications skills** (BICS) and **cognitive-academic language proficiency** (CALP). More than a simple dichotomy between conversational and academic language, the BICS/CALP distinction is based on a functional analysis of linguistic skills required in different situations. There is no sharp line of demarcation between the two types of proficiency, but rather a continuum of evolving skills.

A good example of BICS is "playground English," which relies heavily on nonlinguistic cues and context – gestures, intonations, shared knowledge, etc. – to facilitate communication. In addition, it serves purposes that are primarily social rather than intellectual. Thus BICS involves, according to Cummins's description, "considerably less knowledge of language itself" – that is, a more restricted vocabulary and simpler syntax – than children need in academic pursuits.

At the other end of the continuum is CALP, or "classroom English." This is the kind of proficiency required for abstract, analytical thinking and the expression of complex meaning, with limited support from external context. Children need CALP, for example, when writing a journal entry describing what they have learned or when making a persuasive oral presentation on an issue of the day. While not limited to literacy, these advanced skills are, in Cummins's terms, "literacy-related"; thus they are acquired primarily *through* the written word.

Falling at points in between on the continuum[5] are activities such as copying words from the blackboard or filling out worksheets, which are decontextualized but cognitively undemanding, and reading or discussing books with plenty of illustrations, which may be cognitively demanding but are rich in context. Cummins's framework is represented by the matrix shown in Figure 8–1. The pedagogical implication he draws is that students should be challenged intellectually while being provided the "contextual and linguistic supports" to do academic work in the second language: "In other words, optimal instruction for linguistic, cognitive, and academic growth will tend to move from Quadrant A to B, and from Quadrant B to D. Quadrant C activities may be included from time to time for reinforcement or practice of particular points."

FIGURE 8–1
Conceptual Foundation of the BICS/CALP Distinction

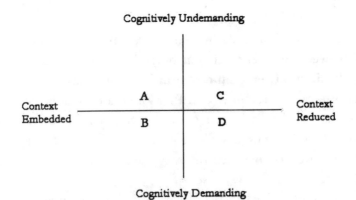

Source: Jim Cummins, *Language, Power and Pedagogy: Bilingual Children in the Crossfire* (Clevedon, U.K.: Multilingual Matters, 2000).

In this developmental process, children are naturally quicker to master BICS – "context-embedded" skills that are linguistically less sophisticated. By contrast, CALP includes command of the "process" words and complex grammatical structures that are needed to succeed in the "context-reduced" tasks of schooling. Empirical studies have found that second-language learners tend to acquire age-appropriate oral skills within three to five years, while it typically takes them four to seven years to catch up academically with native speakers of the target language (see Chapter 9).

Thus when English learners are "transitioned" into mainstream classrooms within three years or less – a common practice and, in some states, a legal requirement – they may have mastered BICS but are still acquiring CALP. No wonder these students are at a disadvantage, Cummins concludes. Lacking the tools needed to do grade-level academic work, they quickly fall behind and tend to stay behind, because English-proficient students "are not standing still waiting for English language learners to catch up."

Still the question remains: Why do these students fail to reap the benefits of bilingualism, such as the transfer of literacy skills and content knowledge, which have been documented for those who make a more gradual transition to English? While acknowledging that various sociopolitical factors are also involved, Cummins has proposed a linguistic explanation known as the **threshold hypothesis**. For the positive effects of bilingualism to be realized and for "cognitive deficits" to be avoided, he asserts, there is a "threshold level" of proficiency that children must reach in their first language, a certain degree of CALP, that is necessary to support academic achievement in the second language. Yet this is precisely what students are denied in subtractive educational programs. Pushing LEP children into the English mainstream prematurely interrupts the development of CALP in the native language. This fosters a gradual loss of mother-tongue skills or, at best, a failure to develop them beyond a basic level. **Partial** or **limited bilingualism** is often the fate of such students, according to Cummins. While they may acquire adequate conversational skills in both languages, they never fully develop their cognitive capacities in either.

Conversely, studies in Sweden, Canada, and the United States have shown that students who immigrate *after* acquiring literacy skills in their native language significantly outperform their counterparts who are schooled entirely through the second language. Indeed, in a relatively short time, "late arrivals" to American schools have scored higher when tested in English, despite having had less **time on task** in English-language classrooms (see Chapter 9). This pattern lends support to the hypothesis that reaching some level of CALP – or, at least, literacy and academic knowledge – in the native language brings important academic benefits.

'Empowering' Linguistic Minorities

Notwithstanding his hypotheses about the role of native-language development, Cummins has come to believe that language of instruction is probably not the most significant variable for English learners. He suggests that "sociocultural determinants of minority students' school failure are more fundamental than linguistic factors." Bilingual instruction is merely one feature of the "educational intervention" that is necessary. To be effective, he argues, schooling must "counteract the power relations that exist within the broader society." That is, it must remove the racial and linguistic stigmas of being a minority child. "Power and status relations between minority and majority groups exert a major influence on school performance," he explains. The lower the status of a "dominated group," the lower the academic achievement.

Cummins cites research on the school failure of Finnish immigrants in Sweden, where historically they have faced discrimination, as compared with their success in Australia, where being a Finn carries no social stigma. Children of the Burakumin minority "perform poorly in Japan, but just as well as other Japanese students in the United States." Rudolph Troike gives the example of Maori children in New Zealand, who enter school speaking English but are soon outperformed by Samoans, a nonstigmatized minority group that arrives with limited English skills. In other words, social expectations seem to exert a significant influence on academic outcomes. The late anthropologist John Ogbu hypothesized that **immigrant minorities**, who voluntarily adopt a new society and tend to see their lowly status as temporary, have an advantage over **caste minorities**, who are acutely aware of ethnocentrism, feel that their options for advancement are limited, and may internalize messages about their "inferiority." This could help to explain why the children of Mexican immigrants generally fare better in school than Mexican American students who have become acculturated to the United States *(see Chapter 1)*.

Schools have tended to perpetuate the marginalization of minority students, Cummins says, by mirroring the "coercive relations of power" that characterize the wider society. Cultures other than those of the dominant group are treated as substandard, primitive, threatening, exotic, or at best irrelevant to American life. Limited English speakers placed in all-English programs inevitably perceive a negative message about the language they brought from home. Even in transitional bilingual programs, the native language is often merely tolerated as a necessary evil rather than respected as a resource. In reaction, many language-minority students exhibit what Cummins calls **bicultural ambivalence**, or shame of the first culture and hostility toward the second. Bilingual teachers often remark on the poignant spectacle of students who stop using their vernacular, even though their English skills remain poorly developed. Peer pressure plays a role here in perpetuating negative messages about minority languages and cultures. In large part, however, children are "disempowered" by their interactions with the school, including their experiences in classrooms where teachers may have the best of intentions but lack the sensitivity or the strategies to counteract the stigmas children feel.

An important part of the solution, Cummins argues, are interventions that lead to the **empowerment** of minority students. To take a simple example, activities that encourage them "to take pride in their cultural background" can bring both social and academic benefits. Ideally, this should include a prominent role for the native language. Where that proves impossible for logistical or political reasons, teaching techniques can still be used that recognize and value children's mother tongue (e.g., by asking them to share with English-speaking classmates a daily word or, for older students, an occasional poem or story from their language).

The success of many developmental bilingual programs, Cummins suggests, may owe more to their affirmation of the English learner's cultural identity than to their linguistic effects. Conversely, he asks, "Is the failure of many minority students in English-only immersion programs a function of cognitive/academic difficulties, or of students' ambivalence about the value of their cultural identity?" Either way, he says, additive bilingualism is the more appropriate treatment.

A 'Theoretical Framework' and Its Critics

The theories elaborated by Cummins and Krashen have considerable explanatory power, accounting for a wide range of classroom phenomena that earlier paradigms did not incorporate. They are also elegant in their simplicity, easy to grasp and communicate. Not surprisingly, the work of the two researchers has had intuitive appeal for educators familiar with the challenges facing English language learners, and it has been enormously influential in program design. In the early 1980s officials at the California Department of Education launched an effort to publicize and test what has become known as the Cummins-Krashen "theoretical framework." The pedagogical result was a research-based, **gradual-exit model** of bilingual education that stressed the development of students' native-language skills *(see Chapter 10)*. Generally speaking, the academic outcomes of such programs have been both impressive and consistent with the paradigm advanced by Cummins and

Krashen – which, it should be noted, is not a unified theory, but rather a constellation of several more or less compatible hypotheses.

Like all scientific theories, these remain "unproven" in any final sense, as the researchers themselves have repeatedly pointed out. Elements of the framework are continually being tested, refined, and debated. While it has provided important guidance to practitioners, many questions – and no doubt, many imperfections – remain.

Academic critics of bilingual education have had remarkably little to say about the theories of Cummins and Krashen, other than to challenge them as empirically unsupported.[6] Christine Rossell and Keith Baker, for example, assert that what they call "the facilitation hypothesis" – the transferability of literacy and academic knowledge between languages – relies on studies that have "major methodological problems," or that it "misinterprets" the findings of more rigorous research. "It is true," they concede, that such studies have shown

> it is easier to teach a second language to individuals who are literate in their native tongue, [but] this tells us nothing about how non-literate individuals should be taught, nor the language in which they should be taught. It is probably also true that a person who has been unable to learn to ride a bike is a harder person to teach to ski, but this does not necessarily mean that the best way to teach a non-bike rider how to ski is to spend years teaching them how to ride a bike. The bilingual education literature, however, is rife with such unwarranted inferential leaps.

This objection is compelling only if one subscribes to the notion of separate underlying proficiency: that children's first- and second-language skills, not to mention their oral and literate skills, develop in ways that are basically autonomous. No linguist in the Chomskyan era would endorse such a theory, for which Rossell and Baker themselves offer no empirical support. It is also worth noting that Cummins and Krashen have never insisted that LEP students must be taught literacy for several years in their first language before being instructed in English – indeed, they have counseled against such practices as unnecessary and possibly harmful. Rather, they have argued that the "transfer effect" has theoretical significance for how second languages are acquired.

More substantive criticisms of their work have come from researchers who acknowledge the effectiveness of well designed bilingual education programs but have raised questions about the adequacy and implications of theories such as the threshold hypothesis, the BICS/CALP distinction, or the input hypothesis. In other words, these concerns are expressed not by opponents in a politicized debate over language of instruction, but by colleagues who share many of the same values and priorities. Hence they merit heightened attention.

Deficit Model?

Challenges to Cummins's work have centered primarily on whether his theories, notwithstanding their emphasis on "empowering minority students," imply what amounts to a **deficit model**. Specifically, does the threshold hypothesis locate the source of academic failure for language-minority children in their own cognitive inadequacies stemming from a failure to acquire full proficiency in any language? In a related vein, does the BICS/CALP distinction confuse academic skills such as literacy with linguistic development, in effect ascribing "superior" properties to the **standard language** of the educated classes?

These are more than semantic quibbles. It matters a great deal in the classroom whether students are conceived as linguistically different or linguistically disabled. "If teachers believe that some children have low language ability in both languages," notes linguist Jeff MacSwan, "then this belief may have a strongly negative effect on their expectations for these children and the curricular content and teaching practices [that] students receive." He argues that such misconceptions are fostered by the notion of **semilingualism**, or lack of full competence in any language.

Semilingualism stems conceptually from **verbal deprivation** theory (a close relative of **cultural deprivation** theory; *see Chapter 4*). An earlier example, proposed by the British sociologist Basil Bernstein, is the hypothesis that children reared in working-class homes acquire only **restricted codes**, defined as "particularistic ... context-bound ... inexplicit" forms of speech that are insufficient for analytical thinking. Higher cognitive activities, Bernstein asserted, require **elaborated codes**, the more abstract, "context-independent," explicit kinds of language that are acquired from literate parents. Applying this hypothesis in the 1960s, some U.S. researchers in educational psychology concluded that many poor, African-American children were so retarded in speech development by their family backgrounds that they effectively had "no language at all." Thus they had no hope of succeeding in school without intensive efforts to "fix" their language deficiencies.[7]

Yet this deficit model, which relied heavily on linguistic arguments, was advanced by social scientists who had no expertise in linguistics. Their methods of assessing children's language proficiency were not only crude but also permeated by class and ethnic prejudices. Essentially their research measured the distance of nonstandard English speakers from the grammar, vocabulary, and speech styles of middle-class speakers of English, and pronounced the former group inferior in logical and analytical capacity. William Labov, a linguist who reviewed some of the test questions used, found that they lacked any scientific basis: "We cannot conclude that the [black] child has no grammar, but only that the investigator does not understand the rules of grammar." Lavov's own research demonstrated that children who spoke **African-American Vernacular English** (AAVE) were just as capable of expressing complex ideas as those who communicated in Standard English. The AAVE speakers simply differed in their form of expression, which happened to carry a social stigma. "There is no reason to believe that any nonstandard vernacular is in itself an obstacle to learning," Labov concluded. "That educational psychology should be strongly influenced by a theory so false to the facts of language is unfortunate; but that children should be the victims of this ignorance is intolerable."

The concept of semilingualism extends verbal deprivation theory to children whose vernacular is undergoing displacement by a socially dominant language, either through subtractive bilingualism in the classroom, unstable bilingualism in the community, or both. It asserts that many such children never achieve "native-like" command of either language, remaining limited in their vocabulary and syntactic knowledge and thus poorly equipped to perform "cognitive tasks" that are essential to school learning: manipulating abstract concepts, drawing analogies and inferences, organizing thoughts systematically, and so forth.

If this reasoning sounds familiar, it is because semilingualism is an essential component of the threshold hypothesis (although Cummins has repudiated the term as pejorative and renamed it "limited bilingualism"). Its purpose is to explain why knowing two languages sometimes has negative rather than positive effects on intellectual growth. Among other limitations, semilingual children are said to have a restricted **repertoire**, or vocabulary size, in literacy-related aspects of both languages – for example, lacking the "process" words needed for abstract thinking. The concept is also relevant to the BICS/CALP distinction because acquiring conversational but not academic English would be considered one, and arguably the most important, form of semilingualism.

At a practical level this theory has exerted a strong influence on language assessment practices. In several states language-minority students enrolling in school, unlike English-background students, are routinely tested for proficiency in their mother tongue. Using assessment instruments based on the threshold hypothesis, schools have classified substantial numbers of children as "non-nons" – that is, "nonverbal in both English and their native language." In Los Angeles, for example, there were 6,800 students in this category in 1996. Although the validity of these assessments is questionable, such children are typically tracked into "low ability groups" or assigned to special education.[8]

Prescriptivism

Cummins has insisted that he is not advancing a deficit theory, in the sense of a blame-the-victim analysis, because he attributes limited bilingualism to sociopolitical and pedagogical factors rather than to inherent deficiencies of language-minority children. For linguists like MacSwan, however, this is a distinction without a difference. Semilingualism and the BICS/CALP dichotomy add up to a deficit theory, he argues, because they assert a form of **prescriptivism**.[9] That is, they imply superior language abilities for those who have acquired the **discourse styles** typical of the middle class, in particular the literary discourse used in the classroom and on achievement tests. It goes without saying that children of any background must learn academic language to succeed in academic domains. Yet MacSwan argues there is no reason to believe that mastery of academic language represents a higher "level" of linguistic competence than, say, the language of boatbuilders or farmers, "who will know many concepts and words utterly foreign to academics." Each of these discourse styles, or **speech registers**, is culturally specific – whether to the school, the shipyard, or the barnyard. Few would argue that, in itself, a lack of cultural knowledge denotes a cognitive deficit.

In effect, however, the concepts of semilingualism and BICS/CALP assert that failure to master one prestigious form of culture – literacy – means failure to acquire full competence in any language. Presumably this linguistic disability would affect not only limited bilinguals but all **nonliterates**, including entire cultures that lack writing systems (MacSwan notes that a majority of the world's languages have none), not to mention the vast majority of humans who lived before 1455, when Gutenberg's invention of movable type began to make literacy accessible on a mass scale. Such persons are no doubt at a disadvantage in print-saturated Western societies. But, by lacking literacy skills, are they less able to use language for higher cognitive functions? Or is this merely a value judgment based on social prejudice? MacSwan adds:

> There are numerous literate practices that are not normally taught in school, such as storytelling, text recital, rapping, songwriting, Morse Code, and Braille, to name a few. Why should an inability to read and write correspond

to deficient levels of linguistic competence in a way that inabilities in these other literate practices do not?

In fact, he says, there is no evidence that nonliterate individuals have less than fully acquired "the linguistic principles that govern their language." Reading and writing skills are not aspects of language competence per se; they are more like "technologies" for using language in various ways. To be sure, mastering these technologies takes time. Children from educated homes have an important advantage because, by the time they start school, they are already quite familiar with the speech registers that are used for educational purposes. Students who have never encountered those registers outside of school have to work much harder to acquire them. Yet they are perfectly capable of doing so, building on the basic competence they have acquired in their native language by age 5 or 6.

English learners naturally face additional hurdles. Simultaneously they must struggle to acquire (1) an entirely new linguistic system, and (2) content knowledge and literacy skills, *including* the literate registers of English. MacSwan and coauthor Kellie Rolstad argue that the tasks should be differentiated in this way – language proficiency on the one hand, academic learning on the other – because confusing the two tends to result in a deficit analysis. They warn that it is not only misleading but potentially harmful to label children as linguistically (and thus cognitively) deficient when they are merely lagging in academic achievement, a lag that is usually due to an incomplete acquisition of English.

In place of BICS/CALP, the two linguists have proposed an alternative construct, which they call **second language instructional competence** (SLIC). It does not refer to native-language proficiency, but simply to the stage of second-language development at which a child is able to function at grade level in a second-language classroom. A student who is still acquiring SLIC "is not considered cognitively less developed; she simply has not yet learned enough L2 to effectively learn through it." To do so, it is necessary to master not one but numerous aspects of academic language. As Kellie Rolstad explains, LEP students

> need to learn all the registers of the subjects they study in school, each with its peculiar vocabulary and whatever other linguistic features that ... [are] required for that student to engage the subject matter at hand. In other words, it matters less what a student scores on some global test of English proficiency than whether that student is able to understand the language of instruction sufficiently well at that moment, in that context, to participate in that lesson and learn from it. ...

Imagine a student who was schooled in Mexico, where she was very good at math, who can easily participate in most math lessons taught in English. She can be said to have SLIC in math, although she may need support whenever word problems are involved. This same student may not have SLIC in social science – except for when her class begins a unit on Mexico. ... SLIC is situational, perhaps even quixotic, and only a teacher who understands the apparent paradox of a student seeming to take two steps forward, then one step back, can recognize by working closely with that student where she has SLIC and where she does not, and hence where she can participate with minimal support and where she needs substantial, perhaps native-language, support.

In response to such criticisms, Cummins has denied any intent to suggest that CALP is "superior" to BICS, or that it is necessarily acquired later in developmental sequence. The two types of language proficiency simply "follow different developmental patterns": basic conversational skills reach an early "plateau," generally by the time children start school, while literacy-related skills such as vocabulary continue to develop "throughout our lifetimes." In addition, he has recently begun to describe BICS and CALP as different "functional registers," albeit with different cognitive-academic properties. The key point to recognize, Cummins argues, is that "conversational fluency in English is [not] a good indicator of 'English proficiency'" in general. Confusing the two "has resulted in countless bilingual children being 'diagnosed' as learning disabled or retarded" – in other words, they have been victimized by a deficit hypothesis. On the importance of avoiding that outcome, he and his critics can firmly agree. Meanwhile the theoretical debate continues.

Other Frameworks

Krashen's input hypothesis has come under criticism of a different sort: as a premature attempt to synthesize existing knowledge about second-language acquisition. Its claims are too "broad and sweeping," argues Barry McLaughlin of the University of California, Santa Cruz. "If the field of second-language acquisition is to advance, it cannot, at an early stage of its development be guided by a theory that provides all the answers. ... More limited and more specific theories are needed at this stage, not a general, all-inclusive theory."

McLaughlin is one of several critics who believe it is simplistic to claim, as Krashen does, that languages are acquired in "one fundamental way," by "understanding messages." While few would deny a role for comprehensible input, they have advanced hypotheses incorporating other factors as well. In contrast to Krashen's theory, these contending explanations put at least some stress on conscious knowledge of grammatical rules and vocabulary, arguing in effect that "learning becomes acquisition." For example:

- The **skill-building hypothesis** asserts that "practicing" the consciously learned rules of a language gradually makes them "automatic."
- The **output plus correction hypothesis** assigns an important role to the negative feedback a student may receive when making errors in speaking the second language.
- The **comprehensible output hypothesis** claims that learning occurs when students struggle to make themselves understood, adjusting their output and internalizing (consciously or otherwise) rules that prove successful.

Krashen has responded that there are virtually no empirical data – from method comparison studies, for example – to support any of these hypotheses, whereas "comprehensible input-based methods are consistent winners." At a theoretical level, he advances the Chomskyan argument that "language is too complex to be consciously learned one rule at a time." While educated speakers of English are estimated to know about 156,000 words on average, "this could not be the result of 156,000 trips to the dictionary, 156,000 flash cards, or 156,000 fill-in-the-blank exercises." Moreover, the most sophisticated rules for English spelling have been shown to produce incorrect results more than 50 percent of the time. Thus it is hard to see how all these elements of language could be mastered through the relatively limited amount of error correction or skill-building that formal instruction can provide. On the other hand, Krashen notes, "clear gains and even high levels of proficiency can take place without ... skill-building, error correction, or comprehensible output. Each time this has occurred, acquirers had obtained comprehensible input."

Another contending framework, advanced by Lily Wong Fillmore of the University of California, Berkeley, portrays second-language acquisition as a multidimensional activity. That is, it incorporates the interactions among learners, speakers of the target language who serve as sources of input, and "the social setting in which the learning takes place." These components are involved in three complex "processes," which she terms

cognitive – what goes on in the heads of learners when they interact with the data on which they base their language learning; ... linguistic – how linguistic knowledge figures in second language learning [including] knowledge ... possessed by persons who provide input for the learners and the knowledge of a first language possessed by the learners; ... [and] *social* – the steps by which learners and speakers jointly create social contexts or situations in which communication in the target language is possible.

Wong Fillmore postulates that cognitive strategies differ significantly between first- and second-language acquisition. Unlike young children, second-language learners tend to be old enough to have well developed capacities for "memory, pattern recognition, induction, categorization, generalization, inference, and the like." Naturally they draw upon such skills to analyze "relationships between forms, functions, and meanings" in the target language. While specialized language-learning mechanisms still operate (Chomsky's language acquisition device), she argues that these are less prominent than in the case of first-language learning.

According to this theory, linguistic processes also differ since, unlike young children, second-language learners have first-language knowledge. Awareness of "linguistic categories such as lexical item, clause, and phrase" helps them make "educated guesses" about comparable features of the second language. Meanwhile speakers of the target language consciously simplify its form and content, using feedback from learners, to make input more comprehensible. Finally, social processes create an environment in which learners use their background knowledge, such as understanding of social rituals, to decipher what target-language speakers are saying. The latter must participate actively to ensure that real communication takes place in a context that is meaningful to both sides.

Notwithstanding differences in explaining how language acquisition/learning takes place, Wong Fillmore's model intersects with Krashen's theory in numerous ways. The pedagogical implications are virtually identical; indeed, they represent an area of wide agreement among researchers in the field. Amid all the sound and fury, even McLaughlin endorses Krashen's "prescriptions about language teaching ... basic assumptions about the need to move from grammar-based to communicatively oriented instruction, the role of affective factors in language learning, and the importance of acquisitional sequences in second-language development."

Bilingualism and the Brain

Preservation of languages and cultures was the overriding goal of bilingual education in the 19th century. Today, however, despite the growing popularity of two-way bilingual programs *(see Chapter 12)*, relatively few schools in the United

States strive to develop lasting bilingualism. Continuing native-language instruction beyond the point at which children become proficient in English is often viewed as politically suspect. At least in part, this resistance is due to lingering suspicions that fluency in more than one language may unduly tax the mind.

Until not long ago, a majority of educational psychologists regarded bilingualism as a cognitive liability for young children. As George Thompson insisted in a widely used college textbook in 1952:

> There can be no doubt that the child reared in a bilingual environment is handicapped in his language growth. One can debate the issue as to whether speech facility in two languages is worth the consequent retardation in the common language of the realm.

This conclusion relied largely on studies conducted in the 1920s and 1930s, when anti-immigrant biases may have influenced researchers. As an example, Kenji Hakuta cites a 1926 study by Florence Goodenough that compared language use among several ethnic groups and found an inverse correlation between median IQ and the amount of foreign speech in the home. Goodenough concluded that either the persistence of minority tongues was "one of the chief factors in producing mental retardation," or that "those nationality groups whose average intellectual ability is inferior" were slow to learn English. In this period, adds Barry McLaughlin, a number of experiments determined that "bilingual children often must think in one language and speak in another, with the result that they become mentally uncertain and confused ... [or that] bilingualism is a mental burden for children, causing them to suffer mental fatigue."

Such studies, however, lacked controls for subjects' socioeconomic status and other factors that could affect test performance, Hakuta explains. Typically the experiments compared lower-class bilinguals with higher-class monolinguals. On the other hand, he expresses some skepticism about research that has reached the opposite conclusion: that proficiency in more than one language is a decided intellectual advantage.

A 1962 study by Elizabeth Peal and Wallace Lambert was the first of several to conclude that bilingualism enhances cognitive flexibility. Testing a group of 10-year-old French Canadian children, Peal and Lambert found that bilinguals significantly outperformed their monolingual counterparts on verbal and nonverbal intelligence tests. The study has been criticized, however, for selecting bilingual subjects whose English and French were equally developed. At a young age, the critics pointed out, such **balanced bilinguals** were likely to be gifted children. Their intellectual edge may have accounted for their bilingualism, rather than vice versa.

In his own research Hakuta sidestepped this methodological problem by focusing solely on children with varying degrees of bilingualism. In a three-year longitudinal study of Hispanic elementary school students in New Haven, Connecticut, he measured nonverbal intelligence (using Raven's Progressive Matrices) and **metalinguistic awareness**, or the aptitude for abstract thinking about language. The results were mixed. More balanced bilingual children clearly performed better on Raven's, but metalinguistic awareness was only weakly related to ability in both languages (it was linked more closely with Spanish proficiency). This was puzzling, Hakuta says, because "the most logical route for bilingualism to have an effect on intelligence is through language."

Over time, however, children in the study who started out with stronger Spanish skills were more likely to become balanced bilinguals. That is, as students progressed through school, there was an increasingly strong correlation between native-language proficiency and English proficiency.[10] This finding is consistent with Cummins's interdependence hypothesis. At the same time, Hakuta observes that bilingualism has social and economic advantages that are unquestionable, if often ignored. He echoes the frustration of many bilingual educators who complain that as a nation we are squandering linguistic resources. Spanish-speaking children, for example, are seldom given an opportunity to continue native-language study after making the transition to English, usually by the 2nd or 3rd grade. As a result, their mother-tongue skills erode or, at best, "fossilize" at that level. On reaching high school, they may enroll in Spanish I – if they are still interested.

Whether the lack of language maintenance programs also represents a wasted opportunity for cognitive development remains a question for further study. Jim Cummins, however, expresses the leaning of most researchers in second-language acquisition when he says, "Bilingualism is not bad for the brain, and it's probably good."

Suggested Reading

Bialystok, Ellen, and Hakuta, Kenji. *In Other Words: The Science and Psychology of Second-Language Acquisition.* New York: Basic Books, 1994.

Cummins, Jim. *Language, Power, and Pedagogy: Bilingual Children in the Crossfire.* Clevedon, U.K.: Multilingual Matters, 2000.

Hakuta, Kenji. *Mirror of Language: The Debate on Bilingualism.* New York: Basic Books, 1986.

Krashen, Stephen D. *The Input Hypothesis: Issues and Implications.* New York: Longman, 1985.

MacSwan, Jeff, and Rolstad, Kellie. "Linguistic Diversity, Schooling, and Social Class: Rethinking Our Conception of Language Proficiency in Language Minority Education." In Christina Bratt Paulston and G. Richard Tucker, eds., *Sociolinguistics: The Essential Readings.* Oxford: Blackwell. 2003.

See also pp. 398–400.

Online
Resource
Guide

Collier, Virginia P. *Acquiring a Second Language for School.* National Clearinghouse for Bilingual Education (1995).

Gándara, Patricia. *Review of Research on the Instruction of Limited English Proficient Students: A Report to the California Legislature.* Linguistic Minority Research Institute (1999).

See also companion CD-ROM.

Internet
Links

Cummins, Jim. "Putting Language Proficiency in Its Place: Responding to Critiques of the Conversational/Academic Language Distinction." In Jasone Cenoz and Ulrike Jessner, eds., *English in Europe: The Acquisition of a Third Language.* Clevedon, UK: Multilingual Matters, 2000.
http://www.iteachilearn.com/cummins/converacademlangdisti.html

Hakuta, Kenji; Bialystok, Ellen; and Wiley, Edward. "Critical Evidence: A Test of the Critical Period Hypothesis for Second Language Acquisition."
http://www.stanford.edu/~hakuta/Docs/Critical%20Evidence.pdf

MacSwan, Jeff. "The Threshold Hypothesis, Semilingualism, and Other Contributions to a Deficit View of Linguistic Minorities." *Hispanic Journal of Behavioral Sciences* 22, no. 1 (2000): 3–45.
http://www.public.asu.edu/~macswan/hjbs2000.pdf

See also companion CD-ROM.

Notes

1. Echoing the view of classical rhetoricians, Locke acknowledged a place for grammar studies in the native tongue: "If Grammar ought to be taught at any time, it must be to one that can speak the Language already, how else can he be taught the Grammar of it. … Grammar being to teach Men not to speak, but to speak correctly and according to the exact Rules of the Tongue"; quoted in Dennis E. Baron, *Grammar and Good Taste: Reforming the American Language* (New Haven: Yale University Press, 1982), pp. 120–21.

2. The audiolingual method was also blessed by its timing. The National Defense Education Act of 1958 opened federal coffers to foreign-language teaching for the first time, authorizing grants for the purchase of costly "language lab" equipment and facilities.

3. Indeed, Eric Lenneberg, the leader of the critical period school, has argued that first-language acquisition in childhood is the key, because "the cerebral organization for language acquisition as such has taken place. … Since natural languages tend to resemble each other in many fundamental respects, the matrix for language skills is present"; quoted in Ellen Bialystok and Kenji Hakuta, *In Other Words: The Science and Psychology of Second-Language Acquisition* (New York: Basic Books, 1994).

4. Krashen calls this "the Paris argument." As he explains in *Under Attack: The Case Against Bilingual Education* (Culver City, Calif.: Language Education Associates, 1996):

   > Pretend that you have just received, and accepted, an attractive job offer in Paris. Your French, however, is limited. (You had two years of French in high school and one semester in college, and it was quite a while ago.) Before your departure, the company that is hiring you will send you the following information, in English: What to do when you arrive in Paris, how to get to your hotel, where and how to find a place to live, where to shop, what kinds of schools are available for your children, how French companies function (how people dress in the office, what time work starts and ends, etc.), and specific information about the functioning of the company and your responsibilities.
   >
   > It would be very useful to get this information right away in English, rather than getting it gradually as you acquire French. If you get it right away, the world around you will be much more comprehensible, and you will thus acquire French more quickly. Anyone who agrees with this, in my opinion, agrees with the philosophy underlying bilingual education.

5. Technically speaking, there are two continuums – relating to contextual support and cognitive demands – as represented by the horizontal and vertical axes of Figure 8–1. Cummins maintains that he is not postulating any direct developmental progression from BICS to CALP.

6. In a 1997 presentation to policymakers in California, Christine Rossell went so far as to claim that "Jim Cummins doesn't do research. … Nevertheless, he does do theories." Perhaps the most charitable response to this charge is that Rossell must be ignorant of Cummins's work, which includes approximately 300 research-related publications over a 30-year career. For a complete listing, see Colin Baker and Nancy H. Hornberger,

eds., *An Introductory Reader to the Writings of Jim Cummins* (Clevedon, U.K.: Multilingual Matters, 2001).

7. This was the genesis of the federal Head Start program.

8. Children were classified using the Language Assessment Scales (LAS) Español. According to Jeff MacSwan, the test is seriously flawed, allowing "very little opportunity for children to demonstrate their linguistic abilities." For example, if they shyly fail to respond, or answer *No sé* ("I don't know"), to questions about a Spanish-language story, a score of zero is entered, which is usually sufficient to classify them as "nonverbal." A study that independently assessed a sample of such students in Los Angeles found them to be no less competent in Spanish than students who had been rated fluent. MacSwan argues that, absent indications of some language disability, there is no reason to assess the native-language proficiency of normal children simply because they are from linguistic minority backgrounds. Yet the states of Arizona, California, Hawaii, New Jersey, and Texas require schools to do so, while Illinois, Indiana, New Hampshire, and Oklahoma recommend the practice; "The Threshold Hypothesis, Semilingualism, and Other Contributions to a Deficit View of Linguistic Minorities," *Hispanic Journal of Behavioral Sciences* 22, no. 1 (2000): 3–45.

9. Early forms of prescriptivism, typified by the European language academies of the 17th and 18th centuries, sought to enforce grammatical "correctness" – which just happened to coincide with the speech patterns of the upper classes. The tradition continues among self-appointed language mavens who bemoan the "corruption" of English by slang, neologisms, and nonstandard dialects. No doubt there is a case to be made for defending literary standards. But such judgments are essentially aesthetic. They have nothing to do with the scientific insights of the past century, which include the following:

    • In living languages, change is constant and unstoppable.
    • Variations in language usage are just that – differences that imply neither superiority nor inferiority.
    • **Language varieties**, often called "dialects," may differ in the number and power of their speakers, but not in expressive potential.
    • As a Yiddish linguist once said, "A language is a dialect with an Army and a Navy."

10. According to Hakuta, "when [children] first entered the bilingual program, their abilities in Spanish and English were unrelated. However, by the end of three years, there were correlations as strong as r = .70 between the languages"; see "Cognitive Development in Bilingual Children," paper presented at a meeting sponsored by the National Clearinghouse for Bilingual Education and the Georgetown University Bilingual Education Service Center, Rosslyn, Va., July 24, 1985.

9 Considering Program Alternatives

*J*im Cummins and Stephen Krashen could hardly be stronger advocates for bilingual education. Yet their work raises a series of logical questions about the potential value of alternative approaches in educating English learners:

- If **comprehensible input** is the key ingredient in acquiring English, why is native-language instruction necessary? Is bilingual education, with its funding demands, teacher shortages, and political headaches, the best pedagogical alternative?
- If **communication-based ESL** looks promising, especially when combined with sheltered English techniques for teaching other subjects, why not devote

more efforts to perfecting all-English programs?

- If English-speaking children in Québec can learn French through **total immersion** in the early grades, with all subjects taught in the second language, why can't language-minority children learn English in the same way in the United States?

These issues have come up repeatedly since the **Baker–de Kanter report** became public in 1981. After reviewing the research literature, this Education Department study concluded: "The case for the effectiveness of transitional bilingual education is so weak that exclusive reliance on this instructional method is clearly not justified." Baker and de Kanter advanced an alternative they hailed as "uniformly successful" wherever it had been evaluated: **structured immersion.**[1] As late as 1985, however, only nine "pure immersion programs" existed nationwide, according to Keith Baker, citing a survey by SRA Technologies as it embarked on a long-term, federally funded evaluation of this methodology (also known as the **Ramírez report**; *see below*).

Thus far the bulk of research evidence about immersion has come from Canada, where the methodology has proven quite successful with language-*majority* children. Immersion "may or may not" be appropriate for language-minority children in the United States, Baker and de Kanter conceded, but it "shows enough promise" that, at minimum, it should be tried. To evaluate this argument, it is necessary to examine what the Canadian immersion model is and is not.

Origins of French Immersion

In the early 1960s a dozen English-speaking parents in the Montreal suburb of St. Lambert began meeting to discuss their frustrations over the linguistic and cultural segregation of their community. This was during the period of Canada's history known as the Quiet Revolution. Longstanding social inequities had resulted in the mutual estrangement of the country's two major language communities. The Francophone minority was starting to protest its second-class status and limited access to government services. Although the nation was bilingual, most individuals were not. Out of economic necessity, French speakers were more likely to speak English than vice versa. Yet neither group seemed to have much to say to the other, a condition that came to be known as the "two solitudes," after a popular book of the postwar period.[2]

The Anglophone parents of St. Lambert, who favored a more integrated and harmonious society, believed it was important for their children to become fluent in

French. Research on language attitudes had shown that Canadians who were bilingual, whether Anglophone or Francophone, had more favorable perceptions of the other ethnic group. Unfortunately, the public schools, segregated by both language and religion, were doing a poor job of cultivating bilingualism. According to Olga Melikoff, a leader of the St. Lambert parents,

> Children were graduating from English Protestant schools in this province with little more knowledge of French than their parents had had, despite claims that the programs had been considerably improved over the years. [After 12 years of French study,] their knowledge was not perceptibly superior to that of graduates from English provinces of Canada and was not sufficient to enable the students to communicate with their French-Canadian neighbors. ... St. Lambert was in 1963 approximately 50 percent French, 50 percent English. It seemed inconceivable to the parents that the children of the two ethnic groups should remain "incommunicado" forever because of language differences.

Clearly something was wrong with the prevalent **audiolingual method** of French instruction.

Working with Wallace Lambert and Wilder Penfield, two McGill University researchers on bilingualism, the parents pressed the local Protestant school board to try a new approach. After initial resistance, in the fall of 1965 the board agreed to an experiment in French immersion, while expressing skepticism about its prospects. Fred Genesee, a psychologist at McGill, describes the program's stated goals:

- to provide the participating children with functional competence in both written and spoken aspects of French;
- to promote and maintain normal levels of English language development;
- to ensure achievement in academic subjects commensurate with students' academic ability and grade level; [and]
- to instill in the students an understanding and appreciation of French Canadians, their language, and culture without detracting in any way from the students' identity with and appreciation for English-Canadian culture.

The initial class of 26 English-speaking kindergartners entered a school program conducted entirely in French. In this **early total immersion** model, children first learned to read in the second language. One period of English language arts was introduced in grade 2.[3] Gradually the proportion of English was increased in other subjects until it reached about 60 percent by the end of elementary school. In grades 7 through 12, students were offered various courses in French "to maintain and further promote second-language competence," according to Genesee.

Immersion students were not mixed with native speakers of French, so that instruction could be conducted in a simplified version of the second language, featuring physical and contextual cues to make input comprehensible. Although the teachers were fluent bilinguals, at the outset they spoke to the children in French only. Recognizing that speech production lags comprehension in a second language – a phenomenon that results in a **silent period** of up to six months – the program's designers allowed students to use English to ask questions in class until the end of 1st grade.

To minimize students' anxiety, instructors avoided "overcorrecting" their errors in French, even as the study of grammar was incorporated. The curriculum placed an emphasis on teaching the second language *incidentally*, without making students conscious of their performance. The expectation, Genesee explains, was that children would be motivated to learn French if instruction fostered "a desire in the student to … learn the language to engage in meaningful and interesting communication." In addition, out of concern that the program might breed negative attitudes toward English-Canadian language and culture, pains were taken to ensure "a respect for English."

Judged against the standard of traditional foreign-language classes, immersion was a nearly unqualified success in teaching French. By the end of elementary school, reports Jim Cummins from his research on this program model, children achieved "native-like levels in the receptive aspects of the language, in their listening skills and their reading skills." Their speaking and writing skills were less developed, probably because they had limited interactions with Francophone peers, he says. Nevertheless, the immersion students became "quite fluent and quite comfortable in speaking French, for the most part."

But what about their overall progress in school? Did becoming bilingual impede their cognitive growth? Were children falling behind in academic subjects taught in French? Was the program retarding their English-language abilities? To the relief of parents and researchers alike, the experiment had none of these consequences. It confirmed the hypothesis that bilingualism could be attained *at no cost* to achievement in English or other subjects. Pupils can achieve functional competence in a second language, Wallace Lambert explains,

> without detriment to their home language skill development; without falling
> behind in the all-important content areas of the curriculum, indicating that

the incidental acquisition of French does not distract the students from learning new and complex ideas; without any form of mental confusion or loss of normal cognitive growth; and without a loss of identity or appreciation of their own ethnicity. Most important of all in the present context, immersion pupils also develop a deeper appreciation for French Canadians and a more balanced outlook toward them by having learned about the group and its culture.

Changes in the students' social attitudes were somewhat contradictory, however. Notwithstanding a strong respect for the culture of France, their reactions to French Canadians were less positive, especially as ethnic tensions heightened in Québec during the late 1960s. Functional bilingualism did enable the young Anglophones to form friendships with French-speaking children. Yet their contacts with members of the other language community remained unrepresentative.[4]

These patterns were confirmed by Genesee in a study of three total immersion programs for English speakers in the United States. Although students lagged in their native-language performance until instruction in English language arts was introduced, they eventually caught up academically. Meanwhile they "attained functional proficiency in the target language," while falling somewhat short of native-like command of grammar and vocabulary.

As Anglophone parents learned about the success of French immersion at St. Lambert, demand for the program spread throughout Canada. The 2001 census reported that 324,000, or more than 7 percent, of English-background students were enrolled (despite some decline during the 1990s, especially in western provinces). Program variations now include **delayed immersion**, beginning in the middle elementary grades, and **late immersion**, beginning early in secondary school. Where school administrators have remained resistant, Genesee says, efforts to persuade them have usually succeeded with the aid of a pesky group known as Canadian Parents for French.

Immersion for Linguistic Minorities?

There are virtually no English immersion programs for French-speaking children in Canada. Nor should there be, in the unanimous opinion of Canadian-immersion researchers, who insist that this approach is appropriate only for language-majority children. Baker and de Kanter's proposal to substitute immersion for bilingual education in the United States is especially dangerous, these experts warn. Richard Tucker, coauthor of the first major study of the St. Lambert experiment, explains: "Although the general assertion that many children can acquire a second language and content material coincidentally is, in all probability correct, it does not imply that the most effective way to educate every child, regardless of demographic, sociopolitical, or other circumstances, is by total [immersion] in a second language." That is, extralinguistic variables can be crucial in determining whether an educational treatment will be helpful or harmful to students.

The St. Lambert curriculum has proved effective because it provides sustained amounts of **comprehensible second-language input** in a low-anxiety environment. But this is only part of the story. As practiced in Canada, immersion is a *bilingual* program, which aims to develop students' academic language proficiency in English as well as French. A measure of its success is that, when tested in English, children do quite well in subjects that they have studied in French – an indication that skills and content knowledge are transferring across languages.

Moreover, early schooling in the second language does not appear to impede the development of first-language literacy for these students. For minority children in the United States, however, the pattern has been different. Initial instruction in English rarely leads to proficient or balanced bilingualism. Why the contrast in outcomes? According to Wallace Lambert, immersion means fundamentally different things to each group. For speakers of a powerful and prestigious language, the program fosters **additive bilingualism**. Children sense no stigma attached to their home language, only an invitation to acquire a new culture. For language-minority students, on the other hand, immersion means **subtractive bilingualism**, an effort to "wean" them from their mother tongue as quickly as possible. This distinction reflects the varying goals of immersion in the two countries, as well as sociolinguistic factors beyond educators' control.

Among English-speaking children in Canada, French immersion poses no threat to native-language development, Lambert says, because English is the high-status tongue throughout the country and even in the province of Québec. If immersion programs ignored English altogether, barring major social upheavals, Anglophone students would probably remain secure in their ethnic identity. Certainly they would have no shortage of opportunities to perfect their English skills. In the St. Lambert model, immersion offers pupils an opportunity to add a language to their repertoire, *without giving up their mother tongue*. Bilingualism thus becomes an educational "extra" that will pay social, academic, and economic dividends in the future. Lambert adds that there are likely to be cognitive benefits as well.

For French-speaking children, by contrast, the social and cultural dominance of English makes the first language "vulnerable to neglect and replacement," he argues. Thus an English immersion program "would result in a slow subtraction of the students' French and its replacement by English." Subtractive bilingualism, Lambert argues,

> can be devastating for children [who] are induced through social pressure in the school, community, and even in the home to put aside their home language and replace [it] as quickly and thoroughly as possible with English. ... The trouble is that for most language-minority children, the home language has been the critical linguistic system associated with the development of basic concepts from infancy on. It would be an enormous mental-gymnastic feat for these children to replace and reprogram these concepts in English ... and at the same time, try to keep up with English-speaking peers in subject matters that introduce new ideas which build on basic concepts.[5]

In choosing among educational treatments for promoting bilingualism, Lambert and Tucker have formulated the following guideline: "Priority in early years of schooling should be given to the language ... least likely to be developed otherwise – in other words, the language most likely to be neglected." This principle, they say, should signal a strong warning against immersion for English learners in the United States. Unlike the **bilingual enrichment** approach of St. Lambert, the Baker–de Kanter model is a **monolingual remedial** method that is likely to replace the languages of minority children. Rather than encouraging proficiency in two languages, structured immersion emphasizes linguistic and cultural assimilation.

'Time on Task'

Keith Baker has rejected what he calls "theoretical" objections to immersion for language-minority children in the United States, insisting that the approach must be judged in practice. In other words, he has generally declined to address the criticisms. This rhetorical strategy, dichotomizing between "mere theory" on the one hand and "hard facts" on the other, proved useful to the Reagan administration in promoting all-English alternatives to bilingual education *(see Chapters 6 and 7)*. Yet it obscures the reality that structured immersion proponents have advanced a language-learning theory of their own. With only one U.S. immersion program to point to in 1981 – and that characterization was disputed *(see below)* – Baker and de Kanter hypothesized why the model *should* be effective: "Practice makes perfect, and English is best learned by using it as much as possible throughout the school day." Christine Rossell and Michael Ross have summed up the rationale as follows: "Time on task – the amount of time spent learning a subject – is ... a good predictor of achievement" generally; therefore, all-English instruction must be a superior way to teach English. Rosalie Porter has also argued: "Education research, we have seen, makes the compelling case for time-on-task as the most important single determinant of success in learning *anything*."

Yet proponents of the **time-on-task hypothesis** have shown little eagerness to debate their ideas in principle. For example, how can this theory be reconciled with Chomskyan linguistics *(see Chapter 8)*, which conceptualizes language acquisition as a special kind of learning, predetermined by "hard-wiring" in the human brain and governed by its own rules? No one denies that English learners need time to acquire second-language proficiency, but what empirical evidence supports the claim that time is the key variable? How can time-on-task be reconciled with scientific studies (acknowledged by Baker, Rossell et al.) in which children who received substantial amounts of native-language instruction learned English at least as rapidly as those who were taught entirely in English?

Thus far answers to these questions have not been forthcoming. Baker, a sociologist, and Rossell, a political scientist, have steered clear of psycholinguistic areas in which they make no claims of expertise.[6] For the most part they have focused on empirical evidence from evaluation studies, maintaining that structured immersion "works better" than bilingual education. In short, they have never subjected time-on-task to a rigorous experimental test – that is, one in which it could be disproven.

Assessing the effects of structured immersion in the United States has been problematic, since until recently only a handful of such programs existed. Before 1998, when Proposition 227 mandated this approach, the state of California gave school districts the option to offer such programs, but few ever petitioned to do so. Under a Texas statute, eight districts were authorized to experiment with all-English approaches for LEP children, but the pilot projects ended in 1987 after most of them failed, according to Ramón Magallanes of the Texas Education Agency. In Houston, for example, the immersion students who scored highest on achievement tests were among the 60 percent who were repeating a grade.

With immersion being hailed as a panacea on the nation's editorial pages, some fear it could function more as a placebo, providing no real help to English learners. In 1986, Philadelphia introduced a curriculum known as ESOL Plus Immersion in response to rising enrollments of immigrants and refugees. The rationale, expressed by one district administrator, was that students would learn English faster if they could "interact with native speakers." In practice, this "immersion" model meant that LEP students would simply spend more time in mainstream classrooms, where they understood little of what went on, and less time receiving ESL or native-language instruction. Community activists, teachers, and parents attacked the program as a return to sink-or-swim.

The ambiguity of program labels also complicates research to evaluate alternatives to bilingual education. Inevitably, when models are compared, disputes arise over terminology. So-called immersion programs that have been favorably evaluated, such as the McAllen, Texas, kindergarten experiment cited by Baker and de Kanter in their 1981 report, often turn out to share key similarities with bilingual education. In this case the "immersion" model featured English instruction in the morning and Spanish reading in the afternoon. Students did well when compared with those in a bilingual model that used the outmoded **concurrent translation** methodology *(see Chapter 8)*. "What apparently happened in McAllen," observes Stephen Krashen, "is that children in a good bilingual program outperformed children in a poor bilingual program."

In the summer of 1987, news of a moderately successful "bilingual immersion" program in El Paso, Texas, became a public relations coup for the opponents of bilingual education when a journalist mischaracterized it as an English-only approach. After being repeated in other press accounts, the error was highlighted by opponents of bilingual education in an advisory report for the Reagan administration.[7] In fact, according to the El Paso school district, this was a "true bilingual education program" that included 60 to 90 minutes of Spanish instruction each day. On some standardized tests the bilingual immersion students performed better, on others worse, than their counterparts in classrooms featuring greater amounts of native-language instruction. In most cases, the district's evaluation found, there were no significant differences between the two groups.

Nevertheless, immersion enthusiasts continued to point to El Paso as proof of their method's superiority. Rosalie Porter, director of the U.S. English–funded READ Institute, released yet another evaluation of the district's programs under the headline "Immersion Boosts Student Achievement, Study Finds." According to this 1993 study by Russell Gersten, John Woodward, and Susan Schneider, "bilingual immersion" students in grades 4 through 6 outscored their peers in the TBE program on tests of language, reading, mathematics, and vocabulary. By the 7th grade, however, the differences between the two programs were "negligible." In other words, children receiving somewhat more native-language instruction eventually caught up with those receiving somewhat less.

Obviously such findings could be interpreted in numerous ways, and the study provided few details about how the native language was used; variables other than language of instruction may also have contributed to the slight differences between the two programs. But Porter had no hesitation in concluding: "The data definitely dispel the notion that transitional bilingual education is a superior approach to English immersion. While both methods seem equally effective for teaching language minority children, they take different periods of time to achieve the same academic results." Because it "boosted" English achievement test scores faster, El Paso's bilingual immersion program proved more "cost effective ... in a time of tightening school budgets," Porter argued.

Such politicized approaches do little to resolve the pedagogical issues. Indeed, they obscure a central question: What exactly distinguishes this form of "structured immersion" from transitional bilingual education, especially in cases where TBE features limited instruction in the native language? Keith Baker has offered contradictory answers, alternately saying that

> immersion programs use the native language only ... to clarify a point that was not understood when it was taught in English;

and that

> most immersion programs also teach language arts [in the native language] for 30 to 60 minutes a day.

Baker's critics maintain that his vagueness on this point muddles the discussion of pedagogical alternatives. Researcher Ann Willig has accused Baker of confusing the concepts **program** and **methodology**. "Immersion is a specific and successful methodology," she says, "that can be used in any type of program, including a bilingual program." For example, sheltered English, an immersion technique, is one component of the successful Case Studies bilingual curriculum *(see Chapter 10).*

Such debates over program labels are hardly trivial. According to the hypotheses of Cummins and Krashen, how first and second languages are employed is critical to the success of an educational treatment. The questions involve quality, not quantity, of instruction. Does the program use the mother tongue merely to provide translations, or does it seek to develop native-language literacy and other academic skills that will transfer to English? Is ESL focused heavily on memorization and skill-building exercises, or does it stress communication in meaningful contexts? Does sheltered instruction simply "water down" academic content, or do teachers consciously use what students already know to make lessons comprehensible and stimulate the growth of academic English?

Longitudinal Immersion Study

The most comprehensive evidence about structured immersion in the United States comes from the Ramírez report, a long-term, $4.1 million study released in 1991.[8] The U.S. Department of Education, which commissioned this research, sought to compare the effectiveness of **early-exit bilingual education** – the transitional model that had received more than 95 percent of Title VII funding up to that time – with two other contenders, all-English **immersion strategies**, and **late-exit** or **developmental bilingual education**. David Ramírez, the principal investigator, worked hard to overcome the design flaws of previous studies, for example, going to great lengths to ensure that comparison groups were carefully matched. Rather than add together apples and oranges, then take an average – as the **AIR report** had done *(see Chapter 7)* – he paid close attention to consistency in program labeling and selected only the best examples of each approach, so as to minimize the effects of poor implementation.

Initial classroom monitoring determined that the immersion programs were conducted in English more than 90 percent of the time, with the native language used "on an informal basis" for purposes of clarification. The early-exit programs, which mainstreamed children after two to three years, used English 65 to 75 percent of the time. The late-exit programs, featuring bilingual instruction through the 6th grade, used increasing amounts of English – from 10 percent in kindergarten to 60 percent by the 4th grade. This was a **longitudinal study**, which tracked the progress of individual students over a four-year period. It involved more than 2,000 Spanish-speaking children enrolled in nine school districts in five states (California, Florida, New Jersey, New York, and Texas). Student achievement was monitored beginning with the 1984–85 school year and ending in 1987–88.

Interim findings from this research became a closely guarded secret after its first-year data were leaked to *Education Week* in 1986. The sneak preview revealed that students in bilingual classrooms were outperforming their peers in immersion classrooms – in reading, language, and mathematics – and that the children who scored highest when tested in English were enrolled in late-exit programs that featured the most Spanish instruction. These findings were "unexpected," according to a memorandum by Ramírez at the time.

The interim results certainly came as a shock to time-on-task theorists, who had confidently predicted that the more English children heard in school, the faster they would progress in English. Among them was Keith Baker, the study's project officer at the Department of Education. Embarrassed by the disclosure, he insisted that no conclusions should be drawn from a single year's scores. "It's like trying to call the winner of the Kentucky Derby based on the horse that reaches the first pole," Baker argued. With his own horse trailing badly, however, he was inclined to modify his theory about the value of "using English as much as possible throughout the school day." Extended exposure to the second language, he hypothesized, "may fatigue the learner so that learning becomes very difficult." (Soon thereafter, he resumed his optimistic statements about the promise of structured immersion.) Meanwhile the Reagan administration clamped a tight lid on the immersion study and refused to release further test data, despite requests to do so from members of Congress. The embargo continued into the first Bush administration.

On both sides expectations for the study remained high, and so did the political stakes. If the early findings held up, they would relieve some of the pressure to divert Title VII grant funding from bilingual to all-English programs. If not, the opponents of bilingual education would have a formidable new weapon to brandish in policy battles.

When its final report was released, however, the Ramírez study provided less clarity than many had anticipated. For the most part, only minor differences in achievement were detected between students in immersion and early-exit bilingual classrooms. While children clearly excelled in the late-exit classrooms, for technical reasons their performance was not directly compared with that of their peers. The Department of Education, in releasing the study, declared "the three most common bilingual education methods" [sic] to be "effective in teaching LEP students." Therefore, "school administrators can choose the method best suited to their students, confident that, if well implemented, it will reap positive results."

This simplistic message was duly disseminated by the news media. While reporters were given the option of purchasing a copy of the full report (for $130), none did so, according to a department spokeswoman. News stories, relying on the official press release and an "executive summary," thus ignored or muddied several of the study's more significant findings. These may be summarized as follows:

- In immersion and early-exit programs – which taught children almost exclusively in English (with Spanish used only for clarification), or mostly in English (two-thirds to three-quarters of the time) – academic growth roughly paralleled that of English-proficient children in regular classrooms. But in both program models, student achievement leveled off well below national norms.
- In late-exit programs, which featured the most native-language instruction (90 percent in kindergarten, declining to 40 percent in grades 4 through 6),

progress in student achievement accelerated over time, approaching national norms by the 6th grade.

- These outcomes were further confirmed by variations among the late-exit programs themselves. In one district that lapsed into an early-exit model during the study, scores fell off dramatically. In another where Spanish was used most extensively, children's progress was most dramatic.

- Regardless of treatment, students generally took five years or longer to acquire academic proficiency in English. Only one-fourth of the children in immersion programs and one-fifth of those in early-exit programs had been mainstreamed after four years.

- In late-exit programs, parents were more likely to help with homework and take an interest in their children's schooling, apparently because of their greater familiarity with the language.

- Across the board, parents favored approaches that would give children a chance to develop competency in their native language as well as in English; only the late-exit programs offered this choice.

- In all three programs, teacher-centered methodologies provided a passive learning environment that gave students limited encouragement to think critically or to speak out in class.

Sensitive to the controversies surrounding bilingual education, David Ramírez chose to take a cautious statistical approach in analyzing his data. This meant paying close attention to issues of comparability among students, teachers, and communities, along with a host of other variables. Because none of the districts that offered late-exit programs also provided immersion or early-exit programs, he explains, it was impossible to make comparisons among all three while controlling for "school-level effects." Only immersion and early-exit approaches could be matched directly against each other.

Ramírez did draw indirect comparisons, however, by analyzing growth curves in student achievement against national norms using a statistical methodology known as TAMP analysis.[10] The study found that the progress of immersion and early-exit students slowed down by 3rd grade; their achievement paralleled but remained well below the 50th percentile. By contrast, late-exit students progressed along a steeper learning curve; while they had yet to overtake their English-speaking peers by 6th grade, they showed promise of doing so. Ramírez believes the implications are significant:

If your instructional objective is to help kids stay where they are – around the 25th percentile – then give them immersion or early exit and they'll keep their place in society. If your concern is to help kids catch up to the norming population, use more primary language. In the late-exit programs, they're growing faster in content areas and in English, too. It's really clear that you will not slow down a child's acquisition of English by providing large amounts of native-language instruction.

While the study concludes that structured immersion can be a viable alternative for LEP children, Ramírez adds a number of qualifiers. Immersion teachers need special training in oral language development and literacy; they need to master sheltered English techniques; and they need to be sufficiently bilingual to provide clarification in students' native language. "The danger," he explains, "is in lifting the cap [on funding for alternative programs] without any clear specifications. When most districts talk about immersion, they mean taking regular teachers and placing them in a bilingual classroom, looking for a way to exit kids as quickly as possible." In such cases students receive little more than **submersion**, with some ESL on the side. "We know that doesn't work," Ramírez says. In a few situations – for example, where bilingual teachers are unavailable or where students speak numerous languages – a quality immersion approach "may be all we can do," he concedes. "But is it really what we want? It doesn't cost you any more to provide a late-exit program than an immersion program. It's just a philosophical or political question. Do you want to help kids catch up? Or do you want to keep them down on the farm?"

Nevertheless, the Ramírez report failed to transcend some perennial pitfalls of evaluation research, according to an expert panel of the National Research Council (NRC).[11] After a detailed review, the panel declined to endorse most of the study's findings because of perceived weaknesses in its design and execution. Statistical techniques used to compensate for pre-existing differences were inadequate, the NRC concluded. It questioned whether comparability had been achieved between programs in different school districts and even in different schools within the same district. Thus it rejected the growth-curve analysis in which late-exit programs had proved superior.

The NRC did, however, accept as "compelling" one finding of the Ramírez report: when comparisons were made between kindergarten and 1st grade classrooms in the same school, early-exit bilingual students scored significantly higher in English reading than the immersion students. More generally, the panel found no evidence that native-language instruction impedes the acquisition of English. To the contrary, it noted the "convergence" of evidence in the Ramírez report and other research that "suggest[s], under certain conditions, the importance of primary-language instruction in second-language achievement in language arts and mathematics."

Submersion, Plus ESL

Where native-language development is absent, its benefits are sometimes most obvious. ESL programs alone, even if well designed and implemented, have failed to provide the short-cut to English acquisition that some enthusiasts had predicted. Opponents of bilingual education often describe ESL as an "alternative method" for teaching children with limited English skills. This is somewhat misleading, considering that ESL is an integral component of virtually every bilingual program in the United States.

Since 1976, the major professional organization in ESL, Teachers of English to Speakers of Other Languages (TESOL), has firmly endorsed native-language approaches and recognized their contribution to second-language acquisition. For various practical and political reasons, however, many English learners are still assigned to ESL-only programs – or, more accurately, to submersion in regular classrooms combined with varying amounts of second-language instruction. Usually this means **ESL pullout** classes for a brief period each day, sometimes in conjunction with sheltered English classes in other subjects *(see Chapter 2).*

Some have argued that "stand alone" programs in **content-based ESL** are the best feasible approach in school districts where LEP students come from diverse backgrounds. Esther Eisenhower, the architect of such a model in Fairfax County, Virginia, says that, "given scattered and multilingual populations like ours, the children can achieve just as well [in an] English-only treatment – if it is provided properly. We would be hard-put to find the number of teachers [needed] to deliver the Fairfax County curriculum" in all the languages spoken there (currently well over 100). In 1980, citing the district's large investment in ESL and achievement test scores suggesting that students were making progress, Eisenhower and her superiors convinced the federal Office for Civil Rights to approve a Lau Plan for the district that included no bilingual education *(see Chapter 5).*

Fairfax thus became a test case for the all-ESL alternative, whose effectiveness was unknown. As Rudolph Troike observed around that time, "There is extraordinarily little evidence for English-only programs showing much promise. There is an enormous methodological base in ESL, oriented toward whether one [ESL] method works better or not," but almost no research assessing the effectiveness of ESL *as a substitute* for bilingual instruction. The Fairfax model represented an improvement over sink-or-swim, most educators agreed, but how significant an improvement remained a matter of debate. Were children likely to catch up with their peers after learning English, or to suffer long-term harm from the neglect of their native language? Were some LEP students more at-risk than others?

Some answers are offered by a 1988 study, the first of its kind in the United States, which compared the rates at which children of different ages acquire proficiency in a second language for academic purposes. The study falls in the category of **basic research**, focusing on a narrow range of issues, and was not a full-fledged **program evaluation**. Yet it provides a rare glimpse of outcomes in an ESL-only treatment.

All subjects in the study were currently or formerly enrolled in Fairfax County's ESL program. Though diverse in ethnic makeup – Latinos, Koreans, Vietnamese, Chinese, and Cambodians, among others – the 2,014 participants were generally regarded as "advantaged children" based on socioeconomic status in their home countries and their parents' strong middle-class aspirations. The researchers, Virginia Collier and Wayne Thomas of George Mason University, analyzed achievement test scores from the district's massive database, covering student performance in the 4th, 6th, 8th, and 11th grades over a six-year period beginning in 1981.

The results came as a shock to Fairfax administrators: the ESL-only students took *four to nine years to reach grade level in English*, according to Collier and Thomas. The age-group differences were even more striking. Children who arrived at ages 5 to 7 scored poorly in all subjects, as compared with their counterparts who entered the ESL program at ages 8 to 11 – usually after learning to read in their native language before immigrating. By the 6th grade, these later arrivals were outperforming earlier arrivals who had been in the United States at least two or three years longer. "The only known variable that differentiated" the two groups, the researchers said, was the limited mother-tongue schooling of the 5-to-7-year-olds. More English instruction did not correlate with more English acquisition.

A third group in the study, students who arrived at ages 12 to 15, did the worst, a phenomenon the researchers attributed to the quicker pace and higher cognitive demands of the upper grades. In mathematics achievement, newly arrived 8th graders scored consistently above the 50th percentile, reflecting the transfer of skills learned back home (particularly in Asia, where math curricula tend to be more demanding than in the United States). Over the next three to four years – the time it took these students to acquire English – they slipped steadily behind. When their scores finally began to rise once more, high school was nearly over. Collier and Thomas concluded that native-language instruction would benefit this oldest group of students by helping them keep up in other content areas, and also the youngest group by providing a foundation for developing academic English proficiency.

Esther Eisenhower conceded that the study's findings, especially the sharp differences in performance by age group, "threw me for a loop." Nevertheless, they did not modify her opposition to bilingual education, she said. "While you're teaching about Mayan culture, you're neglecting to teach the child how to navigate American society. [Educators] are delinquent in their duties if they don't teach these skills from the first day." Yet, at the same time, Eisenhower argued that it would be inequitable to provide native-language instruction to one ethnic group and not others, citing the difficulty of recruiting bilingual teachers in Asian languages. "I cannot, in all fairness, say that the 20 percent of Hispanics we have here are entitled to a treatment that the Asians are not." Although the Collier-Thomas study had little practical impact in the school district,[12] its theoretical significance was widely recognized.

De Facto Bilingual Education

The Fairfax results, which echo those of age-on-arrival studies in several countries, are consistent with Cummins's **threshold hypothesis** that literacy and other skills transfer to a second tongue only after a certain level of competence has been achieved in the first. Stephen Krashen offers an equally plausible interpretation, however, which sidesteps the theoretical debate over semilingualism *(see Chapter 8)*. He calls it **de facto bilingual education**.

According to this hypothesis, children who get a good start in school before immigrating have already begun to develop both literacy skills and subject-matter knowledge through their first language – in other words, "two of the three components of quality bilingual programs." (The third component, Krashen says, is direct support for second-language acquisition.) This academic foundation in the mother tongue, by helping to make English input comprehensible, gave the later-arriving Fairfax children an edge over those who started school in all-English programs. The former group acquired English faster despite receiving less exposure to English – contrary to what the time-on-task hypothesis would have predicted.

Krashen's concept of de facto bilingual education sheds light on some perennial issues in the public debate over how to teach English learners:

- Why do some immigrants succeed without bilingual education?
- Why do some linguistic minorities (e.g., some Asian groups) make dramatic progress in school as compared to others (e.g., some Latino groups)?
- Why do some students in all-English programs learn English faster than those in bilingual programs?

These questions have frequently been raised by the political opponents of bilingual education. U.S. English published a compilation of personal stories by immigrants who had experienced the sink-or-swim treatment in American schools, yet were able to catch up academically and to build professional careers in this country. Analyzing the details of these case histories, Krashen found that the immigrants had all benefited from several years of high-quality schooling in their home countries, and had apparently been good students. It is hardly surprising that, after arriving in the United States, they were able to transfer the skills and knowledge acquired in the first language to support their achievement in English. Their life experiences are certainly not isolated. But neither are they typical of English learners in our schools today, who, as Krashen notes, tend to be "children of poverty who do not have a good education in the primary language, who were not at grade level in their own country, and who did not have high levels of first language literacy." Never having received de facto bilingual education, these students need the real thing.

It is no secret that **socioeconomic status** (SES) plays a significant role in academic outcomes, regardless of student background. As documented by a number of empirical studies, English learners from higher-SES families not only do better in school but acquire academic English more rapidly. Krashen cites some of the likely explanations:

> They have caregivers who are more educated, better prepared to help with school work in the primary language, have more time to interact with the school and more knowledge about interacting with the school. Their greater affluence means their parents can provide tutoring in the primary language. They live in a more print-rich environment, with many more books in the home. ... These children should thus have greater literacy development in the primary language. ... They are more likely to have access to a library. ... They are more likely to have a quiet place to read and study at home, and are more likely to have a good diet.

In other words, it is not high SES per se that gives some English learners an advantage but rather "factors typically associated with high SES." The good news is that most of these factors, which involve literacy development and academic support in the primary language, are also associated with well designed bilingual programs, Krashen says. "We can improve the achievement of LEP children by providing these factors in school."

Failure to consider the kind of de facto bilingual education that high SES provides can lead to unfair program comparisons, as well as invidious ethnic stereotypes. In 1994, a preliminary evaluation of English learner programs in New York City reported that students in bilingual education were slower to acquire English than those who received only ESL. For those who entered the programs in kindergarten, 79 percent of ESL students exited within three years versus only 42 percent of bilingual education students. For those entering in 3rd grade, the rates were 59 percent and 22 percent, respectively.

These findings received widespread publicity, thanks in part to the efforts of U.S. English and Rosalie Porter's READ Institute. The *New York Times* questioned whether bilingual education was holding students back by providing too little time on task in English. Yet, as Luis Reyes, a member of the city's Board of Education, pointed out at the time, the so-called "study" applied no controls whatsoever

> for external factors, like native literacy of the parents, educational level of the parents, and family income. There were a number of middle-class students in the ESL program who came from countries that were more developed. … Kids in the bilingual program came from where they hadn't had full schooling.

While New York's bilingual programs largely served Puerto Rican, Dominican, and Haitian children, ESL was the predominant approach for other nationalities, such as Chinese, Japanese, Koreans, and Russians. Without taking these "confounding" variables into account, there was no reason to conclude that the bilingual programs – or the Spanish- and Haitian Creole–speaking students – were deficient. Meanwhile there was good reason to suspect that the ESL students scored higher in English because, on average, they came from backgrounds with higher SES and higher levels of parental education.

'How Long?' Issue

However imperfectly, the New York City report did seek to address an important issue: How long are English learners likely to need language support before they can succeed in mainstream classrooms? Ever since the early days of the Bilingual Education Act, concerns have been raised about keeping children too long in special programs, which cost money and sometimes carry stigmas for participants. In addition, critics have charged (with little supporting evidence) that students often "languish" in classrooms where native-language instruction predominates at the expense of English. The idea that it could take young children, who seem to "pick up" languages so quickly, as long as five or more years to make the transition seems unreasonable to many laypersons. In the late 1980s English-only advocates seized on this issue and politicians responded. Following the lead of Congress, several states began to impose time limits – typically three years – for a student's participation in a bilingual or ESL program.[13] The Unz initiatives in California, Arizona, and Massachusetts were even more stringent, mandating an English immersion program "not normally intended to exceed one year" as the default approach for all English language learners.

Experts in second-language acquisition have vehemently objected to these limits, which are unsupported by scientific evidence. David Ramírez calls them "absurd and ridiculous … contradicted by 80 years of child development research." He is referring to the considerable variation among individuals in acquiring language, just as in other developmental processes such as physical coordination or spatial perception. In short, psychologists have long understood that children develop at different rates. A recent study in Arizona found that students in bilingual classrooms acquired "native-level proficiency in English" in an average of 3.3 years. Yet there was a wide range, from one year to 6.5 years, in the length of time that they needed. Thus setting limits on language support, whether based on "average" rates of acquisition or arbitrary political decisions, could adversely affect a significant percentage of English learners. Meanwhile no research has shown that staying longer than one to three years in bilingual or ESL classrooms is detrimental. To the contrary, a 1998 study by Ramírez in San Francisco found that formerly LEP students outperformed all other groups in the school district on most achievement tests, after spending an average of 4.6 years in language assistance programs.

Nevertheless, the question persists: How long does it take an "average child" to acquire a second language for academic purposes? It has been difficult to answer with precision. A common shorthand response, based on Cummins's framework and age-on-arrival studies, is to say that **cognitive-academic language proficiency** (CALP) takes from five to seven years to develop. Yet this is not exactly what the data show. The studies found that, on average, second-language learners need five to seven years (or four to nine, according to the Fairfax research) to *catch up academically* with native speakers of that language – that is, to reach the 50th percentile on achievement tests. They did not specify *how many years of support* such students are likely to need before they can understand and benefit from mainstream instruction.

Obviously it is quite possible to master a second language and yet continue to underachieve academically. It is also possible to lag behind because of learning problems that are language-related. How can educators determine whether the source of a child's difficulties is linguistic, academic, or a combination of the two?

As yet, unfortunately, there are no assessment tools that can reliably make such distinctions. Indeed, some tests that were designed to measure oral English skills, such as the Language Assessment Scales (LAS), have been criticized for confounding linguistic and academic development. Judgments about children's academic English are usually made on the basis of how well they perform on achievement tests administered in English and normed for native speakers of English.

It is safe to assume that students who consistently reach the 50th percentile on such tests are no longer LEP. Yet, for purposes of determining whether they are fully English proficient (FEP), this would be an unrealistically high standard. By definition, only half of *all* students score at that level. In most states the bar for redesignating students as FEP is set lower, generally around the 36th percentile. Such cutoff points remain arbitrary rather than scientific, although they do reflect what "feels right" to many practitioners based on years of experience in English learner programs. Scoring at the redesignation level implies that a child is no longer likely to face significant language barriers in a regular classroom, assuming that other important criteria – for example, teacher judgments – are met. Most educators would prefer to err on the side of providing too much, rather than too little, support. Contrary to popular misconceptions, research shows that there is no urgency to exit children from bilingual programs that are providing high-quality instruction. In fact, some of the strongest approaches, such as the Case Studies model *(see Chapter 10)*, enable students to continue developing their native-language skills after they are redesignated as FEP.

Nevertheless, more objective and reliable ways to determine when a child is ready for the mainstream would be extremely helpful, not only in designing and administering effective programs but also in resisting misguided policies to restrict their duration. This issue was at the heart of the debate over Proposition 227 in California *(see Chapter 13)*. Christine Rossell, who worked closely with sponsor Ron Unz in drafting the initiative, has taken credit for the one-year limit on language assistance. She asserts that English learners need "no more than a year and perhaps as little as three months" to understand enough of what a teacher says in English "so that the mainstream classroom is a better learning environment than a sheltered classroom." Lacking hard data to support this claim, however, Rossell has offered only anecdotes. In a deposition defending Proposition 227 against a civil-rights lawsuit, she said:

> Over the years I have asked LEP students in ESL and structured immersion classes, as well as formerly LEP students in my classes at Boston University, "How long was it after you started school before you were understanding

what your teacher was saying in English in your regular classroom?" The most common answer I have received is three months.

While few scientists today would give credence to this type of evidence, many politicians do. Legislation to impose a one-year limit has been introduced in several additional states. For "research" that confirms popular biases, it seems, the burden of proof is none too onerous.

Kenji Hakuta and colleagues at Stanford University recently took a different approach to the "how long" question. They used a variety of assessment tools to gauge oral and academic English proficiency among a diverse sample of language-minority students. Four school districts participated in the study, two in the San Francisco area that were recognized as among California's most successful in teaching English through bilingual and ESL methodologies, and two in the Toronto area, which offered only ESL instruction. Children were tested on a wide range of language skills, including phonology, oral expression, listening comprehension, complex vocabulary, reading comprehension, and written expression.

The researchers found a pattern that was repeated in all four sites: "oral [English] proficiency takes 3 to 5 years to develop, and academic English proficiency can take 4 to 7 years." If anything, they noted, these figures underestimate the time required (because of possible flaws in the study's design). Variations in the rate of English acquisition were closely correlated with socioeconomic status. LEP students from high-poverty backgrounds lagged other students in oral proficiency, reading, writing, and redesignation as FEP. Hakuta and his colleagues concluded:

> We have known that SES is a powerful factor in predicting student achievement in traditional content areas, such as reading and math, regardless of whether they are language minority or native speakers of English. It now appears certain that SES is powerful in predicting the rate of English acquisition.

This finding lends additional support to Krashen's hypothesis that SES is a form of de facto bilingual education.

The policy implications are clear. Arbitrarily limiting instructional programs, on the assumption that young children are rapid language learners, is not only unwarranted. It is especially dangerous for low-SES students, who already face the highest obstacles to academic achievement and are most likely to need special help with English. "A much more sensible policy," the researchers argue, "would be one that sets aside the entire spectrum of the elementary grades as the realistic range within which English acquisition is accomplished, and plans a balanced curriculum that pays attention not just to English, but to the full array of academic needs of the students."

Thomas-Collier Study

Time is also a key factor in evaluating program alternatives for English learners. When academic learning takes place in a context of second-language acquisition, the outcomes of educational treatments can be difficult to gauge. This is not only an assessment problem; it is also a developmental issue. Because learning is a cumulative process that builds on what has gone before, a foundation of concepts and skills acquired today will support intellectual growth in the future. Yet, as we have seen, it takes time to transfer this foundation to a new language.

By the late 1970s, researchers like Rudolph Troike began to notice that successful experiments in bilingual education, while diverse in many ways, shared a salient feature in common: "they all continued through the 6th grade." Moreover, the academic benefits for students only became evident after they had been enrolled in such programs for several years. This may help to explain why short-term evluations have often failed to document "conclusive" advantages for bilingual education *(see Chapter 7)*. In many cases, these studies have measured English learners' progress for one year or less. Yet, as Stephen Krashen has noted, "We're not interested in what kids do at the end of 1st grade. We're interested in their long-term chances of success." Research should be designed accordingly.

The 1991 Ramírez report was the first large-scale study in the United States to take a longitudinal approach in comparing program alternatives for English learners. It was widely seen as a major improvement in research design. Building on this four-year database involving 2,000-odd students in nine school districts, Wayne Thomas and Virginia Collier initiated a study that has continued to expand, incorporating additional districts and 40,000 new students by 1997.[14]

Like Ramírez, they sought to include only well designed and faithfully implemented programs that would cover the spectrum of current strategies for educating English learners. They also took a long-term approach, comparing progress for students enrolled in various treatments over periods ranging from four to 11 years. Unlike Ramírez, Thomas and Collier avoided what they called "laboratory-style research methods." By this the researchers meant **random assignment** to experimental and comparison groups, which they deemed impractical and unethical, and most **quasi-experiments** using complex statistical means to control for pre-existing differences among subjects, which they criticized as unreliable *(see Chapter 7)*. Pursuing a "noninterventionist philosophy," they worked in close collaboration with school district staff to evaluate programs already in place. Rather than focus on classroom-sized samples, in which factors like student attrition can bias results, they followed very large cohorts of English learners enrolled in various program types and compared their achievement against national norms.

Thomas and Collier started with the premise that program effectiveness should be judged by a high standard: "What really matters is how schools are able to assist English learners, as a group, to eventually match the achievement characteristics of native-English speakers, in all areas of the curriculum." Because of the language barrier, LEP students start out considerably behind. At the end of 2nd grade, the researchers found, English learners in all program models typically scored around the 15th percentile (28th NCE) in English reading.[15] To reach eventual parity with their English-speaking peers – that is, to close the **achievement gap** by the end of high school – they needed to make "sustained gains" each year against the norm.

Judged by this criterion, only two-way and developmental bilingual education proved to be successful. On average, Thomas and Collier found, English learners who had received these treatments in elementary school surpassed the 50th percentile in English reading by grade 11. Students in four other program types – ESL pullout, structured immersion, "traditional" TBE (featuring grammar-based ESL and minimal use of the native language), and "current" TBE (interactive teaching methods, along with sheltered English instruction) – fell far short of that mark, scoring between the 11th and 32nd percentiles *(see Figure 9–1)*.

The researchers described these as "consistent patterns across school districts that are very generalizable" to English learner programs throughout the country. As

FIGURE 9–1
Grade 11 Total Reading Scores for Former LEP Students, By Program Type

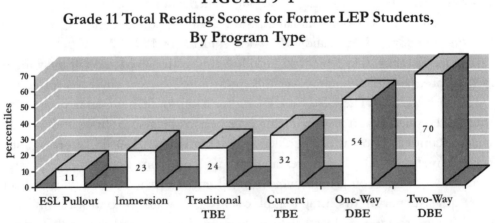

Source: Wayne P. Thomas and Virginia P. Collier, *School Effectiveness for Language Minority Students* (Washington, D.C.: National Clearinghouse for Bilingual Education, 1997).

such, their findings would seem to provide dramatic confirmation of the theoretical framework of Cummins and Krashen. There was a direct relationship between, on the one hand, the amount of cognitively challenging instruction in the primary language and comprehensible input in English that children received in early grades and, on the other hand, their level of academic achievement in secondary school. Differences in program outcomes, which were minimal at first, became increasingly significant over time.

In 1995, Thomas and Collier began circulating a graph that illustrated the learning curves predicted by each program type. It produced excitement among teachers and administrators, many of whom welcomed the clear guidance about "what works" for English learners. Researchers expressed considerable interest as well, although some questioned why the study's conclusions had been announced in advance of supporting data and publicized through news media and informal workshops rather than through a peer-reviewed journal. Thomas and Collier assured colleagues that ample details would soon be published. In late 1997, however, when the first major report on their study appeared, it left many unsatisfied.

The 96-page document, published on the Web site of the National Clearinghouse for Bilingual Education, featured no data tables or statistical analyses; no specifics about the students, teachers, schools, or programs included in the study; and only a general description of its methodology. Thus many questions remained unanswered, for example, about patterns of variance in test scores, comparability of subjects, the role of socioeconomic and sociolinguistic factors, differences in school district practices, and numerous other matters. The report also failed to explain how a large number of diverse programs had been pigeonholed into a few preconceived program types. In the absence of such information, few researchers in second-language acquisition have been eager to endorse or even to make substantive comments about the Thomas-Collier findings.[16]

Opponents of bilingual education, however, were quick to seize on these issues. Christine Rossell noted that the Ramírez report had

> contained 1,148 pages of which there were 478 tables and 228 figures on the characteristics of the sample, the outcomes, and the statistical analysis. The methodology was explained in intricate detail, and the tables and figures represent about 61 percent of the report. The Thomas and Collier report by contrast has no tables at all, no information on the characteristics of the sample and methodology, and no statistical analyses. The two figures represent only one percent of the report. This appears to be a new low in federal grant reporting. Because of the lack of information in this report, it is hard to know exactly what Thomas and Collier have done.

In response to Rossell, Jim Cummins argued that "the credibility of the Thomas/ Collier results is clearly related to their consistency with other data." He reported in 2000 that the researchers were preparing "an overview [that] will address many of the concerns raised regarding the sketchiness of the data reported to date." As yet, no such overview has appeared.

A second report by Thomas and Collier, published in 2002 by the Center for Research on Education, Diversity, and Excellence (CREDE), took a more orthodox approach. This time numerous data tables were included on student achievement in five additional districts – out of 16 sites included in this second, federally funded phase of their study – as well as more detailed descriptions of their research methodology. The results were generally consistent with the achievement patterns reported earlier. Nevertheless, questions persist. No explanation was offered for why data from the remaining 11 districts had been excluded. For the five districts that were included, there are issues involving the **generalizability** of their findings. Two districts featured heritage language programs for Francophone children in northern Maine (who may or may not have been LEP at one time); one was an unnamed district in the Southeast that provided an all-ESL treatment for English learners; and another consisted of a small two-way bilingual school in Oregon.

In the fifth site, the Houston Independent School District, the researchers were able to conduct extensive and detailed studies analyzing the effectiveness of various program models. Again, in long-term outcomes, students who had been enrolled in DBE outperformed those in TBE, who in turn outperformed those in structured immersion. Meanwhile the highest achievers were those who had received two-way bilingual instruction *(for more details on these findings, see Chapter 12)*. The English learners who fared worst over their school careers were "refusers of services," whose parents had insisted that they be assigned to mainstream class-rooms.

Controlled Study in Miami

Social scientists recognize that no single study, however rigorous in design and execution, provides answers that are definitive. For that reason they insist that results be **replicated** by other researchers and in other contexts before firm policy conclusions are drawn. So it is significant that a study in the Dade County Public Schools, contemporaneous with Thomas and Collier's work and published in 2002, found similar – though less pronounced – advantages for programs that stress academic development in students' native language.

This research, led by D. Kimbrough Oller and Rebecca E. Eilers, was on a smaller – some would say, more manageable – scale. It compared the outcomes of 952 children in bilingual, immersion, and monolingual English schools over a four-year period. While random assignment was neither feasible nor desirable, the researchers were able to select participating students and programs in a way that gave them extraordinary control over **background variables**. To ensure comparability, they "matched" children by SES and language spoken at home, and schools by ethnic makeup, percentage of LEP students, per-pupil expenditures, and achievement test scores. This was possible thanks to extraordinary levels of cooperation by the school district, as well as to the community context. Not only is bilingualism widespread in Miami, by comparison to most other U.S. cities, but Spanish speakers are well represented at all levels of society, rather than concentrated disproportionately at the bottom. For all these reasons a "natural experiment" was feasible without statistical acrobatics to compensate for differences between subjects.

The two basic models for educating English learners were well established in Dade County. Indeed, one of the programs in the study, at Coral Way Elementary, dates back to 1963 and the modern rebirth of bilingual education *(see Chapter 4)*. Although it is described locally as a "two-way" school, more than 90 percent of the students are of linguistic minority (Hispanic) background. So it could be argued that this model more closely resembles developmental rather than two-way bilingual education, as practiced elsewhere in the United States *(see Chapter 12)*. Instruction is divided equally between the two languages in all grades (K–5) except in math, which is taught exclusively in English (resulting in a 60/40 percent split, English-Spanish). Dade County's approach to English immersion also differs from "pure" structured immersion, in that children receive an hour each day of Spanish for Spanish speakers (90/10, English-Spanish).[17]

All participants in the study were U.S.-born and had been enrolled in their respective programs since kindergarten. Most students in the English learner programs (though not in the monolingual English schools) were bilingual to varying degrees. The researchers observed that when children spoke among themselves outside the classroom, English was by far the preferred language – more than 65 percent of the time for students in bilingual education, more than 80 percent for those in immersion. Despite the image of Miami as a Spanish-dominant community, language shift is occurring rapidly among younger generations of Latinos, as other studies have confirmed *(see Chapter 1)*.

Children were tested at grades K, 2, and 5 on nine different measures of oral skills, reading, and writing in both English and Spanish. After the achievement data were collected, the researchers performed numerous analyses to determine the role of variables including SES, home language, and educational treatment. When it came to the impact of school programs, students in English immersion made slightly more progress in *oral English* than those in bilingual education, although the researchers noted that these advantages appeared to be "short-term" and "may disappear in elementary school." Conversely, they found that the bilingual group had a somewhat larger edge over the immersion group in various tests of *English literacy*, which became evident by the 2nd grade and widened by the 5th grade. In English phonics tests, the bilingual students even outperformed their monolingual English counterparts in mainstream classrooms (although the difference was "not statistically reliable"). Not surprisingly, their scores in Spanish were superior to those of the other groups on every measure.

Citing Miami's unique features, however, the study's authors cautioned that these patterns may not be generalizable. Unlike many children in immigrant communities, the subjects in Dade County were widely exposed to both languages in the community and often at home. Moreover, they may have started school with higher proficiency in oral English (as well as lower proficiency in Spanish) than Latinos born outside the United States. On the other hand, the absence of monolingual peer models in either language may have limited students' ability to acquire native-like levels of English or Spanish.

Nevertheless, the extensive database enabled the researchers to test a number of theoretical propositions generated by the **interdependence hypothesis** *(see Chapter 8)*. They asked, for example, "Did children tend to show strength in one language if they showed strength in the other … or did achievement in one language drain resources from the second?" Their answers amounted to a qualified endorsement of Cummins's theory:

- There was "no tendency for competence in one language to inhibit competence in another."
- Literacy skills seemed to transfer between languages, exhibiting a "positive interdependence."
- But "oral language skills … tended not to cross the language boundary."

These findings were consistent regardless of SES or home language. Academic proficiency in English was enhanced by academic proficiency in the native language, but conversational proficiency did not seem to transfer. "Why might literacy skills have cohered across languages," the researchers asked, while oral language achievement seemed largely independent across languages? Part of the explanation may lie in the fact that reading and writing skills are dependent on language but not vice versa. Children learn to speak in the home and community. Reading and writing, on the other hand, are usually school-learned skills and as such depend on instruction rather than exposure to models of language at home. Different children have different levels of exposure to Spanish and English at home and through community participation, while they may have relatively more equal access to reading and writing through school instruction. School instruction may, then, create a natural tie between literacy in the two languages of bilingual children.

For educators, this conclusion should be both encouraging and challenging. While English learners may face social disadvantages that affect their academic development in important ways, school can serve as a "great equalizer" – provided that it offers well designed instructional programs.

Suggested Reading

California Department of Education. *Studies on Immersion Education: A Collection for United States Educators.* Sacramento: Office of Bilingual Bicultural Education, 1984.

Krashen, Stephen D. *Under Attack: The Case Against Bilingual Education.* Culver City, Calif.: Language Education Associates, 1996.

Lambert, Wallace E., and Tucker, G. Richard. *Bilingual Education of Children: The St. Lambert Experiment.* Rowley, Mass.: Newbury House, 1972.

Oller, D. Kimbrough, and Eilers, Rebecca E., eds. *Language and Literacy in Bilingual Children.* Clevedon, U.K.: Multilingual Matters, 2002.

See also pp. 400–1.

Online Resource Guide

Collier, Virginia P. *The Effect of Age on Acquisition of a Second Language for School.* National Clearinghouse for Bilingual Education (1988).

Hakuta, Kenji; Butler, Yuko Goto; and Witt, Daria. *How Long Does It Take English Learners To Attain Proficiency?* Linguistic Minority Research Institute (2000).

See also companion CD-ROM.

Internet
Links

Bilingual Research Journal. Special issue on the Ramírez Report, with articles by David Ramírez, Keith Baker, Jim Cummins, David Dolson and Jan Mayer, Christine Rossell, Virginia Collier, and Wayne Thomas (1992). http://www.ncela.gwu.edu/miscpubs/nabe/brj/v16/index.htm#12

Rossell, Christine. "Mystery on the Bilingual Express." *READ Perspectives* 6 (1999). http://www.ceousa.org/READ/collier.html

Ramírez, J. David. *Final Report: Longitudinal Study of Structured English Immersion Strategy, Early-Exit and Late Exit Transitional Bilingual Education Programs for Language-Minority Children* (1991). http://www.ncela.gwu.edu/miscpubs/ramirez/longitudinal.htm

Thomas, Wayne P., and Collier, Virginia P. *A National Study of School Effectiveness for Language Minority Students' Long-Term Academic Achievement: Final Report* (2002). http://www.crede.ucsc.edu/research/llaa/1.1_final.html

Thomas, Wayne P., and Collier, Virginia P. *School Effectiveness for Language Minority Students* (1997). http://www.ncela.gwu.edu/ncbepubs/resource/effectiveness/index.htm

See also companion CD-ROM.

Notes

1. Baker and de Kanter coined this term for English-only immersion to distinguish it from **submersion**. Unlike sink-or-swim, the researchers said, this approach provides a "structured" second-language environment for LEP students *(see Chapter 2)*.
2. Hugh MacLennan, *Two Solitudes* (Toronto: Collins, 1945).
3. Later variations of the program have sometimes postponed use of the native language until grade 3.
4. The immersion students had some contact with French-speaking Protestant children, largely of lower socioeconomic status, who attended separate classes at the St. Lambert school. Stigmatized as academically slow and prone to disciplinary problems, however, the Francophone children were not well accepted when integrated into some of the immersion classes; Wallace E. Lambert and G. Richard Tucker, *Bilingual Education of Children: The St. Lambert Experiment* (Rowley, Mass.: Newbury House, 1972), pp. 160–63.
5. Lambert's distinction between additive and subtractive bilingualism, which influenced Cummins in elaborating the threshold hypothesis, has been criticized as part of a deficit model *(see Chapter 8)*. Indeed, in describing the consequences of subtractive

bilingualism, Lambert asserts that minority children "are placed in a psycholinguistic limbo where neither the home language nor English is useful as a tool of thought and expression." Yet the distinction can also be understood without reference to cognitive disabilities. It is clear that subtractive approaches squander the potential academic benefits of developing native-language literacy.

6. In a 1997 presentation to the California State Board of Education, Baker argued that his lack of a bilingual education background was in fact an advantage. He made an analogy between policymakers choosing programs for English learners and consumers "interested in buying a new car. ... You're thinking about buying a Pontiac [so] who do you want to call to find out if a Pontiac is a good car for you to buy – General Motors or *Consumer Reports*? If you call General Motors and say, 'I'm thinking about buying a Pontiac; is it a good car?' what do you think a General Motors salesman is going to say? ... *Consumer Reports* couldn't build a Pontiac, but they can give you a much better read on whether or not a Pontiac is a good car." By implication, researchers involved in bilingual program design or teacher training could not be trusted to provide an objective evaluation. Baker did not mention his own former directorship of the READ Institute, a venture funded by U.S. English to manufacture research unfavorable to bilingual education.

   Christine Rossell's lack of credentials in language pedagogy has also been cited. Testifying for the defense in the *Teresa P. v. Berkeley* case (a service for which she received $129,000 in fees and expenses), Rossell described an evaluation she had conducted of the district's English-learner programs, which concluded that all-ESL instruction was just as effective as transitional bilingual instruction. Under cross-examination, however, the political scientist acknowledged her limited knowledge of what the program labels represented in practice. It turned out that Rossell's "expert" opinion was based on (1) three minutes of classroom observation, (2) brief conversations with teachers, and (3) a partial comparison of test results for about 20 percent of Berkeley's LEP students.

7. This so-called National Advisory and Coordinating Council on Bilingual Education, a body appointed by Secretary of Education William J. Bennett, was eliminated by Congress soon after. One member was Robert Rosier, a partisan on behalf of U.S. English who described bilingual education as "the new Latin hustle." As editor of the advisory panel's report, Rosier declined to correct several factual mistakes about the El Paso program after they were pointed out to him by Rosita Apodaca, a former administrator in the district as well as the chair of NACCBE. Apodaca and five other members filed a minority report in protest.

8. The original contractor, SRA Technologies, was replaced during the course of the study by Aguirre International, an educational research firm based in San Mateo, California.

9. After reviewing the study's final report, Baker changed his mind once again. In a 1991 interview, he opined: "Bilingual education works, but not the way Cummins says it does. It works in the first three years, but after that point it flips – children do better in all-English programs." Though he had yet to work out any theoretical explanation, he

said, these results could be due to "mental fatigue" among LEP children in English-only classrooms. The 1996 literature review that Baker coauthored with Rossell continued to note this problem with a strict time-on-task hypothesis: "It is possible that bilingual education programs, because they provide a needed rest from constant exposure to the new language, can produce better learning at the early stages of learning a second language." In 1999, Baker took a slightly different tack, arguing in effect that too much time "off task" – that is, time spent in late-exit bilingual programs – results in an "English deficit" that takes "at least 12 years" for children to recover from; "How Can We Best Serve LEP Students? A Reply to Nicholas Meier and Stephen Krashen," *Phi Delta Kappan*, May 1999, pp. 707–10.

10. TAMP is an acronym for Trajectory Analysis of Matched Percentiles.

11. The council, a branch of the National Academy of Sciences, was asked to review the Ramírez report by the U.S. Department of Education. Along with several authorities on statistics and research design, the 14-member panel included two experts in language-minority education, Kenji Hakuta of Stanford University and Luis Moll of the University of Arizona.

12. Following Eisenhower's retirement in 1990, Fairfax quietly initiated some limited experiments with bilingual education, but they have remained largely unpublicized in this politically conservative district.

13. Yet these were rarely hard-and-fast rules. Even in states where such mandates are written into law, exceptions have usually been allowed for students who clearly need additional language support.

14. Confusion has arisen on this point because the researchers' 1997 report, *School Effectiveness for Language Minority Students*, said that the study up to that time "include[d] over 700,000 language minority student records, collected by the five participating school systems between 1982 and 1996, including 42,317 students who have attended our participating schools for four years or more" (p. 30). Some readers have interpreted this to mean that 700,000 students were involved in the study. But it seems clear that, as used by Thomas and Collier, the terms "students" and "student records" are not synonymous. In a 2002 publication, *A National Study of School Effectiveness for Language Minority Students' Long-Term Academic Achievement*, they offer the following definition:

> One student record includes all the school district records for one student collected during one school year, such as student background characteristics, the grade level and school program(s) that student attended, and academic achievement measures administered to that student during the school year. [p. 1]

15. Thomas and Collier, among others, prefer to use **normal curve equivalents** (NCEs) rather than **percentiles** in reporting standardized test scores. Both are relative gauges of student achievement that use a scale from 1 to 99, with 50 denoting "average." But they differ in important ways as units of measurement. Percentiles are essentially ranks (1st, 2nd, 3rd, etc.), in which a score of, say, 66 means that two-thirds of test takers performed worse and one-third performed better. Because more students score in the

middle range on a "normal curve" than at the top or the bottom, a one-percentile change represents different amounts of achievement at different points on the scale – like a yardstick on which the length of an inch varies widely. By contrast, NCEs represent *even intervals* of performance that can be added, subtracted, multiplied, or divided without introducing distortions. Thus they offer a more precise and reliable way to compare the progress of students, not only from year to year but also from study to study. While the 50th percentile is equal to the 50th NCE, above that point percentile ranks are higher than NCEs; below that point they are lower. Despite the advantages of the NCE scale for research purposes, the percentile scale is a more familiar frame of reference for educators and policymakers – for example, in the 36th percentile (42.5 NCE) criterion that is common for redesignating students as fluent in English. So, for the sake of consistency, percentiles are the measure generally used in this volume.

16. To criticisms involving the adequacy of their published data, Thomas and Collier have given various responses:
    - "For maximum understanding and decision-making utility for school personnel, our quantitative findings, including measures of central tendency and variability, are presented in text, charts, and graphics rather than in extensive tables of statistics"; *Study of School Effectiveness* (1997), p. 8.
    - "This is the common way that a study of this type would be reported; it is simply that no one in our field has ever done a study of this type before – a sustained-effects study – so we are having to train the field as to how to apply this type of research methodology to [language-minority] education"; Collier, personal communication, March 22, 1998.
    - "I hope by now researchers in our field understand why we could not present the details of our data analyses for the 1997 report. That 1997 summary of our research to date represented many program evaluations that we conducted over many years, in which we are not allowed by the school districts to identify them – that is typical in program evaluation research and that's why very few program evaluations get published"; Collier, personal communication, March 5, 2003.

17. This component is officially known as Basic Skills in the Home Language.

Practice

10 The Case Studies Project

Bilingual education existed on a tiny scale in the United States before the Title VII program was created. In 1969, the first year of federal funding, there were a few hundred experienced teachers nationwide, virtually no native-language materials, and only limited models for curriculum and methodology. After a 50-year hiatus, bilingual education was starting again virtually from scratch. "Imagine trying to construct an impressive, majestic

A Theoretical Framework
Gradual-Exit Model
Developing the Native Language
Designing a Curriculum
Adapting the Model
Team Teaching
Student Outcomes
Flexibility vs. Leadership
Eastman Replication Project

brick cathedral without bricks or mortar, with inexperienced workers and very limited resources for training them," writes María Medina Swanson, an early president of the National Association for Bilingual Education. "Yet that is how most bilingual programs got off the ground."

It was another decade, following the U.S. Supreme Court's *Lau v. Nichols* decision (1974) and the federal government's aggressive civil-rights enforcement, before most school districts got around to trying the idea. Inevitably, with a limited research base on which to build, there was much trial and error in the design of bilingual programs, and overnight successes were rare. It was a disorderly, uneven process. Still, there was no other way for practitioners to amass experience or researchers to test hypotheses.

Bilingual educators were outraged in 1978 by Title VII's mediocre report card from the American Institutes for Research (AIR). With its crude methodology, the study lumped together the good with the bad, the failures with the successes. It obscured the growing number of schools in which formerly LEP children were beginning to score at or near national norms for the first time *(see Chapter 7)*.

Yet AIR's critics had to admit that serious shortcomings continued to plague many bilingual programs. Some were bilingual in name only, making limited use of LEP students' native language because qualified teachers were in short supply. Other schools favored instruction primarily in English because it was the language of achievement tests, or because officials felt external pressures to "mainstream" children quickly. Many programs continued to employ discredited methodologies, such as concurrent translation and grammar-based approaches to ESL. Bilingual classrooms, perceived as compensatory, were frequently ghettoized within a school or neglected by administrators, while minority languages were treated with disrespect.

English learners tended to perform poorly in such programs, which shared little in common with proven approaches to bilingual education, as identified by both **basic research** and **evaluation research**. Findings were beginning to confirm the importance of native-language development, communication-based ESL, and bicultural efforts to enhance students' self-esteem. But this evidence was often slow to reach classroom teachers. Even where there was enthusiasm for bilingual approaches, educational theory was having a limited effect on educational practice. It was in this context that the Case Studies project began.

Theory First

Recognizing that the implications of research are rarely self-evident, in 1980 the California Department of Education set out to develop a "theoretically sound" model for bilingual education and to test it in selected school districts. Known as **Case Studies in Bilingual Education**, the project was designed "to bridge the gap between educational research and program practices." The emphasis was on school improvement rather than on further effectiveness research. (No attempt was made, for example, to include comparison groups.) At the same time, state officials hoped that Case Studies would yield program experience that could be generalized to help other schools in serving language-minority students.

It was understood that such an ambitious project would take time. "We weren't just going to do a workshop on basic principles and then walk into the classroom and see instruction change overnight," recalls Norm Gold, then a consultant in the California Bilingual Education Office. Schools' needs had to be assessed. A curriculum had to be developed. Teachers had to be trained and, in many cases, won over to a new approach. A range of logistical hurdles had to be cleared.

Before undertaking any of these practical tasks, the first step was to summarize the state of the art in second-language acquisition. The California officials solicited articles from researchers in cognitive psychology, linguistics, and literacy. Contributors included two of the leading theorists, Jim Cummins and Stephen Krashen, as well as researchers on effective teaching for language-minority children: Dorothy Legaretta-Marcaida, an expert on native-language methodologies; Tracy Terrell, an ESL program designer; and Eleanor Thonis, a reading specialist. The result, *Schooling and Language-Minority Students: A Theoretical Framework*, was published in December 1981, a 218-page book that elaborated a coherent theory of second-language acquisition and its practical applications in the classroom. The Bilingual Education Office further synthesized the research into five "basic principles for the education of language-minority students" *(see page 251)*.

Meanwhile the state consultants sought out schools where the theory's validity could be tested. Using a computer search, they identified 134 that met their criteria: K–6 programs, large concentrations of LEP children whose native language was Spanish, and "a core group of qualified bilingual teachers." Of the 30 schools that expressed interest, five were selected for the project in late 1981. While the sites were geographically and demographically diverse, from a small town on the Mexican border to an urban barrio, the students had much in common: poverty, limited English skills, and chronic underachievement. All five schools seemed to be trying hard to make bilingual education work. Still, with LEP enrollments that had increased by 46 percent over the previous four years, their students' test scores were among the lowest in California. The 3rd graders at one site were at the 2nd percentile in English reading, in another at the 6th percentile.

By 1986–87, after five years of the Case Studies treatment, median scores for the 3,500 children in these schools were well above district norms in English read-

Basic Principles of the Case Studies Project

The following theoretical principles, along with their practical implications in the classroom, form the pedagogical basis of the Case Studies project. They are adapted from Basic Principles for the Education of Language-Minority Students: An Overview, *a 1983 publication of the California Department of Education.*

1. For bilingual students, the development of proficiencies in both the native language and English has a positive effect on academic achievement.
2. Language proficiency is the ability to use language for both basic communicative tasks and academic purposes.
3. For LEP students, reaching the "threshold" of native-language skills necessary to complete academic tasks forms the basis for similar proficiency in English. *Implications:*
   • Students are provided substantial amounts of instruction in and through the native language.
   • Initial reading classes and other cognitively demanding subjects are taught in the native language.
   • Sufficient texts and supplementary materials are available in the native language.
   • A sufficient number of well-trained teachers with high levels of native-language proficiency are available to provide instruction.
   • Teachers avoid mixing English and the native language during instruction.
   • Teachers accept regional and nonstandard varieties of the native language.
4. Acquisition of basic communicative competency in a second language is a function of comprehensible second-language instruction and a supportive environment. *Implications:*
   • Comprehensible second-language input is provided through both ESL classes and sheltered English instruction in academic content areas.
   • When content areas are used to provide comprehensible English input, subjects are selected in which the cognitive demands are low to moderate.
   • ESL instruction is communication-based rather than grammar-based and is characterized by the following: (a) content is based on the students' communicative needs; (b) instruction makes extensive use of contextual cues; (c) the teacher uses only English, but modifies speech to students' level and confirms their comprehension; (d) students are permitted to respond in their native language when necessary; (e) the focus is on language function or content, rather than grammatical form; (f) grammatical accuracy is promoted not by correcting errors overtly, but by providing more comprehensible input; and (g) students are encouraged to respond spontaneously and creatively.
   • Opportunities for comprehensible English input are provided for LEP students when grouped by language proficiency and when interacting with fluent English-speaking peers.
5. The perceived status of students affects the interaction between teachers and students and among students themselves. In turn, student outcomes are affected. *Implications:*
   • Teachers use positive interactions in an equitable manner with both language-majority and language-minority students.
   • Language-majority and language-minority students are enrolled in content area classes in which cooperative learning strategies are used.
   • Whenever possible, language-majority students are enrolled in classes designed to develop second-language proficiency in the minority language(s) represented in the school.
   • Administrators, teachers, and students use the minority language(s) represented in the school for noninstructional purposes.

ing, writing, and mathematics. News of this dramatic progress, especially at the Eastman Avenue School in East Los Angeles, the Rockwood School in Calexico, and the Furgeson School in Hawaiian Gardens, prompted numerous other districts to adopt the Case Studies model. Tens of thousands of California students were soon enrolled in variations of the basic curriculum, and its influence was spreading to wider circles of educators throughout the country.

So it came as a surprise to many admirers of the Case Studies approach when the Reagan administration decided in 1986 to terminate the project's Title VII grant two years ahead of schedule.[1] The California Department of Education, facing budgetary problems of its own, declined to fill the gap. While the curriculum remained in place at several schools with local funding, federally financed evaluations and support services were terminated. Apparently, what made Case Studies successful also made it controversial.

Gradual-Exit Model

At the core of the Case Studies approach is intensive native-language development. Its goals are more ambitious than those of many transitional bilingual programs, which strive primarily to keep students from falling behind in content areas while they learn English. The Case Studies curriculum not only teaches LEP children to read in their mother tongue; it also seeks to cultivate a full range of linguistic skills in both languages. Krashen calls it a **gradual-exit model**. From kindergarten to about the 4th grade, Case Studies students receive instruction in ESL, while other subjects are taught in the native language, through sheltered instruction in English, or in mainstream classrooms. Yet there is no hurry to complete students' transition to all-English instruction. Indeed, teachers are trained to resist societal pressures to do so – another break with traditional practices in bilingual education.

The Case Studies curriculum was developed on the theory that academic success demands higher-level academic and literacy skills that, once developed, will transfer readily from the native language to English. On the other hand, the program designers believed, if children leave bilingual programs as soon as they acquire "surface levels" of English, they will be ill-equipped to keep up in class. Thus **cognitive-academic language proficiency** (CALP) became a central goal of the curriculum, even though it takes considerably longer to develop than **basic interpersonal communications skills** (BICS), or "playground English" *(see Chapter 8)*.

In practice this emphasis has paid off, according to the educators who participated in Case Studies. "People are in such a hurry to get kids into English, thinking they're doing the right thing," says Bonnie Rubio, principal of the Eastman Avenue School during the project's first four years. Before Case Studies, she explains, "we were cutting off [native-language instruction] before they developed the thinking process, even the reading comprehension skills, at about 1st grade." Lacking a solid base in their native language, many students were being shortchanged. Rubio says it was common to see 6th graders "still on bunny books" because they had trouble learning to read in English. Initially, she recalls, Eastman's bilingual teachers resisted the gradual-exit approach of Case Studies, but as scores began to rise, "we had converts like you wouldn't believe."

"Most of our 3rd and 4th graders now [make the] transition [into regular classrooms] just about at grade level," says Roqué Berlanga, principal of Furgeson Elementary in suburban Los Angeles. "Whereas before, when we were moving them across earlier, we found there would be a year to a year and a half deficiency. And that would increase as they [rose] through the grades, being frustrated and probably failing."

Before the Case Studies curriculum was launched, a quick-exit philosophy was one of several instructional failings at the five project schools. In their initial site visits, the state consultants noted that, while teachers were generally supportive of bilingual education, few were familiar with effective methodologies in initial literacy or ESL. "Beyond instruction in reading, Spanish was infrequently used as a medium of instruction with any degree of regularity," according to the project's 1986 report. Bilingual teachers were basically on their own in deciding how and when to use Spanish or English. Because there were generally too few Spanish-proficient teachers, untrained aides were conducting lessons in some classrooms. As for Spanish-language materials, the schools had basal readers, but few texts in other subjects or books for supplementary reading.

The assessment also determined that **concurrent translation** was the prevalent method of bilingual instruction. Teachers simply repeated each point of a lesson in both languages, an approach that has been criticized by researchers because it allows students to ignore the English component of the lesson *(see Chapter 8)*. Even though teachers averaged 4.5 years of experience at the five schools, most were uncertain about when to initiate English reading for LEP pupils. Meanwhile ESL instruction stressed memorization of grammar and vocabulary rather than attempts to use the second language for communication. Generally students received little or no **comprehensible input** in English.

Curriculum Design

Dennis Parker, one of the Case Studies consultants, observes that an educational program is like a symphony: without a conductor or score, it can only produce noise, no matter how talented the musicians are. At the outset, Parker says, the project schools "had bilingual teachers who came from the community, they were good ethnic role models, they believed in bilingual education, they were very experienced, [but] the kids were still scoring at the 2nd percentile."

Clearly, if Case Studies was to test a new instructional model, teachers and administrators would have to apply its methods and curriculum with consistency. Toward that end, the state consultants stressed three fundamental points: intensive **staff development**, careful monitoring of classroom practices, and a long-term outlook. Teachers had to be instructed in the *Theoretical Framework* and trained to apply it. Their understanding and implementation of the new approach needed to be evaluated constantly, along with student progress. Administrators had to be

The Case Studies Curriculum Model

	SPANISH	SHELTERED ENGLISH	MAINSTREAM ENGLISH
Phase I K–Grade 1* NEP (SOLOM 5-11)	Language Arts Mathematics Science/Health Social Studies	ESL	Art Music Physical Education
Phase II Grades 2–3* LEP (SOLOM 12-18)	Language Arts Social Studies	ESL Mathematics Science/Health	Art Music Physical Education
Phase III Grades 3–4* LEP (SOLOM 19-25)	Language Arts	Language Arts Social Studies	Art Music Physical Education Mathematics Science/Health
Phase IV Grades 4–6* FEP (SOLOM 25+)	Language Arts (extended Spanish activities)		Art Music Physical Education Language Arts Mathematics Science/Health Social Studies

*Typical grade level for each phase.
NEP = non-English proficient; LEP = limited English proficient; FEP = fully English proficient; SOLOM = Student Oral Language Observation Matrix.

patient but firm, recognizing that it would take time for the treatment's effects to be felt, while ensuring that the curriculum was faithfully taught.

Coordination was also essential because of the complexity of the Case Studies model. With slight variations among schools, it has developed as follows: Students are grouped not by grade, but by language proficiency in both English and Spanish. A child's progress through the program's "phases" reflects his or her performance on the Student Oral Language Observation Matrix (SOLOM), a test of conversational English. All children study essentially the same material; only the language of instruction differs. For Spanish-speaking children the medium gradually moves toward English *(see page 254)*.

Phase I, generally lasting two years for LEP students who start in kindergarten, begins with Spanish-language instruction in subjects that are intellectually challenging and "context reduced": language arts, science, health, social studies, and mathematics. Comprehensible doses of English are provided through ESL and through mainstream classes in art, music, and physical education, subjects that make limited cognitive and linguistic demands while offering a rich context for understanding what is said in the second language.

In *Phase II,* typically grades 2 and 3, Spanish continues as the medium of instruction in language arts and social studies. At the same time, children begin to receive sheltered English classes in math and science, with instruction tailored to their level of English proficiency. In such classrooms, according to the Case Studies program design, "teachers change their speech register by slowing down; limiting their vocabulary and sentence length; repeating, emphasizing, and explaining key concepts; and using examples, props, visual clues, and body language to convey and reinforce meaning carried by the language of instruction." ESL continues in Phase II, and for art, music, and physical education, LEP children are again mixed with fluent English speakers.

In *Phase III,* generally grades 3 and 4, students receive some instruction in English language arts, and social studies becomes a sheltered English subject. All other lessons, including math and science, are taught in mainstream classrooms.

By *Phase IV* children are no longer LEP. The transition to English instruction is complete, except that classes in language arts and sometimes social studies continue in Spanish (a language maintenance feature of the Case Studies model that was never eligible for federal funding). Generally speaking, children who enter the program in kindergarten make the transition to Phase IV sometime in the 4th grade.

Adapting the Model

Although the curriculum looked good on paper, as the schools prepared to adopt it in the 1982–83 school year, they encountered a variety of administrative obstacles. The project schools differed in size, in their concentrations of LEP children, and in the availability and enthusiasm of trained staff. Eastman – with more than 1,700 students in grades K–6, as well as 12 1st grade classrooms – had more flexibility in grouping students than Furgeson did, a suburban school with an enrollment of less than 600. At the same time, Eastman had fewer certified bilingual teachers; only 21 were available to staff 48 bilingual classrooms. Rockwood was located in a small town just across the border from Mexicali – some of its students slipped across from Mexico each day – and about 95 percent of children arrived speaking only Spanish. While their problems differed in particulars, administrators at each site grappled with the realities of low-income communities, from family violence to absenteeism.

Staff resistance had to be overcome at all five Case Studies schools. Although about two-thirds of teachers expressed support for the concept of bilingual education, many resented being told that the methods they had used for years were inadequate, even counterproductive, for their students.

Moreover, the state consultants were theorists rather than practitioners, Rubio explains, and their ideas were sometimes cumbersome. Original plans for sheltered English and mainstream classrooms "would have meant that we'd be juggling children all day long for them to be getting the proper instruction in the right mode," she says. The solution, arrived at after consultation with Eastman's teachers, was **language grouping**. Classrooms would be divided on the basis of English proficiency, an arrangement that necessitated a waiver of California law, which at the time required that English speakers comprise at least one-third of all bilingual classrooms. The new plan led to civil-rights concerns among some teachers, Rubio says, but "it didn't make any difference in East L.A. We were 99.9 percent Hispanic. There was no one else to integrate with." In any case, LEP students were always mixed with fluent English speakers for art, music, and physical education.

Organizationally speaking, language grouping proved to be both cost-effective and educationally effective, says Lilia Stapleton, bilingual coordinator for the ABC Unified School District, where Furgeson is located. "Now the teacher doesn't have to teach in two languages," she explains. "It's cut down on planning time and allows our students to be more on task than before because there's no waiting time [during translations]." And because they no longer spend time with fluent English-speaking children, bilingual teachers are used more efficiently. At Eastman the

Two Models of Bilingual Education

	TRADITIONAL BILINGUAL PROGRAM	CASE STUDIES MODEL
Grouping	1/3 English speakers; 2/3 LEP broad range of English skills; divided by grade level and reading level for all classes	Grouped by levels of language proficiency, grade level, and reading level for core subjects; mixed 1/3 - 2/3 for art, music, and phys. ed.
Methodology	Concurrent translation; grammar-based ESL	Language separated during all subjects (no translation); communication-based ESL
Content Areas	Taught in native language and/or mainstream English	Taught first in native language, then increasingly in sheltered English
Curriculum	Focus is on basics, especially English language arts	Instruction is balanced between language and other subject areas
Exit	Transition before students develop cognitive-academic proficiency in English	Transition after students develop cognitive-academic proficiency in English
Staffing	Requires large number of bilingual teachers; more dependence on aides; little staff development or coordination among bilingual and English-language teachers	Requires fewer bilingual teachers because of language grouping; less dependence on aides; much emphasis on inservice training in teaching strategies; team teaching and cooperative planning
Accountability	Responsibility for teaching LEP students rests primarily on bilingual staff; little or no involvement by principal	Responsibility for teaching LEP students rests on all school staff; requires strong administrative commitment

Source: Los Angeles Unified School District, "Eastman Curriculum Design Project," 1986.

number of bilingual classrooms was reduced by nearly 40 percent and fewer instructional aides were needed.

Case Studies gave teachers no choice. They had to change their methods and they had to work closely with their colleagues. **Team teaching** was mandatory, not a popular idea at the outset, Rubio recalls: "It meant there was more accountability and the need to stay on a tight schedule. [Previously] some teachers did reading for two hours, spelling during math time, health if they thought of it. Some did science

and some didn't do science because they didn't like it." Now teachers had to cooperate and keep on schedule, rather than going at their own pace or favoring one
subject at the expense of another. In the Case Studies program, a team typically
made up of two bilingual teachers and one monolingual English teacher consulted
on the needs of each student, divided children up for various classes, and followed
their progress. This collegial approach, along with growing indications of student
progress, had a salutary effect on staff morale, according to administrators.

In the beginning, recalls Simón López, principal of the Rockwood School in
Calexico, his staff was polarized into "different camps," with bilingual teachers on
one side and monolingual English teachers on the other. "Everybody was doing
their own thing" in the classroom, he says, with teachers usually absorbed by their
own problems. As they began sharing responsibility for instruction, attitudes
changed; the staff began to "focus on the child." A major benefit of Case Studies,
López says, has been in "giving us a real mission, a vision of what it is we're trying
to do." Stapleton adds: "It's really brought the staffs together. And by exposing the
monolingual teachers to ESL techniques, [teaming has helped them to] understand
what the children are going through in the process of acquiring English. And they
have a little bit more empathy for these kids."

Introducing the Case Studies curriculum meant revolutionizing the entire
school program, a process that is never painless. Rubio explains: "It changes [prin-
cipals'] whole lives: 'We want you to redo your school totally; reschedule all your
schedules; change the way you assign children in classrooms; affect all the training
for your school staff, the teachers, the aides; change the way you relate to parents.'"
At the same time, she argues, aggressive leadership by the principal is essential to
the success of the Case Studies model. In an early stage at Eastman, Rubio bluntly
told resisters on her staff either to teach the curriculum – whether they agreed with
it or not – or to transfer out. "It takes the flak of change until you can get to the
benefits of change," she says. "If you're willing to take the flak, believe me, it'll be
worth it in the end."

Tight organization is also necessary to ensure that a **balanced curriculum** is
taught, one that focuses not just on language but on all-round cognitive development as well. John Myers, who initiated a similar instructional model as principal of
Bell Gardens Elementary School near Los Angeles, argues that the mark of a poor-
quality bilingual program is inordinate concentration on language teaching at the
expense of academic content areas:

> Because the kids can't read English, they give them *more* reading in English,
> along with language arts, spelling, and some math. But the thinking areas of

science and social studies and health – these subjects where you're picking up the major ideas you're going to deal with in life – aren't being taught. And so the minority children are set over to one side, most of them being poor and already having a disadvantage, and they're not getting an equal opportunity.

By contrast, in the Case Studies model, no student is treated as a remedial case simply because he or she lacks English proficiency. Language of instruction is incidental to the curriculum, except that LEP children pick up English as they progress from one phase to another. Rubio explains the results:

> One of the things that's exciting is, you can walk into a classroom and the 2nd graders are doing science experiments and – talking, talking – they're doing committee work. These are the same kids that in another [program] would be just sitting there wondering what was going on, or in a corner with a translator. To me, that made it all worthwhile. There's nothing wrong with them. Because they can't speak the English language doesn't mean they can't learn. And for them to be doing the same type of things the other kids are doing – you can imagine how that affects their self-image. We found that it eliminated a lot of the stigma, when they saw the teacher was using their [native] language.

Student Outcomes

Case Studies set the following goals: (1) after three years 100 percent of students would achieve basic oral communicative skills in English, as measured by the SOLOM, and (2) after seven years at least 50 percent would score at or above national norms on the Comprehensive Test of Basic Skills (CTBS) in reading, language arts, and mathematics. These were high expectations at schools where the median reading scores for 6th graders in 1981 ranged from the 1st to the 12th percentile.

By the end of the third year, 1985–86, when funding for the Case Studies project was terminated, only one of the goals had been reached, on average, at all five schools: at least 60 percent of students in grades 2 through 6 who entered the program in kindergarten were scoring at or above California norms in math. In 1984–85, the most recent year for which overall figures are available,[2] 52 percent of 2nd graders had achieved oral English proficiency, along with 72 percent of 3rd graders and 91 percent of 4th graders. (The goal of 100 percent after three years may be unrealistic, say the Case Studies designers, suspecting that the oral SOLOM test may include "aspects of academic language proficiency that take longer to attain.") In English reading, 39 percent of 3rd graders had reached state norms, as

FIGURE 10–1
Eastman School Outcomes
(California Assessment Program, 1980–1987)

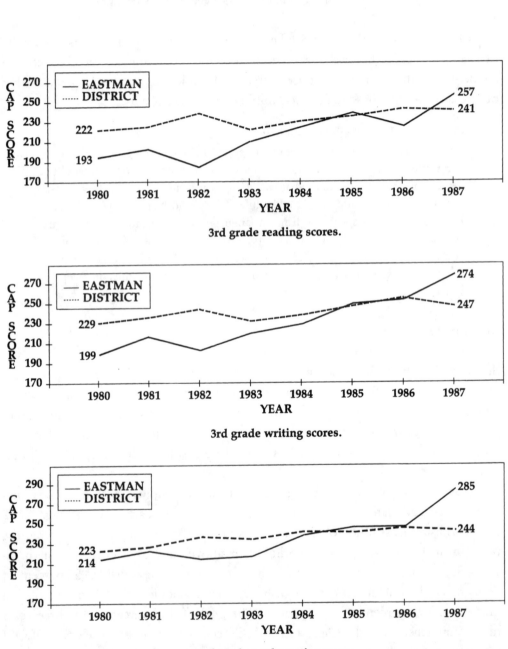

3rd grade reading scores.

3rd grade writing scores.

3rd grade mathematics scores.

FIGURE 10–1
Eastman School Outcomes (cont'd.)
(California Assessment Program, 1980–1987)

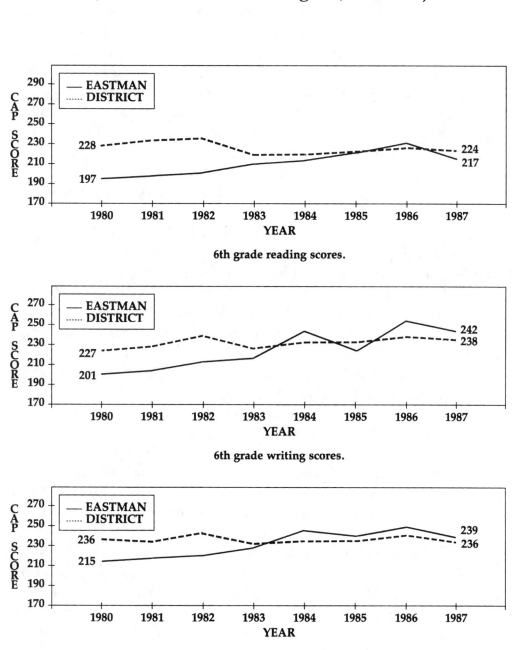

6th grade reading scores.

6th grade writing scores.

6th grade mathematics scores.

had 30 percent of 6th graders.

Despite the project's failure to reach all of its original goals, evaluators were heartened by a steady upward trend in every category of achievement. They documented strong correlations between Spanish reading proficiency and scores in English reading two years later, lending support to Cummins's **interdependence hypothesis** that literacy skills are transferable from the native language to English. Significantly, Norm Gold reports, the "schools where the curriculum was fully implemented" achieved the best results. Administrative problems at two of the Case Studies sites, the Mission Education Center in San Francisco and the Huron Elementary School in the Coalinga-Huron Joint Unified School District, kept the model from being thoroughly tested there, he says. Students progressed more rapidly and consistently at the other three schools.

In 1981–82, the year before Case Studies began, Rockwood Elementary was Calexico's lowest-achieving school; by 1983–84 it was the district's highest, based on California Assessment Program (CAP) results.[3] Under Case Studies there was a steady, upward pattern of achievement; at other schools in the district, scores continued to fluctuate unpredictably from year to year. In 1981–82, Rockwood's 3rd graders were at the 6th percentile in reading on the CTBS. By 1984–85, as 6th graders, this cohort had reached the 38th percentile. In language arts they progressed from the 7th to the 44th percentile over the same period; in math from the 19th to the 64th. For other groups of Rockwood students, the general pattern has been the same. In 1985–86, 6th graders scored at the 32nd percentile in reading, the 46th in language, and the 59th in mathematics.

The Eastman Avenue School posted similar progress.[4] Between 1982–83 and 1985–86, the school's CAP scores climbed from well below average for Los Angeles to generally above average in reading, writing, and mathematics. On the CTBS in 1986, Eastman's 4th graders averaged up to 15 percentiles higher in reading and 25 percentiles higher in math than their counterparts in East Los Angeles (compared against national norms, they scored at the 45th and 66th percentiles, respectively).

Like all achievement test results, Eastman's vary somewhat from year to year. But after Case Studies was introduced, the overall curve was one of substantial improvement. In 1987 CAP scores, the school's 3rd graders made their most impressive gains; in reading (257) they surpassed the Los Angeles citywide median by 16 points; in language (274) by 27 points; and in math (285) by 41 points. Notwithstanding a slight dip in 1987, Eastman's 6th graders also showed substantial improvements since 1980 *(see Figure 10–1).*

Flexibility or Leadership?

For the California Department of Education, Case Studies marked a departure from its normal "top down" approach, says Fred Tempes, who directed the project until 1986. "We [used to] say, 'Here's what's best for all kids, no matter what the concentrations or what languages they speak, because the state law tells us so. And here's what thou shalt do to make it happen." The state's Chacón-Moscone Bilingual-Bicultural Education Act was "very beneficial" before it was allowed to expire in 1987, he adds, "but the law by itself [was not] sufficient." Quality programs for English learners cannot be legislated, according to Tempes. Instead, school districts need to see successful models that they can adapt for their own students.

As the Case Studies project began to demonstrate the advantages of its theory-driven approach, a national debate was raging over whether Title VII should continue to favor bilingual education or – as the Reagan administration proposed – instead give school districts "flexibility" to experiment with nonbilingual approaches. Dennis Parker argues that "local option" can be a recipe for educational neglect or chaos; furthermore, it is not what most school administrators are seeking. He quotes the plea of one district official: "We don't need flexibility. We need leadership. We don't know what to do with these kids. We need some guidance." Parker concludes: "Don't tell people, 'Do whatever you think is right, and we'll reward you if you come up with some good programs,' but rather, 'Here are some things we think you should try.'" Developing and popularizing effective approaches are essential, Tempes adds:

> We worked with [the Eastman] school for five years. People may say that's a poor use of resources. You've got these state consultants who spend 50 percent of their time with one elementary school when you've got 7,000 elementary schools [in California]. What happened was, they were doing an excellent job and – we didn't even promote this – people started calling and asking, "Can we come over and take a look?" Lots of [districts] are on the lookout for innovation. They hear about something, and they want to see what it is; they want to evaluate it and use it if they can. That seems to work better than state laws mandating excellence. The excellence really is out there.

By 1985, following enthusiastic stories in Los Angeles newspapers, Eastman began to give tours of its program. Soon it was receiving more attention than it could handle, and visiting days had to be limited to one per month. Meanwhile other California educators decided to try the Case Studies model. The Ontario-

Montclair School District adopted it for all elementary schools. Los Angeles County began planning a replication project encompassing several medium-sized districts, including a Portuguese bilingual program in ABC Unified. In 1986, the Los Angeles Unified School District appropriated $250,000 and hired Bonnie Rubio to replicate Eastman's approach at seven schools serving 10,000 students; in 1987 the project was expanded to 20 additional sites.

Taking a dimmer view of the Case Studies experiment, the U.S. Department of Education terminated its Title VII grant two years early, claiming that "your project has not made substantial and measurable progress in achieving the specific educational goals contained in the approved application." (The federal director of bilingual education, Carol Pendás Whitten, said the money would be redirected to programs that promised to mainstream children "as quickly as possible.") No one was surprised when the Reagan administration also declined to fund Rubio's replication project. Undaunted by federal opposition, however, the Los Angeles school board voted in 1988 to make the "Eastman model" the cornerstone of a $20 million expansion of bilingual education. It continues today – with federal funding through at least 2004 – in 21 schools known as Project MORE.

Suggested Reading

California State Department of Education. *Schooling and Language Minority Students: A Theoretical Framework.* Los Angeles: California State University, 1981.

Krashen, Stephen, and Biber, Douglas. *On Course: Bilingual Education's Success in California.* Sacramento: California Association for Bilingual Education, 1988.

See also p. 402.

Online Resource Guide

California State Department of Education. *Case Studies in Bilingual Education: Second Year Report (1984–85).* Sacramento: Bilingual Education Office, 1986.

See also companion CD-ROM.

Notes

1. Title VII funding began in the project's second year, 1983–84, and was expected to continue through 1987–88. It was terminated in 1986 following a dispute with the federal Office of Bilingual Education and Minority Languages Affairs.
2. An ambitious final evaluation, which would have tracked the progress of individual students who received the full Case Studies treatment, was canceled for lack of Title VII funding.
3. These scores include the one-third of Rockwood's students who were not enrolled in the bilingual program.
4. Available test data for these years were schoolwide. About 60 percent of Eastman students were receiving bilingual instruction.

11 Indian Language Education

Approximately 175 **indigenous languages** are still spoken in the United States – rivaling the number of immigrant languages – but fewer than one-quarter of these are still being learned by children. Without intergenerational transmission, they are considered **moribund**, or destined to die out in the near future. As many as 45 Native American tongues, spoken primarily by elders in their 70s and 80s, were expected to disappear in the 1990s; at least 100 others face the prospect of extinction in the next

two or three generations. If current trends continue, only 20 will remain alive by 2050, according to Michael Krauss of the Alaska Native Language Center. Even now, relatively few speakers of any indigenous language are school-age children.

In this context, the need for bilingual education among American Indians and Alaska Natives is sometimes questioned. Many who would not dispute the importance of special language programs for newly arrived Cambodians or Salvadorans assume that, since most Native American students are dominant in English when they start school, bilingual instruction is unwarranted. Why waste time teaching them in tribal languages when they already speak English? This assumption stems from a failure to recognize what is special about these students.

Why Bilingual Education?

First, while language shift has affected many Native American communities, it is usually a **nonstandard dialect** of English that has displaced the ancestral tongue among younger generations. Today's parents may retain some of their native language, but tend to be dominant in a variety of **American Indian English**; thus their children learn this dialect at home. While such children grow up with no knowledge, or perhaps passive knowledge, of the indigenous language, they have little exposure to **Standard English** or, in many cases, to literate uses of English before entering school. So they tend to encounter many of the same language barriers as LEP immigrant students, although the barriers may be less obvious. For the first decade of Title VII, programs serving English-dominant children were ineligible for federal funding. Most Indian students therefore went unserved, even when their academic needs resembled those of English learners. Recognizing this problem, in 1978 Congress expanded the definition of limited English proficiency to include "American Indian and Alaska Native students who come from environments where a language other than English has had a significant impact on their level of English language proficiency."[1]

The second thing that needs to be understood is that **cultural loss** has academic consequences. It diminishes Native American children's sense of identity and pride in their origins, which they need to counter society's negative messages about "Indian-ness." Students who lack the cultural tools to define themselves – especially if they come from "disadvantaged," or socially stigmatized, backgrounds – are likely to encounter problems in school. The native language is an essential resource. For indigenous peoples in particular, language serves as the central repository of tribal history, customs, and values, little of which exists in written form. When a language dies, so does much of the culture that it expressed, along with an important symbol of group identity. Preserving and revitalizing **endangered languages** must therefore be recognized as an educational priority.

Bilingual programs, if correctly designed, can address both of these problems. They can help children acquire Standard English while learning other subjects, and they can teach the ancestral language, keeping it alive for future generations.

Nevertheless, Indian bilingual education has faced resistance – and not just from unsympathetic whites. For many Indians, the idea of using tribal languages for instruction represents a confusing reversal of government policy. When Title VII programs were first introduced on Montana reservations in the late 1960s, adults recalled with bitterness their own educational experiences. In Bureau of Indian Affairs (BIA) schools, students had been punished severely for violating **speak-English-only rules**; public and parochial schools, especially in the Southwest, frequently adopted the BIA's policy *(see Chapter 4)*. After being submersed in sink-or-swim classrooms, Indians tended to associate their tribal languages with academic difficulties. Why should a new generation of students, many of whom spoke little Crow or Cree or Cheyenne, risk similar humiliations? parents asked. Some required children to use English in the home, for their own good. Why should the schools do anything less?

Ted Risingsun, a longtime school board member in Busby, Montana, worked hard to change such attitudes. He urged his fellow members of the Northern Cheyenne tribe to take pride in their language and to recognize the benefits of preserving it for future generations. Risingsun also stressed its educational value: "We found that those who learn Cheyenne well learn English well." Parents were invited into the classroom to see for themselves. By the end of the first year, he recalls, the bilingual program had "almost 100 percent support" on the reservation.

Growing up in the 1930s, Risingsun himself had been forbidden by white educators to speak Cheyenne, the only language he knew. "I'd never spoken English," he says, "but at school I was expected to use it. I didn't even know my name [in English] was Ted Risingsun. I hung my head. If there had been a bilingual teacher there, things would have been different."

Rose Chesarek, a Crow educator, tells a similar story about her sink-or-swim experience. "When you come in the school doors, everything is totally foreign. You shed everything at the door, sit at a desk, and you don't understand one word of what goes on. I don't know how I got to 4th grade, because I don't remember too much of anything until then." Her school's ban on using Crow lasted into the 1950s, part of a policy of suppressing everything about students that was Indian, Chesarek says. "All the way through school, I was told they just wanted to make me a white person, so I'd succeed. The teachers would tell me everything about me was bad. I'd go home and think about it: 'What in the hell got me to be an Indian? Why?'"

On becoming a bilingual teacher, Chesarek was determined to break the pattern of low self-esteem and underachievement still suffered by many Crow children. Native-language instruction, she explains, can play an important role in developing students' pride in their Indian identity, a factor that research has linked to improved achievement in school. Based on her own teaching experience, she has no doubts about the long-term, cognitive benefits of bilingual education. In 1973–74, when linguists were still developing the Crow alphabet, Chesarek became the first teacher of reading in that language. Her class of 15 monolingual Crow speakers received initial literacy and mathematics instruction in Crow, along with ESL. Although the children did well, the reading program was abandoned after a year, and Chesarek resigned because of disorganization and controversy within the early Title VII program. Those students have now graduated from high school, she says. "All through the years, I would follow them, talk to their parents and ask how they were doing. And most parents would say, 'Oh, that one is doing so well, but my others are not. I wonder why.'"

Special Case of LEP

A major cause of school failure among Native Americans, and among other language minorities as well, is students' failure to develop literacy and other academic skills in either English or the tribal tongue. The problem, explains William Leap, an American University anthropologist, is that the "variety of English common to their home and community [bears] many similarities (in sounds used, in sentence forms, and in style and structure of speaking) to the ancestral language of the community. It [is] their knowledge of the locally appropriate 'Indian English' code – not their knowledge of their ancestral language per se – which [is] creating the classroom difficulties." Such children tend to have more trouble acquiring the academic registers of English needed in school. Yet attempts to impose Standard English through the correction of errors and other remedial techniques is not the answer, Leap says. It can

> lead to serious consequences for the child ... [whose] control over his community's Indian English variety may be his only link to ancestral language fluency. It may, for example, help explain why Indian students say they "understand" their grandparents when they talk, yet they cannot "speak" to their grandparents in their [tribal] language. Remediation destroys these linkages – hence student rejection of attempts to [impose] standard language

structures, [especially when schools offer them] no alternative other than to acquire it or reject it.

Bilingual education offers a way out of this dilemma, Leap argues. By studying their native language, students can acquire "better control over the non-English grammar" they have internalized. In this way they become conscious of structural differences between the Standard English of academic pursuits and the vernacular used on the reservation.

George Reed, a former Crow educator and linguist, complains that many of his reservation's youth grow up speaking "Crowlish," a blend of the Indian language and English. Native-language instruction can play a role in "helping Indian children sort out their identity" and in slowing the erosion of Indian tongues, he says. "My lexicon is my way of life. Culture is expressed by the language, and my language is tied up with the culture."

Research evidence suggests there are academic advantages for Indian children whose language is preserved and used in the home. This was the conclusion of a five-year longitudinal study conducted in the 1970s by Steve Chesarek, an administrator in several reservation schools, who tracked Crow students' patterns of achievement, with and without bilingual education. In those days native-language instruction at Crow Agency, Montana, was just getting started. After the departure of Chesarek's wife, Rose, it was "basically an oral program," he says. "But what we found was that if you utilize the kids' own language, you see some rapid growth in a number of areas, including English development. Kids who are fluent Crow speakers learn English very quickly, if somebody sets out to teach them English. And they do well in other academic areas, too."

While Crow students at the time were more likely to speak their native language, as compared with students on other Montana reservations, some Crow parents still tried to raise their children in English only. This decision tended to have negative effects on school achievement, according to Steve Chesarek: "English is their only language, but [by kindergarten] they're already limited English speakers. They're hearing two Crow-speaking parents, or maybe a Crow and a Cheyenne, who are dealing in their short suit [when using English]. Typically, if one of the parents was a fluent English speaker, the child had no problem with English. But there weren't very many of those."

Out of tradition or necessity, Indian grandparents play a major role in child-rearing, says Minerva Allen, federal programs director for the Hays/Lodge Pole school district in northeastern Montana. "The grandparents have always raised kids;

it's a cultural value. And a lot are raised by the grandparents because of [parents'] alcoholism, teen-age pregnancy, or the parents go off to look for a job." While this social pattern helps to maintain an appreciation of Indian traditions, it also tends to perpetuate limited English proficiency. Members of the older generations are more likely to be monolingual, or at least dominant, in the tribal language.

As a group, students who grow up in homes where English is spoken, but spoken poorly, are likely to start behind and stay behind, says Steve Chesarek. By contrast, proficient Crow speakers may begin school two to three years behind, but they quickly catch up, according to his research. Crow children who speak only English, he says,

> tend to become somewhat isolated. The Crow-speaking kids aren't as likely to play with them because they don't speak Crow, and the white kids aren't as likely to play with them because they're Indian. And so they form their own play group, and they reinforce the limited English that they have. If you want to draw a generalization: It doesn't matter which language you raise your child[ren] in; as long as you're fluent in it, they'll become fluent in it.[2]

Early Title VII Efforts

The federal government's first foray into Indian bilingual education came in 1969, when it financed a "pan-Indian" project involving the Crow, Rocky Boy, and Northern Cheyenne reservations. Little is known about the results of this early effort, according to Cheryl Crawley, assistant superintendent of the school district that includes the towns of Hardin and Crow Agency. "But people found out that you can't have a pan-Indian bilingual program because of the enormous differences between tribes and languages."

"One of the fallacies that white people have about Indians is that they think we're generic," says Richard Littlebear, a member of the Northern Cheyenne tribe and president of Dull Knife Memorial College. American Indian tongues vary enormously, falling into more than 50 distinct "families" as different from each other as Romance languages and Chinese. Language situations also vary enormously among indigenous communities. The extent to which a vernacular has been preserved, what role it plays in reservation life, whether it is written as well as spoken, how language attitudes fit into tribal politics – such questions are crucial in designing Indian bilingual education programs.

On the Rocky Boy reservation, a long tradition of Cree literacy has been nurtured and guarded by the tribal elders, according to Steve Chesarek:

They already knew how to read and write Cree [when bilingual education programs began], and so they'd teach the young kids who were going to be teachers. There was no question whether it was culturally pure; it was coming from the experts. There's a whole body of Cree literature that's never been translated into English. They're very jealous of their own copyright. For kids old enough to realize this, there's a motivation to learn to read in Cree.

Attempts to put Crow into written form began in the 1960s, when the Wycliffe Bible translators[3] began to develop an orthography, or functional writing system. The project continued into the late 1970s with the aid of academic experts, including G. H. Matthews of the Massachusetts Institute of Technology and two native Crow speakers who had studied linguistics at MIT. The first comprehensive Crow dictionary was finally completed in 1986. When Crow Agency won a new Title VII grant in 1977 and administrators began looking for teachers, there were only 11 adults known to be literate in the language. That number has increased substantially, thanks to teacher training and a Crow Studies curriculum at the reservation's Little Big Horn Community College directed by Dale Old Horn, one of the MIT-trained linguists.

Initially the idea of teaching Crow literacy was foreign to parents who had never read a word in their native tongue. Many questioned whether the program's emphasis on Crow culture was time well spent, an attitude that reflected dissatisfaction with an earlier Title VII program featuring large amounts of beadwork and other traditional crafts. "In the beginning, our biggest goal was public relations," Cheryl Crawley explains, "getting parents to understand what we were trying to do. We emphasized that culture in the classroom meant doing academics embedded in a familiar cultural context that Indian children could understand." Using a newsletter and calendars with monthly messages about bilingual education, the Crow Agency program gradually won over the community. Parents stopped asking for their children to be excused from native-language instruction and stopped insisting on English at home.

Among other pedagogical problems, the Crow Agency program had to cope with a dearth of instructional materials in Crow. Beginning in 1979, Title VII financed a Bilingual Materials Development Center that published tribal legends and history, along with original stories by its staff, in both English and Crow. The center produced bilingual calendars, workbooks, Crow-language flash cards, filmstrips, and bulletin board exhibits. It also took charge of compiling the Crow dictionary.

While located on the Crow reservation, the center also published materials in other Indian languages until the U.S. Department of Education withdrew its funding in 1986. This was a significant setback for Indian bilingual education, Crawley says. "Materials development is vital. No commercial publisher is going to do it because they can't make any kind of profit," owing to the limited market for Indian language publications. Although Crow Agency was able to divert part of its Title VII grant to produce materials, the amount was far short of what was needed, according to Marlene Walking Bear, the program's director. The tribal government wanted to help out, she adds, but its budget was tight, and other expenditures tended to get priority on the economically depressed reservation.

Introducing Crow Literacy

While perhaps an extreme case, Crow Agency illustrates students' pressing need for language assistance on many reservations at the time. As of the mid-1980s, most of the bilingual school's 250 children in grades K through 6 came from homes where Crow was spoken. Although many appeared fluent in conversational English, Walking Bear reports that 99 percent were assessed as LEP: "They don't have the academic language. They can hear and follow directions, but they may not be able to produce."

On entering the program, children are taught oral concepts in Crow, and about half their time is spent in reading-readiness and ESL instruction. Basic reading skills are taught in English. The percentage of native language in other subjects is gradually reduced to about 20 percent by the 4th grade, when Crow reading is introduced. This language enrichment program continues through grade 6, along with lessons in Crow history, and its benefits appear to be more than cultural. "More and more, kids are reading close to grade level" in English, Walking Bear says. While they have yet to reach national norms, students' scores have risen steadily since the program was introduced.

Crawley, who developed this instructional model, says that the lack of a basal reader in Crow has made initial reading instruction impractical in the native tongue. "I think the kids find it easier to learn to read English than to read Crow," she says, "because the Crow words are so long, because the exposure they've had to print already is in English, and they're used to [English] combinations of vowels and consonants." As in many Indian languages, Crow words for some simple concepts can be difficult. For example, the six-syllable word for chair is *baleaalawaache*, or "something to sit on." This is one of many "compound words that came about through contact with whites," Crawley explains. "It's a description of an object rather than a simple, everyday word that has been in the language longer." Thus attempting to decode such words can overwhelm the beginning reader, she argues. "Once kids have learned the techniques in English, and they get to 4th grade motivated to learn to read in their own language, then learning to read in Crow comes quite easy for them [and will help] to build self-esteem."

Other educators and researchers have taken issue with this argument, noting that the Finnish, Magyar, Welsh, and Samoan languages feature word length and syntactical complexity comparable to those of Crow and other Indian tongues. "A foreign language always looks formidable to a person who's going to learn it," says Richard Littlebear. He notes that Americans who saw *Mary Poppins* now "can say 'supercalifragilisticexpialidocious,' and that's longer than any of the Cheyenne words." Rose Chesarek reports that her students in the early 1970s learned Crow literacy with ease and were soon reading "a book a week," because Crow's sounds and phonetic alphabet are similar to those of English, with only a few exceptions.

Needed: Indian Teachers

Crow Agency was fortunate in its ability to train and recruit Crow-speaking staff, who made up eight of its 15 teachers in 1986–87. Those lacking fluency in the language worked with half a dozen Crow-speaking aides from the community. Altogether there were about 40 certified Crow teachers, Crawley estimates, though only about half were still teaching on the reservation, not necessarily in bilingual programs.

It was a different story that year at nearby Busby, Montana, whose Title VII program had no Cheyenne-speaking teachers and needed to rely heavily on instructional aides. Because of low pay and geographical isolation, well-qualified white teachers for Indian children are also difficult to find, explains Norma Bixby, chair of the local school board. She adds that Busby has lost some effective instructors to aggressive recruiting by other Indian schools.

At Hays/Lodge Pole, located on the Fort Belknap reservation, there were just two certified Indian teachers in the Title VII program for 82 students in 1986–87, according to Minerva Allen.[4] Further straining local resources, the "bilingual" program had to be *trilingual* to accommodate children from the two tribes that occupy the reservation. Some speak Assiniboine, a member of the Siouan language family; others speak Gros Ventre, an Algonquian language. The two tongues share no more grammar or vocabulary with each other than they do with English, notes Allen, an Assiniboine. Initial reading is taught in each of the native languages, she reports, and "all the kids seem to learn both" in addition to English, which is used for instruction about 75 percent of the time.

Knowledge of the structure of Native American languages is essential to high-quality ESL instruction, according to Jon Reyhner of Northern Arizona University. For native-English speakers, these languages tend to be among the most difficult to acquire. Yet, in Montana and nationwide, only a tiny proportion of those who teach Indian students are Indians themselves. "It would be a great help to the Indian children to have more," Allen says. "If we could train more teachers, we wouldn't need the federal funds."

Schools might also reduce high rates of staff turnover, a perennial problem in BIA facilities, if more teachers had roots in the surrounding community; non-Indian teachers rarely do. On the other hand, according to Steve Chesarek, recruiting teachers locally can create "a whole new set of social and political problems that can get in the way of how people perceive bilingual education. If you're hiring a local person, it's hard to get rid of him." This is especially true on Montana reservations, where unemployment often approaches 85 percent, he says.

> These are revolutionary programs compared to, say, Chapter 1, in the sense that they lead to dramatic shifts in who controls the schools. You see a different type of involvement from bilingual parents and from teachers who speak the language. And you may find [English-speaking Indians] who feel threatened because [bilingual teaching] is a job that can be done only by someone who knows the language.

At times, Chesarek adds, committed bilingual educators have been "politically pushed out" during struggles between tribal factions.

Indian educators have tackled the bilingual teacher shortage in various ways. In the early 1970s the Navajo Nation launched an ambitious initiative to increase the number of certified Navajo teachers. It combined on-site training of instructors with summer programs on nearby college campuses. The American Indian Language Development Institute (University of Arizona) and the Summer Institute of Linguistics for Native Americans (University of New Mexico) have enabled members of several southwestern tribes to earn certification as well as college degrees. Both programs are oriented toward meeting the needs of bilingual classrooms.

Local teacher recruitment and training have been crucial to the success of bilingual education at Rock Point, Arizona, where a community school board took over the operation of elementary and secondary schools. By the late 1970s Rock

Point students, once among the lowest scoring in the BIA system, were approaching – and occasionally reaching – national norms of school achievement; they were consistently outperforming their peers in other Indian schools. Daniel McLaughlin, a former principal there, explains that in 1968,

> when the bilingual effort began at Rock Point, there were no training programs for teaching in Navajo, nor was there a pool of trained individuals to draw upon. Local people and talent were all that could be relied upon. On-site college classes were offered, and non-credentialed staff were required to make continual progress toward certification. By the late 1980s, approximately 85 percent of all instructional staff were Navajos; more than 60 individuals had gained teaching certificates while working at Rock Point; and increasingly, new teachers came from the ranks of recent bilingual-biliterate graduates of the program itself.

Using this approach, the elementary school achieved a student-teacher ratio of nine to one, enabling it to teach all subjects in both English and Navajo. Self-reliance offered another advantage, McLaughlin says. Teacher training was "Rock Point–centered," focusing on the community's needs and the program's philosophy of developmental bilingualism.

By 1992, Navajos held about 1,500 of 6,000 teaching positions on the reservation in federal, public, private, and community schools, according to a tribal survey. With help from the Ford Foundation, the Navajo Division of Education has provided financial aid to paraprofessionals seeking certification and matched them with teacher-training institutions, many with branches in or near Navajo communities. To participate, candidates must be orally proficient – and willing to become literate – in the Navajo language.

Self-Determination and Its Limits

The Indian Self-Determination Act of 1975, which authorized the Bureau of Indian Affairs to "contract out" the operation of its schools, allowed communities like Rock Point to take control of their children's education. Since then more than 70 have done so, often with excellent results. Local control has brought innovation to stagnant institutions where it was sorely needed, sometimes in the form of exemplary bilingual programs. Given significant decision-making power for the first time, Indian parents frequently feel a new responsibility for educational outcomes. Students tend to respond favorably to higher expectations for their achievement.

Community schools' potential was first tapped by an experiment involving the Navajo Nation, the BIA, and the federal Office of Economic Opportunity. The

Rough Rock Demonstration School, founded in 1966, was also the first bilingual-bicultural program for Native Americans. An all-Navajo school board, largely nonliterate and non-English-speaking, nevertheless set ambitious academic goals while insisting on a Navajo approach to learning. No longer was the school perceived as an alien institution run by outsiders; now it reflected community attitudes, values, and styles of interacting. Using a variety of federal grants, the school established a Navajo Curriculum Center to develop materials, a parent advisory committee, a teacher-training effort, and a transitional bilingual program.

The experiment also brought economic benefits to an isolated area, where cash incomes from farming and sheep-herding averaged $85 a year in the 1960s. The school board not only hired local residents, but also sold hay, milk, fuel, and other commodities at a discount, constructed low-income housing, and helped set up a medical clinic. It secured BIA funding to build new classroom facilities and to pave the first road into the community, opening Rough Rock to the outside world. By 1983, per capita income averaged nearly $2,500 annually. "Though still far below the national average, this greatly enhanced the quality of life for local residents," according to Teresa McCarty, a former curriculum developer at Rough Rock who now teaches at the University of Arizona. The demonstration school also succeeded in developing Navajo leadership, whose impact has been felt beyond the immediate community. Today many of the reservation's most respected educators trace their professional roots to Rough Rock.

So far, however, the school has produced no miraculous gains in academic achievement. McCarty acknowledges that, despite limited assessment data, by the 1980s it became clear that student progress was less than what Rough Rock's founders had anticipated. The main reason, she believes, is "the absence of any stable pedagogical approach over time." In the late 1970s the bilingual program was overshadowed by a prepackaged "basic skills" curriculum that emphasized English phonics and grammar drills. Soon after, two new bilingual-bicultural approaches were developed but became controversial because of their Navajo religious content. School staff divided into factions favoring each of the three curricula, all of which had school board approval; not surprisingly, none was well implemented. Meanwhile self-determination did not erase attitudes that BIA schools had produced through years of indoctrination. Many parents continued to believe that the school's job was to "teach the white man's way," McCarty says.

The most important problem, she believes, was Rough Rock's dependence on short-term funding from federal categorical programs. Oftentimes, when the money ran out at Rough Rock, so did the instructional approach it supported; new pedagogies were then tailored to new funding sources. Unlike Rock Point, whose community school board has never wavered in its financial commitment to bilingual education, Rough Rock has no guarantee that its Navajo-English program would continue without federal or other external assistance.

This is a pervasive problem in Indian education. Reliance on outside financing sacrifices the stability of instructional programs, while local resources are often inadequate to sustain them. Community schools generally have a bare-bones budget provided under contracts with the BIA, supplemented by federal grants that are not designed to be permanent entitlements. Title VII, for example, was expected to be used for **capacity-building** – that is, to make English learner programs self-sufficient. In high-poverty areas, such expectations are unrealistic. On Indian reservations in particular, education is one of numerous programs competing for scarce tribal dollars. Even where public school districts exercise jurisdiction, Indian lands are not subject to taxation. So schools have had to rely heavily on federal assistance under the Johnson-O'Malley Act, Title IV of the 1972 Indian Education Act, and the impact aid program, all of which suffered severe cuts during the 1980s. In 2002, the picture darkened further under **Title III of the No Child Left Behind Act**, which features less generous funding formulas for Indian language programs than the Bilingual Education Act provided *(see Chapter 14)*.

Rough Rock came up with one innovative solution to this problem, however, enhancing pedagogical consistency even as funding for bilingual education remained uncertain. In 1983, it entered into a collaboration with the Kamehameha Early Education Program (KEEP), a Honolulu-based effort that made effective use of Hawaiian culture in the classroom. KEEP wanted to see how its approach would work in a different setting, while Rough Rock teachers were seeking an alternative to their ineffective basic-skills curriculum. The five-year partnership helped to revive a Navajo-English bilingual curriculum and to develop a stable leadership, despite continued turnover among Rough Rock administrators. The key, according to McCarty and bilingual director Galena Dick, was to train and empower Navajo teachers as conscious "change agents." While modeled on KEEP, the new K–3 curriculum was developed and adapted by Rough Rock teachers themselves.[5] Hence there has been a strong feeling of local "ownership," an essential factor in the success of any Indian education program.

Language Survival

When bilingual education began at Rough Rock and Rock Point, at least 90 percent of the students started school as monolingual Navajo speakers. More than three decades later, that pattern has changed dramatically. Although these communities remain relatively isolated, virtually all children now speak some English on arrival and barely 50 percent are assessed as proficient in Navajo. Language shift has proceeded even faster in the reservation's larger towns. In 1992, a tribal survey of 3,328 entering students at 110 Navajo-majority schools found that 32 percent spoke Navajo well, while 73 percent spoke English well; only 16 percent were rated higher in Navajo than in English.[6] Within a generation the native tongue has lost enormous ground.

The number of Navajo speakers remains substantial: 178,014, or 47 percent of all indigenous language speakers in the United States, according to the 2000 census. While a majority of adult Navajos are bilingual, it is not uncommon for elders to speak little or no English. Nevertheless, the rate of language loss among youth is rapid and troubling to tribal members who had until recently taken the survival of Navajo for granted. It suggests that, as their isolated way of life disappears, so too may their tongue – a fate already experienced by many other tribes.

Native American languages began dying out almost as soon as Columbus landed in the so-called New World. While estimates vary, somewhere between 250 and 350 indigenous tongues were spoken in North America in 1492.[7] Certainly scores, perhaps hundreds of these languages became extinct as European settlers carried out policies of Indian enslavement, extermination, removal, containment, and cultural repression. The BIA boarding schools, with their brutal speak-English-only policies, are often blamed as the prime agents of language loss. No doubt this experience robbed many students of skills in their native language as well as pride in its use. Even when able to do so, many have declined to pass on this heritage to their children.

Yet the Navajo experience demonstrates that language shift cannot be explained by repression alone. Indeed, among several Native American groups it began to accelerate in the 1970s – a generation after the BIA abandoned its restrictionist policy and a decade after passage of the Bilingual Education Act. It has been evident even in places like Rock Point, whose schools seek to develop students' Navajo skills through the 12th grade. At Peach Springs, Arizona, where a developmental bilingual program in Hualapai has won federal recognition for academic excellence, language loss has been equally dramatic.

What is happening in these communities? Jimmy C. Begay, director of the Rock Point Community School, offers several answers:

> Back in the '70s, there wasn't a lot of electricity out in the community and there weren't a lot of televisions at the time. Now the kids are watching more

television, VCRs, and so forth. So they're picking up a lot [of English] from the videos. Also, I sense that more parents are teaching their young ones more English than Navajo. From [these] parents' point of view, if you speak more English by the time you get to school, then the better you'll achieve in school. I think that's their mentality. But that isn't the truth. We tell the parents that if you teach your child the native language, then he or she [will do better] in their academics later on.

Daniel McLaughlin, who now trains teachers at Diné College (formerly Navajo Community College), sums up the phenomenon in simple terms: "You pave roads, you create access to a wage economy, people's values change, and you get language shift." Sociolinguist Joshua Fishman calls these "dislocations," structural changes that weaken the bonds of a language community and make it vulnerable to penetration by the dominant culture.

Why have Indian bilingual programs, despite other indications of success, failed to halt or reverse the progress of language shift? First of all, they have rarely been designed to address this problem. Most have been transitional, gradually phasing out the Native American language as a medium of instruction, while giving English top priority. The handful of developmental programs, such as Rock Point and Peach Springs, have emphasized the maintenance of skills in the native tongue, not the cultivation of those skills from scratch.

Moreover, schools alone cannot counteract a community's shifting attitudes and practices regarding its vernacular. Unless a dying language is reinforced in everyday life, on the job, in religious or cultural ceremonies, in tribal functions, and especially in the home, using it in the classroom is unlikely to keep it alive for very long. Unfortunately, parents often take the attitude that "the schools can solve that problem," says Lucille Watahomigie, director of the Peach Springs bilingual program. "That's something that we're trying hard to change. We're saying it's a partnership – we all need to work together to keep Hualapai from being lost."

Tribal Language Policies

Since the mid-1980s several tribes – including the Navajo, Red Lake Band of Chippewa, Northern Ute, Arapaho, Pasqua Yaqui, and Tohono O'odham – have responded to the threat by adopting official policies to promote the use of their languages in government and education. Despite good intentions, however, the impact of these policies has remained largely on paper. Tribes enjoy no legal authority over most reservation schools; so public and private school officials feel no obligation, other than moral pressure, to honor their wishes. When tribes do exercise control, use of the native language remains inconsistent. For example, except in its teacher-training programs, the Navajo Nation's Diné College operates almost exclusively in English. As an abstract idea, language preservation remains popular on most reservations. In practice it tends to give way to more pressing priorities like economic development. Few tribes have committed their own financial resources to the cause.

Indian educators and community activists have had to look elsewhere for funding to cope with language loss. In 1990, they successfully lobbied Congress to pass the **Native American Languages Act**. This broad policy statement stresses the federal government's "responsibility to act together with Native Americans to ensure the survival of these unique cultures and languages." In 1992, a grant program was established to carry out that mission; two years later the federal Administration for Native Americans began to distribute the funds.[8] In 1994, Congress amended the Bilingual Education Act to make programs seeking to conserve Native American languages eligible for Title VII grants. This option continues under the No Child Left Behind Act, although the law also features strong incentives to stress English acquisition.

The availability of external support, albeit limited, combined with a growing awareness that native languages are threatened, has generated new enthusiasm for preservation efforts. Naturally many Indians have pinned their hopes on education as a tool for reversing language shift. Yet questions remain about whether school programs can, in effect, replace the family in transmitting endangered languages to future generations. Three instructional approaches have recently been introduced, although it is too soon to make firm judgments about their effectiveness.

The first could be called a **foreign-language model**: teaching Native

> ## Language: The Psyche of a People
>
> Language is not just another thing we do as humans; it is *the* thing we do. It is a total environment; we live in the language as a fish lives in water. It is the audible and visible manifestation of the soul of a people. ...
>
> Do not let propagandists of any stripe tell you the Native languages are archaic relics of a bygone age, best forgotten. Know that speaking your own tongue along with that of the dominant society is a gain rather than a loss for everyone. Remember that a people who lose their language, and the view of the universe expressed by that language, can no longer survive as a people, but only as rootless individuals. We must continue to use the tongue of the grandfathers and imbibe the wisdom contained therein, for they are the only fixed point in a changing and confusing age, the anchor of identity and meaning.
>
> **Robert Bunge (1987)**

American languages to children who have little or no exposure to them outside of school. Arizona, among several states to mandate foreign-language curricula in elementary schools, allows students to meet this requirement in a few indigenous tongues. Navajo educators in particular have cited the state mandate as a way to justify new language programs. Instruction is limited, however, typically involving 20-to-30-minute classes three to five times per week. Because of a shortage of Navajo-proficient teachers, lessons are often taught by videotape. As in non-Indian schools, where children may get a "taste" of French or Spanish at an early age, Indian students learn numbers, colors, animal names, and other simple vocabulary in their ancestral language. Seldom do they learn to use it for communication.

Still, such programs offer other benefits. The Lawrence Elementary School in Tucson initiated a program to teach the Yaqui language in cultural context by traditional elders, who introduced students to deer dance ceremonies and even took them to visit the tribal homeland in Sonora, Mexico. While children are unlikely to become proficient in Yaqui (or other languages) through such programs, they do acquire a deeper appreciation of their heritage that could motivate some to continue studying the language. Nevertheless, the Yaqui program at Lawrence had to be abandoned in 2002 because the elders, who lacked much formal education, were ruled unqualified to teach under the requirements of No Child Left Behind.

A second approach is **two-way bilingual education**, in which English-speaking children learn a second language while LEP children learn English. In 1992, the Tuba City, Arizona, school district on the Navajo reservation adopted such a model for a portion of its 1st graders and planned to extend it to all eight elementary grades. Half the students in the dual language program were Navajo-proficient, half English-proficient. This enabled each group to learn from the other in daily "immersion activities" such as arts and crafts, games, cooking, storytelling, and drama. The program also featured **whole language** book-publishing projects that focus on a monthly theme – often related to the local culture or environment – which helped to develop children's Navajo and English skills in practical contexts. Other academic subjects were taught in the students' stronger language rather than in both (unlike the practice in many two-way models; *see Chapter 12)*. Tuba City had hoped to expand the program, even though it was a slow process, with only 15 percent of its new kindergartners speaking Navajo well enough to serve as role models for their peers. In the late 1990s, however, the program was dismantled, another casualty to funding instability and personnel turnover in Indian education.

A final alternative – perhaps the best hope of reversing language shift in its advanced stages – is **early immersion**. A preschool "language nest" approach was pioneered by Maori educators in New Zealand who believed that, to acquire an endangered language, children must be sheltered from the influence of the dominant language. Since the mid-1980s this model has been used to teach children Native Hawaiian, a language that had declined to about 2,000 speakers, including only 30 children, mainly on the isolated island of Ni'ihau. (Most Native Hawaiians speak **Hawaiian Creole English**, often called "Pidgin.") Known as 'Aha Pûnana Leo, the program began in private preschools for children as young as two; later it expanded to public elementary schools. The total immersion approach postpones English instruction until the 5th grade. Yet, over the long term, students outscore their English-speaking counterparts on standardized tests, according to William Wilson of the University of Hawaii at Hilo.

In 1986, Wayne Holm, a veteran educator on the Navajo reservation, adapted this model to an elementary school at Fort Defiance, Arizona. In a town where only 2 percent of five-year-olds speak Navajo fluently, parents were eager for help in preserving the language. The Fort Defiance program draws students from the one-third of kindergartners judged to have a "passive knowledge" of Navajo. English instruction is introduced slowly, from 40 minutes per day in kindergarten and 1st grade, to half a day in grades 2 and 3, to virtually 100 percent in grades 4 and 5.[9] Academic outcomes so far have been encouraging. By the 5th grade, Navajo immersion students generally score as well as, and often better than, their peers in English-only classrooms, Holm reports. As in the Hawaiian immersion program, the Navajo students are developing a command of the indigenous language, at no cost to their English or achievement in other subjects.

These approaches remain tentative first steps, however. Only a handful of such programs exist, and funding is limited. Meanwhile the clock is ticking. Already it may be too late to shore up many Native American tongues, which have largely eroded away. Activists are beginning to recognize that, if languages are to be saved, indigenous communities themselves must take the lead rather than wait for outside help.

Suggested Reading

Cantoni, Gina, ed. *Stabilizing Indigenous Languages*. Flagstaff, Ariz.: Center for Excellence in Education, Northern Arizona University, 1996.

Crawford, James. "Seven Hypotheses on Language Loss." In *At War with Diversity: U.S. Language Policy in an Age of Anxiety*. Clevedon, U.K.: Multilingual Matters, 2000.

Fishman, Joshua. *Reversing Language Shift: Theoretical and Empirical Foundations of Assistance to Threatened Languages*. Clevedon, U.K.: Multilingual Matters, 1991.

McCarty, Teresa L. *A Place To Be Navajo: Rough Rock and the Struggle for Self-Determination.* Mahwah, N.J.: Lawrence Erlbaum Associates, 2002.

See also pp. 402–3.

Online
Resource
Guide

Krauss, Michael E., and McCarty, Teresa L. Testimonies before the Senate Indian Affairs Committee on S. 2688, Native American Languages Act Amendments of 2000.

Native American Languages Act (1990).

Senate Select Committee on Indian Affairs, U.S. Hearing on S. 2044, To Assist Native Americans in Assuring the Survival and Continuing Vitality of Their Languages (1992).

See also companion CD-ROM.

Internet
Links

Bilingual Research Journal 19, no. 1 (Winter 1995). Special issue on Indigenous Language Education and Literacy, with articles by Teresa McCarty, Ofelia Zepeda, Richard Ruíz, Cathie Jordan, Galena Sells Dick, Agnes Holm and Wayne Holm, Daniel McLaughlin, Irene Silentman, Lucille Watahomigie, and others. http://www.ncela.gwu.edu/miscpubs/nabe/brj/v19/index.htm#1

Crawford, James. "Endangered Native American Languages: What Is To Be Done, and Why?" In *At War with Diversity: U.S. Language Policy in an Age of Anxiety.* Clevedon, U.K.: Multilingual Matters, 2000.
http://ourworld.compuserve.com/homepages/jwcrawford/brj.htm

Teaching Indigenous Languages Web Site at Northern Arizona University. http://jan.ucc.nau.edu/%7Ejar/TIL.html

See also companion CD-ROM.

Notes

1. By 1986–87, there were 89 Title VII–supported projects serving Indian children, totaling $9.6 million, or 10.7 percent of bilingual education grants to school districts.
2. It is important to note than neither Chesarek nor Leap is espousing the view that LEP Indian children are "semilingual" or that they speak a "restricted code" characteristic of disadvantaged social groups. Such notions, which have supported a "verbal deficit"

explanation for students' academic difficulties, have been discredited by psycholinguistic research *(see Chapter 8)*. Studies have shown that all normal children become competent speakers of natural languages to which they are sufficiently exposed. This does not mean, however, that they will necessarily acquire the standard language used in school. Native American children may grow up hearing their elders speak a **pidgin language**, a simplified variety of English that incorporates elements of the indigenous tongue. Along with their peers, they elaborate this code into a **creole**, a fully developed language that takes on a life of its own. Some may acquire two or more varieties of American Indian English, especially in communities where more than one tribal group is present. While mastering such nonstandard dialects, at home these children receive too little comprehensible input in standard English, or in their ancestral tongue, to become competent speakers of these languages. Hence their need for special assistance in school.

3. This is the U.S. branch of a larger missionary organization, which works with indigenous languages worldwide and is known as the Summer Institute of Linguistics.

4. Meanwhile three other Indian instructors, trained under a previous Title VII grant, were teaching in nonbilingual classrooms.

5. The Rough Rock English-Navajo Language Arts Program (RRENLAP) is a transitional bilingual curriculum, while KEEP uses only English. In 1994, Rough Rock received a Title VII grant to provide a developmental Navajo-English program in grades 4–6.

6. Fewer than one percent of these kindergartners could understand no English whatsoever; 13 percent had no knowledge of Navajo. While 93 percent spoke at least some English, 53 percent spoke some Navajo. The study was conducted by Wayne Holm of the Navajo Nation's Office of Diné Culture, Language, and Community Services. In a Navajo Head Start survey conducted that same year, teachers rated 54 percent of preschoolers as English-only speakers, 18 percent as Navajo-only speakers, and 28 percent as bilingual.

7. These figures cover the United States and Canada, which were relatively less diverse than Central and South America. According to one conservative estimate, "In 1492, as many as 2,000 separate, mutually unintelligible languages were spoken by the many different peoples inhabiting the Western Hemisphere." These included about 250 languages in North America, 350 in Mexico and Central America, and 1,450 in South America. See Joel Sherzer, "A Richness of Voices," in Alvin M. Josephy, Jr., ed., *America in 1492: The World of the Indian Peoples Before the Arrival of Columbus* (New York: Knopf, 1992), p. 251.

8. The program's initial budget was $1 million, providing funds for 18 language preservation projects. Even this modest amount had to be pried out of the Clinton administration with a stern letter from Senator Daniel Inouye of Hawaii to the secretary of health and human services, Donna Shalala. By 2002, $3.7 million was available for tribal language programs nationwide.

9. In the original program design, a daily hour of Navajo activities was scheduled for the upper grades, but in practice it has not always been provided.

12 Two-Way Bilingualism

*M*onolingual Americans are put to shame by the worldwide spread of our national tongue. By some estimates English is spoken today by 1.9 billion people, three-fourths of whom learned it as a second or foreign language. "Fifty million precollegiate Chinese young people are studying English," the American Council on the Teaching of Foreign Languages (ACTFL) reported in 1987, "while less than 5,000 of their counterparts in the United States are studying Chinese, a ratio of 10,000 to one."

Costs of Monolingualism
Impetus for Two-Way Programs
Oyster Experiment
Federal and State Policies
Criteria for Effectiveness
90/10 Model
50/50 Model
Research Questions
Grounds for Optimism
Power Relationships

In recent years Chinese-language study has increased substantially in this country. Yet the growth appears to be occurring mainly among Chinese Americans. Out of the estimated 200,000 U.S. students now enrolled in these classes at all levels, about

140,000 are in heritage language schools, according to the Chinese Language Teachers Association. In 2000, ACTFL counted just 5,304 students in public secondary schools (grades 7–12) who were studying Mandarin or Cantonese as a foreign language.[1] While figures are unavailable by ethnicity, it is likely that many of these students are also from Chinese backgrounds.

Anglo-American complacency about language-learning persists despite warnings that it impairs our national security and economic competitiveness *(see Chapter 3)*. As an employer, the federal government itself faces a crisis in filling many "critical language" positions. Yet it continues to address these shortages with short-term, ad hoc measures rather than long-term investments. In 2004, its assistance to elementary and secondary foreign-language programs across the country totaled just $17 million (about 31 cents per student in grades K–12). The Bush administration proposed to "zero out" even this amount in its budget for 2005. Meanwhile the No Child Left Behind Act eliminated a funding priority, adopted in 1994, that had favored programs designed to maintain and develop proficient bilingualism among English learners.

More than two decades ago, a presidential commission warned that "Americans' gross inadequacy in foreign-language skills is nothing short of scandalous, and it is getting worse." A member of the panel, the late Senator Paul Simon of Illinois, argued that the nation's determination to "Americanize" immigrants was a big part of the problem. "Because of our rich ethnic mix, the United States is home to millions whose first language is not English," Simon wrote in his book *The Tongue-Tied American.* "Yet almost nothing is being done to preserve the language skills we now have or to use this rich linguistic resource to train people in the use of a language other than English."

Opposition to bilingual education often stems from the fear that it will enhance loyalty to minority tongues and retard the process of linguistic assimilation. Ironically, the transitional philosophy that long dominated Title VII is more likely to accelerate **language loss** among minority children. As researchers Catherine Snow and Kenji Hakuta observed in 1989:

> Bilingual education in its present form may be one of the greatest misnomers of educational programs. What it fosters is monolingualism; bilingual classrooms are efficient revolving doors between home-language monolingualism and English monolingualism. ... The bilingual education initiatives that were taken in the 1960s have certainly made the transition easier for students. But the bottom line of all of these programs has been an almost single-minded interest in the extent and the efficiency of English proficiency development.

For students in transitional bilingual education, the results were often disappointing. Sidney Morison, principal of P.S. 84 in New York City, recalls feeling frustrated that in spite of his school's best efforts – recruitment of fluent Spanish-speaking teachers, liberal use of Hispanic culture in the classroom, and success in involving parents – English learners were performing poorly in transitional bilingual education. What's more, they were gradually losing their native language. "Teachers taught mostly in English," he explains, "because they felt tremendous pressure to produce good results on standardized tests. Spanish was used mainly for communication, to translate what was being taught in English." All that would change, however, when P.S. 84 rethought its approach and adopted a program of **two-way bilingual education**. "Hispanic children thought to be intellectually limited, or at least very quiet, are blossoming in Spanish-speaking classes," Morison says.

Impetus for Two-Way Programs

By the late 1980s the quick-exit, remedial mindset was beginning to face a challenge not only in New York but throughout the country. Parents, educators, and even some policymakers were actively seeking alternatives. "One-way" developmental bilingual education, as exemplified by the Case Studies project, was beginning to demonstrate the benefits of extended mother-tongue instruction for English learners. Meanwhile **one-way immersion** for English-background children was yielding results superior to traditional foreign-language instruction. An organization of parents and teachers known as Advocates for Language Learning began pressuring school districts to launch more such programs. Proficient bilingualism and biliteracy were rising in social status.

The new orientation was evident in the 1994 reauthorization of the Bilingual Education Act. It seemed that Congress had finally caught on to what educators were saying: English learners were doing well academically in gradual-exit models of bilingual education. What's more, they were enjoying the added bonus of fluency in two languages. So Title VII was amended to give priority to language maintenance rather than transitional approaches *(see Chapter 6)*. As a direct result of the new policy, developmental programs multiplied manyfold in the 1990s.

Language politics were changing as well. The English-only movement had by no means given up – indeed, it would soon return with a vengeance *(see Chapter 13)*. But its agenda was waning in popularity with many Anglo-Americans. Minority languages not only seemed less threatening than before; increasingly they were perceived as desirable assets to acquire. Significant numbers of Anglo parents now saw bilingualism as an advantage in the global economy and as a source of cultural enrichment, not to mention good preparation for life in a diverse society. In short, this was an opportunity they wanted for their children.

Bilingual educators also saw an opportunity. Programs serving English learners, a constituency with limited political power, had long been forced to cope with external opposition and uncertain funding. Civil-rights lawsuits had brought important gains in the 1970s and early 1980s, but the courts were becoming increasingly conservative on questions of social justice. New allies were needed who could bolster support for bilingual education. What if English-speaking children were invited to participate, enabling them to learn Spanish, Chinese, Navajo, or whatever **target language** the English learners spoke? Would it be possible to serve both groups of students well through a single program? Could language-majority and language-minority children, learning side by side and assisting each other, become fluent bilinguals while making good progress in other subjects? Could English-speaking parents, more accustomed to activism and more likely to influence politicians, become effective ambassadors for bilingual education?

By the late 1980s numerous districts were experimenting with two-way approaches. Los Angeles, as part of its "master plan" for bilingual education *(see Chapter 10)*, featured this model in several parts of the city, from Watts to Koreatown to West L.A. "In the beginning, we were hesitant to get involved," explained Carmen Schroeder of the district's bilingual education office.

> We have such a great need to provide bilingual teachers for LEP kids. But we realized it was a big advantage to have [a Spanish] immersion program, because living in southern California, it's almost a necessity to be bilingual. We believe it will be a wonderful way of joining hands [among] very different ethnic groups. And if the majority of the community understands that to know a second language is to your benefit, that will be a big plus.

Politically speaking, the promise was undeniable. A program model open to all children could hardly be branded a "special interest" subsidy. By treating minority languages as a resource rather than a problem, it would change the social dynamic for English learners and English speakers alike. It also offered a chance to energize Anglo parents who saw diversity as something positive, and might even have an impact on broader community attitudes. But was it pedagogically feasible?

The answer was a resounding yes, according to experts in foreign-language education. Richard Tucker, a pioneer in Canadian immersion research, argued that two-way bilingual education – also known as **dual immersion, dual language, bilingual immersion,** and **two-way immersion**, among other labels *(see Chapter 2)*

– could provide the experience of additive bilingualism for both groups, despite their differing needs:

> For the language-majority youngster, there should be an opportunity to develop a far greater degree of facility in the target language than is the case when participating in a traditional FLES (Foreign Language at the Elementary School) program. The opportunity to actually study meaningful content material via a target language and to interact socially as well as academically with native speakers of the language offers numerous benefits. In addition, for the language-minority youngster the opportunity to spend some portion of the day nurturing and sustaining mother-tongue skills and [another] portion … as a resource person for the language-majority youngster offers numerous social, cognitive, and academic benefits as well.

Tucker noted the successes of French immersion for Anglophone students in Canada *(see Chapter 9)* and developmental bilingual education for language-minority students in the United States.

Indeed, there were theoretical reasons to believe that two-way programs would offer a superior environment for second-language acquisition, especially for the English speakers. Despite their generally impressive performance on achievement tests in the second language, few language-majority students in one-way immersion ever achieve native-like fluency in communicating. The evaluator of a Spanish immersion program in Culver City, California, determined that – even after five to six years in the program – English-background children had not fully acquired grammatical structures or phonology in Spanish: "Both the tenaciousness and systematicity of [students'] errors suggest the development of a classroom dialect peculiar to Spanish Immersion Program students. The children … reinforce each other's incorrect usage, and fossilization at the morphological level results." Another researcher commented that, if Hispanic children made errors of the same type in English, they would be candidates for remedial classes.

By contrast, in a dual immersion program with native Spanish speakers as **peer models**, English-speaking children would likely acquire higher levels of proficiency in the second language, according to Fred Genesee, a researcher who has specialized in immersion models. "Including students from both language groups creates a learning environment that can be truly bilingual and bicultural. Sustained contact with members of the target language group of the same age as the learners may be necessary if students are to develop fundamentally more tolerant and positive attitudes toward each other." Successful two-way programs appear to confirm these predictions, even though data from controlled scientific research remain limited.

Oyster Experiment

While two-way programs were rare until recent years, the model dates back to 1963 at the Coral Way School in Miami *(see Chapters 4 and 9)*. In 1971, a similar experiment was initiated at the Oyster School in Washington, D.C. At the time research on second-language acquisition was in its infancy; in developing the program, administrators worked closely with a community organization representing the city's diverse Hispanic population.[2] The educational philosophy that resulted was additive rather than subtractive. According to Paquita Holland, principal of Oyster in the 1980s and 1990s, the program designers were determined to avoid the segregation of Spanish-speaking children, or any approach that would devalue the native language and culture. Instead, they hoped to exploit linguistic diversity for the benefit of all students. A *Teacher's Handbook* later explained Oyster's philosophy:

> We believe that children from Hispanic cultures will learn to perform better in English in an atmosphere where their native language is respected and where continued growth in their native language is provided. In addition, native English speakers will have their educational experience enriched by achieving competency in a second language, at an age when achieving such competency is easiest. Therefore, the Oyster School staff pledges itself to meeting this challenge by providing a comprehensive bilingual educational program in an atmosphere that is open, concerned and responsive to the needs of students and the community.

With these goals in mind, Oyster organized a single bilingual classroom in the fall of 1971, which gradually expanded into a schoolwide program in all grades, K–6. The entire curriculum was taught in both languages.

Before launching the experiment, the school district consulted parents on the choice of a new principal, and trained staff for a year in bilingual methodologies. With help from the community organization, native Spanish-speaking teachers were recruited from all over Latin America. A further indication of the district's commitment was its decision to hire a staff twice the regular size. With a Spanish-speaking teacher and an English-speaking teacher in each classroom, Oyster may be unique among bilingual education models, at least in U.S. public schools.

In its pedagogical approach Oyster strives for parity between the two languages of instruction, with English and Spanish used in roughly equal proportions, and with majority and minority children mixed throughout the day. Each subject is taught in both English and Spanish – not concurrently, but on alternate days, periods, or semesters – giving students an immersion experience and also a chance to develop conceptually in their native tongue. Since children are mixed, teachers must work hard to make instruction comprehensible to one group and still interesting to the other.

An unusual feature of Oyster's curriculum is that children are taught initial literacy in English and Spanish at the same time. By the middle of the 1st grade, they are reading in both languages. The wisdom of this approach has been questioned by researchers like Merrill Swain of the Ontario Institute for Studies in Education. Citing studies in Canada, Swain warns that children who learn to read in this way may experience confusion due to "interfering and competing surface features" of the two languages. Better to let students transfer literacy skills, once mastered, from one tongue to another, she says. Paquita Holland responds that Oyster has never seen the need to change its reading program because the results have been so favorable. By the 3rd grade, children are reading two years above national norms in English. In 1987, they ranked at the 90th percentile in language and the 95th percentile in mathematics on the Comprehensive Test of Basic Skills; scores for 6th graders were comparable. Nevertheless, it is important to note that, while impressive, these were combined scores for all students; Oyster does not disaggregate test results by language background or by English proficiency.[3]

By 1993, reports researcher Rebecca Freeman, the school's enrollment was 58 percent Latino, 26 percent white, 12 percent black, and 4 percent Asian, with immigrant children representing 25 countries; 24 percent were LEP and 40 percent were eligible for free or reduced-price lunches. Most of Oyster's 300-plus students were drawn from the surrounding community. For the few outsiders admitted, the program has proved extremely popular. In 2002, when 30 new kindergarten "slots" became available, dozens of English-speaking parents camped out in the snow, some for as long as five days, hoping to sign their children up.[4] Despite the unprecedented demand, Holland says the District of Columbia has never considered replicating the Oyster model elsewhere because of its high cost.

Nor does the District offer any public school programs in which English-proficient students can continue their education in Spanish after leaving Oyster at the end of 6th grade. (Affluent parents sometimes transfer their children to private schools that provide this opportunity.) By the time they graduate, Oyster students are usually sold on the advantages of bilingualism, Holland reports, "even though we're fighting all tides in society." As children grow older, the social pressure to speak English intensifies, notes Virginia Collier, speaking from her own experience as an ESL teacher in the district. "Certainly, by the time they reach junior high school, many kids are putting Spanish down. Hispanic students go through a period of having mixed feelings about [their first language]." This pattern was confirmed in Rebecca Freeman's ethnographic study of the Oyster School. Interviewing recent graduates of the program to see how they reacted to pressures for Anglo-conformity, she found mixed reactions:

> Some of the native Spanish speakers may continue to positively evaluate the Spanish language and Spanish-speaking people. ... Others may choose to reject their native language and cultural background in [an] effort to alleviate the negative evaluation of themselves as speakers of Spanish and as different.

In 1987, Collier conducted her own informal survey to see what had become of Oyster's oldest graduates, those who had entered the program in the early 1970s and were now finishing college or starting careers. Had bilingual schooling strongly influenced these students? Or had its effects been transitory? Tracing 11 former students, all native English speakers who had kept in touch with Oyster teachers, Collier found that her "biased sample" had prevailed against the odds. Over the years the graduates had continued to improve their Spanish skills. Five had studied Spanish as a part of a double major in college, and some had lived in Spanish-speaking countries. Several were involved in language teaching, social work, or other jobs in which they could use their Spanish. Perhaps most significant, all the former students expressed positive attitudes toward bilinguals as well as toward bilingualism. Many had native Spanish speakers for friends or chose to live in Hispanic communities. By comparison, Collier notes, French immersion students in Canada, who are "schooled in a segregated setting, tend to come out with good attitudes toward French, but not toward French Canadians."

90/10 Model

Though its successes are well-known, Oyster's approach – two teachers in every classroom and every subject taught in two languages – has failed to catch on elsewhere. Not only are such practices expensive; they are regarded by many as unnecessary, perhaps even undesirable. Numerous two-way designs also feature a 50/50 split in language usage, reflecting the widespread view that the target language must be used at least half the time to meet the needs of English speakers as well as English learners. But most place greater stress than Oyster on **language separation**, teaching subjects either in English or the minority tongue rather than in both.

Others make considerably more use of the target language in the early grades. The **90/10 model** developed by the San Diego public schools in the mid-

1970s could be described as **total immersion** for English speakers, who begin their schooling almost entirely in Spanish. English is limited to 20 minutes a day in preschool, 30 minutes in kindergarten and 1st grade, and one hour in grades 2 and 3. By grades 4 through 6, half the instruction is in Spanish and half in English. In this respect the program resembles immersion in St. Lambert or Culver City, but with an important difference: it simultaneously serves Spanish-speaking children. Meanwhile, for the language-minority students, the program resembles developmental bilingual education.

The main difference is that, because students are mixed for much of the day, subject-matter teaching cannot be **sheltered** in the same way as in one-way immersion. When both native speakers and second-language learners are present, teachers face a difficult trade-off. If they adjust the linguistic level too little, one-half the class will receive the **submersion** treatment – too little **comprehensible input**. If they simplify the language too much, the other half will receive a "dumbed-down" lesson that fails to challenge them with academic content appropriate to their age and grade.

Guadalupe Valdes, an educational researcher at Stanford University, has also cautioned that, by using simplified forms of Spanish to accommodate English-speaking students, two-way programs could have negative linguistic and academic effects for Spanish-speaking students:

> Will hispanophone children acquire native-like academic Spanish? Will they learn as much and as rapidly as they might have in standard bilingual programs? Will they develop the cognitive academic proficiency that Cummins has claimed undergirds development of similar proficiencies in a second language?

From a research perspective, this remains uncharted territory. Even if one takes issue with the **BICS/CALP distinction** *(see Chapter 8)*, the question of whether Latinos' academic needs are slighted because programs cater to Anglos' language-learning needs (or vice versa) is one that cries out for empirical investigation.

Practitioners in two-way programs have long recognized these potential contradictions and have struggled to resolve them. Especially in the early years, techniques must be used to compensate for the disparities in language proficiency among students. A 1982 report by the San Diego Unified School District recommends two approaches:

> First, when the K–1 class's students are receiving Spanish oral language instruction as a total class, visual aids – in the form of pictures, chalkboard

drawings, gestures, and pantomimes – are used to insure that the native speakers of English comprehend what is being discussed. Second, when the class is divided for individualized oral language instruction, the instructional emphasis for native-English-speaking students is on reinforcing beginning Spanish vocabulary and language patterns. (These same techniques apply to native-Spanish-speaking students during the English language period.)

San Diego's two-way program, like many 90/10 models, uses **homogeneous grouping** of students to better serve the needs of each language group. For example, minority children may receive ESL instruction while majority children study English language arts. Other two-way programs, such as Oyster, insist on **heterogeneous grouping** at all times, believing it is important to avoid segregating students by race or ethnicity. According to Kathryn Lindholm-Leary of San Jose State University, research has yet to determine whether one approach is pedagogically superior, but many effective programs use both.

No one disputes the chief advantage of mixing the two groups: children have an opportunity to acquire a second language from native speakers of their own age. Peers tend to be more influential role models than teachers when it comes to language learning. Simply throwing the two groups together, however, is not enough. The San Diego approach features a variety of structured activities that encourage children to interact, communicate, and assist each other in becoming bilingual. Such **peer tutoring** may reinforce the salutary effects of immersion, researchers predict, especially for language-majority students. It can also transform the status of language-minority students from "disadvantaged" underachievers to experts in a valuable set of skills, boosting their self-confidence in academic pursuits.

The outcomes of the 90/10 experiment in San Diego were encouraging. According to periodic evaluations, students of both language groups did well, although the benefits tended to manifest themselves late in the program. Children formerly limited in English made rapid gains in their oral skills from the very beginning. But generally speaking, it took them until the 6th grade to score at the 50th percentile on reading and mathematics tests administered in English. This pattern was consistent with other developmental bilingual models *(see Chapters 9 and 10)*. Native-English speakers reached the 30th to 36th percentile range in Spanish reading, while exceeding national norms in their other subjects. Researcher Fred Genesee reported that, for the Anglo children, "there is generally a lag in English language literacy skills development during those grades of early total immersion programs when English language arts are not taught."

Two-Way Fervor Spreads

Beginning in the mid-1980s, these promising results inspired similar experiments in California, Connecticut, New York, and Massachusetts. The Center for Language Education and Research (CLEAR) at the University of California, Los Angeles, played an important role in spreading the word. In 1987, it published the first national directory of two-way programs – 30 met its strict criteria – along with a description of effective practices *(see page 297)*. Yet federal support was slow in coming. Consistent with its quick-exit philosophy for English learners, the Reagan administration was unenthusiastic about two-way programs, only two of which received Title VII grants in the 1980s.

Policies began to change under the first President Bush, thanks to his bilingual education director, Rita Esquivel, who had witnessed firsthand the success of a dual immersion model in Santa Monica, California. The Clinton administration was even more supportive. In the year following the 1994 reauthorization of Title VII, the U.S. Department of Education funded 61 two-way projects. Republicans in Congress quickly moved to block these grants; one year they voted to cut funding for all forms of developmental bilingual education. Still, the number of two-way programs multiplied in the 1990s *(see Figure 12–1)*. They have become especially popular in Texas, where in 2001 the legislature unanimously passed a bill to promote "dual language immersion."

The most recent directory, compiled in 2003 by the Center for Applied Linguistics (CAL) identified 271 "two-way bilingual immersion" programs in 24 states and the District of Columbia. In 94 percent of these, Spanish and English

FIGURE 12–1

Growth of Two-Way Bilingual Programs in the United States, 1987–2002

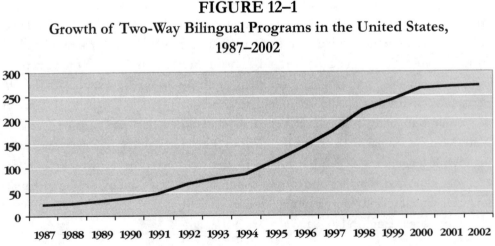

Source: Center for Applied Linguistics.

Criteria for Effective Two-Way Bilingual Education

Basic research provides the following guidelines, which apply equally to 90/10 and 50/50 program models. These criteria are adapted from Kathryn J. Lindholm, Directory of Bilingual Immersion Programs *(Los Angeles: Center for Language Education and Research, 1987).*

- **Long-term treatment.** A program must last from four to six years for students to achieve bilingual proficiency.
- **Optimal input in two languages.** Second language input, provided through language arts and subject-matter instruction, must be *comprehensible*, that is, adjusted to students' level; *relevant*, so as to stimulate student interest; *sufficient* in quantity; and *challenging*, so that it requires students to "negotiate meaning."
- **Focus on academic subjects.** Children need more than language development. The curriculum should emphasize *concept development* as well, beginning in the second language for English speakers, in the native language for minority students.
- **Integration of language arts with curriculum.** Sheltered instruction alone has failed to produce native-like proficiency in the second language; students also need formal language arts. Linguistic structures are best mastered in connection with subject-matter instruction, rather than through isolated grammar exercises.
- **Separation of languages for instruction.** Sustained periods of monolingual instruction promote linguistic development better than concurrent approaches that mix languages during the same lesson.
- **Additive bilingual environment.** Enrichment approaches, in which children acquire a second language without abandoning their mother tongue, lead to higher levels of bilingual proficiency, along with improved self-esteem and more favorable attitudes toward other cultures.
- **Balance of language groups.** To ensure equity in the classroom, as well as maximum interactions among language-minority and language-majority children, the two groups should be mixed in roughly equal proportions. The ratio should never slip below 2/3 to 1/3.
- **Sufficient use of minority language.** At least 50 percent of instruction should be conducted in the minority language, both to provide English-speaking students optimal input and to ensure that minority students develop cognitive-academic language proficiency in their native tongue.
- **Opportunities for speech production.** To become proficient in a second language, children need opportunities to practice it orally with native speakers, preferably including exercises on which language-minority and language-majority students can collaborate.
- **Administrative support.** Bilingual programs should be treated equitably within a school for many reasons; not least of these are the language-status implications that will be communicated to students.
- **Empowerment objective of instruction.** Breaking with the authoritarian "transmission model," in which teachers impart and children receive knowledge, instruction should be a dialogue in which students learn to think for themselves rather than simply to memorize information.
- **High-quality teachers.** Even though languages are separated, teachers need to be competent bilinguals, so they can respond to children's needs and provide comprehensible input.
- **Home-school collaboration.** Especially for language-minority students, parental involvement is essential to reinforce children's native-language development and to communicate high expectations about academic achievement.

were used for instruction; other target languages were French, Chinese, Korean, and Navajo. CAL defines the model using the following criteria:

- **Integration:** Language-minority and language-majority students are integrated for at least 50% of instructional time at all grade levels.
- **Instruction:** Content and literacy instruction in both languages is provided to all students.
- **Population:** Within the program, there is a balance of language-minority and language-majority students, with each group making up between one-third and two-thirds of the total student population.

Only programs that feature all three of these characteristics are listed in the directory. Schools serving primarily language-minority children, such as most of those in the Rio Grande Valley, are excluded from consideration even though many offer approaches labeled "two-way" or "dual immersion." So is the Coral Way program, where more than 90 percent of students are either English learners or **heritage language learners** from Hispanic backgrounds. The rationale for limiting the definition of two-way bilingual education in this way is that student characteristics obviously affect the sociopolitical environment within a school. Power relationships are quite different with – or without – the presence of language-majority children (along with Anglo parents championing their interests). Ethnic composition is likely to have linguistic effects as well. When virtually all students live in communities where they are exposed to both languages, it may be easier to shelter instruction for both groups than when programs include students from monolingual English backgrounds.

TABLE 12–1
Key School Two-Way Program Compared to Mainstream Programs, 4th Grade Achievement Test Scores* (percentile ranks)

	Language	Math	Reading	Social Studies	Science
Two-Way (Key)	79	93	89	86	84
All-English (Key)	45	68	53	49	66
Arlington District	71	81	74	76	79
State of Virginia	64	66	61	65	71

Source: Donna Christian et al., *Profiles in Two-Way Immersion Education* (McHenry, Ill.: Center for Applied Linguistics and Delta Systems, 1997).
*Iowa Test of Basic Skills, 1995; average scores for students of all language backgrounds.

50/50 Model

Parents of two-way students – of whatever language background – are generally quite eager for their children to become fully bilingual and biliterate. At the same time, some express worries about the potential of 90/10 programs to neglect English in the early years. This concern inspired an alternative, **50/50 model** – sometimes called **two-way partial immersion** – in which the languages of instruction are equally balanced from the outset. The Key School in Arlington, Virginia, adopted this approach in 1986. Students are taught in English in the morning (language arts and mathematics) and Spanish in the afternoon (language arts, social studies, and science). Music, art, and physical education classes are conducted in English.

Early results were encouraging, and the program expanded as it became popular with local Spanish- and English-speaking communities. Like Oyster, Key remains in part a neighborhood school, but "magnet" students are allowed to transfer in; priority is given to those with siblings already in the program. By 1995, enrollment reached 318 in grades K–5, about half of Key School's students. Arlington County has also opened similar programs in two other elementary schools. Unlike the situation in most districts, children have the option to continue in two-way programs in a middle school and a high school nearby.

An evaluation of the program by the Center for Applied Linguistics found that children were far outperforming their counterparts in Key School's all-English track by the 4th grade. They were also scoring well above average in the district and in the state of Virginia *(see Table 12–1)*. This was true even when students were tested in English on subjects they had been taught in Spanish, such as science, math, and social studies. Academic content knowledge was clearly transferring between the two languages. As expected, Spanish speakers – who received ample exposure to both languages in the community – made better progress toward bilingualism, with virtually all scoring fluent in oral English (level 4 or 5) on the Language Assessment Scales by 3rd grade. English speakers, on the other hand, received most of their Spanish exposure at school; 43 percent were judged fluent in oral measures of Spanish by 4th grade.

Research Questions

Though impressive, reported results from the Key School program leave some important questions unanswered. As has often been the case in evaluations of two-way models, achievement test scores were not disaggregated by language background or by initial level of English proficiency. In addition, there were no controls for **socioeconomic status** (SES). Many English-speaking children in the program come from high-SES families and are expected to do well academically. The performance of low-SES Latino students, who face higher hurdles, remains more of a question mark. How well does two-way bilingual education serve their needs? It is hard to say when their scores are combined with those of English speakers (even when the averages are quite high). More important, how do English learners fare in this model as compared to their counterparts in, say, one-way developmental bilingual education? To answer this question, it is necessary to identify which students are LEP at the outset and to examine their progress over several years – as the **Ramírez study** did for transitional, developmental, and immersion models *(see Chapter 9).*

Thus far, rigorous research on two-way programs has been limited – too limited to yield definitive conclusions. Most studies have either included no comparison groups or used no controls for pre-existing differences among subjects *(see Chapter 7).* In reporting academic achievement, several have failed to distinguish between LEP students and heritage language learners who are English-dominant. Some have involved very small samples. Others have published minimal program details or outcomes data to justify their findings. To date, none has solved the problem of **selection bias,** the fact that parents who choose this approach have special characteristics, such as a tendency to value bilingualism, which are likely to affect their children's academic performance.

Sweeping claims about the two-way model have nevertheless been made. In a 1997 report, Wayne Thomas and Virginia Collier describe it as "the program with the highest long-term academic success" for English learners. According to their study, which is summarized in Chapter 9, graduates of two-way bilingual education are predicted to reach the 70th percentile in English reading by the 11th grade – significantly higher than LEP students who receive other treatments *(see Figure 9–1, page 236).* Except for a widely circulated graph, however, the researchers have offered no supporting evidence for this conclusion.

In a 2002 publication, Thomas and Collier do include details of controlled studies they conducted in Houston that involved three program types: transitional bilingual education (TBE), one-way developmental bilingual education (DBE), and a 90/10 model of two-way bilingual education. Using a **cross-sectional analysis,** the researchers compared student achievement at various grade levels, along with a smaller **longitudinal analysis** that followed cohorts of individual children. Overall the study involved more than 3,500 Spanish-speaking students enrolled in bilingual programs for periods ranging from one to five years.

In Houston, unlike the practice in most districts, all three program designs featured "the same ratio of Spanish-English instruction for Grades PK–3," with the native language predominating until grade 4. (In other words, TBE departed from the more common "quick-exit" approach taught primarily in English.) As shown in Table 12–2, student outcomes in TBE and DBE were similar in English reading, while those in two-way classrooms were considerably higher. Thomas and Collier attribute the difference to

> the inclusion of native-English speakers in the two-way bilingual classes. The research to date has found that interacting with same-age native-speaking peers assists the natural second language acquisition process and creates an additive bilingual context, with a positive social and emotional climate for all. Thus both groups are peer teachers for each other.

The researchers offer no explanation, however, for why scores declined over time in all three programs.

TABLE 12–2
English Reading Achievement in Three Bilingual Program Models,*
Houston Independent School District, 1996–2000 (percentile ranks)†

Grade	TBE	DBE	TBE	Two-Way
1	53	50	54	68
2	45	46	40	59
3	44	44	48	58
4	40	39	39	55
5	34	34	30	52

Source: Wayne P. Thomas and Virginia P. Collier, *A National Study of School Effectiveness for Language Minority Students' Long-Term Academic Achievement* (Santa Cruz, Calif.: Center for Research on Education, Diversity & Excellence, 2002).
* Cross-sectional analysis of Stanford 9 scores.
†Converted from normal curve equivalents (NCEs).

Still more troubling is the question of why children "initially classified as LEP" scored so high at the outset – well above the 36th percentile level that is often used as a criterion for academic English proficiency. If the two-way students were reading in English, on average, at the 68th percentile in 1st grade, by what measure where they limited in English? Even their 52nd percentile scores in 5th grade are considerably higher than has been documented in other studies of two-way programs *(see below)*. One likely explanation is that many of the subjects in Houston were heritage language learners rather than English language learners. Their advantage over counterparts in TBE and DBE may also reflect **background variables** that the researchers did not control for: students' socioeconomic status,[5] parental attitudes toward bilingualism, and prior attendance in bilingual preschools. By all indications, Spanish-background children are performing well in Houston's two-way bilingual program. The Thomas-Collier study does not necessarily show, however, that LEP students are performing well, much less that this model is their best hope for "long-term academic success."[6]

Cautious Optimism

As of late 2003, Stephen Krashen argues that the research evidence on two-way bilingual education is "supportive and encouraging," but there is still too little scientific data "to state with 100% confidence that [this] is the best possible program for English learners." He adds that

> two-way and other options should be evaluated with respect to other factors as well as English language development. ... We also need to consider long-term cognitive development, social and attitudinal factors, the ease of implementation and efficacy of different versions of two-way bilingual education, and the effect on majority language students, especially those from low-income families who may have little opportunity for first-language development outside of school because of print-poor environments.

In other words, more and better studies are needed to investigate the model's effectiveness for varying groups of students under varying conditions. Too few have been published thus far to warrant unbounded optimism. This is not to minimize the difficulties in designing and conducting such research, nor to claim that any findings yielded by less than perfect methodologies should be discarded. It is also worth remembering that, despite their flaws, most studies of two-way bilingual education thus far have pointed toward similar – generally favorable – conclusions.

Perhaps the most ambitious of these is a study by Kathryn Lindholm-Leary involving 16 two-way programs, divided equally between 90/10 and 50/50 models for Spanish- and English-background children, all but one located in California. Student backgrounds were primarily Hispanic or white Anglo-American; few Asian or Native Americans participated, and African-American enrollment was significant (30 percent) at just one school. For comparative purposes, sites were grouped by SES level and ethnic concentration as well as by two-way model; four TBE pro-

TABLE 12-3
Second-Language Reading Achievement in Two-Way Bilingual Education, By Grade and Language Background (percentile ranks)*

Grade	English Speakers In Spanish	Spanish Speakers in English	California English Learners in English
1	66	16	
2	68	19	22
3	65	25	18
4	52	29	17
5	42	29	16
6	61	27	18
7	58	39	14
8		39	

Source: Kathryn J. Lindholm-Leary, *Dual Language Education* (Clevedon, U.K.: Multilingual Matters, 2001).
* Converted from normal curve equivalents (NCEs).

grams were also included. Yet, because there was no **random assignment** or other measures to compensate for background variables, these were not **controlled scientific experiments**. For the most part, standardized test scores were compared against national norms and state averages; cross-sectional and longitudinal analyses were conducted.

Lindholm-Leary found that both English and Spanish speakers rated high in oral and academic skills in their respective native languages. After English reading was introduced in grade 3, English speakers scored at or above the statewide average in that subject. Spanish speakers generally reached average levels of Spanish literacy as well, although they tended to acquire better reading skills in the 90/10 model. English speakers in 90/10 programs, regardless of ethnicity or SES, made substantial gains in oral Spanish, outperforming their counterparts in 50/50 programs. In the researcher's words, "receiving a much larger percentage of instruction in Spanish (80-90% as compared to 50%) in the early grade levels produced a larger gain in Spanish proficiency," just as in one-way immersion programs. Thus, for students whose only exposure to the second language came in school, **time on task** appeared to be a factor. Nevertheless, the English speakers failed to acquire the levels of second-language proficiency that Spanish speakers did. For Spanish speakers, by contrast, there was no significant difference between the two models in students' acquisition of oral English. "Whether they spent 10 to 20% or 50% of their instructional day in English, the students were equally proficient in English," Lindholm-Leary reports – another blow to the time-on-task hypothesis for language-minority students *(see Chapter 9)*.

When it came to reading in the second language, English speakers outperformed Spanish speakers – which is not atypical in two-way programs – and again they fared considerably better in the 90/10 approach. Spanish-background students scored about the same in both models in English reading. According to the longitudinal analysis, they made steady progress throughout elementary school, reaching the 29th percentile by the 5th grade *(see Table 12–3)*.[7] This was well above the California average for LEP 5th graders (16th percentile) but still below the 36th percentile criterion for redesignation as FEP. In addition, as Krashen notes, the comparison was not entirely fair because the state average includes English learners who have only recently arrived in California schools.

Lindholm-Leary reported no correlation between oral proficiency in first and second languages, echoing the findings in Dade County, Florida, described in Chapter 9. On the other hand, she found a strong relationship between academic skills in both languages: "Across the grade levels, as students became more proficient in both languages, the correlation between reading achievement in English and Spanish increased." Reading achievement, in turn, was strongly associated with mathematics achievement in both English and Spanish. These findings are consistent with Cummins's **interdependence hypothesis** on the transferability of literacy and other academic skills.

Based on extensive surveys of two-way students, Lindholm-Leary found "very positive attitudes toward the program, their teachers, their parents, and the classroom environment, as well as positive learning attitudes and behaviors." Low-SES African-American students were somewhat less satisfied with the program and less likely to enjoy learning in two languages. But all groups expressed positive perceptions of other cultures and enthusiasm about becoming bilingual, believing it would help them get better jobs, make them smarter, and improve their academic performance. There was no difference between Hispanic and white Anglo students in how they rated themselves academically. These findings are "pedagogically encouraging," Lindholm-Leary concludes, because they "suggest that ethnic minority children in a high-quality educational program that incorporates the language and culture of both groups and fosters academic achievement could also enhance the perceived scholastic competence and global self-worth of those students."

Caveats

Notwithstanding the demonstrated benefits of bringing together diverse groups of students and pursuing the goal of bilingualism for all, there is also a downside to consider. By definition, two-way programs must meet diverse needs while working within a societal context of racial, ethnic, economic, and linguistic inequality. These realities do not stop at the schoolhouse door. Thus **power relationships** – between communities of widely differing status and resources, parents with conflicting priorities, educators with varied professional interests, and children with different life experiences – must be managed skillfully to ensure success. This is no small challenge. Two-way bilingual education is a delicate balancing act that depends on the cooperation and good will of everyone involved, as well as on administrators with well honed political skills.

Guadalupe Valdes relates an anecdote that begins to illustrate these contradictions. It involves Andrew, an English-speaking child whose affluent parents recognize the opportunities that fluent bilingualism can bring for their son:

> Andrew is enrolled in a dual-language immersion program offered in a magnet school in a large city in California. At recess one day, Andrew and a group of three other boys were engaged in a noisy game, chasing and pushing each other. As often happens with seven-year-olds, what started as a game turned into a fight. Andrew felt outnumbered and said, red in the face and almost in tears, "If you can't play fair, I'm going off to another school, and all of you will be here, all by yourselves." At seven, Andrew already understands a great deal about power and about the fragile relationships between groups in our society. His remarks, said in childish anger and frustration, reflect a fundamental difference between the two groups of children enrolled in this particular dual-language immersion program.

Unlike many affluent whites, Andrew's parents are "deeply committed to social justice." No doubt they support the two-way bilingual concept on that basis and hope that their child, by experiencing other cultures, will come to embrace those ideals. Nevertheless, they are active in advocating for Andrew's needs, which are not the same as those of his low-SES Latino classmates. Yet all these children are being taught simultaneously by the same teachers in the same classrooms.

Active involvement by parents is a key component of effective bilingual education, both in promoting academic success and as a source of political support. Thanks to their efforts, most two-way programs have survived thus far in states that have adopted English-only initiatives.[8] Yet there are great disparities in the skills, experiences, and attitudes that language-majority and language-minority parents bring to the table. Not surprisingly, well educated Anglos tend to dominate parent councils in two-way schools. Rebecca Freeman, in her study of Oyster, reported that Latino parents were far more likely to attend small conferences organized by individual teachers.

In addition, Valdes notes that different groups of educators have come together to develop this program model: those whose primary interest is promoting foreign-language proficiency among English speakers and those who are primarily concerned with guaranteeing equal opportunities for English learners. Although teachers and administrators generally strive to ensure equal respect for the two languages, children are quick to perceive status differences – if not in school, then in the community. Bilingual skills, for example, are usually seen as a praiseworthy accomplishment by English-speaking students, while taken entirely for granted among English learners. There is a fine line between treating Spanish, say, as a valuable resource and treating Spanish-speaking students as a resource who are there to "service" the needs of English-speaking classmates. While two-way programs are never consciously organized in this way, the potential for inequity is something they must constantly guard against.

"If we are truthful," Valdes concludes, "perhaps we will admit that supporters and proponents of dual-language immersion programs face a dilemma. They want to find ways to support language study among majority group members, and they want to provide minority children with access to the curriculum in a language they can understand." The contradictions are by no means insuperable. But affirmative efforts by educators are required to overcome them in a way that serves the interests of all children.

At the level of public policy, making two-way programs the primary model of bilingual education poses other dangers. One is the dilution of scarce resources originally set aside for language-minority students. Another is the reality that, despite the rapid growth of this pedagogy in recent years, there remain far too few English-speaking parents who want their children to participate. Precise enrollment figures are unavailable. By a generous estimate, however, two-way programs currently serve about 2 percent of LEP students in the United States. For the model to become widespread, a large-scale attitude adjustment will be necessary among Anglo-Americans. Meanwhile English learners need other bilingual options, not just English-only approaches.

On the brighter side, it is clear that the growth opportunities are considerable. With immigrants, refugees, and indigenous minorities swelling the U.S. school population, two-way programs are feasible not only in Spanish, French, Chinese, and Korean, but also in Japanese, Russian, Arabic, Mandarin, and other world languages. All that is needed is the foresight to tap these linguistic resources, instead of squandering them through assimilationist education policies. Some day, perhaps, to become Americanized will no longer mean to become monolingual.

Suggested Reading

Christian, Donna et al. *Profiles in Two-Way Immersion Education*. McHenry, Ill.: Center for Applied Linguistics and Delta Systems, 1997.

Lindholm-Leary, Kathryn J. *Dual Language Education*. Clevedon, U.K.: Multilingual Matters, 2001.

Snow, Catherine E., and Hakuta, Kenji. "The Costs of Monolingualism." In James Crawford, ed., *Language Loyalties: A Source Book on the Official English Controversy*. Chicago: University of Chicago Press, 1992, pp. 394–94.

Valdes, Guadalupe. "Dual-Language Immersion Programs: A Cautionary Note Concerning the Education of Language-Minority Students." *Harvard Educational Review* 67, no. 3 (Fall 1997): 391–429.

See also pp. 404-5.

Online Resource Guide

Howard, Elizabeth R., and Loeb, Michael I. *In Their Own Words: Two-Way Immersion Teachers Talk About Their Professional Experiences*. ERIC Digest (1998).

Lindholm-Leary, Kathryn J. *Biliteracy for a Global Society: An Idea Book on Dual Language Education*. National Clearinghouse for Bilingual Education (2000).

National Center for Research on Cultural Diversity and Second Language Learning. *Two-Way Bilingual Education Programs in Practice: A National and Local Perspective*. ERIC Digest (1994).

Torres-Guzmán, María E. *Dual Language Programs: Key Features and Results*. National Clearinghouse for Bilingual Education (2002).

See also companion CD-ROM.

Internet
Links

Cazabon, Mary T.; Nicoladis, Elena; and Lambert, Wallace E. *Becoming Bilingual in the Amigos Two-Way Immersion Program.* Santa Cruz, Calif: Center for Research on Education, Diversity & Excellence, 1998.
http://www.cal.org/crede/pubs/research/rr3.htm

Center for Applied Linguistics. *Directory of Two-Way Bilingual Immersion Programs in the U.S.* http://www.cal.org/twi/directory/

de Jong, Esther. "Effective Bilingual Education: From Theory to Academic Achievement in a Two-Way Bilingual Program." *Bilingual Research Journal* 26, no. 1 (2002). http://brj.asu.edu/content/vol26_no1/pdf/ar5.pdf

Draper, Jamie B. and Hicks, June H. *Foreign Language Enrollments in Public Secondary Schools, Fall 2000: Summary Report.* Yonkers, N.Y.: American Council on the Teaching of Foreign Languages, 2002.
http://www.actfl.org/public/articles/enroll2000.pdf

See also companion CD-ROM.

Notes

1. At the college level there were 28,456 students enrolled in Chinese language courses in 1998, according to a survey by the Modern Language Association. But the National Security Education Program and the American Council of Teachers of Russian have found that "the median speaking proficiency of American college graduates, before study abroad, in five languages critical to national security (Chinese, Arabic, Russian, Korean, and Japanese) is 1 on a scale of 5, with 2 being the absolute minimum for functional proficiency, and 3 the minimum for professionals to practice in another language"; Richard D. Brecht and William A. Rivers, *Language and National Security: The Federal Role in Building Language Capacity in the U.S.* (Washington, D.C.: National Foreign Language Center, 2001).

2. Unlike the situation in most parts of the United States, no single Hispanic nationality dominated; by the 1980s, Oyster's Latino students were primarily immigrants from El Salvador and other Central American countries.

3. School officials seem unconcerned about the problems this poses for researchers. In her comprehensive ethnographic study of Oyster, Rebecca Freeman reports: "I was unable to obtain a statistical breakdown of Oyster students' test scores according to socioeconomic class or cultural background. The Guidance Counselor told me that Oyster did not analyze test scores that way because they believed that such groupings were discriminatory"; *Bilingual Education and Social Change* (Clevedon, U.K.: Multilingual Matters, 1998), pp. 23–24.

4. The school district has since replaced this chaotic process with a lottery system.
5. Program models being compared were matched by school characteristics, including SES, but participating students were not – unlike, e.g., in the Oller-Eilers study in Dade County *(see Chapter 9)*.
6. The same report includes a controlled study of a 50/50 two-way model at the Grant Community School in Salem, Oregon. Sample sizes were quite small, however, and student mobility was a problem in analyzing achievement data. Moreover, by the 5th grade, outcomes were disappointing.
7. In Lindholm-Leary's cross-sectional analyses, results for Spanish-background 5th graders varied among two-way models – from the 9th to the 30th percentiles in English reading; in 6th grade they ranged from the 23rd to the 30th percentiles.
8. Under Proposition 227 in California, liberal interpretation of parental "waiver" provisions meant that not a single two-way program was dismantled. After Massachusetts adopted Question 2, the legislature passed a law specifically exempting this approach from the English-only mandate. In Arizona following passage of Proposition 203, two-way programs have come under pressure from a state school superintendent who was elected on an English-only platform in 2002, but at this writing most are still in operation.

Politics

13 Disaster at the Polls

*I*t all started at Ninth Street Elementary. In early 1996, a group of Spanish-speaking parents pulled their children out of the school to protest its alleged failure to teach English. They blamed bilingual education. The boycott lasted for nearly two weeks and received extensive coverage in the *Los Angeles Times* – suggesting a new trend, perhaps even a sea-change, in Latino attitudes. These reports soon caught the eye of a Silicon Valley businessman named Ron Unz. "Parents shouldn't have to carry pick-

et signs to get English instruction for their kids," Unz declared. Dipping into his personal fortune, he organized a statewide ballot initiative requiring that "all children ... be taught English by being taught *in* English." The measure, known as

Proposition 227, passed overwhelmingly on June 2, 1998. It virtually outlawed bilingual education in California.

That is the official account, the story as conveyed by the victors and the news media. What actually happened – during the Ninth Street boycott and the Proposition 227 campaign – is more complicated. It is also instructive in understanding the political adversity surrounding bilingual education. California's experience highlights a second wave of English-only activism, one with a narrower agenda but a broader appeal than the first. Avoiding the rhetoric of ethnic bigotry, it evokes the principles of equal opportunity, parental choice, and pedagogical effectiveness. Instead of warning about the menace of "bilingualism," it stresses the importance of "English for the Children." In effect, it embraces key premises of bilingual programs to undermine their public support. This strategy proved to be an unqualified success in California, as voters dealt the most serious setback to bilingual schooling since World War I.

Manufacturing a Myth

Located in downtown Los Angeles, on the edge of Skid Row, the Ninth Street School faces more than its share of challenges. It serves about 460 students in pre-kindergarten through the 5th grade. About half are classified as homeless, living in downtown shelters and single-room-occupancy hotels. Others are bused into the area each morning with their parents, mostly recent immigrants from Mexico who work in garment factories nearby. Nine out of 10 children are LEP; 99 percent are eligible for free or reduced-price meals. All but a few come from homes where only Spanish is spoken. These factors help to explain why Ninth Street students, like their counterparts in similar schools, score well below national norms when tested in English.

Nevertheless, prospects brightened following the appointment of Eleanor Vargas Page as principal in 1993. The school entered into partnerships with local businesses, civic groups, and social service agencies. Academic expectations increased and so did the amount of English instruction.[1] Ninth Street won a $600,000 Title VII grant to support extended learning opportunities, before and after school, and to expand the school library. Student attendance and parent participation soared. The results were impressive: children's English scores rose by 35 percent over a four-year period.

So when a reporter called on February 9, 1996, with news that a meeting of 63 Ninth Street parents had just voted to boycott the school, "I was in shock," Vargas Page recalls. She had always been proud of her close ties with parents and their high attendance at school functions, where complaints about bilingual education had never come up. None of the boycotting parents had asked for their children to be removed from the program; in fact, all had recently signed forms consenting to their children's enrollment. "The conflict was not here in the school," the principal believes. "The complaints were initiated by [an outsider], not by the parents."

The outsider was Alice Callaghan, an Episcopal priest who ran a community center, Las Familias del Pueblo, that provided daycare for about one-quarter of Ninth Street students. Callaghan was also a veteran political organizer who had skirmished with city officials on numerous issues. Now she took up a new cause: abolishing bilingual education. For months she wrote to the Los Angeles Unified School District demanding English-only instruction at Ninth Street. After receiving little response, Callaghan urged the parents to take direct action.

Sensational headlines followed: *"80 Students Stay Out of School in Latino Boycott … Bilingual Schooling Is Failing, Parents Say."* For the news media, conflict means "good copy." This is especially true when the conflict seems unlikely – known in the trade as a "man bites dog" story. Journalists found the Ninth Street saga irresistible. Here were downtrodden immigrants, led by a colorful activist, who were using civil-rights tactics to protest a "politically correct" program supported by their own ethnic leaders. Amazing, but true!

The news accounts neglected, however, to clarify a key point. This was a needless conflict – a drama that was staged precisely to generate sensational headlines.

California, like other states, has long recognized parents' right to remove their children from bilingual instruction if they so choose. At Ninth Street, all they had to do was come to the school, meet with their child's teacher and principal, and hear about the educational options. Then, if the parents preferred to enroll their children in the school's alternative program taught mostly in English – as a few had done earlier that year – they merely needed to sign a consent form.[2] Vargas Page felt this procedure was essential "for a parent to make an informed decision." Callaghan called it "harassment" and "intimidation." She advised the parents to refuse to attend any such conference, keep their children out of school, and send them to Las Familias (where "we will speak only English with them") until the district gave in to their demands. Several days into the boycott, she circulated a form for parents to sign – in English, although few could read the language – authorizing student transfers to the alternative program.[3]

No doubt some of Alice Callaghan's followers were convinced that bilingual education was to blame for their children's academic problems. But others told school staff that they had no choice but to join the boycott and remove their children from the program, believing that otherwise they would lose the free daycare at Las Familias. In an interview, Callaghan denied making any explicit threats along these lines. Whatever the case, it is clear that she failed to assuage such concerns or to reassure parents that these decisions were entirely their own. Virtually none of those with children at Las Familias resisted her advice to transfer their children out of bilingual education (although a few would later change their minds).

What was the effect on LEP students? Two years later, only two out of the 74 moved into intensive English instruction had been redesignated as fluent in English. On state-mandated achievement tests, the 5th graders scored at the 11th percentile in reading, the 15th percentile in language, and the 16th percentile in math – well below peers who had remained in bilingual classrooms.[4] Questioned about these disappointing outcomes, Callaghan refused to accept responsibility. "If it's the older kids, that's not our fault," she said. "It's a result of their terrible bilingual program" provided to these children in the early grades.

Despite its dismal academic results, the boycott was a public relations bonanza for opponents of bilingual education. Soon it mushroomed into a national story. Spanish-speaking parents were quoted, often in translation, citing the importance of English to their children's future. Los Angeles Mayor Richard Riordan endorsed their protest. Ninth Street was portrayed as indicative of bilingual education's ineffectiveness and unpopularity among those it was intended to serve. Critics' views were prominently featured. Misinformation about the school went unchallenged. The *Los Angeles Times* asserted that bilingual education "trapped" children in all-Spanish classrooms for "six or seven years. ... That's much too long." Readers never heard an effective response.

This imbalance was not entirely the fault of the news media. Los Angeles School Board members and district officials reacted as though the controversy concerned practices at a single school and promised to "look into it." Few bilingual education advocates came forward to assist their beleaguered colleagues at Ninth Street. Facing a hostile press, Eleanor Vargas Page and her staff were largely on their own in defending the school. Their side of the story usually came out garbled – when it came out at all. By and large, the public never heard a coherent case for bilingual education. L.A. Unified's failure to provide one conveyed an impression of arrogance and unresponsiveness to parents' legitimate demands for English.

Thus the Ninth Street myth was born. Over the next two years, it would prove more damaging than anyone had foreseen.

Calls for 'Reform'

Critics had long complained that, despite the "sunset" of California's bilingual education law in 1987, the state kept most of the old requirements in place. Citing federal and state civil-rights guarantees for LEP students, the California Department of Education (CDE) continued to mandate – and enforce – the use of native-language instruction "when necessary ... [to] provide equal opportunity for academic achievement." The policy also required school districts to staff bilingual and ESL programs with an adequate number of qualified teachers. In the prevailing political climate, however, Sacramento could offer them little practical help in achieving these goals.

To come from behind and win re-election in 1994, Governor Pete Wilson promoted a crackdown on undocumented immigrants known as **Proposition 187**. One of its key provisions would have thrown their children out of public schools.[5] Not surprisingly, the Wilson administration saw little political gain in funding programs to train teachers for language-minority students. By 1996–97, the CDE estimated the shortage of bilingual teachers at 25,000 and rising. This left districts unable to provide bilingual classrooms for more than a minority of their LEP students – about 30 percent, on average, statewide.[6]

Meanwhile the California Association for Bilingual Education (CABE) resisted proposals in the legislature to allow more **local flexibility** in pedagogical matters. Since the mid-1980s CABE had built an effective lobbying operation. It remained committed to the prescriptive philosophy of mandating bilingual education, based on its experience with districts that had to be prodded constantly to meet their obligations to English learners. The problem remained prevalent, for example, in the Central Valley, where language-minority communities often lacked political influence on school boards. Year after year, CABE relied on the clout of Latino legislators in Sacramento to block any attempt to relax state requirements and oversight.

Yet **prescriptiveness** proved to be a double-edged sword. On the one hand, districts could be required to respond to the needs of English learners, providing additional resources, trained staff, and better designed programs. On the other hand, mandates inevitably bred resentment. The same had been true in the 1970s, when the U.S. Office for Civil Rights imposed **Lau Plans** forcing districts to try native-language approaches *(see Chapter 5)*. Aggressive enforcement created a backlash that forced OCR to retreat – but not before it had established bilingual education as a viable pedagogy. The tradeoff was harder to justify in the 1990s, when that pedagogy was embraced, for the most part, by California's "education

establishment." Public skepticism, English-only campaigns, and attacks by conservative politicians posed more formidable challenges than resistance at the school
district level.

The CDE's encroachment on local control – and CABE's vigorous defense
of the policy – presented an inviting target for anti-bilingual forces. Their charges
of bureaucratic "heavy-handedness" and "one-size-fits-all" schooling were effective, if exaggerated. No one seemed to notice that, by 1997, only five school boards
– all in conservative Orange County – had petitioned the State Board of Education
for waivers of the native-language requirement; none was denied. California's other
districts also enjoyed considerable flexibility in designing programs for English
learners, as exemplified by wide variations in program design. Nevertheless, the
native-language requirement made bilingual education an easy scapegoat when
schools failed these students.

Prescriptiveness also put the burden on advocates of bilingual approaches to
prove their superiority in practice over all-English approaches. Given the limited
quantity and quality of achievement data for LEP students in California, that was
rarely possible. At the national level, program evaluation research continued to provide relatively weak support – as compared with basic research in second-language
acquisition – for the effectiveness of bilingual instruction *(see Chapters 7 and 8)*. It has
become routine to blame bilingual educators for failing to "prove" the worth of their
methodology. Yet scientific comparisons of LEP program models are difficult to
design and expensive to execute. Federal and state policymakers have seldom been
generous in funding such research. Since the **Ramírez report**, commissioned in 1984
and completed in 1991, the U.S. Department of Education has funded only one large-
scale study, the **Thomas-Collier report** *(see Chapter 9)*. Otherwise it has de-emphasized research on English-learner programs, except for reviews of the literature.

National Research Council Report

The most significant of these reviews appeared in 1997. *Improving Schooling for
Language-Minority Children: A Research Agenda* summarized the findings of an expert
panel of the National Research Council. In addition to its chair, Kenji Hakuta of
Stanford, several other participants were prominent supporters of bilingual education. On the effectiveness question, however, their conclusions were equivocal:

> It is difficult to synthesize the program evaluations of bilingual education
> because of the extreme politicization of the process. Most consumers of the
> research are not researchers who want to know the truth, but advocates who
> are convinced of the absolute correctness of their positions. The beneficial

effects of native-language instruction are clearly evident in programs that are labeled "bilingual education," but [beneficial effects] also appear in some programs that are labeled ... "structured immersion," although a quantitative analysis of such programs is not yet available.

Complaints about politicization had been heard before. When the discussion of English learner policies became polarized in the 1980s, focusing almost exclusively on language of instruction, it tended to discourage open-minded efforts to analyze research evidence and improve programs. The restructuring of Title VII grant categories in 1994 was one attempt to mitigate this problem *(see Chapter 6)*.

What was new in the NRC report was its suggestion that the debate is no longer relevant. That both bilingual and English-only program models can be beneficial. That the federal government should stop funding expensive yet futile attempts to determine which is superior. That researchers on both "sides" needed to behave more like scientists and less like advocates.[7] "We need to think in terms of program components," the NRC panel recommended, "not politically motivated labels." It called for "theory-based interventions" that could be evaluated more scientifically and "a developmental model ... for use in predicting the effects of program components on children in different environments."

The report also raised eyebrows with its generous, albeit ambiguous, words about structured immersion. Its favorable assessment relied heavily on studies of an El Paso program whose English-only character had long been disputed; this so-called "bilingual immersion" model featured substantial amounts of Spanish instruction *(see Chapter 9)*. Some suspected that, in pursuit of even-handedness, the NRC panel was stretching the evidence to fit a preconceived agenda of its own.

Depoliticizing the research debate ... considering the diversity of LEP students and their needs ... restoring a measure of scientific detachment – these goals sounded worthy on paper. In reality they proved problematic. Opponents of bilingual education were quick to seize on the NRC's findings as a vindication of their views. Rosalie Porter's READ Institute, a project funded in part by U.S. English, published a lengthy analysis of the report by Charles Glenn of Boston University. Its main theme was that, despite a generation of experience with bilingual education, virtually nothing was known about whether it "works." Hakuta disputed this interpretation, condemning what he called "the far from impartial attempt by READ to place its own political spin on this matter." His statements, however, did little to settle what the NRC panel had meant to say. Like the research literature it criticized, the report had something for everyone, enabling partisans to pick and chose findings that served their purposes.

Meanwhile the political divide showed no sign of narrowing. Language of instruction was becoming, if anything, a more heated point of contention. Journalists and commentators highlighted the panel's complaints about the quality of program evaluation studies – "design limitations ... poorly articulated goals ... extreme politicization" – and pronounced all research in the field useless to policy-makers. If the science was inconclusive about what works, why not encourage experimentation and flexibility? they argued, reviving a familiar theme of the 1980s *(see Chapter 6).*

In California, state senator Deirdre Alpert and assemblyman Brooks Fire-stone sponsored a bipartisan bill along these lines. It proposed to relax the mandate for native-language instruction and allow local districts to choose their own approach, while requiring them to assess English learners annually and show progress over time. Programs would have to be restructured if children failed to meet goals within three years. Some bilingual education advocates saw the measure as a compromise worth exploring, believing that few districts were likely to disman-tle existing programs. Others objected that its accountability provisions were too weak and its sanctions too vague, thus encouraging schools to scale back their efforts for LEP children. Although the Alpert-Firestone bill easily passed the California Senate in the summer of 1997, for the third year in a row CABE man-aged to kill it in the Assembly. Self-described "moderates" expressed frustration and blamed bilingual educators for obstructing change. It was an opening tailor-made for Ron Unz.

English Only, Phase II

A software millionaire, aged 36 and single, with no children in school and no background in education, Unz seemed an unlikely antagonist. His first experience in politics had come three years earlier, when he challenged Pete Wilson for the Republican gubernatorial nomination and won about a third of the vote, mainly from Far Right critics of the incumbent. Yet he also emerged as a staunch oppo-nent of Proposition 187, earning "pro-immigrant" credentials that distinguished him from other English-only advocates. Unz believed that Republicans needed to face demographic realities and reach out to fast-growing minorities in states like California. Rather than side with nativists, he argued, the party should cater to the "natural conservatism" of Hispanic and Asian Americans on issues like welfare, crime, and abortion. Campaigning in 1994, the challenger preached the gospel of upward mobility through assimilation, while denouncing "the poisonous brew of bilingual education, multiculturalism and other ethnic-separatism policies."

These views and the wherewithal to promote them gave Unz access to prominent conservatives like Linda Chávez. He helped to endow her so-called Center for Equal Opportunity, a Washington advocacy group that opposes affirmative action and bilingual education on "civil rights" grounds. Impressed with the ideas of Peter Salins, Unz commissioned the sociologist to write *Assimilation, American Style*, a tendentious history that portrays earlier immigrants as eager to abandon their native languages in favor of English. Meanwhile he kept his distance from traditional English-only lobbies.

The influence of groups like U.S. English already appeared to have peaked, reaching its high-water mark on August 1, 1996. That day, by a vote of 259-167, the House of Representatives approved the so-called **English Language Empowerment Act**, the first Official English bill to receive serious consideration in Congress. (The logic was that, in terminating bilingual services, the bill would "empower" limited English speakers by forcing them to learn the language.) But the measure died without action in the Senate after a veto threat from President Clinton. If enacted, it would have banned most federal publications in languages other than English, repealed bilingual voting rights, mandated English-only naturalization ceremonies, and shielded English speakers from "discrimination." Republicans claimed that the legislation was essential to preserve the nation's "common bond." Democrats condemned it as divisive, mean-spirited, and potentially unconstitutional in its restrictions on minority access to government. In practice, the bill would have affected relatively few people. It was the precedent that stimulated interest on both sides.[8]

Likewise, in criticizing bilingual education, English-only advocates had always stressed symbolism over substance. Rhetorical attacks aside, they never dared to mount a legislative campaign to destroy the program. Concerned about being seen as callous toward children, leaders of U.S. English always included an exemption for bilingual education in their Official English proposals. Evidently they failed to grasp the program's vulnerability.

Ron Unz brought a different approach to English-only politics. In place of official-language declarations opposing "bilingualism" in government, he launched a frontal assault on the most important bilingual program. Rather than gauzy rhetoric about English and American identity, he used specific arguments about educational effectiveness. Instead of blaming immigrants for failing to learn English, he posed as their advocate against unresponsive schools.

It was a more sophisticated strategy than the visceral politics of resentment that had guided Phase I of the English-only movement. Unz's arguments sounded rational and public-spirited by contrast. They also exploited ignorance about language acquisition, which extended into liberal and progressive sectors of the electorate. As a result, he effectively changed the terms of the debate. Instead of *Should English learner policies be made more "flexible," supporting all-English as well as bilingual approaches?* the question became: *Should bilingual education be eliminated?*

Crafting Proposition 227

Unz's first step was to disassociate himself from California's anti-immigrant fringe. In the spring of 1997, he recruited prominent Latinos to help spearhead his ballot initiative, which he dubbed **English for the Children**. These included his cosponsor, Gloria Matta Tuchman, a 1st grade teacher from Santa Ana and a perennial candidate for state superintendent of public instruction.[9] Jaime Escalante, the legendary calculus teacher of *Stand and Deliver* fame, agreed to serve as "honorary chairman." Several lesser luminaries also lent their support. Alice Callaghan helped to kick off the campaign with a media event at Las Familias del Pueblo, where scenes of brown-skinned children provided a backdrop for speeches attacking bilingual education. Unz established his headquarters nearby, just a few blocks from the Ninth Street School.

Petitions for Proposition 227 began circulating in July. Qualifying an initiative statute for the ballot required sponsors to gather 433,000 valid signatures from registered voters – an enormous hurdle for grassroots volunteers, but not for those able to pay. Unz simply opened his checkbook and spent $650,000 to hire canvassers, paying a dollar per signature.

He made a point of circulating petitions in East Los Angeles, home to a large Mexican American community. Claims of minority support became a key selling point for the initiative after a Los Angeles Times Poll, conducted in October, reported that it was favored by 84 percent of Latinos. Small wonder, since the survey portrayed the measure as primarily an effort to improve English instruction for children who needed to learn the language.[10] Few Californians had heard about its extreme provisions, much less read the fine print.

Proposition 227 was a complex, often confusing proposal crafted to meet conflicting political and policy goals. Unz sought to outlaw a program that many parents wanted without appearing to restrict parental choice; to tie the hands of school boards that favored bilingual education without seeming to usurp their authority; and to eliminate protections for LEP students while shielding the law from civil-rights litigation. In the name of ending top-down mandates, he offered a far more prescriptive, one-size-fits-all system than any state had yet adopted. While

Preamble to Proposition 227
Chapter 3. English Language Education for Immigrant Children
Article 1. Findings and Declarations

300. The People of California find and declare as follows:

(a) WHEREAS, The English language is the national public language of the United States of America and of the State of California, is spoken by the vast majority of California residents, and is also the leading world language for science, technology, and international business, thereby being the language of economic opportunity; and

(b) WHEREAS, Immigrant parents are eager to have their children acquire a good knowledge of English, thereby allowing them to fully participate in the American Dream of economic and social advancement; and

(c) WHEREAS, The government and the public schools of California have a moral obligation and a constitutional duty to provide all of California's children, regardless of their ethnicity or national origins, with the skills necessary to become productive members of our society, and of these skills, literacy in the English language is among the most important; and

(d) WHEREAS, The public schools of California currently do a poor job of educating immigrant children, wasting financial resources on costly experimental language programs whose failure over the past two decades is demonstrated by the current high drop-out rates and low English literacy levels of many immigrant children; and

(e) WHEREAS, Young immigrant children can easily acquire full fluency in a new language, such as English, if they are heavily exposed to that language in the classroom at an early age.

(f) THEREFORE, It is resolved that: all children in California public schools shall be taught English as rapidly and effectively as possible.

questioning the effectiveness of bilingual pedagogies, he proposed a short-term, all-English approach that had never been tried and whose effectiveness had never been studied. Neither the news media nor the public seemed to appreciate the ironies.

The initiative's highlights, as adopted by California voters, include the following:

- LEP students must be taught in **sheltered English immersion** classrooms "during a temporary transition period not normally intended to exceed one year."

- Instruction must be delivered "overwhelmingly [in] English" by teachers who "possess a good knowledge of the English language."
- Students may be mixed by age and grade in immersion classrooms.
- They must be transferred to mainstream classrooms after they have attained "a good working knowledge of English."
- Parents may request **waivers** of the English-only rule under limited circumstances: (a) if children already score at or above grade level in English; (b) if they are at least 10 years old and educators believe that a bilingual program would foster "rapid English acquisition"; or (c) if they are under 10, have spent at least 30 days in English immersion, and can be shown to have "special physical, emotional, psychological, or educational needs" that would be better served through native-language instruction.
- Individual schools where at least 20 waivers are granted to students at the same grade level must offer a bilingual program; if fewer waivers are granted, children have the right to transfer to another school.
- Yet schools are under no obligation to grant waivers, regardless of students' special needs, and parents have no right to appeal denials.
- Teachers, administrators, and school board members who "willfully and repeatedly" violate the law's provisions may be sued by any parent and held personally liable for financial damages and plaintiffs' legal fees.
- The California legislature must appropriate $50 million each year to provide ESL instruction for adults who agree to tutor children in English.
- The law may be repealed or amended only by a two-thirds vote of the legislature and approval of the governor, or by another ballot initiative.

Campaign Strategies

When Proposition 227 was unveiled, California's education and civil-rights communities were naturally alarmed. A long list of advocates came together to plot strategy, including CABE, the California Teachers Association, the Association of California School Administrators, the Mexican American Legal Defense and Educational Fund, California Tomorrow, and the Northern California Coalition for Immigrant Rights. But an opposition campaign was slow to get under way. Finally, in mid-November, a coalition calling itself Citizens for an Educated America held its first press conference – four months after Ron Unz had launched his campaign. Meanwhile his charges against bilingual education had gone largely unchallenged. Though not unreported.

News media were drawn to the high-stakes controversy and covered it in lav-

PRO
COMMON SENSE ABOUT LEARNING ENGLISH

- Learning a new language is easier the younger the age of the child.
- Learning a language is much easier if the child is immersed in that language.
- Immigrant children already know their native language; they need the public schools to teach them English.
- Children who leave school without knowing how to speak, read, and write English are injured for life economically and socially.

English for the Children ballot argument

ish detail. Unz took to the campaign trail full-time. He carefully stayed "on message," repeating the same arguments at every stop. His pitch was straightforward: "Begun with the best of theoretical intentions some twenty or thirty years ago, bilingual education has proven itself a dismal practical failure. ... Enormous numbers of California children today leave years of schooling with limited spoken English and almost no ability to read or write English." He blamed "government efforts to prevent young immigrant children from learning English," despite the wishes of parents at schools like Ninth Street. "During the past decade, the number of these non-English-speaking immigrant children has more than doubled. Yet under the current system, centered on bilingual education, only about 5 percent of these children each year are found to have gained proficiency in English. *Thus our state's current system of language instruction has an annual failure rate of 95 percent.*"

Unz's mantra was simplistic but powerful. It was widely disseminated by journalists, who seldom challenged his evidence or assumptions. Few prospective voters understood that, because of teacher shortages, fully 70 percent of California's LEP students were not enrolled in bilingual classrooms. If the "current system" was indeed failing, it was more logical to blame the scarcity, not the excess, of native-language instruction. Moreover, Unz's arbitrary standard of success – one year to learn English – bore no relation to the realities of second-language acquisition. It defied research evidence that, while children quickly acquire "playground English," they need several years to acquire the decontextualized, cognitively demanding English required to excel in school *(see Chapter 9)*.

The annual **redesignation rate** – which averaged 7 percent statewide in 1997 – fluctuated significantly from district to district. It was affected by socioeconomic status, immigration trends, variations in assessment procedures, and other factors unrelated to achievement. Using this dubious statistic to "hold schools accountable" implied that rapid English acquisition was the best measure of student progress. Yet research showed the opposite: programs that stressed a gradual transition to English were correlated with long-term academic success.

On the other hand, there was limited research evidence supporting the sheltered English immersion approach (a term used interchangeably with **structured immersion**) that Unz sought to impose by law. There was none whatsoever that this model could successfully mainstream children within 180 school days. One of the few rigorous studies in this area, the 1991 Ramírez report, found that after one year in English immersion programs only 4 percent of students had become fully English-proficient (FEP). After four years 67 percent had been redesignated FEP, as compared with 72 percent of those in transitional bilingual education and 51 percent in developmental bilingual education.

While such rebuttals occasionally appeared in the press, they did not lend themselves to snappy "sound-bites." On the other hand, voters tended to remember the "95 percent failure rate." In candid moments Unz conceded the figure was misleading, but he found it too useful to abandon. Journalists never exposed the fraud. Appealing to folk wisdom about how languages are acquired – "the younger the better" ... through "total immersion" ... without the "crutch" of bilingual support – he dismissed all research in the field as worthless, motivated by ethnic politics or ivory tower "looniness." Many reporters and editorial writers, after a cursory glance at the NRC report, were inclined to agree.

Unz also played to their habitual cynicism, portraying bilingual educators as a vested interest – resistant to legislative reform and more interested in taxpayer subsidies than in student achievement. The news media recycled these charges, while rarely questioning Unz's own motives once it was established that he was not a nativist zealot.

Meanwhile it seemed that every story trumpeted his lead in the polls, implying that Proposition 227 was unbeatable. This seemed to intimidate the politicians who had traditionally supported bilingual education, includ-

CON

Children in California must learn English. In thousands of classrooms all over California, they are. Good teachers. Good local school boards. Good parent involvement.

Those successes are not the result of one instructional method imposed on every school by state government. Sadly, there have been failures too. However, these failures can best be remedied by reasonable program changes that maximize local control.

California should be returning more decisions to parents, teachers, principals, and local school boards. A growing number of school districts are working with new English teaching methods. Proposition 227 stops them.

The San Diego Union-Tribune editorial said it best: "School districts should decide for themselves."

Citizens for an Educated America
ballot argument

ing Latinos and liberal Democrats. Few spoke out aggressively against the measure. Those who finally did, in the late stages, were quick to concede that the program needed a complete overhaul.

How to Respond?

Bilingual education advocates were in a quandary. Anti-immigrant bias was an obvious factor in the initiative's popularity; yet Unz had seemingly immunized his campaign from the charge of racism. Voters who truly cared about English learners were badly misinformed; yet there was little time to give them a crash course in the theory and practice of bilingual education. Media bias had become a major obstacle; yet the No on 227 campaign needed the help of journalists to get its message out. The California Teachers Association was a potential source of funds to buy TV advertising; yet the giant union was ambivalent in its support for bilingual programs. A deal remained within reach on bilingual education "reform" legislation that might head off the initiative; yet the coalition was divided over whether to compromise.

Citizens for an Educated America recognized its need for professional help. It hired campaign and media consultants, along with pollsters to conduct surveys and focus groups. The professionals recommended a counterattack against Proposition 227. This election should not be a referendum on bilingual education, they argued, but a referendum on Unz's proposal. Highlighting its extreme provisions — mixing students by age and grade, usurping local control, threatening lawsuits against educators — would help to win over "swing voters" yet to form an opinion. Such voters were not to be found among immigrants, many of whom were noncitizens and thus ineligible to vote, nor among Latinos and other language minorities, who usually turned out in small numbers. Given California's electoral realities, the swing voters would have to be found among white, affluent, older, English-speaking moderates. In particular, the consultants argued, the No campaign should target "Republican women over 50." A winning message — one that would appeal to the undecided — could not be built on challenging the conventional wisdom. It could not claim success for programs that were widely perceived to be failing. In short, the consultants recommended: *Don't defend bilingual education.*

This advice came as a bitter pill for many educational practitioners and advocates for English learners. It seemed like a betrayal of everything they had worked for, a capitulation to demagogues who would risk children's futures for political gain. Lies about bilingual education were everywhere. How could Citizens fail to refute them? Still, it was hard to deny that the situation was desperate. With their polling results and political savvy, the professionals were convincing. "Put aside your personal feelings," they said in effect. "This strategy is the only hope of saving bilingual education. Given a free rein and sufficient resources, we can beat Proposition 227." After much internal debate, the coalition agreed.

Others viewed the decision as not merely misguided but suicidal. In private, some said, the strategy could have hardly served Ron Unz's purposes better if he had designed it himself. Indeed, when school officials came forward to defend bilingual education, Unz warned that they could be prosecuted under a California law that prohibited public employees from taking sides on pending legislation. Now bilingual educators and even immigrant advocates working in Latino communities were feeling the same pressure from their own campaign. Whenever pedagogical issues came up in debates or press interviews, the Citizens consultants advised them to change the subject, saying: "I'll be happy to discuss bilingual education on June 3 [the day after the election] – assuming the Ron Unz Initiative fails and we can still have a meaningful conversation." Predictably, Unz cited the Don't Defend strategy as evidence that the program was indefensible.

Journalists were incredulous, not to mention frustrated, when Citizens refused to respond to his attacks. But they did not stop writing about issues of educational effectiveness. For the press and the public, Proposition 227 remained very much a referendum on bilingual education. Ron Unz and his surrogates maintained a steady barrage of attacks on the program, which were duly recycled by the news media. (Newspapers in California and other states ran nearly 700 separate articles during the campaign.) Yet No on 227 rarely if ever responded, continuing to discourage bilingual researchers and practitioners from speaking out to correct the misconceptions that Unz was exploiting.

Some advocates chose to go their own way. Notwithstanding his long alliance with CABE, Stephen Krashen was among those who broke with its leadership. By the winter of 1998, it was clear that the No campaign was faltering, as opinion polls consistently reported overwhelming support for Proposition 227. Unless voters heard the case for bilingual education, Krashen reasoned, who could blame them for accepting the critics' claims? He recalls an incident that drove home this point:

> It had been a frustrating day. I had been scheduled to debate Ron Unz at Cal State LA, my first chance to debate him face to face. To my disappointment, Unz did not show up ... and therefore the press wasn't there. On the way home [I] was standing in line [and] the woman behind me asked why I looked so depressed. I explained the situation briefly. ... She asked what the debate was about, and I said that it was with Ron Unz and had to do with Propo-

sition 227. Her response was immediate and animated: "Oh, yes, English for the children! I've heard of that. I'm voting for it. I'm for English." I was stunned. I realized right then that my strategy of carefully presenting the research that contradicted the details of 227 had been all wrong. The woman had no idea what 227 was about: she was "voting for English," but she clearly had no idea that a major goal of bilingual education was English language development.

Krashen saw the initiative as a rare opportunity to educate Californians about the issue. The more they learned about the rationale and aims of bilingual education, he believed, the more likely they were to oppose Proposition 227. So he joined with like-minded colleagues in a project to influence media coverage by debunking Unz's claims.[11] Numerous other researchers, teachers, and administrators also seized opportunities – acting as individuals – to defend bilingual education in public forums. Yet without central coordination by the No campaign, these efforts were sporadic, unfocused, and poorly covered by the news media; their impact on the voters was minimal.[12] Bilingual teachers and immigrant advocates formed local committees, especially in Latino communities, to activate parents, staff phone banks, and get out the vote. They enjoyed some success. Apart from fundraising drives, however, grassroots organizing received limited support from Citizens for an Educated America.

No on 227 needed large sums because its strategy relied heavily on TV advertising. Based on private opinion surveys, the campaign singled out one feature of the initiative for special attack: the $50 million annual appropriation for adult English instruction. Even though that represented barely one-sixth of one percent of the state's K–12 education budget, Californians resented such spending to benefit immigrants, according to the Citizens polls. Ironically, Unz had inserted this provision to guard against attacks from the Left. It was intended to enhance his "pro-immigrant" guise and draw criticism from anti-immigrant zealots, making him look moderate by comparison. Now Citizens took the bait. Advocates who had lobbied over the past decade for more immigrant ESL classes suddenly sounded like fiscal conservatives, denouncing "a new spending program – not in our schools – but to teach adults English." The hypocrisy was hard to conceal. Unz charged that his opponents were so desperate that they were willing to abandon cherished principles. For once he was right.

A lion's share of No on 227 spending, which exceeded $4.7 million for the campaign, went for media buys in the final two weeks. Unz ran little advertising; there was simply no need, considering the lopsided polls. Contrary to expectations,

Citizens outspent him nearly five to one overall.[13] Proposition 227 still passed easily, by a margin of 61 to 39 percent.

The only surprise was the Latino vote – two to one against the initiative – exactly the opposite of pollsters' predictions.[14] In at least this one respect, bilingual educators were vindicated. The program's strongest constituency had not forsaken it, contrary to opponents' claims. Indeed, a survey by Spanish-language media found no decline in approval rates: 68 percent of Latino parents in Los Angeles favored bilingual education, including 88 percent of those with children in bilingual classrooms.[15] Spanish-speaking parents campaigned actively to defeat Proposition 227 in some areas. In Santa Barbara and Orange County, respectively, hundreds staged boycotts and filed litigation against local decisions to terminate native-language instruction. Journalists paid little attention, however, even as they continued to publicize the two-year-old protest at Ninth Street.

Nevertheless, parent activism against the initiative remained more the exception than the rule – an unhealthy sign. When beneficiaries of a controversial program offer mainly passive support, political trouble cannot be far away. Thus the Proposition 227 story is a cautionary one for bilingual educators across the country. Ron Unz went on to finance successful anti-bilingual initiatives in Arizona (2000) and Massachusetts (2002). Although their provisions were harsher than those in California – severely limiting parental choices and making it easier to sue educators – they passed by even larger margins (63-37 percent and 68-32 percent, respectively). Opponents failed to mount effective campaigns in either state.

Education and Latino advocacy groups in Arizona were unable to raise significant resources, mobilize many of their constituents, or unite behind a single campaign organization (three splinter groups competed for leadership). The only exception to this pattern was Native American activism, especially on the Navajo reservation, where the initiative known as Proposition 203 was defeated by nearly 10-1. Latinos appear to have voted no statewide, although a reliable estimate is impossible because no exit polling was conducted. In Phoenix, where the opposition campaign was weakest, the measure passed narrowly in several working-class, heavily Latino precincts (which meanwhile gave 70 percent support to Democrat Al Gore). Small cadres of volunteers worked hard in various parts of Arizona, but could not overcome the lack of central direction or the limited number of educators willing to participate actively.

In Massachusetts, the official campaign against English Only seemed determined to replicate the failed strategy of No on 227 four years earlier: avoid any serious discussion of bilingual education. The chief diversionary tactic became

"Don't Sue Teachers" – an issue that generated limited enthusiasm among the electorate. Another blow came when the Republican candidate for governor, Mitt Romney, made support for Unz's Question 2 a centerpiece of his winning campaign. Once more, volunteer activists waged their own grassroots efforts, often working to educate the public about the benefits of bilingual education. But, as in the other states, they were no match for Unz's sophisticated, media-driven effort.

The one surprise in the 2002 election came in Colorado, where Unz's Amendment 31 to the state constitution was soundly defeated, winning just 44 percent of the vote. Opponents again hired professional campaign consultants, who conducted opinion research and recommended a strategy of diverting voters' attention to issues other than bilingual education – for example, the initiative's threat to parental choice and local control of schools. They also benefited from a $3 million contribution from a local heiress who happened to have a child in two-way bilingual education; this enabled them to orchestrate a massive advertising effort. Perhaps most important was the No on 31 campaign's message, which struck a chord with conservative, white, affluent voters. A dark, brooding television commercial warned that Unz's initiative would "force children who can barely speak English into regular classrooms, creating chaos and disrupting learning." By implication, a vote to preserve bilingual education would be a vote to preserve the segregation of Latino students. This approach, which might be described as *If you can't beat racism, then try to exploit it*, was successful in the short run. Yet it remains questionable whether abandoning appeals to social justice, along with efforts to win support for bilingual education on its merits, will serve the interests of English learners over the long term.

Post-Mortem

Meeting at Lake Tahoe in August 1998, veterans of No on 227 shared their views about what had gone wrong. Some defended the campaign strategy and argued that defeat was inevitable, given the demographics of California voters and their appetite for anti-immigrant initiatives. Others insisted that the outcome might have been different if Citizens had offered a straightforward rationale for bilingual education – something most voters had never heard – instead of insulting their intelligence with diversionary gimmicks. No consensus was achieved on these matters. Still, there was no shortage of mea culpas in explaining the victory of Proposition 227:

- *Inattention to the public image of bilingual education.* Facing increasing opposition since the mid-1980s, the field has failed to respond proactively. Professional organizations have rarely used the news media to showcase success stories, or to elaborate the mission of bilingual education, or to challenge widespread misunderstanding among the public and "disinformation" by English-only groups. School districts have often neglected to communicate with parents, for example, to assuage worries about programs that stress a gradual transition to English. Researchers have seldom made their findings accessible to a broad audience. Bilingual educators have tended to circle the wagons and complain to each other about unsympathetic colleagues in their schools rather than work systematically to challenge misconceptions. It is no wonder that the field has become politically isolated.

- *Limited efforts to marshal data on outcomes.* The field has tended to ignore the importance of test scores to combat skepticism about bilingual education. Notwithstanding the difficulties in assessing English learners, the public is not unreasonable to demand accountability for programs that have been in place for years. To their credit, a few California districts (including Los Angeles and Calexico) scrambled during the campaign to release data comparing the outcomes of children in bilingual and all-English classrooms. Unfortunately, the data sometimes had flaws that tended to discredit legitimate claims of success. Trained researchers are needed to assist in analyzing these results. In their large-scale evaluation studies, Wayne Thomas and Virginia Collier have reported results that confirm theories underlying bilingual education, such as a correlation between native-language development and long-term academic achievement *(see Chapter 9).* Their work would seem to offer powerful evidence against the claims of Ron Unz. Yet in their 1997 report, released during the Proposition 227 campaign, Thomas and Collier declined to release sufficient data – in the view of many colleagues – for others to assess their findings. As a result, the researchers missed an opportunity to influence debate over the initiative.

- *Resistance to legislative compromise.* During the 1990s – an era of conservatism, fiscal and otherwise – bilingual educators adopted a defensive posture, relying on backroom deal-making to block change. They continued to stress legal mandates to force schools to meet their obligations to LEP students. In other words, they became defenders of the status quo. Refusal to compromise may be "principled," but it can also sacrifice chances to win needed improvements – for example, to remedy the chronic shortage of qualified teachers. In addition, it strengthens the stereotype of bilingual educators as a vested interest rather than a group of dedicated professionals, sometimes inviting more extreme measures like Proposition 227.

- *Loss of ties to the grassroots.* Bilingual education was not a gift from above, but a victory of mass struggle from below. Without the efforts of determined parents and community leaders, the Bilingual Education Act and the *Lau v. Nichols* decision would never have materialized. Increasingly the program was supported by government, accepted by school boards, studied by researchers, and sustained by a corps of experts, lawyers, and bureaucrats. In short, it became institutionalized. To the extent that it became a domain of professionals, it became less of an activist cause, less of a social movement. Parents, once its strongest political base, were reduced to a passive role – as consumers of bilingual education rather than participants.

Whether any single decision by No on 227 could have altered the outcome is impossible to say. There is little doubt, however, that greater attention to these problems during the campaign would have left advocates in a better position to cope with the initiative's aftermath. Because of legal challenges and ambiguous language, the final interpretation of Proposition 227 could take years to sort out *(see Chapter 15)*. Its ultimate impact on children will depend not only on litigation but, more importantly, on the pressures that each side can bring to bear to influence school boards, district administrators, and state officials.

These efforts are complicated by a new political climate in which policies for educating English learners are no longer considered in isolation, seen as a simple conflict between English Only and English Plus. They are now inseparable from larger debates over **school reform.** The No Child Left Behind Act of 2002 eliminated the direct federal role in sustaining bilingual education. Moreover, in the name of "accountability," it created new carrots and sticks that may ultimately prove more powerful than Unz's initiatives in pressuring schools to adopt all-English instruction.

Suggested Reading

Crawford, James. "Boom to Bust: Official English in the 1990s." In *At War with Diversity: U.S. Language Policy in an Age of Anxiety* (Clevedon, U.K.: Multilingual Matters, 2000).

Unz, Ron. "Immigration or the Welfare State: Which Is Our Real Enemy?" *Policy Review*, Fall 1994.

See also pp. 405–6.

Online Resource Guide

Arizona Secretary of State. *Proposition 203*. Voter information pamphlet (2000).

California Secretary of State. *English Language in Public Schools: Initiative Statute.* Information Guide and Ballot Pamphlet on Proposition 227 (1998).

Colorado Legislative Council. *Amendment 31: English Language Education in Public Schools.* Initiative text (2002).

Massachusetts Secretary of State. *Question 2: Law Proposed by Initiative Petition – English Language Education in Public Schools.* Information for voters (2002).

See also companion CD-ROM.

Internet Links

Crawford, James. "The Campaign against Proposition 227: A Post Mortem." *Bilingual Research Journal* 21, no. 1 [Winter 1999]. http://brj.asu.edu/archives/1v21/articles/Issue1Crawford.html

Crawford, James. "Agenda for Inaction: A Critique of the National Research Council Report." *International Journal of the Sociology of Language* 155/156 (2002). http://ourworld.compuserve.com/homepages/jwcrawford/agenda.htm

Language Policy Web Site. Unz initiative page, including commentaries, litigation, polls, voters pamphlets, and extensive media coverage. http://ourworld.compuserve.com/homepages/jwcrawford/unz.htm

Shultz, Jim. "Proposition 227 – The Morning After." *Democracy Center On-Line* (1998). http://democracyctr.org/newsletter/vol14.htm

See also companion CD-ROM.

Notes

1. According to Vargas Page, students in 1997–98 were receiving a minimum of two hours of English daily in the early years, with the amount of Spanish instruction decreasing until children were redesignated as fluent English proficient (R-FEP), usually by the 4th or 5th grade.

2. Critics have frequently charged that children are misassigned to bilingual programs, typically on the basis of Hispanic surnames, and that parents' requests for all-English instruction are denied. Such mistakes may sometimes occur. There is no evidence,

however, that they are common, much less pervasive. Norm Gold, the official in charge of enforcing civil-rights guarantees for English learners in California, said in 1998 that his department had received "scores of written complaints" each year from parents unable to get bilingual instruction for their children. "But records going back over more than a decade show that there have been no complaints alleging that parents have been unable to remove their children from bilingual instruction."

3. One parent who checked off the English-only box wrote below: "Quiero que mi hijo siga en la clase bilingüe porque quiero que es mejor para su futuro" (I want my son to continue in the bilingual classroom because I believe it is better for his future).

4. By contrast, 5th graders in bilingual programs at Ninth Street scored at the 27th, 31st, and 38th percentiles respectively. These scores are from the Stanford 9 test administered in the spring of 1998. Direct comparisons are difficult because some students were excused from taking the test owing to their limited English proficiency.

5. This feature of Proposition 187 (among others) was ruled unconstitutional in 1998, a question the U.S. Supreme Court had previously decided in a 1982 case, *Plyler v. Doe*.

6. Even in these classrooms, about one-third of teachers were still working toward their bilingual certification. According to the CDE's annual language census, another 21 percent of LEP students received lessons taught in English with "native-language support" from paraprofessionals. Various forms of all-English instruction were provided to 32 percent of English learners, and 16 percent received no language assistance of any kind *(see Table 2–2, page 34)*.

7. The plague-on-both-houses theme came through even stronger in an NRC press release announcing the study on January 14, 1997:

    Political debates over how children with limited English skills should be taught are hampering research and evaluation of educational programs established to meet the needs of these children. ... Much research has been used in trying to determine which type of instruction is better – English-only or bilingual. However, there is little value in using research for this purpose. ... Instead of attempting to single out one method for all students, research should focus on identifying a variety of educational approaches that work for children in their communities, based on specific local needs and available resources. ... *Evaluations have proved inconclusive about which teaching approaches work best.* ... Because many current studies are attempting to compare different types of programs that vary widely in such areas as funding, classroom setting, student background, and subject matter, the studies are unlikely to settle the debate over which type of instruction is best. ... Advocates on many sides of the issue have been able to use research to uphold their arguments because there are study results that support a wide range of positions. These debates confuse policy-makers and muddle research agendas. [Emphasis added]

8. Speaker Newt Gingrich championed the English-only cause during House floor debate, hoping to give Republicans a boost in the fall campaign. But the issue seemed to have little impact at the polls, except to drive Latinos further from the party. Gingrich would not make the same mistake again. In the 105th Congress, he refused to

allow another vote on the legislation, even in committee. Subsequent Republican leaders have done the same.

9. Cosponsoring Proposition 227 gave her the name recognition to wage a serious challenge to the incumbent, Delaine Eastin, in November 1998. Tuchman lost narrowly.

10. Here is how the question was posed:

> There is a new initiative trying to qualify for the June primary ballot that would require all public school instruction to be conducted in English and for students not fluent in English to be placed in a short-term English immersion program. If the June 1998 primary election were being held today, would you vote for or against this measure?

Overall, 80 percent of likely voters said yes and 18 percent said no. Later surveys by the Los Angeles Times Poll and the Field Poll were nearly as misleading. So was California's official ballot summary, which failed to mention the virtual ban on bilingual programs. It seems likely that many voters never got that message.

11. The author was also an organizer of this effort, known as UnzWatch – http://ourworld.compuserve.com/homepages/jwcrawford/unzwatch.htm.

12. Spokespersons hired by Citizens, who had little background in education or knowledge of research, devoted most of their energies to debating Ron Unz and to lobbying editorial boards to oppose Proposition 227. But they held few press conferences and generated few news stories of any kind. Meanwhile Unz faxed daily press releases to journalists – setting the campaign agenda and defining the terms of debate.

13. English for the Children raised $1,289,815 but spent only $976,632, according to its reports to the California Secretary of State. Of this amount, $752,738 came from Ron Unz. Citizens for an Educated America raised and spent $4,754,157, including $2.1 million from the California Teachers Association and $1.5 million from Jerrold Perenchio, owner of the Spanish-language network Univision.

14. A week before the election, the Los Angeles Times Poll reported 62 percent Latino support for Proposition 227. By contrast, its exit interviews with voters on June 2 found that Latinos had opposed the initiative by 63 to 37 percent. African Americans also voted no, 52-48, while Asian Americans voted yes, 57-43, and whites voted yes, 67-33, according to the exit poll.

15. Still, because of confusion about Proposition 227, 43 percent were inclined to support it, too. The poll was conducted in February 1998 by the newspaper *La Opinión* and KVEA-TV, the Los Angeles affiliate of Telemundo.

14 No Child Left Untested

*T*he debate over Proposition 227 high-lighted an important but often neglected issue in educating English learners: **program quality**. Virtually no one denied that many California classrooms, bilingual and all-English alike, were poorly serving language-minority students, whose overall test scores and dropout rates were too dismal to ignore. Yet, because of polarized conflicts over language policy in recent years, constructive discussion of how to improve programs has been difficult. It

seems that whenever supporters of bilingual education concede weaknesses in implementation, opponents seize on their statements and use them, usually out of context, to attack the concept of teaching in two languages.

Researcher Kenji Hakuta, for example, offered this forthright assessment in his 1986 book *Mirror of Language*: "An awkward tension blankets the lack of empirical demonstration of the success of bilingual education programs. Someone promised bacon, but it's not there." Hakuta was criticizing pedagogical practice, not the theory behind it. Citing basic research, he went on to outline a strong rationale for native-language instruction *(see Chapter 7)*. Nevertheless, his statement was widely exploited by enthusiasts of English-only approaches. Over the next decade it was quoted in numerous forums – federal courts, state legislatures, and the U.S. Congress, not to mention the popular press – to allege that even the supporters of bilingual education have "no proof" that it "works." In this adversarial climate, both researchers and practitioners have had to confront the unsavory choice of mincing their words or inviting unprincipled attacks on their profession.

The risks of candor were well illustrated during the high-stakes conflict over Proposition 227. Supporters of bilingual education were often willing to concede that too many bilingual programs were still not working as they should. Indeed, groups like the California Association for Bilingual Education had been pressing state officials for years to improve the situation – for example, by devoting more resources to train bilingual and ESL teachers and by riding herd on school districts that continued to neglect the needs of English learners. It was obvious that until such problems could be solved, "bad bilingual programs" would remain a fact of life. Such admissions, however, inspired little confidence in the status quo that the ballot initiative was targeting. In news accounts like this one from the *Sacramento Bee*, advocates seemed to be making excuses:

> Even supporters of bilingual education admit that the current system is flawed. But they blame a lack of structure, consistency and accountability in programs for children learning English, as well as a shortage of qualified teachers. The answer is not to gut the program, but to fix it, they argue. "We don't stop teaching biology because some teachers aren't doing a good job. We don't give up algebra because we don't have the algebra teachers," said Norman Gold, manager for bilingual compliance for the California Department of Education.

However reasonable in the abstract, this argument had little impact on voters. A generation earlier it might have proved compelling, but by the late 1990s overall confidence in the public schools had been shaken by years of ideological attacks and negative media reports. Journalistically speaking, the *Bee* article was "balanced," striving to represent the viewpoints of both sides. Yet it did so in a larger context of crisis: children were continuing to fail year after year, but "politicians have been unable to pass bilingual reforms." Ron Unz, the sponsor of Proposition 227, was quoted as follows: "What really is shocking to me is … that the system is so totally nuts and nobody has done anything about it for all this time." This was more than an appeal to anti-bilingual sentiment; Unz also perceived a deep skepticism toward the public schools. Taxpayers increasingly wanted **accountability** in education, and they no longer trusted the "system" to reform itself. For many, Proposition 227 promised a way to force change from without.

Bilingual educators, whose job it was to serve minority students with low to abysmal test scores in controversial programs that few outsiders understood, were especially vulnerable to these attacks. English-only forces sought to demonize them as a "vested interest" and a "self-serving bureaucracy," beneficiaries of a "jobs program" for Latinos. Such charges even came from fellow teachers who resented the extra resources, classroom aides, and higher salaries often available to their bilingual colleagues. In part because of **categorical funding** from state and federal governments, English learner programs had operated autonomously within most school districts. The arrangement was advantageous in some respects – financially, for example – but it also bred isolation. Not only were other educators generally ignorant (if not outright skeptical) of bilingual education, but the field was rarely included in broader initiatives affecting all students. With few defenders outside their own ranks, bilingual educators were convenient scapegoats for the **achievement gap** between LEP and non-LEP students.

This was as shortsighted as it was unfair. Language of instruction is just one of many variables affecting the academic progress of English learners. Their schooling has been, and continues to be, afflicted by the same ills that affect many of their English-proficient peers: unequal resources and facilities, uncaring bureaucracies, insensitive treatment of parents, poorly trained staff, unchallenging curricula, low expectations for minority children – any of which can limit achievement, no matter what language is used for instruction.

Conversely, while bilingual education is hardly to blame for failing schools, neither is it a panacea. The most creative use of the native language cannot overcome a hostile learning environment or an incompetent administration. Not that creativity is the norm. Mediocrity is no stranger to bilingual programs, as any professional in the field can confirm (even if many hesitate to do so in an adversarial climate). Although bilingual pedagogies have advanced enormously since 1968, they have developed unevenly among states, districts, and schools. Local attitudes toward bilingualism, relations among ethnic groups, availability of resources, and quality of educational leadership have all played a role.

Above all, this experience has shown that improving outcomes for language-minority students is a complex undertaking. It requires not merely appropriate instruction, but fundamental changes in the way schools relate to students, parents, and communities. It demands that the unique needs of LEP children be considered in every step toward **school reform**. In addition, as bilingual educators began to recognize over the past decade, it necessitates their active participation. No longer can they remain a field apart. English learners need to be represented in deliberations over education policies that affect them just as directly as they affect other students.

School 'Reform' in Context

Reform is a loaded word. Although journalists and politicians now seem to apply the term whenever any change in policy is proposed, it also carries connotations of *improvement, elimination of abuses,* and *correction of faults.* More often than not, these are matters of debate. In education policy over the past two decades, the debate has developed largely along partisan and ideological lines. Some might argue that the **No Child Left Behind Act of 2002**, which was approved by large bipartisan majorities in Congress, contradicts this pattern. In fact, the law resulted from a convergence of political currents flowing from very different directions. This may help to explain why the climate that produced the legislation has become increasingly turbulent. To understand the contending philosophies involved, a bit of history is necessary.

Today's **reform movement** – another misnomer, because all the "motion" has been among elites, with nary a sit-in or street demonstration – began in 1983, with the release of *A Nation at Risk: The Imperative for Educational Reform.* The study was conducted by a "blue-ribbon commission" appointed by the Reagan administration, which had previously shown limited interest in education. Suddenly the quality of public schools became a front-burner issue, assuming a prominence unseen since the panic over *Sputnik.* Educators were understandably grateful for the attention, even if the report exaggerated the "crisis" with its breathless rhetoric:

> If an unfriendly foreign power had attempted to impose on America the mediocre educational performance that exists today, we might well have viewed it as an act of war. As it stands, we have allowed this to happen to ourselves. … We have, in effect, been committing an act of unthinking, unilateral educational disarmament.

This assessment, coming from a panel of Nobel laureates and other notables, inspired public concern and, in many cases, public willingness to spend more on schools to promote "excellence," however vaguely defined.

The strong response to *A Nation at Risk* also caught the notice of White House advisers, who recognized the potential benefits for Republicans in championing school reform. Conservatives inside and outside the administration saw an opportunity to advance their agenda, by making education a site of ideological conflict. As one writer for *Commentary* explained, "Far more than any other institution in American society, the schools have become an arena for the struggle between the values of traditionalism and modernity." Politicians on the Right articulated a critique that made sense to frustrated taxpayers. They drew connections between declining test scores, innovations like whole language and the "new math," child-centered approaches that de-emphasized rote learning, and moral relativism, as exemplified by sex education and the ban on school prayer. They had no trouble identifying the main enemy: the "education establishment," portrayed as a bureaucratic leviathan dependent on Big Government. Liberals, on the other hand, tended to blame the schools' difficulties on inadequate funding, arguing that budget cuts by the Reagan administration were exacerbating these problems. But conservatives rejected that explanation, noting that spending for public education had increased sharply during the 1960s and 1970s, with no discernible impact on academic outcomes. "Throwing money at the problem" was no solution, they insisted.

Neither Democrats nor Republicans questioned the dire portrait of public schools presented by *A Nation at Risk*. The study found that the scores of U.S. "high school students on most standardized tests [are] now lower than 26 years ago when Sputnik was launched." On 19 measures of academic achievement, American children reportedly ranked lower than their counterparts in other industrialized nations. This was especially worrisome at a time when many feared that Japan, with its highly touted educational system, would soon displace the United States as the world's leading economic power. Yet, as researchers David Berliner and Bruce Biddle later pointed out, *A Nation at Risk* featured no actual evidence and cited no published research to support its claims. In fact, on virtually every kind of standardized assessment, American students had shown modest increases in the years prior to the report.[1] Moreover, the international comparisons often pitted a representative sample of American students, including English learners, against select groups of students from high-status schools in other countries. To the extent that a crisis existed, Berliner and Biddle concluded, it was a "manufactured crisis" designed to advance political ends.

Meanwhile there were two factors with a significant impact on achievement – the growing diversity of American students and the difficulties of American schools in serving them – that received scant attention in this discussion. So did the reality that racial, cultural, and linguistic minorities were receiving far less than their fair share of educational resources. In his best-selling book *Savage Inequalities*, Jonathan Kozol documented the segregation and despair of urban schools, with decaying buildings, overcrowded classes, and burnt-out teachers – in contrast to the ample and sometimes lavish facilities found in predominantly white suburbs. He illustrated in vivid strokes the failure of Great Society programs to abolish a **two-tier educational system**; if anything, inequities had increased since the 1960s. Unequal allocation of resources among school districts remained a contentious legal and political issue in several states.[2]

Nevertheless, educational quality – not equality – became the rallying cry of the new reformers. Many agreed with neoconservatives Diane Ravitch and Chester E. Finn, Jr., that excessive egalitarianism was to blame for U.S. schools' low standards and limited accountability. By this way of thinking – and it appealed to many *non*conservatives – "dumbing-down" the curriculum had ended up depriving poor and minority children of academic opportunities. Schools that emphasized cognitive skills over factual knowledge were turning out "cultural illiterates" unprepared for anything but menial jobs *(see Chapter 6)*. From his bully pulpit as U.S. secretary of education, William J. Bennett denounced the "dangerous theory that content is not really important because American culture has become too fragmented and pluralistic to justify a belief in common learning." As an antidote, the critics proposed intensive efforts to instill in students the basic facts of American culture, by establishing **academic standards** that would specify what each child "needs to know."

Despite massive and often supportive coverage by the national media, by decade's end this ideological trend had done little to remold the schools' values, curricula, or philosophies. Although conservatives controlled the federal Department of Education, they failed to develop a legislative strategy for imposing their vision (other than abolishing the department itself, an idea that President Reagan had championed in his 1980 campaign but never seriously pursued). Secretary Bennett proposed only a handful of practical initiatives, and most of these were blocked by Democrats in Congress.

Strategies for Change

One bold education proposal did emerge from Ronald Reagan's administration: **school choice**. This idea was promoted heavily by his successor, George H. W. Bush, who announced his intention to become "the Education President" (another promise that soon fell by the wayside). Choice was a radical idea in the strictest sense. It was not intended to reform the existing school bureaucracy, but to break its "monopolistic" control and allow "free market" forces to operate. Under such a plan, parents could use **vouchers** or tax credits to enroll their children in any school, public or private, at government expense. It was argued that poor and minority parents would thereby receive the same opportunities enjoyed by the privileged classes to purchase a superior education for their children. Simultaneously the competition would create incentives for excellence in public schools, by rewarding innovation and penalizing inefficiency, all at no additional cost – or so the theory went. In sum, school choice promised to empower parents, expand opportunities, and enhance quality while keeping taxes down. It sounded almost too good to be true.

Many critics believed that it was. They noted that proposed subsidies to parents would fall far short of expenses at most private schools, which would have no obligation to admit voucher students in any case. In practice, the conservatives' choice plans, if enacted, would mainly provide a windfall to families whose children were already enrolled there. More to the point, opponents cited the potential harm to the majority of students who would remain in public schools, including those with special needs or other traits that made them undesirable to private schools. How would these children fare when the free market diverted resources, disrupted programs, forced staff reductions, and allowed facilities to deteriorate? Further concerns were voiced about whether choice would violate the constitutional separation of church and state. Troubled by such prospects, Congress has thus far refused to sanction any form of choice that might bankrupt public education or subsidize religious instruction – although Republicans continue to push voucher experiments, despite their limited popularity in opinion surveys.[3]

It was at the state level where the most substantive school reforms were taking place in the 1980s. Moderate governors in both parties, such as Bill Clinton (Democrat of Arkansas) and Lamar Alexander (Republican of Tennessee), struck a deal with voters. In exchange for higher taxes for education, requirements would be stiffened in such areas as teacher certification, academic course loads, participation in extracurricular programs, grade promotion, and graduation. Other innovations included honors diplomas for advanced students; magnet schools dedicated to mathematics, science, and the arts; and "pay for performance" and career ladders for teachers. These changes had the most impact in the South, where school systems were most starved for resources and generally had the most room for improvement. Politically the reforms proved popular, even though the overall effect on student achievement was modest.

Meanwhile, as new regulations and categorical programs proliferated, the

National Education Goals
from the Goals 2000: Educate America Act*

SCHOOL READINESS. By the year 2000, all children in America will start school ready to learn.

SCHOOL COMPLETION. By the year 2000, the high school graduation rate will increase to at least 90 percent.

STUDENT ACHIEVEMENT AND CITIZENSHIP. By the year 2000, all students will leave grades 4, 8, and 12 having demonstrated competency over challenging subject matter including English, mathematics, science, foreign languages, civics and government, economics, arts, history, and geography, and every school in America will ensure that all students learn to use their minds well, so they may be prepared for responsible citizenship, further learning, and productive employment in our Nation's modern economy.

TEACHER EDUCATION AND PROFESSIONAL DEVELOPMENT. By the year 2000, the Nation's teaching force will have access to programs for the continued improvement of their professional skills and the opportunity to acquire the knowledge and skills needed to instruct and prepare all American students for the next century.

MATHEMATICS AND SCIENCE. By the year 2000, United States students will be first in the world in mathematics and science achievement.

ADULT LITERACY AND LIFELONG LEARNING. By the year 2000, every adult American will be literate and will possess the knowledge and skills necessary to compete in a global economy and exercise the rights and responsibilities of citizenship.

SAFE, DISCIPLINED, AND ALCOHOL- AND DRUG-FREE SCHOOLS. By the year 2000, every school in the United States will be free of drugs, violence, and the unauthorized presence of firearms and alcohol and will offer a disciplined environment conducive to learning.

PARENTAL PARTICIPATION. By the year 2000, every school will promote partnerships that will increase parental involvement and participation in promoting the social, emotional, and academic growth of children.

Public Law 103-227 (1994). The first six goals were adopted by the National Governor's Association and the first Bush administration in 1989; the last two were added by Congress.

operation of schools became increasingly complex. Educational expenditures, administrative staff, and layers of bureaucracy all expanded as a result. Changes were harder to detect in the classroom. Notwithstanding some creative and promising new programs, the success of top-down reforms had been limited, according to most observers. For the most part, teachers continued to teach and students continued to learn pretty much as before.

This recognition generated a second wave of reform efforts, more holistic than the first and less ideologically motivated. Variously described as "restructuring," "rethinking the process of schooling," and "systemic reform," the new approaches criticized the fragmentation and incoherence of education policy at all levels. They sought to overcome what Stanford University researchers Marshall Smith and Jennifer O'Day called the "project mentality," a tendency to initiate and abandon short-lived programs "soon to be replaced by a different 'concept,' a new panacea. ... Few leave much of a lasting trace." While some of these add-on initiatives were worthwhile in themselves, rarely were they coordinated to bring fundamental, qualitative changes in the way schools are run. Without a strategic vision, the first wave of school reform inevitably fell victim to institutional resistance. Systemic reformers, like choice advocates, saw bureaucracy as a key obstacle to change, but they worked to "reinvent" rather than wreck it. One mechanism for doing so was an effort to develop national **standards and goals**.

The first step was a 1989 "summit meeting" on education, sponsored by the National Governors Association and the first Bush administration. Participants agreed on six broad goals for American education by the year 2000, involving school readiness, high school graduation, student achievement and citizenship, mathematics and science, adult literacy, and protection from drugs and violence. In many cases the policymakers knew that these objectives were wildly unrealistic, such as: "By the year 2000, the high school graduation rate will increase to at least 90 percent," or "By the year 2000, United States students will be first in the world in mathematics and science achievement" *(see page 343)*. Their philosophy could be summed up as: S*et targets that will encourage schools to aim high*. Pleased by the prospect of increased resources, few educators demurred.

Soon afterward Congress authorized a National Education Goals Panel to measure progress in these areas and a National Council on Education Standards and Testing to study whether it would be feasible to develop national standards for *content* (what students should know), *performance*, (what levels of competence they should achieve), and *delivery* (what schools must do to ensure students an adequate "opportunity to learn"). In 1992, to no one's surprise, the council returned an affirmative verdict. Standards were portrayed as an important step forward – provided that they reflected high expectations for achievement, were nonbinding rather than federally mandated, and took the form of general guidance rather than a national curriculum.

Two years later Congress adopted this approach in the **Goals 2000: Educate America Act**, which established a federal panel to oversee the development of voluntary standards and assessment systems. The legislation also provided funding to help state education agencies plan systemic reforms that would, among other things, raise expectations for student learning and "hold schools accountable" for meeting them. In addition, it required state grant recipients to specify a minimum level of school resources and services needed to meet academic goals. Yet observance of such **opportunity-to-learn standards** would remain strictly voluntary (the Democratic majority had hastily retreated on this issue after Republicans raised objections).

Sprinkled throughout Goals 2000 were provisions addressing the special situation of "at-risk students, students with disabilities, students with limited-English proficiency, and students from diverse cultural backgrounds" – for example, in developing appropriate assessments and preventing biased ones from unfairly penalizing these children. The overall thrust, however, was toward comprehensive reforms that would enable all U.S. students to meet "world class" standards. For critics of the **compensatory education** model, which addresses "academic deficits" by stressing basic skills, this was a welcome change in philosophy. Limited goals had brought limited results and limited accountability, as documented by studies of the costly but ineffective Chapter 1 program. Now schools would challenge all children, whether at-risk or advantaged, to perform at high levels.

What remains to be seen is whether making the course tougher will help underachievers catch up with their peers, or whether it will leave them farther behind and more likely to drop out. In the past compensatory programs have, in effect, removed such children from competition and steered them into dead-end tracks. Achievement gaps could easily be ignored. But to include these students in the race without accommodating their diverse needs could intensify inequities and reverse gains that have been achieved through special programs. In a society that is ambivalent about its diversity, such accommodations remain a low priority for policymakers. Yet the consequences for academic failure are increasingly severe. This is the environment for educating English learners in the standards-and-goals era.

Accountability Mechanisms

By late 1992, it was clear that major policy initiatives were in the offing. In addition to Goals 2000, Congress would soon consider a five-year reauthorization of the Elementary and Secondary Education Act (ESEA), including Title VII and Chapter 1. Meanwhile the transition to a new presidential administration was under way. President-Elect Bill Clinton, who had been a leader among governors in pursuing school reform, was expected to bring his activism to the federal level. Scores of Washington-based interest groups, representing virtually every aspect of education, were poised to take advantage of the favorable climate for change. But few of these lobbies had much acquaintance with the needs of language-minority students, which had thus far been a low priority for the standards-and-goals movement.

To ensure that educators and advocates for English learners were included in these deliberations, the Stanford Working Group, led by Kenji Hakuta, convened meetings among leaders in the field to discuss the opportunities – as well as the perils – presented by the political trends under way. In the spring of 1993, this ad hoc panel released its report, *A Blueprint for the Second Generation*. It criticized the compensatory model that characterized most federal programs for English learners, such as transitional bilingual education, and called on policymakers to raise academic expectations: "Language-minority students must be provided with an equal opportunity to learn the same challenging content and high-level skills that school reform movements advocate for all students." Most of its recommendations that addressed the specific needs of LEP children – such as giving priority to Title VII programs designed to cultivate bilingualism – were embraced by the Clinton administration and later adopted by Congress *(see Chapter 6)*.

Yet, on larger questions of how English learners fit into plans for more ambitious content and performance standards, the impact of the panel's ideas was limited. On the one hand, it endorsed a trend that was already gathering steam: the full inclusion of students – regardless of English proficiency, disability status, or other special characteristics – in standardized testing programs. The Working Group argued that "to exclude LEP students from such assessments until they are proficient in English ... would be dangerous because *it would leave no way to hold anyone accountable for the progress of LEP students*." This recommendation was widely accepted. On the other hand, it warned that "until the new accountability assessments are determined to be fully valid and reliable, and until mechanisms to ensure opportunities to learn have been implemented, these assessments should not be used for high-stakes purposes for students." As discussed below, this concern has largely been ignored by state and federal policymakers.

Nevertheless, the Working Group did crystallize the views of many professionals in language-minority education who were tired of making excuses for program quality. While continuing to support bilingual instruction in principle, they recognized that teaching children in the native language was, in itself, insufficient to guarantee academic success. Despite a generation of experience with bilingual programs, a substantial achievement gap persisted. While the quality of instruction had improved, it remained uneven. If English learners were thriving in some places, why not in all? Expectations needed to be raised – not just for students but for educators as well. One way to do that would be to institute higher standards and stricter accountability mechanisms.

This line of reasoning paralleled that of the broader "reform movement" in the 1990s. Because conservatives in Congress remained suspicious of a larger federal role in education, most of the action continued to take place at the state level. Academic content and performance standards were soon adopted in 49 out of the 50 states.[4] But the idea of developing opportunity-to-learn standards – designed to guarantee adequacy and equity in school resources, among other things – was quietly dropped.

Thus, over the past decade, accountability came to mean a heavy emphasis on **educational outputs**. Inputs were less important, as far as most policymakers were concerned, whose attitude was summed up by the slogan: "No Excuses." In other words, production targets would be raised without any assurance that additional investments would be forthcoming. Instead, there would be a new system of incentives – rewards as well as punishments – that relied on **high-stakes testing** to ensure that goals would be met. The primary focus, however, was on consequences for schools, administrators, teachers, and students who failed to make the grade.

All of these ideas reflected the growing role of corporate leaders in school reform, who tended to regard underachievement by students as essentially a management problem. Hence they stressed the need to rationalize the educational process, set measurable objectives and monitor progress toward meeting them, and take corrective action against underperformers when necessary. As Louis Gerstner, former chief executive of IBM, advised teachers: "Know what your job is; know what your outcomes should be; know how you will measure output." In short, businessmen believed that schools should be "run like a business."

Increasing numbers of taxpayers and politicians have adopted this viewpoint over the past decade. As education consultant Alfie Kohn points out, virtually nobody opposes the idea that American schools need standards and goals. But *what kinds* of standards and goals, set *by whom*, to serve *what purposes?* Different, sometimes conflicting, interests are at stake in this discussion:

> Ultimately the goals of business are not the same as those of educators and parents. … When business thinks about schools, its agenda is driven by what

will maximize its profitability, not necessarily what is in the best interest of students. Any overlap between these goals is purely accidental – and, in practice, turns out to be minimal. What maximizes corporate profit often does not benefit children, and vice versa. To a significant extent, the push for Tougher Standards is about the former more than the latter.

The philosophy of **standardization** was applied with special force in attacking the persistent achievement gap between children of different races, ethnicities, classes, and language backgrounds. It was even extended to students with physical, mental, and emotional disabilities. New York State's approach was typical, announcing that its "standards apply to all students, regardless of their experiential background, capabilities, developmental learning differences, interests or ambitions." Unlike New York, however, most states have been slow to consider the special circumstances of LEP children. Thus far, with only a few exceptions, they have simply developed standards in academic content areas, including English language arts, that all students are expected to meet. "High expectations," to be sure, but how helpful is this approach for English learners? Indeed, could it be harmful to organize classroom instruction and adopt accountability measures on the basis of standards that are unrealistic? Would children and their schools be unfairly penalized by high-stakes testing that takes no account of the language barrier? As momentum mounted for standards-based education, few policymakers showed much interest in addressing these questions.

> ### Hooked on Hype
>
> Standardistos proclaim that standards are in and of themselves a guarantee of educational equity. State commissioners of education promise that standards won't be watered down for anybody. Therefore, by fiat, everybody will achieve equal excellence. And get that Fortune 500 job. Creating new skills empires in the name of excellence for all, raising the bar for high school graduation, is at best an empty promise; at worst, it is criminal malfeasance. Handing out standards in the name of preparing everyone to meet the high skills that will be demanded for employment in the twenty-first century is as cynical as handing out menus to homeless people in the name of eradicating hunger. ... Let them eat cake. Let them take calculus.
>
> **Susan Ohanian, *One Size Fits Few* (1999)**

ESL Standards

Stepping into this vacuum, in 1997 the Teachers of English to Speakers of Other Languages (TESOL) published a detailed set of **ESL standards**. Drawing on the latest research in second-language acquisition, TESOL approached the question of standards and goals as a developmental process for English learners at diverse ages, school experiences, and levels of English proficiency. The ESL standards were designed to help teachers understand students' language needs and plan instruction accordingly. They featured "progress indicators" – sometimes called **benchmarks**, or specific skills that children should master at various stages of second-language acquisition – along with "vignettes" to illustrate appropriate classroom activities to develop each proficiency. For example:

> **Goal 2, Standard 2.** To use English to achieve academically in all content areas: Students will use English to obtain, process, construct, and provide subject matter information in spoken and written form.
>
> **Sample Progress Indicator:** Construct a chart or other graphic showing data.
>
> **Grade 4–5 Vignette:** Students read a Native American myth and share myths from their own cultures.
> - *Beginning.* Draw a sequence chart to illustrate the story line of the myth that was read and describe the chart orally, using words and phrases.
> - *Intermediate.* Draw a sequence chart to illustrate the story line of the myth that was read and write simple sentences describing the chart.
> - *Advanced.* Develop a comparison chart to compare two nature myths with regard to characters, setting, and conflict resolution.
> - *Limited formal schooling.* Make rebus symbols for key vocabulary and then copy part of the myth using rebus symbols for appropriate words.

A few states, such as New York, have adopted standards for English learners that incorporate TESOL's framework, while "aligning" them with English language arts standards that were previously adopted. Numerous school districts have also used the ESL standards, with their extensive practical guidance for teachers, to guide their staff development programs.

So far, however, TESOL's approach has yet to be widely embraced. One reason is that the progress indicators and vignettes illustrated above, while useful in the classroom, are often difficult to measure with standardized tests. **Alternative assessments** – such as those that rely on portfolios of student work – can often provide more useful feedback to teachers. TESOL also stresses the importance of integrating assessment closely with instructional planning. The idea is to test English learners on the actual content of their lessons, which are organized to help them meet the ESL standards. Generally speaking, this approach does not generate scores that can be compared across schools, districts, and states. So it has inspired little enthusiasm among policymakers whose prime focus is accountability.

By contrast, the English Language Development (ELD) Standards adopted by the California State Board of Education were tailored to fit that purpose. They specify literally hundreds of discrete skills that English learners must master while advancing through five levels of proficiency. Here are two examples:

> [Grades K–2, Intermediate; Reading]: Track (move sequentially from sound to sound) and represent the number, sameness/difference, and order of two and three isolated phonemes (e.g., /f, s, th/, /j, d, j/) …

> [Grades 3–5, Early Advanced; Writing]: Spell correctly one-syllable words that have blends, contractions, compounds, orthographic patterns (e.g., qu, consonant doubling, changing the ending of a word from -y to -ies when forming the plural), and common homophones (e.g., hair-hare).

The California English Language Development Test (CELDT), administered for the first time in 2001, was designed to assess mastery of the ELD standards. Unlike a **norm-referenced test**, which simply ranks a student's performance against that of others, the CELDT is a **criterion-referenced test** that measures whether English learners are making "satisfactory yearly progress" toward predetermined levels of English proficiency. These levels – beginner, early intermediate, intermediate, early advanced, and advanced – are intended to correspond to the five-point Language Assessment Scales. Yet they have been criticized as essentially arbitrary. Jill Kerper Mora of San Diego State University notes that, in second-language acquisition, "the learning curve is far from being neatly incremental. … So what is an 'average' rate of 'growth' in language proficiency?" Moreover, studies have shown wide variations in the time students need to acquire oral and academic English skills *(see Chapter 9)*. Thus the precise meaning and relevance of CELDT scores are difficult to determine. According to Edward De Avila, one of the test's authors, the problem of setting reasonable expectations for annual gains in English is further complicated by children's diverse levels of English proficiency when they enter school programs. Thus far, he adds, research on "relationships between [English] proficiency and academic performance-over-time has been suggestive … not definitive." Additional studies in this area, especially longitudinal studies, are needed. Yet, scientific uncertainties notwithstanding, the CELDT results are reported each year, posted on the Internet, and published in newspapers throughout the state, with the aim of "holding schools accountable."

High Stakes, High Anxiety

At least the CELDT was designed with English learners in mind. In addition, California requires a full battery of achievement tests in grades 2–11 for all students, no matter how limited their English proficiency. These norm-referenced assessments, such as the Stanford 9, were neither designed nor normed for English learners, who represent about one-quarter of California schoolchildren. Thus the results are not very meaningful for these students or for their schools, according to experts in educational measurement, or **psychometrics** (including experts employed by the test publishers themselves). Nor do they provide specific guidance to teachers about students' progress, or lack thereof. Perhaps needless to say, undergoing such assessments can also be stressful and discouraging for children who find them incomprehensible. In the "no excuses" era, however, the tests are mandatory for all.[5] The purpose is neither to diagnose the needs of individual students nor to provide feedback on instructional practices – the traditional reasons for assessment – but to appease pressures for "reform."

Every year, using results from these achievement tests, the California Department of Education computes an Academic Performance Index (API) for each school in the state. Those with the highest API rankings, along with their staff, are eligible for financial rewards. In 2000, these amounted to more than $700 million and up to $1,300 per employee. Schools with the lowest API rankings – which tend to enroll large numbers of English learners and other minority students – are also eligible for state aid to spur improvements. But failure to meet performance targets can bring serious sanctions. Under the state's Public Schools Accountability Act of 1999, these include "reorganizing the school" with new staff, allowing parents to convert it to a charter school, bringing in a nonprofit organization to run the school, reassigning school employees elsewhere, and closing the school entirely. API rankings also have a major community impact – on real estate values in particular – and thus receive considerable attention from local news media. Yet all of these effects flow from achievement tests whose relationship to student learning is questionable.

California, like most states, has introduced yet another level of assessment: criterion-referenced tests to measure progress toward mastery of state standards in various content areas. High stakes for students are increasingly attached. Failure to pass can mean denial of grade promotion or high-school diplomas for students whose work is otherwise judged satisfactory. In 2003, for example, 23 percent of Florida's 3rd graders – 43,000 children – were prevented from advancing to the 4th grade because of their performance on a state reading test. English learners have been disproportionately affected by these new barriers. In Massachusetts, LEP students in the high school class of 2003 failed the MCAS, the state exam required for graduation, at four times the rate of white, English-proficient students.[6] Many others dropped out after failing the MCAS before reaching the 12th grade.

Not surprisingly, the intensified focus on **assessment for accountability** has brought significant changes in the classroom. Many teachers complain that instruction is often reduced to little more than rote exercises designed to teach skills that are easy to measure, such as English phonics. This comes at the expense of other beneficial activities, such as **free voluntary reading**, and often to the exclusion of subjects that will not be assessed, especially art, music, and physical education. Recess is being eliminated in elementary grades including kindergarten, so that teachers can squeeze in more time for test preparation. The greatest impact has been felt in schools with concentrations of poor and minority students, which are under heavy pressure to improve test scores. At higher-SES schools, where there is less anxiety about meeting academic standards, children are more likely to have access to enrichment programs – another example of the "two-tier" trend in public education.

Alfie Kohn draws a distinction between **horizontal standards**, such as TESOL's systematic guidelines for educating English learners, and **vertical standards**, which are increasingly connected to high-stakes assessments. The latter represent an effort to "raise the bar" – for example, to increase the redesignation rate for LEP students – as well as a "top-down" way to engineer reform, designed to exert pressure on districts, schools, teachers, and ultimately children. This is the dominant approach among policymakers today, especially at the federal level. In 2002, it produced the most sweeping legislative changes in American education since Elementary and Secondary Education Act of 1965.

'No Child Left Behind'

Historically speaking, the federal government has played a modest role in American education. To be sure, its initiatives in such areas as civil rights and compensatory education had a substantial impact on state and local policies over the past generation. Yet the financial contribution from Washington remained small – just 6 to 7 percent of total K–12 expenditures during the 1980s and 1990s. As much as budget pressures, this reflected the nation's longstanding tradition of local control of schools. Federal mandates in education, especially those of the unfunded variety, were often resented by citizens whose state and local taxes had to be raised as a result. Politicians of both parties have therefore been cautious in this area, even while advocating "world-class standards" for American students.

Over the past decade, Republicans were especially skeptical of moves toward national assessments or a national curriculum, insisting that such matters should be left to the states. Many of the party's members in Congress continued to prescribe "choice" – primarily in the form of private-school vouchers – as an all-purpose remedy for the ills of public schools. While this position pleased free-market enthusiasts (as well as constituents who opposed tax increases to support education), it tended to confirm the image of conservatives as unconcerned with programs that benefit less affluent Americans. It also led to an impasse with Democrats, who managed to block privatization bills yet lacked the political strength to pass major education initiatives of their own.

The advent of George W. Bush put an end to the stalemate. Aware of his party's vulnerability on the class-warfare front, Bush espoused a strategy of "compassionate conservatism." As governor of Texas, he had made school reform his top priority; when he became president, fellow Republicans in Congress had little choice but to follow his lead. Democrats, despite lingering bitterness over the disputed election of 2000, saw an opportunity to work with Bush in reauthorizing the ESEA. In recent years they had been frustrated by spending limits imposed by a Republican-dominated Congress. They hoped the new president would continue the approach he had endorsed in Texas: increased education funding in exchange for increased accountability by educators. At any rate, bipartisan cooperation was what the voters seemed to want; minority obstructionism was not.

For both parties, it seemed, the stars were perfectly aligned to produce an agreement. Although numerous issues had to be resolved, the basic outlines of legislation to replace the ESEA soon fell into place. Republicans would approve significant new resources if Democrats would accept a school accountability system that not only demanded higher standards but accepted no excuses for failure. Under considerable pressure from the White House, legislative leaders on each side, including conservative Representative John Boehner of Ohio and liberal Senator Edward Kennedy of Massachusetts, were willing to make significant compromises. Among other things, Republicans abandoned proposals to authorize private-school vouchers and eliminate funding for bilingual education. Democrats set aside concerns about resource inequities, high-stakes testing, and adverse outcomes for poor and minority children. Education interest groups, many attracted by the promise of substantial funding increases, were largely won over as well. The result was the No Child Left Behind Act, signed into law on January 8, 2002, after passing easily in both houses of Congress.[7]

'Failing' Schools

While preserving some popular ESEA programs, such as Title I assistance for "the disadvantaged," No Child Left Behind (NCLB) creates a complex new structure of goals, incentives, and penalties. Each state is required to develop accountability plans to move *all* students to "proficient" levels of achievement in language arts, mathematics, and science by 2013–14. The plans must include a "timeline" specifying "measurable objectives" for **adequate yearly progress** (AYP) for students in general and for those who are LEP, economically disadvantaged, belong to racial or ethnic minorities, or have learning disabilities. At least 95 percent of students in each subgroup must participate in annual achievement testing, which is mandated in grades 3–8. In addition, English learners must be assessed for English proficiency each year.

Schools are required to meet performance targets – not just overall, but for *every subgroup* of students – and to publish annual "report cards" on student progress. Those that fall short of AYP or fail to test a sufficient percentage of children, even in one out of numerous categories, will be labeled "in need of improvement" – that is, as **failing schools** – and will be targeted for special help. Parents must be notified and be given the option of transferring their children elsewhere, with districts required to pay for transportation. For schools that fail to meet AYP targets in subsequent years, increasingly severe penalties will apply, ultimately leading to reassignment of their staff, takeover by external managers, or closure of the

> ### Making the Grade
>
> The most striking thing about the sweeping educational reforms débuting this fall is how much they resemble, in language and philosophy, the industrial-efficiency movement of the early twentieth century. In those years, engineers argued that efficiency and productivity were things that could be measured and managed, and, if you had the right inventory and manufacturing controls in place, no widget would be left behind. Now we have "No Child Left Behind," in which Congress has set up a complex apparatus of sanctions and standards designed to compel individual schools toward steady annual improvement, with the goal of making a hundred per cent of American schoolchildren proficient in math and reading by 2014. It is hard to look at the new legislation and not share in its Fordist vision of the classroom as a brightly lit assembly line, in which curriculum standards sail down from Washington through a chute, and fresh-scrubbed, defect-free students come bouncing out the other end. It is an extraordinary vision, particularly at a time when lawmakers seem mostly preoccupied with pointing out all the things that government cannot do. The only problem, of course – and it's not a trivial one – is that children aren't widgets.
>
> **Malcolm Gladwell, *New Yorker* (2003)**

school. Various sanctions are in store for failing districts as well.

By 2003, about 8,000 schools nationwide were identified as needing improvement. There were large disparities between states, however, each of which defines its own standards under NCLB. In Missouri, for example, only 8 percent of 4th graders were judged to be proficient in math that year, versus 79 percent in Colorado. States also make determinations about when to excuse schools' failure to achieve AYP if only small numbers of a subgroup are enrolled. Again, procedures vary widely. So, in 2003, 87 percent of the schools in Florida failed to make the grade, as compared with 57 percent in Delaware, 45 percent in Virginia, and just 8 percent in Minnesota.

Naturally the inconsistencies led to protests about the arbitrariness and unfairness of this form of accountability. No doubt some of the schools singled out did need corrective action. But the ranks of the "failing" also included many that were perceived to be successful by parents, and even some Blue Ribbon Schools recognized as exemplary by the U.S. Department of Education. More often than not, these schools were stigmatized because of poor test performance by special education, racial minority, or LEP students. This was no accident. The authors of NCLB, backed by some advocates for these groups, made the requirements strict in hopes of focusing attention on achievement gaps that have often been ignored. They seem to have succeeded. The question is whether this type of attention will bring the benefits for children that have been promised.

How No Child Left Behind Helps English Language Learners

Under No Child Left Behind, the academic progress of every child will be tested in reading and math, including those learning English. All English language learners will be tested annually to measure how well they are learning English, so their parents will know how they are progressing. States and schools will be held accountable for results...

No Child Left Behind gives states the freedom to find the best methods of instruction.

- The new law does not dictate a particular method of instruction for learning English and other academic content.
- States and local education agencies must establish English proficiency standards and provide quality language instruction, based on scientific research for English acquisition, in addition to quality academic instruction in reading and math.
- States and local education agencies must place highly qualified teachers in classrooms where English language learners are taught.
- Children who are becoming fluent in English are also learning in academic content areas such as reading and math, and they will be tested in these areas so they are not left behind.

U.S. Department of Education (2002)

English Learner Provisions

No Child Left Behind has certainly brought radical changes in federal programs for English learners. With remarkably little protest from its erstwhile supporters, the Bilingual Education Act, a component of the ESEA for 34 years, was replaced with the English Language Acquisition Act. Just eight years earlier, Congress had given funding priority to programs that cultivate bilingual proficiencies for language-minority students *(see Chapter 6)*. Now it voted to expunge the word bilingual from federal education law.[8] Lawmakers turned all choices about language of instruction, along with most decisions on how to spend federal funds, over to the states. To emphasize a thorough break with the past, they even renumbered the section governing English learner programs, from Title VII to Title III.

The political deal-making was delicate. House Republicans had proposed provisions that would have banned developmental bilingual education, demanded written parental consent for children to receive native-language instruction, and required English learners to exit any kind of language assistance program within three years. But the Bush administration, ever-solicitous of Hispanic voters, wanted to avoid an emotional debate on these issues.[9] So did Senate Democrats and members of the Congressional Hispanic Caucus, mindful of the popularity of English-only measures like Proposition 227. The two sides reached a compromise by which Democrats agreed to repeal Title VII, provided that Republicans would support additional resources under Title III. The guarantee was that, if annual appropriations ever fell below $650 million, the traditional Bilingual Education Act would be resuscitated.

The bottom-line result was an increase in federal spending for LEP and immigrant students of nearly 50 percent.[10] These resources, however, were now spread more thinly than before. Title VII had authorized a **competitive grant** system that concentrated federal funding to support school programs judged to be well designed by experts in the field. Title III initiated a **formula grant** system, in which federal money is distributed to states on the basis of their LEP and immigrant enrollments; funds are then allocated to districts on the same basis. In 2002, this worked out to roughly $150 per English learner, far less than Title VII grantees had received.[11] One-half of one percent of Title III appropriations, or at least $5 million annually, was set aside for Native American programs, although this amount is likely to be far less than what reservation schools will lose under the formula grant system. In addition, states may reserve up to 5 percent of their allocations for planning, administration, teacher training, and other purposes.

NCLB also authorizes a National Professional Development Project for bilingual staff, awarding competitive grants to universities similar to those under Title VII. Funding for this purpose has been "capped," however, at levels considerably lower than the $100 million spent in 2001. After an initial round of Title III professional development grants, totaling $37.5 million in 2002, no funding was available for new projects the following year. Fellowships for graduate study in English learner education are no longer available under NCLB.

State officials who had felt short-changed under Title VII, especially those with recently arrived immigrant populations, were generally pleased by the new formula. Still, the overall impact of federal funds will likely be diluted. Program quality controls, inherent in a competitive grant-making process, will be eliminated. So will special projects previously funded under Title III, including grants for field-initiated research, academic excellence demonstration programs, and instructional materials development.

'Scientifically Based Research'
As Defined By the No Child Left Behind Act

The term 'scientifically based research'—
(A) means research that involves the application of rigorous, systematic, and objective procedures to obtain reliable and valid knowledge relevant to education activities and programs; and
(B) includes research that—
   (i) employs systematic, empirical methods that draw on observation or experiment;
   (ii) involves rigorous data analyses that are adequate to test the stated hypotheses and justify the general conclusions drawn;
   (iii) relies on measurements or observational methods that provide reliable and valid data across evaluators and observers, across multiple measurements and observations, and across studies by the same or different investigators;
   (iv) is evaluated using experimental or quasi-experimental designs in which individuals, entities, programs, or activities are assigned to different conditions and with appropriate controls to evaluate the effects of the condition of interest, with a preference for random-assignment experiments, or other designs to the extent that those designs contain within-condition or across-condition controls;
   (v) ensures that experimental studies are presented in sufficient detail and clarity to allow for replication or, at a minimum, offer the opportunity to build systematically on their findings; and
   (vi) has been accepted by a peer-reviewed journal or approved by a panel of independent experts through a comparably rigorous, objective, and scientific review.

Public Law 107-110, Sec. 9101 (2002)

Meanwhile there are several new accountability provisions, all of which emphasize a rapid transition to English. States must set benchmarks for the percentage of LEP students redesignated as FEP and for their adequate yearly progress toward English proficiency. In addition, the English learner subgroup is expected to meet the same AYP targets in language arts and mathematics as other students. After complaints that these targets are unrealistic, in 2004 federal officials announced a policy change allowing states to exclude English learners' scores in language and math for their first year in U.S. schools – and to include those of re-designated-FEP students for up to two years – in calculating AYP.[12] Schools failing to meet performance goals will naturally be subject to the sanctions outlined above.

In the Name of 'Science'

Title III also requires that instructional and teacher-training programs be guided by **scientifically based research**. This phrase appears more than 100 times throughout the text of NCLB. While few would dispute the goal, questions remain about what legislating it will mean. Specifically, who will make determinations about whether programs are "scientifically based," using what processes and what criteria, and with what consequences? In defining the term, NCLB elaborates experimental protocols that are laudably stringent in principle *(see page 357)*. In practice, they are more stringent than those used in the vast majority of research studies in all branches of education. Today only a tiny handful of school programs and practices could pass this test. According to the legal definition, the rest are clearly *un*scientific. That goes for the entire edifice of school accountability plans on which NCLB is founded. Thus far there is no research base that supports it, "scientific" or otherwise. Conversely, there is plenty of evidence to suggest that high-stakes initiatives to "raise standards" are in fact high-risk initiatives for many children.

Disputes over scientific claims are commonplace in most fields. When it comes to educating English learners, they are compounded by societal conflicts over immigration, ethnicity, class, and culture. This is the context in which policy decisions must be made, usually on the basis of imperfect evidence. Government can and should play a role in improving the quality of educational research. But setting a legislative standard for research methodology that is, in most cases, unattainable could open the door to politicized decision-making in the name of science.

In the field of reading, for example, the Bush administration has indicated that only **phonics-intensive** programs will be eligible for funding under NCLB – grants that approached $1 billion in 2003 – because these are the only "scientifically based" approaches. Yet that is far from the consensus view among literacy researchers, many of whom favor a balance of **whole language** methods and phonics training. It is no accident that conservative advocacy groups who are influential with the Bush White House have made this an ideological debate, championing phonics and demonizing whole language.[13]

Thus far the U.S. Department of Education has revealed no plans to favor, on "scientific" grounds, any particular pedagogical approach for English learners. Yet, by the same token, there is no legal barrier that would prevent policymakers from doing so at federal, state, or local levels. Such efforts would hardly be surprising, since supporters of English-only mandates have long argued that research supporting bilingual education is unscientific. No doubt this debate will continue, with higher stakes, in the coming years. All the more reason for researchers and practitioners who serve language-minority students to take an active role in educating the public.

Suggested Reading

Kohn, Alfie. *The Schools Our Children Deserve: Moving Beyond Traditional Classrooms and "Tougher Standards."* Boston: Houghton Mifflin, 1999.

Ohanian, Susan. *One Size Fits Few: The Folly of Educational Standards.* Portsmouth, N.H.: Heinemann, 1999.

Teachers of English to Speakers of Other Languages. *ESL Standards for Pre-K–12 Students.* Alexandria, Va.: TESOL, 1997.

Toch, Thomas. *In the Name of Excellence: The Struggle To Reform the Nation's Schools, Why It's Failing, and What Should Be Done.* New York: Oxford University Press, 1991.

See also pp. 406–7.

Online Resource Guide

De Avila, Edward. *Setting Expected Gains for Non and Limited English Proficient Students.* National Clearinghouse for Bilingual Education (1997).

New York State Department of Education. *The Teaching of English Language Arts to Limited English Proficient/English Language Learners: Learning Standards for English as a Second Language* (n.d.).

No Child Left Behind Act, P.L. 107-110 (2002)

See also companion CD-ROM.

Internet
Links

Crawford, James. "Programs for English Language Learners (Title III)." In *ESEA Implementation Guide.* Alexandria, Va.: Title I Report, 2002. http://our-world.compuserve.com/homepages/jwcrawford/new.htm#T3_Guide

Department of Education, U.S. Gateway to the No Child Left Behind Act. http://www.ed.gov/nclb/landing.jhtml?src=fb

Hakuta, Kenji, et al. *Federal Education Programs for Limited-English-Proficient Students: A Blueprint for the Second Generation.* Report of the Stanford Working Group (1993). http://www.ncela.gwu.edu/miscpubs/blueprint.htm

Wright, Wayne E. "The Effects of High Stakes Testing in an Inner-City Elementary School: The Curriculum, the Teachers, and the English Language Learners." *Current Issues in Education* 5, no. 5 (2002). http://cie.asu.edu/volume5/number5/

See also companion CD-ROM.

Notes

1. The only apparent exception was the Scholastic Aptitude Test (SAT), which Reagan's second-term education secretary, William J. Bennett, often cited to illustrate what he called "the worst educational decline in our history." While there had indeed been a decline in average SAT scores since the 1950s, Berliner and Biddle showed that it reflected the changing demographic profile of the high-school students who took the test. No longer were they primarily white, affluent, and headed to elite universities; in recent years the number of poor and minority test-takers had increased substantially. Taking this into account, the researchers found that the picture looked quite different: "*Disaggregated* SAT scores suggest that student achievement in the nation has either been steady or has been climbing over the past 18 years"; *The Manufactured Crisis: Myths, Fraud, and the Attack on America's Public Schools* (Reading, Mass.: Addison-Wesley, 1995).

2. School finance litigation has continued, occasionally resulting in more equitable funding formulas. In June 2003, New York State's highest court ruled that New York City students had been consistently short-changed. It ordered the legislature to develop a comprehensive school-finance plan to provide them a "sound basic education."

3. In early 2004, they pushed through the first federally sanctioned voucher program, as part of a District of Columbia appropriations bill, over the fierce opposition of the local school board in a jurisdiction that lacks full self-rule.

4. Iowa, the last holdout for local autonomy, was forced to set state standards by the No Child Left Behind Act.

5. When the testing program was introduced in 1998, the San Francisco school board refused to include English learners who had been enrolled in school for less than 30 months. Superintendent Waldemar Rojas argued that not only was the Stanford 9

invalid for these students, but that being subjected to an incomprehensible test could damage children's self-esteem. The district later backed down after Governor Pete Wilson threatened to withhold millions in state funding.

6. The overall failure rate for Latino students was five times as high.

7. The final "conference agreement" on the bill passed in the House by 381-41, with only six Democrats voting no. In the Senate the margin was 87-10, with just three Republicans opposed.

8. Actually the word appears in two provisions of the 670-page bill – once in connection with Indian education and once in a section that renames the federal Office of Bilingual Education and Minority Languages Affairs (OBEMLA) as the Office of English Language Acquisition, Language Enhancement, and Academic Achievement for Limited English Proficient Students (OELA). In addition, the National Clearinghouse for Bilingual Education has become the National Clearinghouse for English Language Acquisition and Language Instruction Educational Programs (NCELA).

9. As governor of Texas, George W. Bush had supported bilingual education, even speaking out against Proposition 227 when it passed in California. As president, he has remained silent on the issue. His secretary of education, Rod Paige, once presided over successful bilingual programs as superintendent of the Houston Independent School District in the 1990s. But soon after arriving in Washington, Paige told a journalist: "The idea of bilingual education is not necessarily a good thing. The goal must be toward English fluency"; Thomas Hargrove, "Many Hispanics in Charter Schools," *Rocky Mountain News*, Nov. 2, 2001.

10. In 2001, Congress had approved $296 million for Title VII programs and $150 million under the Emergency Immigrant Education Act (EIEA), for a total of $446 million. In 2002, the combined appropriation was $665 million. ESEA programs overall received an 18 percent increase in the first year and an additional 9 percent in 2003. By 2004, however, the Bush administration no longer supported the full funding of NCLB that Democrats said they had been promised. Education officials in several states complained that federal subsidies would be inadequate to cover the increased cost of mandated assessments and record-keeping.

11. Data that would allow precise calculations of per-capita amounts awarded under Title VII are unavailable. Under EIEA, supplemental payments to districts based on their enrollment of recently arrived immigrants amounted to $184 per student in 2001. Existing Title VII grantees, including instructional programs and professional development projects, were allowed to complete their multiyear projects, some of which extend through 2005.

12. Delia Pompa of the National Association for Bilingual Education called the new policy "a good first step," but argued that "more has to be done to ensure States and school districts are held accountable for the academic achievement of LEP students."

13. In addition, the president himself has close personal and political ties to the chairman of McGraw-Hill, publisher of the *Open Court* phonics program; Stephen Metcalf, "Reading between the Lines," *Nation*, Jan. 28, 2002.

15 Advocating for English Learners

*I*n its 34 years of existence, the Bilingual Education Act enjoyed consistent support from liberal Democrats, who controlled Congress for most of that period, and from Latino legislators regardless of party affiliation. Although the idea of teaching in two languages was widely misunderstood and often unpopular, bilingual education not only survived but expanded in a climate of political adversity. Many local officials were won over on nonpolitical grounds, after witnessing the

Changing Political Currents
Impact of Public Attitudes
Conflicting Opinion Surveys
Racism or Ignorance?
Media Bias
Advocacy Imbalance
Legal Challenge to English Only
Disputed Outcomes in California
Proposition 227 in the Classroom
Educators and Advocacy

outcomes of well designed bilingual programs. But it was powerful allies in places like Washington, Sacramento, Austin, and Albany who kept federal and state subsidies flowing. These resources proved crucial to program design and professional training. Title VII, in particular, was instrumental in developing expertise and leadership for a field that barely existed in 1968.

So, in 2002, when Congress passed the No Child Left Behind Act (NCLB), reversing a generation of policies on educating English learners, the acquiescence of liberal Democrats was unprecedented. More remarkable still was the role of the Congressional Hispanic Caucus. The Bilingual Education Act was repealed with hardly a murmur of dissent – and not a single attempt to amend the bill – by Latino members of Congress, every one of whom voted for NCLB.[1] What's more, they did so with the explicit approval of Hispanic advocacy groups. Raul Yzaguirre, president of the National Council of La Raza, issued a statement praising lawmakers for their "statesmanship" in reaching a bipartisan compromise on English learner programs.[2]

Even the National Association for Bilingual Education portrayed the final outcome as a victory, after lobbying successfully to increase funding levels and to remove provisions restricting native-language instruction *(see Chapter 14)*. Executive director Delia Pompa went so far as to assert: "Through this legislation, Congress has strengthened the core of bilingual programs – which have as their mission ensuring that ALL students, regardless of their native tongue have a chance to succeed academically." NABE's enthusiastic statements about NCLB made no mention of the demise of Title VII, an outcome that all participants in the process seemed to regard as inevitable.

Thus a longstanding federal policy of supporting bilingual education, strongly reiterated in 1994, proved politically unsustainable just eight years later. Advocates for Title VII and their Congressional allies made some efforts at damage control, but effectively they surrendered without a fight. Not a single legislative hearing was held to consider the consequences, even during the second half of 2001, when Democrats controlled the Senate. Before most stakeholders learned about the backroom deal-making, a system that had served English learners well for more than three decades was dismantled. How did this come to pass? What are the implications for the future of language-minority programs? How should professionals in the field respond?

Public Attitudes

To the frustration of many educators, politicians are frequently unaware of program details and research findings, casually passing bills that have little connection with the real problems facing schools. Yet, unlike educators, politicians tend to have extensive knowledge of how their constituents feel about education issues.

These are among the realities they must consider in formulating positions; otherwise they risk early retirement by the voters. Elected representatives can and do take risks, of course, demonstrating what in hindsight is labeled either courage or foolhardiness, depending on the result. But seldom, on a given issue, are more than a few of them willing to challenge the popular will. In short, the politician's role is circumscribed by **public attitudes**.

When it comes to native-language instruction for LEP students, public attitudes are increasingly negative. Or, at least, that is the politicians' perception, following landslide victories for English-only initiatives in California, Arizona, and Massachusetts *(see Chapter 13)*. What laypersons actually think about a subject can be difficult to determine when their knowledge base is limited. In such cases, the way opinion pollsters or initiative drafters frame an issue is generally decisive in the responses elicited. "Slight differences in question wording, or in the placement of the questions in the interview, can have profound consequences," concedes David Moore, vice president of the Gallup Poll. Polling results "are very much influenced by the polling process itself." No doubt this helps to explain the widely varying opinions expressed in surveys about educating English learners *(see page 365)*.

In 2003, the Gallup Poll asked a representative sample of American adults: "In general, do you favor or oppose school districts offering bilingual education for non-English-speaking students?" A surprising 58 percent of those surveyed said yes, including 72 percent of Latinos and 73 percent of African-Americans. But the findings were quite different in another nationwide poll, conducted in 1998, when Gallup asked respondents to choose between bilingual and all-English approaches:

> When there are a large number of non-English-speaking students in a public school, these students are usually taught using one of the following two methods. After I read both methods, please tell me which one you prefer — immersion, which means teaching these students all of their subjects in English, while giving them *intensive training* in how to read and speak English; or bilingual education, which means teaching these students their core subjects in their native language, while providing them *gradual training* in how to read and speak English. [Emphasis added]

This time bilingual education was favored by only 33 percent, with 63 percent preferring the all-English alternative; 4 percent were undecided. Broken down by race and ethnicity, opinions were virtually identical. Shortly thereafter, this pattern was echoed by California voters' 61 percent support for Proposition 227.

How can such disparate poll results – a swing of 25 percentage points in sup-

Opinion Surveys on Educating English Learners

"[Would you] require bi-lingual education be available in the public schools?"
(Houston Metropolitan Area Survey; 1983)

Yes – 68%   No – 29%   Not Sure – 3%

"Do you think government policy should promote bilingual education programs that teach English and teach other substantive subjects in a child's native language, or should policy mandate that substantive subjects be taught in English?"
(Harris Poll; non-Hispanic teachers, 1993)

Bilingual – 34%   All-English – 64%   Not Sure – 2%

"Which one of the following three approaches do you think is the best way for public schools to deal with non-English-speaking students? (1) Require children to learn English in special classes at their parents' expense before they are enrolled in the public schools. (2) Provide public school instruction in all subjects in the students' native languages while they learn English? (3) Require students to learn English in public schools before they receive instruction in other subjects?"
(Gallup Poll for *Phi Delta Kappan;* national sample, 1993)

Option #1 – 25%   Option #2 – 27%   Option #3 – 46%

"Should children of Hispanic background living in the United States be taught to read and write Spanish before they are taught English, or should they be taught English as soon as possible?"
(Center for Equal Opportunity; Hispanic sample, 1996)

Spanish – 17%   English – 63%   Same Time – 17%

"Which [statement] comes closest to your point of view about how to educate students who are not fluent in English? (1) Students should be taught only in English because that is the best way for them to learn English. (2) Students should be assisted in their native language for only a brief period of time, such as a year or two. (3) Students should be taught in both their native language and English as long as their educators and parents believe it is necessary.
(Los Angeles Times Poll; California registered voters, 1998)

Option #1 – 32%   Option #2 – 39%   Option #3 – 25%   Don't Know – 4%

"Should English be the only language used in school classrooms, or should immigrant children be able to take some classes in their native language?"
(*Chicago Tribune;* Chicago area suburbanites, 2001)

Bilingual – 33%   English-only – 61%   Don't Know – 6%

port for bilingual education – be explained? Could negative public attitudes have diminished that much between 1998 and 2003? Such a change seems unlikely, with English-only initiatives continuing to win by wide margins in 2000 and 2002. Moreover, the trend in opinion surveys over the past two decades has been toward increasing opposition to native languages in the classroom. An analysis by Stephen Krashen detected "a shift of about one-third of the public from mild support (those who would allow one to two years of bilingual education) ... to the all-English position, with only about 33 percent of the public remaining solid supporters of bilingual education."

A more plausible explanation for Gallup's 2003 findings is that respondents tended to interpret its question to mean: Should English learners get *some kind of special help* in overcoming language barriers? A majority believed that they should. But when opinion surveys mention alternatives to bilingual education – as the 1998 Gallup Poll did – an "intensive" English program has consistently proved more popular than a "gradual" transition to English. This has been especially true when bilingual education is inaccurately described as teaching "core subjects" entirely in the native language.

For most Americans, including the parents of language-minority students, several polls suggest that learning English is a higher priority than helping children keep up academically. Consider, for example, the responses to a 1998 survey question posed by Public Agenda: "Should public schools teach new immigrants English as quickly as possible even if this means they fall behind, or teach them other subjects in their native language even if this means it takes them longer to learn English?" Among all parents with children in public schools, 67 percent favored all-English instruction and 27 percent favored native-language instruction; among immigrant parents the differential was even larger: 73 percent for all-English versus 20 percent for native-language.[3]

The majority's logic here is obvious: English is the key that opens the doors to academic achievement in the United States. After acquiring English proficiency, children can catch up academically; without acquiring English proficiency, they will surely be left behind. Bilingual education – as portrayed by most pollsters, politicians, and news media – minimizes or at least postpones the teaching of English, while immersion is presented as "intensive training in how to read and speak English." Ergo, immersion seems to offer the best hope of long-term success for English learners.

These are, of course, false premises and false choices. Both pedagogical approaches strive to teach both English and academic content. While programs vary in quality, there is no evidence that immersion offers any short-cut to second-language acquisition. To the contrary, most research to date favors bilingual education – in particular, the **gradual-exit model** – as an effective way to develop English and academic skills over the long term, not to mention fluent bilingualism and biliteracy *(see Chapters 8–10)*. Yet most Americans, whatever their ethnic or language background, seem to be unaware of these findings.

Krashen has noted that when survey questions describe the principles underlying bilingual education, laypersons tend to support its pedagogical rationale. In several studies, researcher Fay Shin of California State University, Long Beach, found that majorities of Latino, Korean, and Hmong parents of English learners agreed with the idea that developing skills in the native language supports the transfer of literacy and content knowledge, thereby facilitating English acquisition. Such questions, however, are rarely asked in the mainstream opinion polls that influence policymakers.

Racism or Ignorance?

Of course, pedagogical effectiveness is hardly the only factor for members of the public in formulating attitudes toward English learner programs. External concerns involving the assimilation of immigrants, stereotypes about certain ethnic groups, and opposition to public expenditures that benefit minorities always seem to be part of the equation *(see Chapter 3)*. No doubt such sentiments motivate some Americans to oppose bilingual instruction.

Following the civil-rights movement of the 1960s, explicit forms of racism are no longer acceptable in most social contexts. Few people who harbor such views will readily acknowledge them when interviewed by pollsters. So indirect means are necessary to gauge the impact of, say, nativist animosity on attitudes toward educating English learners. In what is thus far the most comprehensive study in this area, political scientists Leonie Huddy and David Sears surveyed a national sample of non-Hispanic adults, identifying various responses that were symptomatic of ethnocentrism. Such attitudes, grouped together under the term **symbolic racism**, included "resistance to special favors for minorities, anti-Hispanic sentiment, nationalism [directed against immigrants], a general desire for lower levels of government spending, and a resistance to foreign-language instruction." Not surprisingly, the researchers found that symbolic racism was a significant predictor of hostility toward bilingual education.

This did not mean, however, that racism was the *primary* source of support for all-English instruction. The symptomatic factors that Huddy and Sears identified accounted for just 26 percent of the opposition to native-language instruction. Opinion research on Proposition 227, conducted shortly before the election, tends to confirm this conclusion. Asked by the *Los Angeles Times* to explain their support for the English-only initiative, only one to 5 percent of likely yes voters cited statements that could be interpreted as symbolic racism, such as complaints about the cost of bilingual education, hostility toward undocumented immigrants, and fears about ethnic divisions. By contrast, 73 percent cited the statement: "If you live in America, you need to speak English." In other words, a substantial majority focused on what was best for children – at least in their explicit remarks.

Another important finding by Huddy and Sears was that most non-Hispanic Americans, surveyed in 1983, had very limited knowledge about educating English learners. Sixty-eight percent were unable to provide a "substantially accurate" description of bilingual education, and 55 percent said they had given little or no thought to it. Nevertheless, 60 percent said they favored the concept. To the extent that respondents understood bilingual education as a way to ease the transition to English for a disadvantaged group of children – as news media generally portrayed it at the time – they saw the program as beneficial. But the more they knew about the language maintenance goal of bilingual education, the more likely they were to oppose it.

These findings may help to explain Californians' contradictory attitudes about Proposition 227. In the Los Angeles Times Poll cited above, just 23 percent of likely voters said they planned to vote against the initiative; yet 64 percent expressed support for various forms of bilingual education. One obvious explanation is that many respondents were confused about the wording of Proposition 227 and the impact it would have in the classroom. Few voters, it seems, like to read the fine print of ballot measures, which are numerous, lengthy, and technical in nature. (California's official voter guide, issued shortly before each election, often runs to hundreds of pages.) Thus it is likely that at least some people did not realize they were voting for a strict English-only mandate.

Another possible reason for the disparity is that many Californians – 39 percent in this 1998 poll *(see page 365)* – favored bilingual education that featured a quick exit to the mainstream, but this was not the approach they perceived to be the norm. Thus, given a choice between extended native-language instruction and all-English instruction, most preferred the latter. This thought process may have been a significant factor in the passage of Proposition 227. No doubt there were other factors as well, including hostility toward immigrants, that motivated some of the initiative's supporters. But the available evidence shows that substantial numbers of voters were focusing on what pedagogical approach would be effective for English learners.[4] They simply lacked information about the role of native-language instruction in fostering English acquisition.

The complexity of public attitudes obviously complicates the task of advocacy. If racism were the primary factor in opposition to bilingual education – as it was in opposition to school desegregation, for example – a straightforward strategy would be in order: expose the bigots, activate linguistic minorities, and appeal to the moral conscience of the majority. Opinion research, however, suggests that in this case opposition is more often due to misunderstanding of pedagogical methods, goals, and outcomes. Ignorance about English learner programs not only appears to shape attitudes among the dominant group; it also extends deep into language-minority communities. If this analysis is accurate, it would suggest a very different strategy, one based on educating the public. That, in turn, would require a different message – stressing the effectiveness of bilingual education – and also a different approach to disseminating that message through the news media.

(Mis)Reporting Bilingual Education

Over the past two decades, as **school reform** became a high-profile "movement," media coverage of education has undergone a transformation. Once a journalistic backwater, concerned primarily with local school budgets, student awards, and cute class projects, the education beat now focuses on ideological conflicts with national implications, issues that are often crucial in electing candidates for high office. Education reporting has become, in many respects, a branch of political reporting. Conversely, political reporters increasingly function as education reporters, applying a frame of reference, background, and expertise that have only a tenuous connection with what goes on in the classroom. Media coverage nevertheless exerts a significant influence on policies that have a very real impact in the classroom.

One result of these changes has been a more influential role for external pressure groups, such as the English-only movement. In the 1980s, using sophisticated media strategies, U.S. English began to reframe the issue of bilingual education from a matter of equal opportunity to a threat of ethnic divisiveness *(see Chapter 6)*. Ideological lines were quickly drawn. Complex questions about meeting the diverse needs of English learners were reduced to a simplistic debate over language of instruction. News stories began to present the policy question as whether to stress English acquisition or whether to teach primarily in the native language.

Opponents of bilingual education, such as the READ Institute, sponsored conferences and published journals that appeared to be academically oriented but were primarily aimed at shaping public opinion. Others filed lawsuits and organized boycotts by Latino parents, such as the Ninth Street School protest in Los Angeles *(see Chapter 13)*, again with the news media in mind. These staged events generated sympathetic coverage in major newspapers. A Brooklyn school boycott in 1995 led to a *New York Times* editorial entitled "New York's Bilingual 'Prison,'" which alleged that children were being held against their parents' will in non-English classrooms. Over the past decade articles by advocates for all-English instruction were featured prominently in the *Reader's Digest, Wall Street Journal, Atlantic Monthly,* and other national publications. By contrast, opinion pieces praising bilingual education rarely appeared in mass-circulation organs.

Nevertheless, journalists came to regard all "sides" in the debate as politically motivated – English-only advocates as encouraging the rapid assimilation of immigrants; minority rights advocates as promoting the maintenance of Spanish; and bilingual educators as defending the status quo, including their own livelihoods. Thus the conventions of "objective journalism" came into play: give equal time to contending positions and let the best sound-bite win. In other words, leave it to readers or viewers to sort out the truth – a difficult task when limited pedagogical information was provided.

This format, designed to ensure fairness in covering political campaigns, has serious drawbacks in conveying the myriad details of policymaking. First, it tends to give equal credence, on the one hand, to the real experts – in this case educational researchers and practitioners who understand the challenges and complexities of educating English learners – and, on the other hand, to political advocates, whose expertise is in crafting messages for public consumption. In the battle of sound-bites, this is hardly a fair fight. Simplistic arguments, such as "Let's teach children English by teaching them *in* English," tend to win out when an audience is unfamiliar with the facts.

Second, the notion of "journalistic objectivity" ignores the problem of **framing**. Journalists cannot avoid making judgments about what to include and what to leave out, which facts are important enough to feature in the "lead," or opening, of a news story and which can be "buried" in the 32nd paragraph, where they will often go unnoticed. In this way news accounts provide a *context* – an "angle," in reporter lingo – for making sense of the information conveyed; otherwise they would lack any interest for readers or viewers. Too often, journalistic context serves primarily to enhance dramatic effect or cater to popular attitudes, rather than to foster a broad and balanced understanding of an issue.

The Proposition 227 debate could have been framed in several ways: as a conflict over the impact of societal bilingualism, differing views on immigration, parental choice and local control of school programs, resource allocation for English learners, or the merits of various pedagogies, among others. As it happened, news media usually framed the issue as follows: "Most Californians agree that the current system is failing to teach English to immigrant students; the issue is whether we should scrap bilingual education or attempt to reform it." No doubt this statement summed up – and reinforced – the conventional wisdom about the political choice facing voters. It did little, however, to supply relevant evidence, such as research findings about program alternatives, that voters needed to make a wise decision for children.

Whether intentional or not, the result has been a pattern of **media bias**. Education researchers Jeff McQuillan and Lucy Tse reviewed opinion articles on bilingual education that appeared in major publications from 1984 to 1994 and found that only 45 percent were supportive. Yet, over the same period, 87 percent of research studies published in academic journals were supportive. Less than half of the journalistic articles cited any research evidence; a third relied entirely on anecdotes to make their case. "This was true," the researchers noted, "even though the primary reason for opposing bilingual education hinged on the empirical question – answered by research in the affirmative – of whether or not the programs were effective."

Advocacy Imbalance

Since the McQuillan-Tse study was completed, no systematic effort to analyze journalistic bias in this area has been published. Yet, if anything, the slant against bilingual education would appear to be more pronounced following passage of Proposition 227 and similar English-only initiatives. Press coverage has become a self-reinforcing cycle: journalists disseminate negative messages, which help to shape public attitudes, which lead voters and politicians to adopt anti-bilingual policies, which influence journalists to disseminate more negative messages about bilingual education.

For many professionals who educate English learners, these media images bear little relation to reality. Authoritative-sounding reports are full of misinformation and superficial judgments. English-only advocates with no pedagogical credentials are routinely treated as experts. Meanwhile those closest to bilingual education – teachers, parents, and children – appear to be shut out of the journalistic process, their perspectives largely ignored. Sometimes it seems there is a "news blackout" whenever the news is favorable to bilingual programs. Frustrated educators often attribute media bias to journalists' personal attitudes: anti-immigrant prejudice, or a tendency to cater to whatever ideology happens to be fashionable at the moment. There may be some truth in that analysis. The extent to which it applies is difficult to gauge, however, in the absence of dispassionate research. Certainly it overlooks another important factor in the equation: the advocacy efforts, or lack thereof, of bilingual educators and their supporters.

Since the founding of the English-only movement in 1983, anti-bilingual activists have worked full-time and spent tens of millions of dollars in a campaign to shape public opinion. Advocates for bilingual education have not responded in kind. Taking a reactive rather than a proactive approach, they have launched few efforts to publicize successes in their field or otherwise generate favorable media coverage. As a result, most members of the public are well aware of arguments advanced by the English-only side, but they have rarely if ever heard a research-based rationale for bilingual education. Important opportunities have been missed.

In 1991, when the Ramírez report announced encouraging outcomes for developmental bilingual education *(see Chapter 9)*, one district's program stood out as exceptional. Located in Brooklyn, New York, School District 19 enrolled students who were 99 percent Latino or African-American, a majority from welfare families. The impoverished neighborhood resembled "a bombed-out area," recalls researcher David Ramírez. Schools were equipped with chains and grates, metal shields over the doors, and guards to keep muggers and crack dealers at bay. "I've never seen a district that faced as many challenges," Ramírez says. Nevertheless, over a four-year period, English learners in School District 19 rated highest in the national study, approaching national norms in English and math by the 6th grade. Here was hard evidence that bilingual education could make a difference for the children most in need of help. Yet neither the public nor the influential media in New York ever heard about this success story. It simply was never publicized. While the district's performance in the Ramírez study was well known in bilingual education circles, no one seemed to grasp the importance of writing up a press release or even phoning an education reporter. This is not an isolated case.

Another problem has been the difficulty of mobilizing experts to participate in the public discourse. Over the years researchers in second-language acquisition have testified frequently and effectively in institutional settings, such as Congressional committees, federal courts, and state boards of education. Meanwhile the same researchers have had limited success in influencing news media, a less organized or predictable forum. This has also been true of practitioners who have valuable insights and experience to share. Occasionally their voices are heard, but these messages are often distorted or truncated, and they rarely reiterate common themes. In short, there has been a lack of central coordination, which is key to any effort to shape media coverage. Professional organizations in many fields have learned the necessity of developing ties with key journalists, having a list of experts on call, organizing media training, circulating "talking points" for members, framing news stories and suggesting them to reporters, commissioning policy-oriented research, and generally keeping abreast of developments that require comment or provide opportunities to educate the public. English learner education is not yet one of those fields.

Still, the shock of Proposition 227 and subsequent political defeats has raised awareness of bilingual education's image problem. Advocates are beginning to recognize the importance of public opinion. So an increasing number are educating themselves about current issues, monitoring press coverage, reaching out to reporters, writing letters to the editor and guest editorials, and building networks of likeminded individuals. Widespread use of the Internet – notably, email listservs – has facilitated these grassroots efforts. Passage of English-only initiatives did not end the policy debates over bilingual education. To the contrary, these debates have intensified in states where such laws were passed. Among the key issues have been the implications, both legal and pedagogical, of Proposition 227.

'Irreparable Harm'?

On June 3, 1998, the day after the initiative passed in California, advocates for language-minority students filed a lawsuit asking a federal court to block its implementation. They argued that, by mandating a scientifically untested, one-year immersion program, Proposition 227 would violate the civil rights of English learners under the *Castañeda* standard *(see Chapter 5)*. That is, the program was not based on a sound educational theory designed to help students overcome language barriers and give them equal access to the school curriculum. Thus the new law would likely do "irreparable harm" unless the court issued a preliminary injunction while it decided the merits of the legal challenge. The litigation was supported by expert testimony from well known researchers in second-language acquisition, including Kenji Hakuta and Lily Wong Fillmore, and by numerous school-district officials.

On the defendants' side, Governor Pete Wilson marshaled academic authorities in support of the initiative, including Christine Rossell, Charles Glenn, and Rosalie Porter. Their testimony, summarized in court documents, was that the one-year immersion model was "based upon a sound educational theory, which is not only tested but is the predominant method of teaching immigrant children in many countries in Western Europe, Canada and Israel." No research evidence was cited for these claims, however, because a one-year approach has never been scientifically evaluated *(see Chapter 9)*.

Judge Charles Legge, a Reagan appointee to the federal court, ruled that the *Castañeda* test did not apply in this case because "the experts disagree over whether the implementation of Proposition 227 will <u>benefit</u> or <u>harm</u> LEP students." Moreover, he found "insufficient evidence to demonstrate that there will be harm, or that any actual harm would be irreparable." In effect, he told civil-rights advocates that their arguments would be in vain until they could prove that English learners were being adversely affected. Meanwhile, he ruled, Proposition 227 would take effect as scheduled on August 2. The 9th U.S. Circuit Court of Appeals refused to overturn Legge's decision, and the plaintiffs later dropped the case rather than risk a binding precedent from a conservative judge.

Other lawsuits against Proposition 227 were brought in state courts. While none was successful, one decision – supplemented by a California attorney general's opinion – did help to mitigate its impact. These rulings interpreted the law's **waiver provisions** broadly, essentially guaranteeing parents' right to choose bilingual education for their children. Not all districts have fully complied. But, over the objections of initiative sponsor Ron Unz, many schools have kept bilingual programs intact by routinely granting parents' requests to exempt their children from the English-only rule. As a result, in 2002–03, about 141,000 English learners remained in bilingual classrooms – 9 percent of California's LEP enrollment in grades K–12 – down from 410,000, or 29 percent, the year before Proposition 227 took effect. One other result was that Unz tightened the waiver provisions in ballot measures that later passed in Arizona and Massachusetts, severely restricting parental choice.

Disputed Outcomes

The easy passage of these initiatives naturally encouraged anti-bilingual forces to promote similar laws in other states. So a key issue has become: How are these English-only mandates working out? What has been their impact on children's academic achievement and acquisition of English? Since the Arizona and Massachusetts laws only became effective in 2001 and 2003, respectively, most attention thus far has focused on California. Outcomes data under Proposition 227 remain limited as well – no controlled studies have been conducted – but the lack of reliable evidence has failed to discourage sweeping judgments by news media, conservative politicians, and English-only advocates.

As early as the summer of 2000, two years after passage of the initiative, the *New York Times* published a lengthy front-page article suggesting that the imposition of all-English immersion programs was a "striking" success. Its conclusion was based on rising achievement test scores among English learners statewide and especially in one school district, Oceanside Unified, which had entirely eliminated bilingual programs. Here is how the *Times* framed its report:

> Many educators had predicted catastrophe if bilingual classes were dismantled in this state, which is home to one of every 10 of the nation's public school children, many of them native Spanish speakers. But the prophecies have not materialized.
>
> In second grade, for example, the average score in reading of a student classified as limited in English increased 9 percentage points over the last two years, to the 28th percentile from the 19th percentile in national rankings, according to the state. In mathematics, the increase in the average score for the same students was 14 points, to the 41st percentile from the 27th. ...
>
> At the very least, the results so far in California represent a tentative affirmation of the vision of Ron K. Unz. Mr. Unz is the Silicon Valley entrepreneur who almost single-handedly financed and organized the initiative that has all but eliminated bilingual education in California.

The article noted that the implications of these results "reach beyond California's borders, most immediately in Arizona, where voters will be presented with a ballot initiative in November asking them whether the state should outlaw bilingual education."

Several paragraphs later, after the *Times* had made its case, Kenji Hakuta was quoted, warning that no meaningful conclusions could be drawn from these test data. But the reporter failed to mention a study that Hakuta and some colleagues at Stanford University had recently completed, which directly refuted the *Times*'s claims. That analysis documented a significant increase in Stanford 9 scores[5] for virtually every subgroup of California students – rich, poor, white, minority, English-proficient, LEP. The study found that English learners' performance was roughly the same in school districts that had continued bilingual education, those that had eliminated bilingual education, and those that had never offered bilingual education. It concluded: "Scores rose for all students, and in no clear pattern that could be attributable to Proposition 227."

A more plausible explanation, the Stanford researchers said, was that the Stanford 9 had been administered in California for the first time in 1998. Scores typically rise as teachers become familiar with an achievement test and are better

TABLE 15–1

Stanford 9 Total Reading Scores and Redesignation Rates* for English Language Learners, Oceanside and San Francisco Unified School Districts and California Statewide Average, 1998–2002

Grade	2	3	4	5	6	7	8	9	10	11	Rate*
1997–98†											
Oceanside	12	9	8	6	9	4	9	5	2	3	5.4%
San Francisco	44	27	26	22	18	16	16	13	8	9	12.6%
Statewide	19	14	15	14	16	12	15	10	8	10	7.0%
1998–99											
Oceanside	26	15	16	16	16	12	15	9	6	6	6.6%
San Francisco	54	30	31	22	23	21	22	13	11	12	10.6%
Statewide	23	18	17	16	18	14	17	11	9	11	7.6%
1999–00											
Oceanside	32	22	23	19	20	13	18	11	6	8	4.1%
San Francisco	59	34	36	28	24	21	22	16	10	13	8.3%
Statewide	28	21	20	17	19	15	18	12	9	11	7.8%
2000–01											
Oceanside	32	22	19	16	16	12	15	8	7	7	17.8%
San Francisco	47	38	38	29	26	19	19	12	9	10	8.3%
Statewide	31	23	21	18	21	16	19	12	9	11	9.1%
2001–02											
Oceanside	33	24	20	17	18	14	18	12	8	9	8.4%
San Francisco	50	39	39	30	24	20	20	14	9	11	16.4%
Statewide	34	26	24	20	21	17	19	12	9	11	7.8%

Source: California Department of Education.
*Redesignation rates are calculated by dividing the number of ELLs who are reclassified as FEP each year by the total ELL enrollment in the previous year.
† The year before Proposition 227 took effect.

able to prepare their students. In addition, schools had begun to take the Stanford 9 more seriously because, beginning in 2000, it was used to compute the state's high-stakes Academic Performance Index *(see Chapter 14)*. Finally, the study noted that the test had been "developed to distinguish academic achievement among native speakers of English, and it is not a measure of English language development for LEP students."

Viewed in this context, the *Times*'s report on Oceanside looked considerably less impressive. Scores in 2000 were higher, to be sure, but there had been much room for improvement in the district. English learners in grades 3–11 had averaged in the single percentiles in English reading the year before Proposition 227 took effect. Ken Noonan, school superintendent in Oceanside and a self-described convert to English immersion, acknowledged that in the past LEP students had received virtually no English instruction for four or more years – unlike the practice in most bilingual programs. It is little wonder that English reading scores improved, especially in the early grades, after English instruction was introduced.

Even more important was the role of **redesignation rates** in computing test scores. In the year that Oceanside reported the greatest gains on the Stanford 9, it redesignated only 4 percent of English learners as fluent in English, about half the statewide rate. This meant that LEP students who scored highest on achievement tests – and who might have qualified for redesignation in other districts – were averaged in with the LEP group. If they had been redesignated at higher rates, mean LEP scores on the Stanford 9 almost certainly would have dropped. Indeed, that is exactly what happened over the following two years *(see Table 15–1)*. In 2001 and 2002, when larger percentages of LEP students in Oceanside were reclassified as fully English proficient (FEP), their test performance lagged in most grades. The *New York Times*, however, did not return to reconsider its verdict on Proposition 227.

Over the same period the San Francisco Unified School District continued to provide bilingual programs, as ordered by the 1974 *Lau v. Nichols* decision, which remains in effect *(see Chapter 5)*. English learners there recorded test scores and redesignation rates far superior to those of counterparts in Oceanside. Their performance, as shown in Table 15–1, was also well above statewide averages. Yet the district's accomplishments have received no media attention whatsoever. Of course, this is hardly a scientific comparison. There is no way to know the extent to which results in either San Francisco or Oceanside are generalizable statewide, or whether background variables – such as student characteristics and the percentage of English learners tested – would bias any conclusions about program effectiveness.

In any case, the variability of redesignation patterns makes achievement test scores virtually meaningless in gauging the impact of Proposition 227. The LEP category is constantly changing, as children enter and exit bilingual or immersion programs at different rates, in different districts, which use different criteria for English proficiency. Thus when English learner test scores are compared from one year to another – say, 4th graders in 1998 versus 4th graders in 2002[6] – it is impossible to know exactly who is being compared with whom. This comparability problem, among others, invalidates partisan claims on both sides of the issue. Just as rising Stanford 9 scores cannot vindicate the dismantling of bilingual programs, neither can the initiative be labeled a failure – as some opponents have done –

because of an increasing achievement gap between English learners and English-proficient students in some statewide comparisons. To accurately measure the effects on English acquisition and academic achievement, **controlled scientific studies** will be required; thus far none has been forthcoming.[7]

Redesignation data are useful in one respect, however. They illustrate how far short Proposition 227 has fallen on its promise to provide a shortcut to English acquisition. After five years of the mandated "one year" immersion program, the percentage of LEP students redesignated as FEP in California remained virtually unchanged. In 1998, the annual redesignation rate stood at 7 percent; in 2003, at 7.7 percent *(see Table 15–2)*. Over the entire period, a total of 590,289 English learners acquired full proficiency in English – or roughly 42 percent of the state's LEP enrollment (1.4 million) when the ballot measure was enacted. Thus it appears that more than half of California's English learners in 1998 either remained LEP in 2003 or had left school before becoming FEP.

The rate of English acquisition was a central issue of the Proposition 227 campaign. To win voters' support, Ron Unz repeatedly alleged that bilingual education had a "95 percent annual failure rate" in teaching English. News media made this one of the most memorable sound-bites of the campaign *(see Chapter 13)*. Yet since the election, they have failed to hold Proposition 227 to the standard set by its sponsor. It seems that redesignation rates have largely been forgotten, except by the Spanish-language press.[8]

TABLE 15–2

English Language Learner Enrollments and Redesignations as FEP, California Public Schools, 1998–2003

	ELL Enrollment	Annual Growth	ELLs Redesignated	Redesignation Rate*
1997–98†	1,406,166	1.2%	96,545	7.0%
1998–99	1,442,692	2.6%	106,288	7.6%
1999–00	1,480,527	2.6%	112,214	7.8%
2000–01	1,511,299	2.1%	134,125	9.1%
2001–02	1,559,244	3.2%	117,450	7.8%
2002–03	1,599,542	2.5%	120,122	7.7%

Source: California Department of Education.
*Redesignation rates are calculated by dividing the number of ELLs who are reclassified as FEP each year by the total ELL enrollment in the previous year.
† The year before Proposition 227 took effect.
ELL = English language learner; FEP = fully English proficient.

Qualitative Changes

Despite the lack of quantitative data, substantial evidence has been gathered in **qualitative studies** of the initiative's impact. One of the most common findings has been confusion on how to interpret Proposition 227. This has resulted in a wide variation in district policies and practices. From the outset, teachers and administrators who feared being sued and held liable for violating the English-only mandate *(see Chapter 13)* tended to exercise extreme caution.[9] According to a survey commissioned by the California legislature, "many principals forced their teachers to box up or discard Spanish-language materials." One educator reported: "To keep from being sued, the district gave teachers a directive of zero percent Spanish use."

Yet in this area, as in several others, the law's requirements remained vague. What did it mean to say that children must be taught "overwhelmingly in English" until they achieved a "good working knowledge of English"? Proposition 227 offered few precise definitions. Some administrators noted that Ron Unz had called his 61 percent victory at the polls "overwhelming." So they reasoned that 61 percent of instructional time in English should be legally sufficient.

Districts also varied in their application of the law's waiver provisions. Many failed to inform parents of their rights to choose bilingual programs or did a poor job of explaining the pedagogical options, the state survey found. In at least one district, "waiver" was mistranslated as *renuncia*, which implied to Spanish speakers that signing the form would mean renouncing, or giving up, something of value for their children. Some districts that welcomed a move to all-English instruction, including Oceanside Unified, routinely denied all parental requests for waivers. By contrast, those that hoped to continue bilingual education actively invited parents to apply for them.

Not surprisingly, Proposition 227 has brought major changes in classrooms that were transformed from bilingual education to structured immersion. Because districts had only 60 days to prepare for implementation following the vote, in the first year there was no time to train teachers in sheltered instruction methodologies, develop curriculum, or purchase materials. Many schools had to teach English reading with prepackaged commercial programs that were inappropriate for English learners. The results were often frustrating for teachers and students alike, according to case studies sponsored by the Linguistic Minority Research Institute.

One research team led by Kris Gutiérrez of the University of California, Los Angeles, found that the combination of all-English instruction and high-stakes testing in English led to "reductive literacy practices" that tended to "equate oral English fluency with proficiency in academic English," while stressing the mechanics of reading at the expense of comprehension. Patricia Gándara of the University of California, Davis, elaborates:

> Often teachers told us that they did not feel good about what they were doing – leapfrogging much of the normal literacy instruction to go directly to English word recognition or phonics bereft of meaning or context. However, they worried greatly that if they spent time orienting the children to broader literacy activities – storytelling, story sequencing activities, reading for meaning or writing and vocabulary development in the primary language – that their students would not be gaining the skills that would be tested on the standardized English test. ...
>
> Language and literacy were rarely used as tools for learning, but rather English language learning (oral fluency) was becoming the target of instruction. Heavy emphasis was placed on decoding skills (phonics) and vocabulary development rather than developing broader literacy skills such as reading for meaning, or writing.

These strategies may sometimes succeed in raising English learners' Stanford 9 scores in the early grades, when test questions focus disproportionately on decontextualized skills. But they are unlikely to teach the more complex forms of literacy demanded in middle and high school. One indication that LEP students are not receiving the support they need is the precipitous decline of their English reading scores in California after the 2nd grade *(see Table 15–1)*. The pattern is consistent year after year: the older the English learner, the wider the achievement gap. Yet for these students, the emphasis on teaching primarily what can be tested with multiple-choice questions only seems to increase.

Wayne Wright of Arizona State University conducted a case study of an inner-city elementary school after bilingual education was eliminated under Proposition 227. He found an impoverished curriculum that revolved around four commercial programs: (1) *Open Court,* a one-size-fits-all phonics approach that is not adapted to the needs of English learners, who made up 87 percent of the school's enrollment; (2) a basal spelling program; (3) *Math Steps,* which the researcher describes as "essentially a series of worksheets emphasizing paper and pencil practice"; and (4) *Test Best for Test Prep,* whose purpose is to familiarize students with the format of the Stanford 9. Little time in the school day was left for anything else, Wright reported:

> Since the Stanford 9 tests only language arts and math, there is no room for science, social studies, PE, music and art. Even English Language Develop-

ment (ELD), which is required by State law as essential instruction for ELL students, is beginning to be cut back. Teachers have little time during the day to develop the oral language skills of their students. ...

The teachers are stressed and overwhelmed by all the curricular changes and pressure to teach to the test and raise scores. They feel they are disempowered as professionals, and are no longer able to make decisions on how to best meet the needs of their students. ...

The students feel the stress as well. Students often break down and cry because of test-related anxiety. Some are developing apathetic test-taking behaviors in the primary grades because they deem it pointless to read a test question before bubbling in a wrong answer. ... Teachers want to see their students as more than candidates for high and low test scores, but this is difficult when pressures are placed on teachers to post gains year-to-year and meet academic targets set outside of the classroom.

Educators and Advocacy

Teachers once employed a tried-and-true remedy for "reforms" they perceived to be irrelevant or harmful to their students. They simply closed the classroom door and taught as they saw fit. In the standards-and-accountability era, that prescription is no longer effective. Or, to extend the analogy, it can have dire side-effects on educators' careers and on students' chances for promotion and graduation. Top-down mandates like Proposition 227 and No Child Left Behind have also diminished the ability of administrators, parents, community members, and school boards to resist policies that have a harsh impact on children, intended or otherwise. There has been a dramatic power shift in decision-making, from the local level to state and federal officials far removed from the classroom. Thus influencing education policy today increasingly requires political action.

Advocacy has been an unfamiliar role for the vast majority of educators, even in politicized fields such as language-minority education. Most have been content to leave such matters to their unions or professional associations, which hire full-time staff and devote considerable resources to lobbying policymakers. While educators have supported these efforts, in the past they have rarely seen advocacy as part of their own work – or as the kind of work they were willing to perform. That is beginning to change. Alarmed at the transformation of their classrooms by rigid policy mandates and worried about adverse impacts for their students, growing numbers of teachers and administrators are getting involved.

Grassroots organizing on behalf of English learners, combined with more traditional forms of advocacy, produced two significant victories in 2003. Parent advocates in California joined with the California Association for Bilingual Education and a coalition of education and civil-rights groups known as Californians Together to oppose a state decision to deny funding for native-language literacy programs in grades K–3. At stake was $133 million in subsidies under the Reading First section of No Child Left Behind, which the State Board of Education had voted to reserve for all-English programs. These groups successfully sued the state board and also persuaded the California legislature to strike down the policy, making the federal literacy funds available to children in bilingual classrooms.

Meanwhile in New York City, activists came together to oppose Mayor Michael Bloomberg's threat to terminate the ASPIRA Consent Decree *(see Chapter 5)* and institute English immersion programs for all LEP students. The Coalition for Educational Excellence for English Language Learners mobilized parents and community members to make their views known at rallies and public hearings, with support from sympathetic local politicians. As a result, the mayor not only backed down from his original plan. He also committed $20 million in additional resources to strengthen bilingual and ESL programs, hire additional staff, establish an academy to train teachers for English learners, and create 14 two-way bilingual programs, including a new high school specializing in Asian studies, to be taught in Mandarin and English.

Both of these victories were primarily defensive, preventing a further weakening of native-language programs. Nevertheless, they reversed a long losing streak for English learner advocates, while demonstrating the promise of grassroots activism by parents and educators. This formula could become increasingly important in the coming years. With the field's first generation of leaders now approaching retirement, much will depend upon the understanding and dedication of those now entering the profession.

Suggested Reading

Huddy, Leonie, and Sears, David O. "Qualified Public Support for Bilingual Education: Some Policy Implications." *Annals of the American Academy of Political and Social Science* 508 (1990): 119–34.

Krashen, Stephen. "Bogus Argument #5: Public Opinion Is against Bilingual Education." In *Condemned without a Trial: Bogus Arguments against Bilingual Education.* Portsmouth, N.H.: Heinemann, 1999.

See also pp. 407–8.

Online
Resource
Guide

Documents from Civil-Rights Litigation on Proposition 227 (1998):
- Plaintiffs' Legal Brief Requesting Preliminary Injunction
- Declarations by Plaintiffs' Authorities
- Declarations by Defendants' Authorities
- Decision by Denying Request for Preliminary Injunction

Gándara, Patricia, and Rumberger, Russell. *The Inequitable Treatment of English Learners in California Public Schools.* Linguistic Minority Research Institute (2003).

See also companion CD-ROM.

Internet
Links

Bilingual Research Journal 24, nos. 1–2 (Winter-Spring 2000). Special issue on the implementation of Proposition 227.
http://www.ncela.gwu.edu/miscpubs/nabe/brj/v24.htm

Crawford, James. "The Bilingual Education Story: Why Can't the News Media Get It Right?" presentation to the National Association of Hispanic Journalists (1998).
http://ourworld.compuserve.com/homepages/jwcrawford/NAHJ.htm

Crawford, James. "Hard Sell: Why Is Bilingual Education so Unpopular with the American Public?" Education Policy Studies Laboratory, Arizona State University (2003). http://www.asu.edu/educ/epsl/LPRU/features/brief8.htm

McQuillan, Jeff, and Tse, Lucy. "Does Research Matter? An Analysis of Media Opinion on Bilingual Education, 1984–1994." *Bilingual Research Journal* 20, no. 1 (1996).
http://www.ncela.gwu.edu/miscpubs/nabe/brj/v20/20_1_mcquillan.pdf

Parrish, Thomas B., et al. *Effects of Proposition 227 on the Education of English Learners, K–12: Year 1 Report* (American Institutes for Research and WestEd, 2001). http://lmri.ucsb.edu/resdiss/2/pdf_files/070301_yr1_finalreport.pdf

See also companion CD-ROM.

Notes

1. The only complaints came from Democratic Representatives Rubén Hinojosa and Silvestre Reyes of Texas, Hilda Solis and Joe Baca of California, and Ed Pastor of

Arizona. Each of these legislators made a brief statement in the *Congressional Record* opposing Republican attempts to limit access to native-language instruction. When those provisions were later dropped, so were the complaints. No objections were raised against turning Title VII into a state-administered, formula-grant system or against imposing accountability rules likely to promote all-English instruction *(see Chapter 14).*

2. In contrast to "the demagoguery that has characterized the debate over bilingual education in California, Arizona, and Massachusetts," Yzaguirre said, Congressional negotiators had "eschewed political rhetoric and maintained a focus on truly helping ELL students achieve academically while mastering English."

3. A similar question by the Henry J. Kaiser Foundation in 1999 yielded similar results: Americans in general favored immersion over bilingual education by 62-36 percent; immigrants, by 63-32 percent.

4. It is also worth noting that exit polling on election day reported that significant numbers of Latinos (37 percent), Asian Americans (57 percent), Democrats (47 percent), political moderates (59 percent), and self-identified liberals (36 percent) had voted for Proposition 227.

5. The Stanford Achievement Test, 9th Edition, is published by Harcourt Brace Educational Measurement. It has no connection with Stanford University.

6. In 2003, the Stanford 9 was replaced by the California Achievement Test, 6th Edition (CAT/6), whose results are not directly comparable with those of the Stanford 9.

7. A five-year research project on Proposition 227, commissioned by the California legislature, published an interim report in 2002 that analyzed statewide patterns in Stanford 9 scores. But the available data from the California Department of Education were so limited that the study was unable to match individual student outcomes with particular program models. Researchers simply compared test scores by schools, depending on whether they continued to provide bilingual instruction or had switched to all-English programs – a procedure conceded to be "somewhat crude." On average, for example, only 54 percent of students at the so-called "bilingual" schools were actually receiving bilingual instruction. Overall the study's findings were equivocal. It reported that the achievement gap had slightly widened between LEP and non-LEP students under Proposition 227, but had slightly narrowed if redesignated-FEP students were included in the calculation; Thomas B. Parrish et al., *Effects of Proposition 227 on the Education of English Learners, K–12: Year 2 Report* (Palo Alto, Calif.: American Institutes for Research and WestEd, 2002).

8. See, e.g., José Fuentes-Salinas, "Sopesan efectos de Prop. 227," *La Opinión*, Aug. 22, 2003: http://www.latinosonline.com/cabe/showarticle.cfm?titleID=1137.

9. To date no serious litigation has been brought under Proposition 227, although threats of litigation no doubt seemed serious to many educators. As schools began to implement the measure, Ron Unz warned them not to resist: "There is a real possibility that some administrators and teachers will lose their homes and be forced into bankruptcy over this"; Louis Sahagun, "Responses to Prop. 227 All over the Map," *Los Angeles Times*, Sept. 2, 1998.

Sources and Suggested Reading

This book relies in part on journalistic sources – that is, interviews, press briefings, public records, legislative hearings, oral statements at conferences, school visits, and reporting of events during and after the author's tenure at Education Week *(1985–87). Bibliographic sources, along with recommendations for further reading, are provided below. Many of the "public domain" documents listed are included on the CD-ROM companion to this book, along with numerous Internet links to copyrighted materials. For a full listing, see the* Online Resource Guide.

Introduction

Sabine R. Ulibarrí describes the experience of Latino students before the bilingual education era in "The Word Made Flesh: Spanish in the Classroom," in Luís Valdez and Stan Steiner, eds., *Aztlán: An Anthology of Mexican American Literature* (New York: Alfred A. Knopf, 1972).

Einar Haugen analyzes American attitudes toward bilingualism in *The Norwegian Language in America: A Study in Bilingual Behavior* (Bloomington: Indiana University Press, 1969), and "The Curse of Babel," in Haugen and Morton Bloomfield, eds., *Language as a Human Problem* (New York: Norton, 1973).

Joel Perlmann provides immigrant school attendance figures (extrapolated from the 1911 report by the federal Dillingham Commission) in "Bilingualism and Ethnicity in American Schooling before 1960: An Historical Perspective," paper presented at the Institute on Bilingual Education, Harvard Graduate School of Education, Dec. 11, 1987. See also Perlmann's "Historical Legacies: 1840–1920," *Annals of the American Academy of Political and Social Science* 508 (Mar. 1990). Further discussion of the human costs of Americanization may be found in Stanley Feldstein and Lawrence Costello, *The Ordeal of Assimilation: A Documentary of the White Working Class* (Garden City, N.Y.: Anchor Books, 1974).

The *Washington Post* editorial that blamed bilingual education for the growing number of LEP youth ("Teach English") appeared on Aug. 9, 2001.

Kenneth G. Wilson's misinformed tirade against bilingual education appears in his otherwise urbane and entertaining book, *Van Winkle's Return: Change in American English, 1966–1986* (Hanover, N.H.: University Press of New England, 1987).

Chapter 1. Bilingualism, American Style

Studies by the Urban Institute are unparalleled sources of statistical information about immigrants and demographic change. Especially useful are two presentations by Michael E. Fix and Jeffrey S. Passel:

- "U.S. Immigration at the Turn of the 21st Century," testimony before the U.S. House Judiciary Committee, Subcommittee on Immigration and Claims, Aug. 2, 2001; and
- "U.S. Immigration – Trends & Implications for Schools," presentation at the National Association for Bilingual Education NCLB Implementation Institute, New Orleans, Jan. 28–29, 2003.

See also Jorge Ruiz-de-Velasco and Michael Fix, *Overlooked & Underserved: Immigrant Students in U.S. Secondary Schools* (Washington, D.C.: Urban Institute, 2000).

For a broad sociological overview, see Alejandro Portes and Rubén G. Rumbaut, *Immigrant America: A Portrait*, 2nd ed. (Berkeley: University of California Press, 1996).

Naturally, the U.S. Census Bureau offers enormous amounts of raw data through its Web site. Gateway to Census 2000 is a good starting point: http://www.census.gov/main/-www/cen2000.html. It also publishes numerous useful publications (many included on the companion CD to this volume). See in particular:

- *Profile of the Foreign-Born Population in the United States: 2000*; and
- *Language Use and English Ability: 2000*.

See also the annual *Yearbook of Immigration Statistics* published by the U.S. Department of Homeland Security.

The premier source for English learner statistics is the National Clearinghouse for English Language Education (NCELA). See in particular Anneka L. Kindler, *Summary of the States' Limited English Proficient Students and Available Educational Programs and Services: 2000–2001 Summary Report* (2002).

For more perspective on the limitations of census language data, see James Crawford, "Making Sense of Census 2000," an article published by the Education Policy Studies Laboratory at Arizona State University: http://www.asu.edu/educ/epsl/LPRU/-features/article5.htm.

François Grosjean explains some of the forces driving language shift in *Life With Two Languages: An Introduction to Bilingualism* (Cambridge, Mass.: Harvard University Press, 1982). Another helpful book is Nancy Faires Conklin and Margaret A. Lourie, *A Host of Tongues: Language Communities in the United States* (New York: Free Press, 1983).

Calvin J. Veltman presents another view in "The American Linguistic Mosaic: Understanding Language Shift in the United States," in Sandra Lee McKay and Sau-ling Cynthia Wong, eds., *New Immigrants in the United States: Readings for Second Language Educators*

(New York: Cambridge University Press, 2000). See also Veltman's *The Future of the Spanish Language in the United States* (Washington, D.C.: Hispanic Policy Development Project, 1988) and *Language Shift in the United States* (Berlin: Mouton Publishers, 1983).

Dorothy Waggoner's critique of Veltman appeared in a review of *The Future of the Spanish Language* in *NABE Journal* 13, no. 3 (Spring 1989): 253–61. During the 1990s Waggoner published *Numbers and Needs*, an analytical newsletter on census data relevant to English language learners. Some back issues may be found at http://www.asu.edu/educ/-sceed/n_n/index.html.

The Children of Immigrants Longitudinal Survey is described in two articles by Alejandro Portes and Lingxin Hao:

- "*E Pluribus Unum:* Bilingualism and Loss of Language in the Second Generation," *Sociology of Education* 71 (1998): 269–94; and
- "The Price of Uniformity: Language, Family, and Personality Adjustment in the Immigrant Second Generation," *Ethnic and Racial Studies* 25 (Nov. 2002): 889–912.

Stephen Krashen's comments about today's levels of diversity are from *Under Attack: The Case against Bilingual Education* (Culver City, Calif.: Language Education Associates, 1996).

Lucy Tse's study of successful biliterates is reported in *"Why Don't They Learn English?" Separating Fact from Fallacy in the U.S. Language Debate* (New York: Teachers College Press, 2001).

The New York City exit rates for English learners come from Shelley Rappaport's study for the Puerto Rican Legal Defense and Education Fund, *Beyond Bilingual Education: Meeting the Needs of English Language Learners in the New York City Public Schools* (Nov. 2002). The San Francisco study on long-term outcomes is *Performance of Redesignated Fluent-English-Proficient Students* (Feb. 1998), by J. David Ramírez.

Patrick Welsh comments on the work ethic of immigrant students in "Motivation, Focus Send Foreign-Born Students Soaring," *USA Today*, Aug. 25, 2003.

New York State dropout rates for English learners are reported by Catherine Man in "Should New Immigrants Take Regent Exams?": http://www.insideschools.org/view/-ed_elled. Russell Rumberger's conclusions on school completion appear in "Dropping Out of Middle School: A Multilevel Analysis of Students and Schools," *American Educational Research Journal* 32 (1995): 583–625.

Chapter 2. Options for English Learners

The National Research Council provides a broad overview of programs and practices for English learners in Diane August and Kenji Hakuta, eds., *Improving Schooling for Language-Minority Children: A Research Agenda* (Washington, D.C.: National Academy Press, 1997).

A rich resource, not only on bilingual program types but on a multitude of related issues, is Colin Baker and Sylvia Prys Jones, *Encyclopedia of Bilingualism and Bilingual Education* (Clevedon, U.K.: Multilingual Matters, 1998).

The study on native-language usage in bilingual programs is Paul Hopstock et al.,

Descriptive Study of Services to Limited English Proficient Students, vol. 2, *Survey Results* (Arlington, Va.: Development Associates, 1993).

Lt. Richard Henry Pratt offered his thoughts on immersion in an 1883 address to the World Convention of Baptists; quoted in Francis Paul Prucha, *American Indian Policy in Crisis: Christian Reformers and the Indian, 1865–1900* (Norman: University of Oklahoma Press, 1976).

Results of California's annual Language Census since 1980–81 are available at: http://www.cde.ca.gov/demographics/.

Daniel Domenech described his sink-or-swim experience to Welsh in "Motivation, Focus." Comments on speak-English-only rules by Edgar Lozano and state senator Joe Bernal appeared in U.S. Commission on Civil Rights, *The Excluded Student: Educational Practices Affecting Mexican Americans in the Southwest,* Mexican American Education Study, Report III, 1972.

A useful overview of program models is Fred Genesee, ed., *Program Alternatives for Linguistically Diverse Students* (Santa Cruz, Calif.: Center for Research on Education, Diversity and Excellence, 1999). See also Carlos Ovando, Virginia P. Collier, and Mary Carol Combs, *Bilingual and ESL Classrooms: Teaching in Multicultural Contexts,* 3rd ed. (New York: McGraw-Hill, 2003); Colin Baker, *Foundations of Bilingual Education and Bilingualism,* 3rd ed. (Clevedon, U.K.: Multilingual Matters, 2001); and Judith Lessow-Hurley, *Foundations of Dual Language Education* (New York: Longman, 2000).

ESL/EFL Teaching: Principles for Success (Portsmouth, N.H.: Heineman, 1998), by Yvonne S. Freeman and David E. Freeman, offers an especially helpful overview of all-English approaches.

The views of José Cárdenas on transitional and maintenance bilingual education are detailed in James Crawford, *Hold Your Tongue: Bilingualism and the Politics of "English Only"* (Reading, Mass.: Addison-Wesley, 1992).

Stephen Krashen describes the gradual-exit model in *Condemned without a Trial: Bogus Arguments against Bilingual Education* (Portsmouth, N.H.: Heinemann, 1999).

Kathryn J. Lindholm-Leary's encyclopedic treatment of two-way programs is *Dual Language Education* (Clevedon, U.K.: Multilingual Matters, 2001). Former education secretary Richard W. Riley gave the Clinton administration's blessings to this approach in "Excelencia para Todos – Excellence for All: The Progress of Hispanic Education and the Challenges of a New Century," a speech delivered at Bell Multicultural High School in Washington, D.C., Mar. 15, 2000.

Useful sources on newcomer programs include Monica Friedlander, *The Newcomer Program: Helping Immigrant Students Succeed in U.S. Schools* (Washington, D.C.: National Clearinghouse for Bilingual Education, 1991), and Lorraine M. McDonnell and Paul T. Hill, *Newcomers in American Schools: Meeting the Educational Needs of Immigrant Youth* (Santa Monica, Calif.: Rand Corporation, 1993). Leona Marsh details the newcomer program at Liberty High School in "A Spanish Dual Literacy Program: Teaching to the Whole Student," *Bilingual Research Journal* 19 (1995), nos. 3–4: 409–28.

Chapter 3. Language Policies in the USA

For a broad overview of this subject, see James Crawford's Language Policy Web Site: http://ourworld.compuserve.com/homepages/jwcrawford/. A wealth of information about language issues in Europe can be found at a web site funded by the European Commission, which is known as Mercator: Linguistic Rights and Legislation: http://www.ciemen.org/mercator/index-gb.htm. For background about language policies in Australia, see Joseph LoBianco, *National Policy on Languages* (Canberra: Australian Government Publishing Service, 1987). Further information is available through http://languageaustralia.com.au/.

For the latest information about Executive Order 13166, see the U.S. Justice Department web site: http://www.usdoj.gov/crt/cor/13166.htm.

Various historical documents in the Online Resource Guide are useful in understanding national myths that influenced American attitudes toward language:
- James Madison, *The Federalist*, No. 51 (1788);
- Alexis de Tocqueville, "Unlimited Power of the Majority in the United States, and Its Consequences" (from *Democracy in America*, 1835); and
- Theodore Roosevelt, "Children of the Crucible" (1917).

Geoffrey Nunberg analyzes many of these themes in "The Official English Movement: Reimagining America," in James Crawford, ed., *Language Loyalties: A Source Book on the Official English Controversy* (Chicago: University of Chicago Press, 1992). See also Richard B. Morris, *Witnesses at the Creation: Hamilton, Madison, Jay, and the Constitution* (New York: Holt, Reinhart and Winston, 1985).

Herbert Kelman is quoted in Richard Ruíz's influential article, "Orientations in Language Planning," *NABE Journal* 8, no. 2 (1984): 15–34; rpt. in Sandra Lee McKay and Sau-ling Cynthia Wong, eds., *Language Diversity: Problem or Resource?* (Cambridge, Mass.: Newbury House, 1988), pp. 3–25.

Nathan Glazer's observation about the paradox of linguistic laissez-faire appears in "The Process and Problems of Language Maintenance: An Integrative Review," in Joshua A. Fishman, ed., *Language Loyalty in the United States: The Maintenance and Perpetuation of Non-English Mother Tongues by American Ethnic and Religious Groups* (The Hague: Mouton Publishers, 1966; rpt. New York: Arno Press, 1978), pp. 358–68.

Milton M. Gordon traces the drive for Anglo-conformity in his seminal work, *Assimilation in American Life: The Role of Race, Religion, and National Origins* (New York: Oxford University Press, 1964). See also John Higham, "Ethnic Pluralism in Modern American Thought," in *Send These to Me: Jews and Other Immigrants in Urban America* (New York: Atheneum, 1975), pp. 196–230.

Rolf Kjolseth analyzes Americans' "schizophrenic" attitudes about language in "Cultural Politics of Bilingualism," *Society*, May–Jun. 1983, pp. 40–48. Noam Chomsky discusses language as a "question of power" in *Language and Responsibility* (New York: Pantheon, 1979).

The *Washington Post* article on U.S.-born English learners was Brigid Schulte, "Trapped Between Two Languages," Jun. 9, 2002.

Fascinating background about English learner programs in Georgia can be found in Stanton Wortham, Enrique G. Murillo Jr., and Edmund T. Hamann, *Education in the New Latino Diaspora: Policy and the Politics of Identity* (Westport, Conn.: Ablex Publishing, 2002).

John Hawgood describes German parents' efforts at language maintenance in *The Tragedy of German-America* (New York: Putnam, 1940). The two works by Horace Kallen are "Democracy versus the Melting Pot," *Nation*, Feb. 25, 1915; and *Culture and Democracy in the United States* (New York: Boni and Liveright, 1924).

The critical importance of language resources in a time of terrorism is highlighted by the National Foreign Language Center at the University of Maryland – http://www.nflc.org/security/background.htm.

A useful introduction to questions of policy and politics is David L. Weimer and Aidan R. Vining, *Policy Analysis: Concepts and Practice*, 3rd ed. (Upper Saddle River, N.J.: Prentice Hall, 1999).

Maxwell F. Yalden describes Francophones' situation in "The Bilingual Experience in Canada," in Martin Ridge, ed., *The New Bilingualism: An American Dilemma* (New Brunswick, N.J.: Transaction Books, 1981), pp. 71–87. Another useful work on language rights is Reynaldo F. Macías, "Choice of Language as a Human Right: Public Policy Implications in the United States," in Raymond V. Padilla, ed., *Bilingual Education and Public Policy* (Ypsilanti, Mich.: Department of Foreign Languages and Bilingual Studies, Eastern Michigan University, 1979), pp. 39–57.

Chapter 4. A Forgotten Legacy

A more detailed history of language policy in the United States can be found in Crawford, *Hold Your Tongue*. Various supporting documents are reprinted in Crawford, *Language Loyalties*. See also Crawford, *At War with Diversity: U.S. Language Policy in an Age of Anxiety* (Clevedon, U.K.: Multilingual Matters, 2000).

A comprehensive and readable history of bilingual education is Diego Castellanos, *The Best of Two Worlds: Bilingual-Bicultural Education in the U.S.* (Trenton, N.J.: New Jersey State Department of Education, 1983). Useful anecdotal material may be found in Colman B. Stein, Jr., *Sink or Swim: The Politics of Bilingual Education* (New York: Praeger, 1986).

For researchers of U.S. language policy, the starting point is Heinz Kloss, *The American Bilingual Tradition* (Rowley, Mass.: Newbury House, 1977; rpt. Washington, D.C.: Center for Applied Linguistics and Delta Systems, 1998), which is unmatched for encyclopedic detail about language-minority schooling, particularly before 1968. See also Kloss, "German-American Language Maintenance Efforts," in Fishman, ed., *Language Loyalty in the United States*, pp. 206–52.

Franklin's English-only inclinations are described in Glenn Weaver, "Benjamin Franklin and the Pennsylvania Germans," in Leonard Dinnerstein and Frederick Jaher, eds., *The Aliens: A History of Ethnic Minorities in America* (New York: Appleton-Century-Crofts, 1970), pp. 47–64. See also Whitfield J. Bell, Jr., "Benjamin Franklin and the German Charity Schools," *Proceedings of the American Philosophical Society* 99, no. 6 (Dec. 1955): 381–87.

Shirley Brice Heath has traced the history of language attitudes in the colonial era in "A National Language Academy? Debate in the New Nation," *International Journal of the Sociology of Language* 11 (1976): 9–43; and "English in Our Language Heritage," in Charles A. Ferguson and Heath, eds., *Language in the USA* (Cambridge: Cambridge University Press, 1981), pp. 6–20. See also Allen Walker Read, "American Projects for an Academy to Regulate Speech," *Publications of the Modern Language Association* 51, no. 4 (1936): 1141–79. Noah Webster's efforts to standardize American English are described in Dissertations on the English Language (1789) and Dennis Baron, "Federal English" (1987); both are reprinted in Crawford, *Language Loyalties*, pp. 33–40. See also Baron's *Grammar and Good Taste: Reforming the American Language* (New Haven: Yale University Press, 1982.

Lewis William Newton paints a fascinating picture of conflicts over language policy following the Louisiana Purchase in *The Americanization of French Louisiana: A Study of the Process of Adjustment between the French and the Anglo-American Populations of Louisiana, 1803–1860* (New York: Arno Press, 1980).

For details on language usage by minority groups before and after the American Revolution, see Marcus Lee Hansen, *The Atlantic Migration, 1607–1860: A History of the Continuing Settlement of the United States* (New York: Harper Torchbooks, 1961). Another useful source is Louis B. Wright, *The Cultural Life of the American Colonies, 1607–1763* (New York: Harper & Row, 1957).

An excellent study of schooling for German–Americans in the mid-19th century is Stephen L. Schlossman, "Is There an American Tradition of Bilingual Education? German in the Public Elementary Schools, 1840–1919." *American Journal of Education* 91, no. 2 (1983): 139–86. Joel Perlman's work (cited above) is also noteworthy.

The Wisconsin and Illinois conflicts over English-only instruction are detailed in Louise Phelps Kellogg, "The Bennett Law in Wisconsin," *Wisconsin Magazine of History* 2 (1918): 3–25; William F. Whyte, "The Bennett Law Campaign in Wisconsin," *Wisconsin Magazine of History* 10 (1927): 363–90; and Daniel W. Kucera, *Church-State Relationships in Education in Illinois* (Washington, D.C.: Catholic University of America Press, 1955.)

The nativist poem for the *Atlantic* was by Thomas Bailey Aldrich; quoted in Daniel Boorstin, *Hidden History: Exploring Our Secret Past* (New York: Vintage Books, 1989).

Probably the most prolific writer on language restrictionism in the United States has been Arnold H. Leibowitz. Three important works are "Language as a Means of Social Control: The United States Experience," paper presented at the 8th World Congress of Sociology, Toronto, Aug. 1974; "English Literacy: Legal Sanction for Discrimination," *Notre Dame Lawyer* 45, no. 7 (Fall 1969): 7–67; and *The Bilingual Education Act: A Legislative Analysis* (Rosslyn, Va.: National Clearinghouse for Bilingual Education, 1980).

Repression of the German language during and after World War I is well documented in Carl Wittke, *German-Americans and the World War: With Special Emphasis on Ohio's German-Language Press* (Columbus: Ohio State Archaeological and Historical Society, 1936), pp. 163–79. See also Hawgood, *The Tragedy of German-America.*

The seminal political and sociological analysis of the Americanization era is John Higham, *Strangers in the Land: Patterns of American Nativism, 1860–1925,* 2d ed. (New

Brunswick, N.J.: Rutgers University Press, 1988). See also Edward George Hartmann, *The Movement to Americanize the Immigrant* (New York: Columbia University Press, 1948). Ellwood P. Cubberly's views on schooling immigrants are detailed in *Changing Conceptions of Education* (Boston: Houghton Mifflin, 1909). Josué M. González provides insights into ethnic politics and assimilationist pressures in "Coming of Age in Bilingual/Bicultural Education: A Historical Perspective," *Inequality in Education* 19 (Feb. 1975): 5–17.

The Language Policy Task Force examines education as an instrument of colonial rule in "Language Policy and the Puerto Rican Community," *Bilingual Review* 5, nos. 1–2 (1978): 1–39. See also Aída Negrón de Montilla, *Americanization in Puerto Rico and the Public-School System, 1900–1930* (Río Piedras, P.R.: Editorial Edil, 1971); and Pastora San Juan Cafferty and Carmen Rivera-Martínez, *The Politics of Language: The Dilemma of Bilingual Education for Puerto Ricans* (Boulder, Colo.: Westview Press, 1981).

For analyses of linguistic repression directed at American Indians, see Senate Labor and Public Welfare Committee, Special Subcommittee on Indian Education, *Indian Education: A National Tragedy – A National Challenge*, 91st Cong., 1st Sess. (1969); Jon Reyhner and Jeanne Eder, *A History of Indian Education* (Billings: Eastern Montana College, 1989); and James Park, "Historical Foundations of Language Policy: The Nez Percé, Case," in Robert St. Clair and William Leap, eds., *Language Renewal among American Indian Tribes: Issues, Problems, and Prospects* (Rosslyn, Va: National Clearinghouse for Bilingual Education, 1982). An excellent account of Indian education reform in the John Collier era can be found in Margaret Connell Szasz, *Education and the American Indian: The Road to Self-Determination Since 1928* (Albuquerque: University of New Mexico Press, 1977).

Leonard Pitt documents ethnic conflicts in early California in *The Decline of the Californios: A Social History of the Spanish-Speaking Californians, 1846–1890* (Berkeley: University of California Press, 1966). The modern Chicano experience is described by the U.S. Commission on Civil Rights, *The Excluded Student*. See also Mario T. García, *Mexican Americans: Leadership, Ideology, and Identity, 1930–1960* (New Haven: Yale University Press, 1989); and Guadalupe San Miguel, Jr., *"Let All of Them Take Heed": Mexican Americans and the Campaign for Educational Equality in Texas, 1910–1981* (Austin: University of Texas Press, 1987). Lyndon B. Johnson's enforcement of English-only rules is chronicled by Robert Caro in *The Path to Power* (New York: Alfred A. Knopf, 1982).

Stephen Steinberg critiques cultural theories of school failure in *The Ethnic Myth: Race, Ethnicity, and Class in America*, 2nd ed. (Boston: Beacon Press, 1989).

On the misclassification of language-minority children, see Alba A. Ortiz and James R. Yates, "Incidence of Exceptionality among Hispanics: Implications for Manpower Planning," *NABE Journal* 7, no. 3 (Spring 1983): 41–53.

Kenji Hakuta details the Coral Way experiment and analyzes its outcomes in *Mirror of Language: The Debate on Bilingualism* (New York: Basic Books, 1986). For additional details, see William Francis Mackey and Von Nieda Beebe, *Bilingual Schools for a Bicultural Community: Miami's Adaptation to the Cuban Refugees* (Rowley, Mass.: Newbury House, 1977).

Chapter 5. The Evolution of Federal Policy

In their general histories, Castellanos, Kloss, and Stein describe the political circumstances surrounding the passage of Title VII. The educational context is sketched in *The Invisible Minority: Report of the NEA–Tucson Survey* (Washington, D.C.: National Education Association, 1966). Leibowitz summarizes the law's subsequent development in *The Bilingual Education Act*. See also Carlos J. Ovando, "Bilingual Education in the United Status: Historical Development and Current Issues," *Bilingual Research Journal* 27, no. 1 (Spring 2003).

For details of state legislation in the 1970s, see Tracy C. Gray, H. Suzanne Convery, and Katherine M. Fox, *The Current Status of Bilingual Education Legislation, Bilingual Education Series*, no. 9 (Washington, D.C.: Center for Applied Linguistics, 1981). See also Kloss, *American Bilingual Tradition.*

Key documents from this era, included in the Online Resource Guide, include:
- U.S. Department of Health, Education, and Welfare, "Memorandum to School Districts with More Than Five Percent National Origin-Minority Group Children" (1970);
- *Lau v. Nichols* (Supreme Court, 1974);
- U.S. Office for Civil Rights, "Task-Force Findings Specifying Remedies Available for Eliminating Past Educational Practices Ruled Unlawful under *Lau v. Nichols*" (Lau Remedies, 1975);
- *Serna v. Portales Municipal Schools* (10th Circuit Court of Appeals, 1974); and
- *Castañeda v. Pickard* (5th Circuit Court of Appeals, 1981).

Fascinating details about the civil-rights context are provided in *Revisiting the Lau Decision: 20 Years After* (Oakland, Calif.: ARC Associates, 1996). Martin Gerry's recollections about drafting the Lau Remedies appear in Thomas Toch, "The Emerging Politics of Language," *Education Week*, Feb. 8, 1984, pp. 1, 12–16.

Noel Epstein's influential attack on bilingual education, *Language, Ethnicity, and the Schools: Policy Alternatives for Bilingual-Bicultural Education* (Washington, D.C.: Institute for Educational Leadership, 1977), includes thoughtful responses by José A. Cárdenas and Gary Orfield.

A helpful article in untangling the legal issues is Sau-ling Cynthia Wong, "Educational Rights of Language Minorities," in McKay and Wong, *Language Diversity*. Complete texts of several precedent-setting court decisions are reprinted in Arnold H. Leibowitz, ed., *Federal Recognition of the Rights of Minority Language Groups* (Rosslyn, Va.: National Clearinghouse for Bilingual Education, 1982).

For a detailed analysis of Office for Civil Rights activity under the Reagan administration, see James Crawford, "U.S. Enforcement of Bilingual Plans Declines Sharply," *Education Week*, Jun. 4, 1986.

Congressional hearings on Title VII, its periodic reauthorizations, and related issues are a treasure trove of information about federal policy and about the condition of bilingual education over the past three decades. The more significant of these include:

- Senate Labor and Public Welfare Committee, Special Subcommittee on Bilingual Education, 90th Cong., 1st Sess. (1967), hearing on S 428; rpt. by Arno Press (New York: 1978).
- House Education and Labor Committee, General Subcommittee on Education, 90th Cong., 1st Sess. (1967), hearings on HR 9840 and HR 10224; rpt. by Arno Press (New York: 1978).
- Senate Select Committee on Equal Educational Opportunity, 91st Cong., 2nd Sess. (1970), hearings on Mexican American Education.
- Senate Labor and Public Welfare Committee, Subcommittees on Education and Human Resources, 93rd Cong., 1st Sess. (1973), joint hearing on bilingual education, health, and manpower programs; rpt. by Arno Press (New York: 1978).
- Senate Labor and Human Resources Committee, Subcommittee on Education, Arts, and Humanities, 97th Cong., 2nd Sess. (1982), hearing on S 2002.

Chapter 6. English Only or English Plus?

The debate over the English Language Amendment and, more generally, over bilingualism in the United States has produced a voluminous literature since 1983. Analyses, editorials, legislation, court decisions, and organizational positions on both sides of the issue are reprinted in Crawford, *Language Loyalties*, along with information about the English Plus alternative; *Hold Your Tongue* offers the author's own overview of language politics in the United States. See also Harvey A. Daniels, ed., *Not Only English: Affirming America's Multilingual Heritage* (Urbana, Ill.: National Council of Teachers of English, 1990); Karen L. Adams and Daniel T. Brink, eds., *Perspectives on Official English: The Campaign for English as the Official Language of the U.S.A.* (Berlin: Mouton de Gruyter, 1990); Dennis Baron, *The English Only Question: An Official Language For Americans?* (New Haven: Yale University Press, 1990); Roseann Dueñas González, ed., *Language Ideologies: Critical Perspectives on the Official English Movement* (Urbana, Ill: National Council of Teachers of English and Lawrence Erlbaum Associates, 2000); and Carol L. Schmid, *The Politics of Language: Conflict, Identity, and Cultural Pluralism in Comparative Perspective* (New York: Oxford University Press, 2001).

The charge that Hispanics are resisting English is elaborated by Gerda Bikales and Gary Imhoff in *A Kind of Discordant Harmony: Issues in Assimilation*, Discussion Series, no. 2 (Washington, D.C.: U.S. English, 1985). Bikales outlines her views immigration in remarks at the Georgetown University Round Table on Languages and Linguistics, Mar. 12, 1987. Imhoff carries these arguments further in a book he coauthored with Colorado Governor Richard D. Lamm, *The Immigration Time Bomb: The Fragmenting of America* (New York: E. P. Dutton, 1985).

The intimate ties between U.S. English and the immigration-restrictionist lobby are documented in William Trombley, "Prop. 63 Roots Traced to Small Michigan City," *Los Angeles Times*, Oct. 20, 1986, Pt. I, pp. 3, 20–21; and Laird Harrison, "U.S. English's Links to Anti-Immigration Groups," *Asian Week*, Aug. 15, 1986, pp. 1, 21. See also Trombley, "Norman Cousins Drops His Support of Prop. 63," *Los Angeles Times*, Oct. 16, 1986, Pt. I, p. 3.

Linda Chávez, as president of U.S. English, outlined her views in "English: Our Common Bond," speech to the Los Angeles World Affairs Council, Dec. 4, 1987. The "cultural conservative" educational philosophy, which underlies attacks on bilingual education by Chávez and others, is elaborated in E. D. Hirsch, Jr., *Cultural Literacy: What Every American Needs To Know* (Boston: Houghton Mifflin, 1987), pp. 92–93, 232–33.

Events leading to the resignations of Chávez, Walter Cronkite, and John Tanton as officers of U.S. English are detailed in Crawford, *Hold Your Tongue*.

Joshua A. Fishman looks at the movement's social psychology in "'English Only': Its Ghosts, Myths, and Dangers," paper presented at the 12th annual conference of the California Association for Bilingual Education, Anaheim, Jan. 30, 1987, excerpted in Crawford, *Language Loyalties*, pp. 165–70. See also Ana Celia Zentella, "Language Politics in the U.S.A.: The English-Only Movement," in Betty Jean Craige, ed., *Literature, Language, and Politics* (Athens: University of Georgia Press, 1988), pp. 39–53.

Linguists from several countries attack the notion of an official language for the United States in *International Journal of the Sociology of Language* 60 (1986), a special issue devoted to "The Question of an Official Language: Language Rights and the English Language Amendment." The lead article is by David F. Marshall, with responses by Tom McArthur, Eric Maldoff, Michael Clyne, Shirley Brice Heath and Lawrence Krasner, Heinz Kloss, Kathryn A. Woolard, and James E. Alatis.

Other noteworthy criticisms include: Mary Carol Combs and John Trasviña, "Legal Implications of the English Language Amendment," in *The English Only Movement: An Agenda for Discrimination* (Washington, D.C.: League of United Latin American Citizens, 1986); Geoffrey Nunberg, "An 'Official Language' for California?" *New York Times*, Oct. 2, 1986; Roseann Dueñas González, Alice A. Schott, and Victoria F. Vásquez, "The English Language Amendment: Examining Myths," *English Journal*, Mar. 1988, pp. 24–30; Elliot L. Judd, "The English Language Amendment: A Case Study on Language and Politics," *TESOL Quarterly* 21, no. 1 (Mar. 1987): 113–35; and Amado M. Padilla et al., "The English Only Movement: Myths, Reality, and Implications for Psychology," *Journal of the American Psychological Association* 46, no. 2 (Feb. 1991): 20–30.

Rosalie Porter's *Forked Tongue: The Politics of Bilingual Education* was published by Basic Books (New York: 1990). Keith Baker reviews the book in "*Forked Tongue*'s Forked Tongue," unpublished article, 1990. Arthur Schlesinger, Jr., confounds bilingual with multicultural and Afro-centric education in *The Disuniting of America: Reflections on a Multicultural Society* (New York: Norton, 1992).

Several Congressional hearings have been held on the Official English question, including:

- Senate Judiciary Committee, Subcommittee on the Constitution, 98th Cong., 2nd Sess., hearing on SJ Res 167, Jun. 12, 1984.
- House Judiciary Committee, Subcommittee on Civil and Constitutional Rights, 100th Cong., 2nd Sess., hearing on HJ Res 13, 33, 60, and 83, May 11, 1988.
- Senate Committee on Governmental Affairs, 104th Cong., 1st & 2nd Sess., hearings on S 356, Dec. 6, 1995, and Mar. 7, 1996.

For an excellent history and analysis of English Plus, see Mary Carol Combs, "English Plus: Responding to English Only," in Crawford, *Language Loyalties*, pp. 216–24. Further information on English Plus and a wide range of policy issues is provided by Rosa Castro Feinberg, *Bilingual Education: A Reference Handbook*. Santa Barbara, CA: ABC-CLIO, 2002.

Editorials favorable to Secretary Bennett's "bilingual education initiative" include the *New York Times*, "Language Is the Melting Pot," Sept. 27, 1985, and the *Washington Post*, "Secretary Bennett Makes Sense," Sept. 27, 1985.

Criticisms of Bennett's position may be found in James J. Lyons, "Education Secretary Bennett on Bilingual Education: Mixed Up or Malicious?" *NABE News* 9, no. 1 (Fall 1985): 1, 14; José, A. Cárdenas, "Education Secretary Bennett and the Big Lie," *Intercultural Development Research Association Newsletter*, Oct. 1985, pp. 7–8; and "A Forked Tongue," *Miami Herald*, Sept. 29, 1985, p. 2E.

Two 1987 reports by the U.S. General Accounting Office that played a role in the legislative battles that year are *Bilingual Education: A New Look at the Research Evidence*, GAO/PEMD-87-12BR, and *Bilingual Education: Information on Limited English Proficient Students*, GAO/HRD-87-85BR. See also U.S. House Education and Labor Committee, *A Compendium of Papers on the Topic of Bilingual Education*, serial no. 99-R (Jun. 1986).

Policy controversies during Bennett's tenure are recounted in *Education Week* articles by James Crawford: "Bilingual-Education Proposals Spark Politically Charged Debate," Feb. 12, 1986; "Bennett Proposes Bilingual Legislation," Mar. 12, 1986; "Immersion Method Is Faring Poorly in Bilingual Study," Apr. 23, 1986; "Lawmakers, Lobbyists Challenge E.D.'s Bilingual-Education Data," Apr. 30, 1986; "Bennett Pushes Bilingual Bill in Congress," Jun. 11, 1986; "Bilingual-Ed. Measure Is Vetoed in California," Oct. 8, 1986; "G.A.O. Refutes Bennett's Criticism of Bilingual Education," Nov. 19, 1986; "Finn Criticizes G.A.O.'s Handling of Bilingual Study," Jan. 14, 1987; "E.D.'s Bilingual-Education Plan Faces Second Test in Congress," Jan. 21, 1987; "Battle Lines Redrawn over Bilingual Education," Apr. 1, 1987; "Bilingual Educators Challenge E.D.'s 'English Only' Proposal," Apr. 15, 1987; "Accord Is Reached on Bill to Extend Bilingual-Ed. Act," Apr. 29, 1987; "Senate Panel Would Expand Bilingual-Ed. Funding Options," May 13, 1987.

Lyons's letter on the 1988 House-Senate conference deliberations on reauthorizing Title VII is reprinted in *NABE News* 11, no. 6 (Apr. 1988). Relevant Congressional hearings include:

- Senate Labor and Human Resources Committee, Subcommittee on Education, Arts, and Humanities, 99th Cong., 2nd Sess., hearing on S 2256, Jun. 4, 1986.
- House Education and Labor Committee, Subcommittee on Elementary, Secondary, and Vocational Education, 100th Cong., 1st Sess., hearing on HR 1755, Mar. 24, 1987.

The Stanford Working Group's report, released in June 1993, is Kenji Hakuta, ed., *Federal Education Programs for Limited-English-Proficient Students: A Blueprint for the Second Generation* – http://www.ncela.gwu.edu/miscpubs/blueprint.htm.

Chapter 7. The Effectiveness Debate

The politicization of bilingual education research is critiqued in August and Hakuta, *Improving Schooling for Language-Minority Children*, chap. 6, "Program Evaluation." Barry McLaughlin summarizes and rebuts many of the popular misconceptions surrounding bilingualism in *Second-Language Acquisition in Childhood*, 2d ed. (Hillsdale, N.J.: Lawrence Erlbaum Associates, 1984).

The American Institutes for Research study – Malcolm N. Danoff et al., *Evaluation of the Impact of ESEA Title VII Spanish/English Bilingual Education Programs* – had two significant installments: vol. 1, *Study Design and Interim Findings* (1977) and vol. 3, *Year Two Impact Data, Educational Process, and In-Depth Analysis* (1978). For criticisms of this first major evaluation of Title VII, see Tracy C. Gray and M. Beatriz Arias, "Challenge to the AIR Report," Center for Applied Linguistics, 1978; Rudolph C. Troike, "Research Evidence for the Effectiveness of Bilingual Education," *NABE Journal* 3, no. 1 (1978): 13–24; Merrill Swain, "Bilingual Education: Research and Implications," Ontario Institute for Studies in Education, 1979; and Heidi Dulay and Marina Burt, *Bilingual Education: A Close Look at its Effects*, National Clearinghouse for Bilingual Education Focus Series, no. 1 (1979).

Jim Cummins describes alternative research models in *Language, Power, and Pedagogy: Bilingual Children in the Crossfire* (Clevedon, U.K.: Multilingual Matters, 2000). Rudolph Troike stresses the importance of longitudinal studies of bilingual education in "Synthesis of Research on Bilingual Education," *Educational Leadership* 14 (Mar. 1981): 498–504.

Keith A. Baker and Adriana A. de Kanter question the effectiveness of Title VII programs in "Federal Policy and the Effectiveness of Bilingual Education," which appears in a volume they edited, *Bilingual Education: A Reappraisal of Federal Policy* (Lexington, Mass.: Lexington Books, 1983). The literature review by Laraine T. Zappert and Roberto B. Cruz is *Bilingual Education: An Appraisal of Empirical Research* (Berkeley, Calif.: Bay Area Bilingual Education League, 1977).

Kenji Hakuta and Catherine E. Snow elaborate the lessons of basic research in "The Role of Research in Policy Decisions about Bilingual Education," *NABE News* 9, no. 3 (Spring 1986): 1, 18–21 (rpt. in House Education and Labor Committee, *Compendium of Papers*). See also Carrol E. Moran and Kenji Hakuta, "Bilingual Education: Broadening Research Perspectives," in James A. Banks and Cherry A. McGee Banks, eds., *Handbook of Research on Multicultural Education* (New York: Macmillan, 1995), pp. 445–62.

Chester E. Finn's argument about the burden of proof in bilingual education research appears in an appendix to the 1987 GAO report, *Bilingual Education: A New Look at the Research Evidence*, pp. 63–70.

For a different view on the role of theory in educational research, see Cummins, *Language, Power, and Pedagogy*, and Stephen Krashen, *Inquiries and Insights: Second Language Learning, Immersion & Bilingual Education, Literacy* (Hayward, Calif.: Alemany Press, 1985). Karl Popper's major articles on the philosophy of science can be found in David Miller, ed., *Popper Selections* (Princeton, N.J.: Princeton University Press, 1985).

There are two versions of the Baker–de Kanter report. The earlier one – Keith A.

Baker and Adriana A. de Kanter, *Effectiveness of Bilingual Education: A Review of the Literature* (U.S. Department of Education, Office of Planning, Budget, and Evaluation, 1981) – received wide publicity in unpublished form but was never officially released. "Federal Policy and the Effectiveness of Bilingual Education," as published in *Bilingual Education*, is more concise and accessible; this 1983 version is relied upon here.

Ann C. Willig has produced the most influential critique of Baker and de Kanter, "A Meta-Analysis of Selected Studies on the Effectiveness of Bilingual Education," *Review of Educational Research* 55, no. 3 (Fall 1985): 269–317. See also Willig, "The Effectiveness of Bilingual Education: Review of a Report," *NABE Journal* 6, nos. 2–3 (Winter/Spring 1981–82): 1–19. An exchange between Baker and Willig on their points of disagreement appears in the *Review of Educational Research* 57, no. 3 (Fall 1987): 351–76.

The literature review by Christine Rossell and Keith Baker is "The Educational Effectiveness of Bilingual Education," *Research in the Teaching of English* 30, no. 1 (1996): 7–74. Jay P. Greene's reanalysis of their conclusions is described in "A Meta-Analysis of the Rossell and Baker Review of Bilingual Education Research," *Bilingual Research Journal* 21, nos. 2–3 (1997). Krashen's critique can be found in *Under Attack*.

Chapter 8. Basic Research on Language Acquisition

The American Council on the Teaching of Foreign Languages reports statistics on Americans' limited linguistic abilities in *ACTFL Public Awareness Network Newsletter* 6, no. 3 (May 1987).

Historical overviews and theories of language education may be found in Barry McLaughlin, *Second-Language Acquisition*, and Stephen D. Krashen and Tracy D. Terrell, *The Natural Approach: Language Acquisition in the Classroom* (Hayward, Calif.: Alemany Press, 1983). See also Charles A. Ferguson, "Linguistic Theory," in *Bilingual Education: Current Perspectives*, vol. 2, *Linguistics* (Arlington, Va.: Center for Applied Linguistics, 1977). Wilga M. Rivers makes a case for the audiolingual method in *Teaching Foreign Language Skills* (Chicago: University of Chicago Press, 1968).

An accessible introduction to Noam Chomsky's work, presented in the form of an extended interview, is *Language and Responsibility*. For a discussion of the "language faculty," see his *Language and Problems of Knowledge: The Managua Lectures* (Cambridge, Mass.: MIT Press, 1988). See also John Lyons, *Noam Chomsky*, rev. ed. (New York: Viking Press, 1970). Jeff MacSwan and Kellie Rolstad offer a Chomskyan view of the language faculty in "Linguistic Diversity, Schooling, and Social Class: Rethinking Our Conception of Language Proficiency in Language Minority Education," in Christina Bratt Paulston and G. Richard Tucker, eds., *Sociolinguistics: The Essential Readings* (Oxford: Blackwell, 2003). Kenji Hakuta discusses Chomsky's relationship to psycholinguistic research in *Mirror of Language*, pp. 109–11.

Ellen Bialystok and Hakuta evaluate the critical period hypothesis in *In Other Words: The Science and Psychology of Second-Language Acquisition* (New York: Basic Books, 1994). See also Hakuta, Bialystok, and Edward Wiley, "Critical Evidence: A Test of the Critical Period Hypothesis for Second Language Acquisition," *Psychological Science*, Jan. 2003.

Lily Wong Fillmore and Barry McLaughlin's study of variability in second-language acquisition is *Learning English through Bilingual Instruction: Final Report to the National Institute of Education* (NIE-80-0030), 1985. The findings are summarized by Wong Fillmore in "Teachability and Second Language Acquisition," in R. Schiefelbush and M. Rice, eds., *The Teachability of Language* (Baltimore: Paul Brookes, 1989), pp. 311–32. See also Wong Fillmore, "Second-Language Learning in Children: A Model of Language Learning in Social Context," in Ellen Bialystok, ed., *Language Processing in Bilingual Children* (New York: Cambridge University Press, 1991), pp. 49–69.

An early summary of basic research on second-language acquisition, along with its implications for the bilingual classroom, can be found in a book compiled by California's state Office of Bilingual Bicultural Education: *Schooling and Language Minority Students: A Theoretical Framework* (Los Angeles: California State University, 1981). This collection includes Jim Cummins, "The Role of Primary Language Development in Promoting Educational Success for Language Minority Students"; Stephen D. Krashen, "Bilingual Education and Second Language Acquisition Theory"; Dorothy Legaretta-Marcaida, "Effective Use of the Primary Language in the Classroom"; Tracy D. Terrell, "The Natural Approach in Bilingual Education"; and Eleanor W. Thonis, "Reading Instruction for Language Minority Students."

Krashen discusses the input hypothesis and related issues in a series of absorbing essays, *Inquiries and Insights*. He outlines and documents his theory more formally in *The Input Hypothesis: Issues and Implications* (London: Longman, 1985) and *Principles and Practice in Second Language Acquisition* (Oxford: Pergamon Press, 1982). See also his *Bilingual Education: A Focus on Current Research*, Occasional Papers in Bilingual Education, no. 3 (Washington, D.C.: National Clearinghouse for Bilingual Education, 1991).

Cummins further elaborates his theories – and responds to critics – in "Empowering Minority Students: A Framework for Intervention," *Harvard Educational Review* 56, no. 1 (Feb. 1986): 18–36; *Negotiating Identities: Education for Empowerment in a Diverse Society* (Sacramento: California Association for Bilingual Education, 1996); and *Language, Power, and Pedagogy*.

For more on the distinctions between "immigrant minorities" and "caste minorities," see John U. Ogbu and María Eugenia Matute-Bianchi, "Understanding Sociocultural Factors: Knowledge, Identity, and School Adjustment," in *Beyond Language: Social and Cultural Factors in Schooling Language Minority Students* (Sacramento: California State Department of Education, 1986), pp. 73–142.

Rossell and Baker attack the so-called "facilitation hypothesis" in "The Educational Effectiveness of Bilingual Education."

MacSwan's critique of Cummins's theory is "The Threshold Hypothesis, Semilingualism, and Other Contributions to a Deficit View of Linguistic Minorities," *Hispanic Journal of Behavioral Sciences* 22, no. 1 (2000): 3–45. William Labov's refutation of verbal deprivation theory, "The Logic of Nonstandard English," originally appeared in *Georgetown Monographs on Language and Linguistics* 22 (1969); rpt. in Pier Paolo Giglioli, ed., *Language and Social Context* (Harmondsworth, U.K.: Penguin Books, 1972). See also

MacSwan and Rolstad, "Linguistic Diversity, Schooling, and Social Class," and Kellie Rolstad, "Second language Instructional Competence," in Kara McAlister et al., eds., *Proceedings of the 4th International Symposium on Bilingualism* (Somerville, Mass.: Cascadilla Press, in press).

Barry McLaughlin elaborates his critique of Krashen's work in *Theories of Second-Language Learning* (London: Edward Arnold, 1987). Krashen responds to these and other objections in "The Input Hypothesis and Its Rivals," in Nick C. Ellis, ed., *Implicit and Explicit Learning of Languages* (London: Academic Press, 1994). See also Krashen, *Explorations in Language Acquisition and Use: The Taipei Lectures* (Portsmouth, N.H.: Heinemann, 2003).

Hakuta reviews the research on bilingualism and cognition in *Mirror of Language*. See also Bialystok and Hakuta, *In Other Words*.

Chapter 9. Considering Program Alternatives

A helpful introduction to immersion – its theoretical underpinnings, the development of program models in Canada and the United States, and arguments about its appropriateness for language-minority students – is provided in *Studies on Immersion Education: A Collection for United States Educators* (Sacramento: California State Department of Education, Office of Bilingual Bicultural Education, 1984). This anthology includes Wallace E. Lambert, "An Overview of Issues in Immersion Education"; Fred Genesee, "Historical and Theoretical Foundations of Immersion Education"; and Eduardo Hernández-Chávez, "The Inadequacy of English Immersion Education as an Educational Approach for Language Minority Students in the United States."

The genesis and development of French immersion is described in detail by Lambert and G. Richard Tucker, *Bilingual Education of Children: The St. Lambert Experiment* (Rowley, Mass.: Newbury House, 1972). Tucker argues that the Canadian immersion model is inappropriate for language-minority children in "Implications of Canadian Research for Promoting a Language Competent American Society," in Joshua A. Fishman, ed., *The Fergusonian Impact*, vol. 2, *Sociolinguistics and the Sociology of Language* (Berlin: Mouton, 1986).

Keith Baker and Adriana de Kanter's arguments for the time-on-task hypothesis can be found in *Bilingual Education*. See also Christine H. Rossell and J. Michael Ross, "The Social Science Evidence on Bilingual Education," *Journal of Law and Education* 15 (1986) 385–418; and Rosalie Porter, *Forked Tongue*.

Philadelphia's ESOL Plus Immersion program and the controversy surrounding it are described in Martha Woodall, "As Refugees' Grades Sink, English Immersion Faulted," *Philadelphia Inquirer*, Mar. 30, 1986, pp. 1B, 8B.

Baker and Willig's differences over program definitions may be found in their exchange in the *Review of Educational Research*, Fall 1987.

The El Paso pilot program is described in El Paso Independent School District, Office for Research and Evaluation, "Bilingual Education Program Evaluation: 1986–87 School Year," Jul. 1987. Robert Rosier's erroneous characterization appears in the "Twelfth Annual Report of the National Advisory and Coordinating Council on Bilingual Education," Mar. 31, 1988. The READ study by Russell Gersten et al. is "Bilingual Immersion: A Longitudinal Evaluation of the El Paso Program" (1993).

Gersten and John Woodward discuss the limited research evidence that exists on English-only immersion approaches in "A Case for Structured Immersion," *Educational Leadership*, Sept. 1985, pp. 75–79, 83–84. See also Ramón L. Santiago's response in the same issue, "Understanding Bilingual Education – or The Sheep in Wolf's Clothing," pp. 79–83.

As released in 1991, the Ramírez study's full reference is: J. David Ramírez, Sandra D. Yuen, and Dena R. Ramey, *Final Report: Longitudinal Study of Structured Immersion Strategy, Early-Exit, and Late-Exit Transitional Bilingual Education Programs for Language-Minority Children* (San Mateo, Calif.: Aguirre International, 1991). For analyses of, and debate over, its findings, see the *Bilingual Research Journal* 16, nos. 1 & 2 (Winter/Spring 1992).

The review of the Ramírez study by the National Research Council is summarized in Michael M. Meyer and Stephen E. Fienberg, eds., *Assessing Evaluation Studies: The Case of Bilingual Education Strategies* (Washington, D.C.: National Academy Press, 1992).

The research on Fairfax County's ESL-only program was conducted by Virginia P. Collier and Wayne P. Thomas, who describe their findings in "Acquisition of Cognitive-Academic Language Proficiency: A Six-Year Study," paper presented at the annual meeting of the American Educational Research Association, New Orleans, Apr. 7, 1988. See also Collier, "Age and Rate of Acquisition of Second Language for Academic Purposes," *TESOL Quarterly* 21, no. 4 (Dec. 1987): 617–41. Reactions by the school district and others are reported in James Crawford, "Study Challenges 'Model' E.S.L. Program's Effectiveness," *Education Week*, Apr. 27, 1988.

Stephen Krashen outlines his theory of de facto bilingual education in *Under Attack*.

The Arizona study on the time required for second-language acquisition is Lisa C. Pray and Jeff MacSwan, "Different Question, Same Answer: How Long Does It Take for English Learners to Acquire Proficiency?" a paper presented at the annual meeting of the American Educational Research Association, New Orleans, Apr. 4, 2002. The Stanford University study on this topic is Kenji Hakuta, Yuko Goto Butler, and Daria Witt, *How Long Does It Take English Learners to Attain Proficiency?* (Santa Barbara, Calif.: Linguistic Minority Research Institute, 2000).

Rudolph Troike's comments about late-exit programs appear in "Synthesis of Research on Bilingual Education."

The Thomas-Collier reports are *School Effectiveness for Language Minority Students* (Washington, D.C.: National Clearinghouse for Bilingual Education, 1997) and *A National Study of School Effectiveness for Language Minority Students' Long-Term Academic Achievement: Final Report* (Santa Cruz, Calif.: Center for Research on Education, Diversity, and Excellence, 2002). Christine Rossell criticizes the 1997 study in "Mystery on the Bilingual Express," *READ Perspectives* 6 (1999).

The controlled study in Dade County, Florida, is D. Kimbrough Oller and Rebecca E. Eilers, eds., *Language and Literacy in Bilingual Children* (Clevedon, U.K.: Multilingual Matters, 2002).

Chapter 10. The Case Studies Project

The most comprehensive description of this program is California State Department of Education, *Case Studies in Bilingual Education: Second Year Report* (1984–85), evaluation report to the U.S. Office of Bilingual Education and Minority Languages Affairs (Federal Grant #G008303723), May 1986.

Implications of basic research for curriculum design are developed in California Office of Bilingual Bicultural Education, *Basic Principles for the Education of Language-Minority Students: An Overview* (Sacramento: California State Department of Education, 1983).

A detailed analysis of student scores in Case Studies schools and other exemplary programs is provided in Stephen Krashen and Douglas Biber, *On Course: Bilingual Education's Success in California* (Sacramento: California Association for Bilingual Education, 1988). See also F. Samaniego and L. Eubank, *A Statistical Analysis of California's Case Study Project in Bilingual Education* (Davis: University of California, Intercollegiate Division of Statistics, 1991).

For a summary of early experience in replicating the Eastman/Case Studies model, see Jesús Salazar, *Eastman Curriculum Design Project, 1986–87, First Year Implementation Report,* Publication no. 512, Los Angeles Unified School District, Research and Evaluation Branch, Feb. 1988.

Chapter 11. Indian Language Education

Michael Krauss quantifies the threat to endangered languages, including those spoken by Native Americans, in "The World's Languages in Crisis," *Language* 68, no. 1 (Mar. 1992): 6–10. In the same issue, see also Lucille J. Watahomigie and Akira Y. Yamamoto, "Local Reactions to Perceived Language Decline," pp. 10–17; and Ken Hale, "Language Endangerment and the Human Value of Linguistic Diversity," pp. 35–42. An excellent overview of the problem is Ofelia Zepeda and Jane H. Hill, "The Condition of Native American Languages in the United States," in Robert H. Robins and Eugenius M. Uhlenbeck, eds., *Endangered Languages* (Oxford: Berg, 1991).

Leanne Hinton provides a unique and readable account of language preservation efforts now under way in *Flutes of Fire: Essays on California Indian Languages* (Berkeley, Calif.: Heyday Books, 1994). See also Gina Cantoni, ed., *Stabilizing Indigenous Languages* (Flagstaff, Ariz.: Center for Excellence in Education, Northern Arizona University, 1996).

For more perspective on these issues from the author, see James Crawford, "Endangered Native American Languages: What Is To Be Done, and Why?" and "Seven Hypotheses on Language Loss," in *At War with Diversity*.

William L. Leap describes the unique language situation of American Indian children in "Title VII and the Role It Plays in Indian Education: A Background Statement," paper for the National Conference of American Indians, 1982. See also his *American Indian English* (Salt Lake City: University of Utah Press, 1993), and Bea Medicine, "Speaking Indian": *Parameters of Language Use Among American Indians*, Focus series, no. 6, National Clearinghouse for Bilingual Education, Mar. 1981.

Steve Chesarek's research on the influence of native language development on later school achievement is summarized in "Cognitive Consequences of Home or School Education in a Limited Second Language: A Case Study in the Crow Indian Bilingual Community," paper presented at the Language Proficiency Assessment Symposium, Airlie, Va., Mar. 1981.

For a detailed description of the Crow Agency bilingual program (although the district is not identified by name), see "A Well-Organized Indian Project," in *ESEA Title VII Case Studies* (Arlington, Va.: Development Associates, 1983), pp. 111–29.

A wealth of information about Navajo bilingual programs may be found in a special issue of the *Bilingual Research Journal* 19, no. 1 (Winter 1995), including Sally Begay et al., "Change from the Inside Out: A Story of the Transformation in a Navajo Community School," pp. 121–39; Agnes and Wayne Holm, "Navajo Education: Retrospect and Prospects," pp. 141–67; and Daniel McLaughlin, "Strategies for Enabling Bilingual Program Development in American Indian Schools," pp. 169–78.

For detailed, first-person accounts of bilingual education at Rock Point, see the Holms' "Rock Point, A Navajo Way to Go to School," *Annals of the American Association of Political & Social Science* 508 (1990): 170–84; and McLaughlin's *When Literacy Empowers: Navajo Language in Print* (Albuquerque: University of New Mexico Press, 1992).

Teresa L. McCarty relates the complex and compelling story of Rough Rock in "School as Community: The Rough Rock Demonstration," *Harvard Educational Review* 59, no. 4 (Nov. 1989): 484–503. See also McCarty, *A Place To Be Navajo: Rough Rock and the Struggle for Self-Determination* (Mahwah, N.J.: Lawrence Erlbaum Associates, 2002); Galena Sells Dick and Teresa L. McCarty, "Reclaiming Navajo: Language Renewal in an American Indian Community School," in Nancy H. Hornberger, ed., *Indigenous Literacies in the Americas: Language Planning from the Bottom Up* (Berlin: Mouton de Gruyter, 1997); and John Collier, Jr., "Survival at Rough Rock: A Historical Overview of Rough Rock Demonstration School," *Anthropology & Education Quarterly* 19 (1988): 253–69.

For an overview of Indian bilingual education policy, see McCarty, "Federal Language Policy and American Indian Education," *Bilingual Research Journal* 17, nos. 1 & 2 (Spring 1993): 13–34. See also Jon Reyhner, ed., *Teaching American Indian Students* (Norman: University of Oklahoma Press, 1992).

Joshua Fishman provides a worldwide perspective on the problem of language loss and efforts to solve it in *Reversing Language Shift: Theoretical and Empirical Foundations of Assistance to Threatened Languages* (Clevedon, U.K.: Multilingual Matters, 1991). See also Fishman's edited volume, *Can Threatened Languages Be Saved? Reversing Language Shift, Revisited: A 21st Century Perspective* (Clevedon, U.K.: Multilingual Matters, 2001).

Details of the Pûnana Leo immersion program may be found in Larry Lindsey Kimura, "The Hawaiian Language and Its Revitalization," in Freda Ahenakew and Shirley Fredeen, eds., *Our Languages: Our Survival, Proceedings of the 7th Annual Native American Languages Issues Institute* (Saskatoon: Saskatchewan Indian Languages Institute, 1987). Robert Bunge, "Language: The Psyche of a People," appeared in the same volume. See also William G. Demmert, Jr., "Language, Learning, and National Goals: A Native American View," in Center for Applied Linguistics, *The National Education Goals: The Issues of Language and Culture* (Washington, D.C.: CAL, 1992), pp. 25–33.

Chapter 12. Two-Way Bilingualism

The estimate for speakers of English worldwide comes from the English Speaking Union, cited in Chris Redman, "Wanna Speak English?" *Time Europe*, Jun. 24, 2002. See also Chinese Language Teachers Association, *CLTA Newsletter* 25, no. 2 (Sept. 2001), and Jamie B. Draper and June H. Hicks, *Foreign Language Enrollments in Public Secondary Schools, Fall 2000: Summary Report* (Yonkers, N.Y.: American Council on the Teaching of Foreign Languages, 2002).

Then-Representative Paul Simon, a member of the President's Commission on Foreign Languages and International Studies (1979), documented the sad state of our linguistic resources in *The Tongue-Tied American: Confronting the Foreign Language Crisis* (New York: Continuum, 1980). See also Catherine E. Snow and Kenji Hakuta, "The Costs of Mono-lingualism," in Crawford, *Language Loyalties*, pp. 394–94.

Russell N. Campbell and Kathryn J. Lindholm of the Center for Language Education and Research (CLEAR) make a case for two-way bilingual education in *Conservation of Language Resources*, Educational Report Series, no. 6 (Los Angeles: University of California, CLEAR, 1987). See also two related publications by CLEAR: Marguerite Ann Snow, *Innovative Second Language Education: Bilingual Immersion Programs*, Educational Report Series, no. 1 (1986); and Lindholm's *Directory of Bilingual Immersion Programs: Two-Way Bilingual Education for Language Minority and Majority Students*, Educational Report Series, no. 8 (1987).

The Center for Applied Linguistics compiles an annual *Directory of Two-Way Bilingual Immersion Programs in the U.S.*: http://www.cal.org/twi/directory/.

G. Richard Tucker explains how two-way programs serve both language-majority and language-minority students in "Encouraging the Development of Bilingual Proficiency for English-Speaking Americans," Center for Applied Linguistics, Jun. 1986.

Sidney Morison describes the rationale for launching a two-way program at New York City's P.S. 84 in "Two-Way Bilingual Education: The Time Has Come," paper presented at the 17th annual conference of the National Association for Bilingual Education, Houston, Apr. 30, 1988. See also Morison, "A Spanish-English Dual Language Program in New York City," *Annals of the American Academy of Political & Social Science* 508 (1995): 160–69.

Campbell, who helped design the Culver City Spanish immersion program in the early 1970s, outlines its history and effects in "The Immersion Approach to Foreign Language Teaching," in California Office of Bilingual Bicultural Education, *Studies on Immersion Education*, pp. 114–43. Also in that volume, Merrill Swain voices theoretical objections to teaching literacy simultaneously in two languages in "A Review of Immersion Education in Canada: Research and Evaluation Studies," pp. 87–112.

Rebecca Freeman's ethnographic study of the Oyster School is *Bilingual Education and Social Change* (Clevedon, U.K.: Multilingual Matters, 1998). Greg Toppo describes parents camping out in the snow to enroll their children in "Unique Public Schools Highlighted," *Los Angeles Times*, Feb. 24, 2002. Virginia Collier traces the outcomes of Oyster graduates in

"Two-Way Bilingual Programs: The Longitudinal Impact of Integrated Majority-Minority Bilingual Classes on Majority Students' Attitudes and Career Goals," paper presented at the annual meeting of Advocates for Language Learning, Washington, D.C., Oct. 17, 1987.

Guadalupe Valdes expresses reservations about the two-way model in "Dual-Language Immersion Programs: A Cautionary Note Concerning the Education of Language-Minority Students," *Harvard Educational Review* 67, no. 3 (Fall 1997): 391–429.

Fred Genesee analyzes San Diego's experiment in two-way total immersion in "Considering Two-Way Bilingual Programs," *Equity and Choice* 3, no. 3 (Spring 1987): 3–7. The program's effects on student achievement are reported in Krashen and Biber, *On Course*.

Kathryn J. Lindholm-Leary provides the most comprehensive overview of two-way programs to date in *Dual Language Education* (Clevedon, U.K.: Multilingual Matters, 2001).

Deborah L. Gold compliles useful details about two-way programs and policymakers' responses in "2 Languages, One Aim: 'Two-Way' Learning," *Education Week*, Jan. 20, 1988, pp. 7, 24–25.

The evaluation of the Key School partial dual immersion program appears in Donna Christian, Christopher L. Montone, Kathryn J. Lindholm, and Isolda Carranza, *Profiles in Two-Way Immersion Education* (McHenry, Ill.: Delta Systems, 1997).

The Thomas-Collier data in Houston are reported in *A National Study of School Effectiveness*.

Stephen Krashen expresses cautious optimism about two-way bilingual education in "The Acquisition of Academic English by Children in Two-Way Programs: What Does the Research Say?" unpublished, Oct. 2003.

Chapter 13. Disaster at the Polls

Initial coverage of the Ninth Street School boycott appeared in the *Los Angeles Times*, Feb. 13– 26, 1996. Another side of the story was provided by James Crawford, "The Ninth Street Myth: Who Speaks for Latino Parents?" an article syndicated by the Hispanic Link News Service, May 25, 1998.

The National Research Council report is August and Hakuta, eds., *Improving Schooling for Language-Minority Children*. Charles Glenn's "political spin" on the report is posted at http://www.ceousa.org/READ/nrc.html. Hakuta responds at http://ourworld.compuserve.com/homepages/jwcrawford/hakuta.htm.

For more on the changing face of the English-only movement, see Crawford, "Boom to Bust: Official English in the 1990s" and "The Proposition 227 Campaign: A Post Mortem," in *At War with Diversity*.

Ron Unz outlines his strategic ideas for Republicans in "Immigration or the Welfare State: Which Is Our Real Enemy?" published in the Heritage Foundation journal *Policy Review*, Fall 1994. Peter Salins's *Assimilation, American Style* was published by Basic Books (New York: 1997).

Stephen Krashen's campaign experience is detailed in "The Two Goals of Bilingual

Education: Development of Academic English and Heritage Language Development," in Josefina V. Tinajero and Robert A. DeVillar, *The Power of Two Languages 2000: Effective Use Across the Curriculum* (New York: McGraw-Hill, 2000).

Unz makes his case against bilingual education on a campaign Web site: http://onenation.org/. Commentaries, analysis, debates, poetry, opinion polls, research briefs, study guides, resource links, and an archive news articles on Proposition 227 can be found at http://ourworld.compuserve.com/homepages/jwcrawford/unz.htm.

Chapter 14. No Child Left Untested

The *Sacramento Bee* article is Janine DeFao, "Choice Looms: Fix or End Bilingual Education System," Oct. 5, 1997.

David Berliner and Bruce Biddle debunk the claims and conclusions of *A Nation at Risk* in *The Manufactured Crisis: Myths, Fraud, and the Attack on America's Public Schools* (Reading, Mass.: Addison-Wesley, 1995). See also Gerald Bracey, "20 Years of School Bashing," *Washington Post*, Apr. 25, 2003.

Jonathan Kozol's *Savage Inequalities* was published by Crown Publishers (New York: 1991).

Thomas Toch provides a useful account of 1980s school reform efforts in *In the Name of Excellence: The Struggle to Reform the Nation's Schools, Why It's Failing, and What Should Be Done* (New York: Oxford University Press, 1991). A discussion of the movement's limitations can be found in Marshall S. Smith and Jennifer O'Day, "Systemic School Reform," *Politics of Education Association Yearbook*, 1990, pp. 233–67.

For a history of the standards-and-goals movement, see Cynthia D. Prince and Pascal D. Forgione, Jr., "Raising Standards and Measuring Performance Equitably: Challenges for the National Education Goals Panel and State Assessment Systems," in Center for Applied Linguistics, *National Education Goals*, pp. 11–22.

IBM's Louis Gerstner is quoted in Susan Ohanian, *One Size Fits Few: The Folly of Educational Standards* (Portsmouth, N.H.: Heinemann, 1999), a passionate critique of top-down "reform." Alfie Kohn further analyzes the role of business ideology in *The Schools Our Children Deserve: Moving Beyond Traditional Classrooms and "Tougher Standards"* (Boston: Houghton Mifflin, 1999).

The *ESL Standards for Pre-K–12 Students* were developed by Teachers of English to Speakers of Other Languages (Alexandria, Va.: TESOL, 1997). The *English-Language Development Standards for California Public Schools, Kindergarten through Grade Twelve* were adopted by the California State Board of Education in 1999.

Jill Kerper Mora's comments on the California English Language Development Test (CELDT) can be found at: http://coe.sdsu.edu/people/jmora/Prop227/celdt.htm. On LEP assessment, see also Edward De Avila, *Setting Expected Gains for Non and Limited English Proficient Students* (Washington, D.C.: National Clearinghouse for Bilingual Education, 1997).

The Florida grade retention figures are from Michael Winerip, "A Pupil Held Back, a Heavier Burden," *New York Times*, May 21, 2003. For media coverage of the impact of the No Child Left Behind Act, see Malcolm Gladwell, "Making the Grade," *New Yorker*, Sept.

15, 2003; Erik W. Robelin, "State Reports on Progress Vary Widely," *Education Week*, Sept. 3, 2003; Rosalind S. Helderman and Ylan Q. Mui, "Comparing Schools' Progress Difficult," *Washington Post*, Sept. 25, 2003; and Perry Bacon, Jr., "Struggle of the Classes," *Time*, Sept. 22, 2003. See especially Susan Ohanian, "Bush Flunks Schools," *Nation*, Dec. 1, 2003.

Wayne E. Wright describes the classroom impact the Stanford 9 testing program in California in "The Effects of High Stakes Testing in an Inner-City Elementary School: The Curriculum, the Teachers, and the English Language Learners," *Current Issues in Education* 5, no. 5 (2002): http://cie.asu.edu/volume5/number5/.

James Crawford considers the implications of NCLB for English learners in "The Bilingual Education Act, 1968–2002: An Obituary," Education Policy Studies Laboratory, Arizona State University (2002): http://www.asu.edu/educ/epsl/LPRU/features/brief2.-htm.

Gerald Coles debunks extravagant claims about "scientifically based" literacy programs in *Misreading Reading: The Bad Science That Hurts Children* (Portsmouth, N.H.: Heinemann, 2000). See also Elaine Garan, "Beyond the Smoke and Mirrors: A Critique of the National Reading Panel Report on Phonics," *Phi Delta Kappan* 82, no. 7 (2001): 500–6.

Chapter 15. Advocating for English Learners

Statements on NCLB by Raul Yzaguirre and Delia Pompa were made in press releases dated Dec. 14, 2001, and Nov. 30, 2001, respectively.

The Gallup executive is quoted in Norman Solomon, "Polls Give Numbers, But the Truth Is More Elusive," Creators Syndicate, May 20, 1996. The Gallup Poll results on bilingual education are reported in Eric Hubler, "Bilingual Ed Backed by 58% in U.S., Poll Says," *Denver Post*, Jul. 9, 2003"; and "Bilingual Education, June 6," in *Public Opinion*, 1998 (Wilmington, Del.: Scholarly Resources, Inc., 1999).

Stephen Krashen analyzes changing opinions on bilingual education in "Evidence Suggesting That Public Opinion Is Becoming More Negative: A Discussion of the Reasons, and What We Can Do About It" (2002): http://ourworld.compuserve.com/-homepages/jwcrawford/Krash11.htm. He summarizes the findings of several studies by Fay Shin in *Under Attack*; see also *Condemned without a Trial*.

The Public Agenda and Kaiser surveys are detailed in Steve Farkas, Ann Duffett, and Jean Johnson, *Now That I'm Here: What America's Immigrants Have To Say about Life in the U.S. Today: A Report from Public Agenda* (New York: Public Agenda, 2003).

Opinion patterns on Proposition 227 were reported in two Los Angeles Times Polls conducted in 1998: *Study #410: California Politics* (Apr. 13) – http://www.latimes.com/-extras/timespoll/stats/pdfs/410ss.pdf – and *Study #413: Exit poll, California Primary Election* (Jun. 2) – http://www.latimes.com/extras/timespoll/stats/pdfs/413ss.pdf.

The *New York Times* editorial, "New York's Bilingual 'Prison,'" appeared on Sept. 21, 1995, p. A22.

For advocates of progressive causes, the best all-round guide to understanding and working with news media is Charlotte Ryan, *Prime Time Activism: Media Strategies for Grassroots Organizing* (Boston: South End Press, 1991).

McQuillan and Lucy Tse report their findings on media bias in "Does Research Matter? An Analysis of Media Opinion on Bilingual Education, 1984–1994," *Bilingual Research* Journal 20, no. 1 (Winter 1996): 1–27.

The federal court case against Proposition 227 was *Valeria G. v. Wilson*, 12 F.Supp.2d 1007 (N.D. Cal. 1998). The state case that expanded parental waiver rights was *McLaughlin v. State Board of Education*, 75 Cal.App.4th 196 (1999). The opinion by California Attorney General Bill Lockyer was Opinion No. 99-802. See also Multicultural Training, Education, and Advocacy, "Prop. 227 Vests Program Choice with Parents, Not Administrators," *Education Equity* 10, no. 1 (Spring 2000).

The *New York Times* report is Jacques Steinberg, "Increase in Test Scores Counters Dire Forecasts for Bilingual Ban," Aug. 20, 2000. The Stanford analysis of California achievement test results is Evelyn Orr, Yuko Goto Butler, Michele Bousquet, and Kenji Hakuta, *What Can We Learn about the Impact of Proposition 227 from SAT-9 Scores?* (Aug. 15, 2000): http://www.stanford.edu/~hakuta/SAT9/SAT9_2000/analysis2000.htm.

Ken Noonan describes his "conversion" experience in "I Believed That Bilingual Education Was Best … Until the Kids Proved Me Wrong," *Washington Post*, Sept. 3, 2000.

The study of Proposition 227 commissioned by the California legislature is Thomas B. Parrish et al., *Effects of Proposition 227 on the Education of English Learners, K–12: Year 1 Report* (Palo Alto, Calif.: American Institutes for Research and WestEd, 2001).

Results of the Linguistic Minority Research Institute studies of Proposition 227 are reported in a special issue of the *Bilingual Research Journal* 24, nos. 1–2 (Winter 2000). See especially Patricia Gándara, "In the Aftermath of the Storm: English Learners in the Post-227 Era," and Tom Stritikus and Eugene E. García, "Education of Limited English Proficient Students in California Schools: An Assessment of the Influence of Proposition 227 on Selected Teachers and Classrooms."

Wayne Wright's case study is reported in "The Effects of High Stakes Testing."

The California law allowing Reading First grants for bilingual programs is A.B. 1485 (signed into law on Oct. 10, 2003). The court decision is summarized by Multicultural Education, Training, and Advocacy at: http://www.latinosonline.com/cabe/show-article.cfm?titleID=1006. For information on New York City's expansion of English learner programs, see David M. Herzsenhorn, "Mayor Steps back from English Immersion," *New York Times*, Jun. 25, 2003; and Clara Hemphill, "Mike Likes 'Dual Language'": http://www.insideschools.org/nv/NV_bilingual_plan_june03.php.

Index

ALSO AVAILABLE FROM

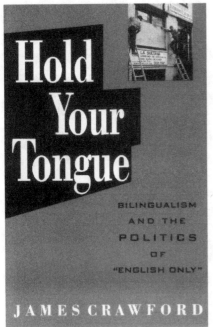

Hold Your Tongue:

Bilingualism and the Politics of "English Only"

by

James Crawford

Now in paperback, this award-winning exposé of the English Only campaign traces the hidden agenda and social consequences of today's backlash against bilingualism.

"A very timely book that is more timely than ever."

Los Angeles Times

"Crawford is at once a scholar, advocate, and journalist – all those voices are heard in this book and masterfully woven into a gripping indictment of seemingly innocent attempts to legislate English."

Kenji Hakuta, *Stanford University*

"Readers looking for insight into the tangled politics of language are well served by Crawford['s] . . . extensive and illuminating discussions."

The Nation

"Jim Crawford's news-gathering prowess and insider's knowledge shine through *Hold Your Tongue*. Rich in anecdotes, majestic in its sweep and scope . . . a ground-breaking study of the English Only movement."

Henry Cisneros, *U.S. Secretary of Housing & Urban Development*

"Richly informative . . . a valuable discussion of the US' past and present difficulties with intolerance and discrimination against immigrants."

Harvard Educational Review

"Convincingly argues that multilingualism is a significant economic resource and that English Only sends a xenophobic message to the rest of the world."

The Washington Post

Hold Your Tongue:
Bilingualism and the Politics of "English Only"

by **James Crawford**

Author of

*Bilingual Education: History,
Politics, Theory, and Practice*

As a journalist who closely monitors developments in legislation, research, and the classroom. James Crawford examines bilingual education from all sides:

CONTENTS

1. Guardians of English
2. Polygot Boarding-House
3. Strangers in Their Own Land
4. Tribal Politics
5. Old Ethnics and New

6. Hispanophobia
7. Language Rights and Wrongs
8. Problem or Resource?
9. Babel in Reverse

Conclusion: Democracy and Language

324 pages • Paperback

- -